D1233178

Also in the Variorum Collected Studies Series:

RICHARD L. CROCKER
Studies in Medieval Music Theory and the Early Sequence

DAVID FALLOWS
Songs and Musicians in the Fifteenth Century

AMNON SHILOAH
The Dimension of Music in Islamic and Jewish Culture

D.P. WALKER
Music, Spirit and Language in the Renaissance

HELMUT GNEUSS
Language and History in Early England

JOHN J. CONTRENI
Carolingian Learning, Masters and Manuscripts

P. SIMS-WILLIAMS
Britain and Early Christian Europe
Studies in Early Medieval History and Culture

ROSAMOND MCKITTERICK
Books, Scribes and Learning in the Frankish Kingdoms, 6th–9th Centuries

GILES CONSTABLE
Culture and Spirituality in Medieval Europe

NEIL WRIGHT
History and Literature in Late Antiquity and the Early Medieval West
Studies in Intertextuality

VALERIE J. FLINT
Ideas in the Medieval West
Texts and their Contexts

YAKOV MALKIEL
Theory and Practice of Romance Etymology
Studies in Language, Culture and History

PETER DRONKE
Latin and Vernacular Poets of the Middle Ages

VARIORUM COLLECTED STUDIES SERIES

Music and Instruments of the Middle Ages: Studies on Texts and Performance

Dr Christopher Page

Christopher Page

Music and Instruments of the Middle Ages: Studies on Texts and Performance

VARIORUM
1997

This edition copyright © 1997 by Christopher Page.

Published by VARIORUM
> Ashgate Publishing Limited
> Gower House, Croft Road,
> Aldershot, Hampshire GU11 3HR
> Great Britain
>
> Ashgate Publishing Company
> Old Post Road,
> Brookfield, Vermont 05036-9704
> USA

ISBN 0-86078-623-4

British Library CIP Data
> Page, Christopher.
> Music and Instruments of the Middle Ages: Studies on Texts and Performance. —
> (Variorum Collected Studies Series: CS562)
> 1. Music—500–1400. 2. Musical instruments—History. I. Title. II. Series.
> 780.9'02

US Library of Congress CIP Data
> Page, Christopher.
> Music and Instruments of the Middle Ages: Studies on Texts and Performance /
> Christopher Page.
>   p.   cm. — (Collected Studies Series: CS562)
> Includes index (cloth: alk. paper)
> 1.Music—500–1400—History and criticism. 2. Music—15th century—History and
> criticism. 3. Musical instruments. 4. Performance practice (music)—500–1400.
> 5. Performance practice (music)—15th century. I. Title. II. Series: Collected Studies:
> CS562.
> ML170.M83 1997   97-2605
> 780'.9'02—dc21   CIP

Printed by Galliard (Printers) Ltd
> Great Yarmouth, Norfolk, Great Britain

VARIORUM COLLECTED STUDIES SERIES CS562

CONTENTS

This volume contains xii + 328 pages

PREFACE

The articles published in this volume were inspired by a desire to learn what medieval texts reveal about the musical life and resources of the Middle Ages. Many of them are devoted to instruments, for the years between 1970 and 1980 were propitious ones for such research. During the first half of the decade, David Munrow, a gifted instrumentalist, was famous for his performances of medieval music; his distinguished book *Instruments of the Middle Ages and Renaissance* was published by Oxford University Press in 1976, shortly before his untimely death.[1] At the same time Professor Howard Mayer Brown – perhaps the only world-class musicologist ever to devote a substantial part of his research endeavours to medieval organology – was continuing his important research. In 1973 the journal *Early Music* was founded by John M. Thomson (in close consultation with Howard Brown) to unite the interests of scholars and performers; with its lavish provision for the reproduction of pictures, a vital resource for medieval organology, *Early Music* matched the spirit of its times; nearly half of the articles on instruments and instrumentation published here, first appeared in its pages during the middle years of John Thomson's editorship (I, II, IV–VI, IX–XI). Among the leading organologists of the 1970s, Ephraim Segerman, Jeremy Montagu and others involved in the establishment of the Fellowship of Makers and Restorers of Historical Instruments (founded in 1975) were powerful and inspiring presences. So too was David Fallows; many of the articles published here have benefited from his knowledge and breadth of interest.

Those of us interested in the literary sources for medieval music, especially musical instruments, were not ploughing a new field in 1970. The *Galpin Society Journal* for 1950 contains Anthony Baines' translation of material pertaining to instruments in Tinctoris' *De Inventione et Usu Musicae*, while the standard edition of the writings by Arnaut de Zwolle and others – the richest of all written sources for medieval organology – had been published even further back, in 1932. However, research during the decade 1970–1980 was given a fresh impetus by the publication of Norma Deane's translation of Werner Bachmann's *Die Anfänge des Streichinstrumentenspiels* (first German edition 1964); in English as *The Origins of Bowing*, this masterly work set new standards for the study of medieval instruments

---

1 The current of interest in early instruments was flowing so strongly in the mid 1970s that another important book was published in the same year, Jeremy Montagu's *The World of Medieval and Renaissance Musical Instruments* (London, 1976).

and some of the articles assembled here were directly inspired by its example. Hugo Steger's *Philologia Musica* appeared soon after, in 1971, and it suddenly began to seem that the study of early instruments had been catapulted to a new level of rigour and comprehensiveness, thanks to the force of German linguistic and historical scholarship which had newly been brought to bear upon it. This was also the decade of Laurence Wright's article on the medieval gittern and citole in the *Galpin Society Journal* for 1977, probably the most rigorous and searching study of any medieval instrument which had appeared in English until that time; several of the articles published here (VII, VIII, XII and XIII) were printed in the same journal under the editorship of the late Anthony Baines.

By the early 1980s many of the fundamental Latin texts had been made available with translations and organological commentaries, among them the texts given here in articles IV, VII, VIII and X; other scholars had accounted for Tinctoris, Ramos de Pareja and Paulus Paulirinus of Prague. My own work in this area continued in some studies of the earlier 1980s (IX, X, XII, XIII and XV), culminating in *Voices and Instruments of the Middle Ages: Instrumental Practice and Songs in France 1100–1300* (London, 1987). This study preserves the 'literary' basis of the 1970–1980 articles but its fundamental thesis – that troubadour and trouvère songs in the High Style were generally performed unaccompanied – reflects the new *a capella* movement of the 1980s, a movement in which articles II and XVII played a part which some scholars have subsequently been kind enough to overestimate. During the period 1983–1993 I was mostly occupied in writing books, but some articles of that period show the same fascination with textual sources and with the task of translating them with accompanying commentary (XI, XVIII and XX).

I would like to take the opportunity to thank all the publishers and copyright holders who have granted permission to reproduce the articles which appear in this volume.

CHRISTOPHER PAGE

Cambridge
February, 1997

PUBLISHER'S NOTE

The articles in this volume, as in all others in the Collected Studies Series, have not been given a new, continuous pagination. In order to avoid confusion, and to facilitate their use where these same studies have been referred to elsewhere, the original pagination has been maintained wherever possible.

Each article has been given a Roman number in order of appearance, as listed in the Contents. This number is repeated on each page and quoted in the index entries.

Biblical instruments in medieval manuscript illustration

It is difficult to think ourselves back into the minds of men for whom [a sense of the past] did not exist . . . in the Middle Ages, and long after, it did not. It was known that Adam went naked till he fell. After that, they pictured the whole past in terms of their own age.   C. S. Lewis[1]

When we consider the vast amount of medieval musical iconography devoted to the past—principally the range of subjects associated with King David—we find little evidence of 'a sense of the past'. For the most part medieval artists were content to represent the Old Testament king with the instruments of their own

Detail plate 22, page 307

Reprinted from *Early Music* 5 (1977), pp. 299—309. By permission of Oxford University Press.

day (plate 1), and even well-informed scholars like Nicholas Trivet (?1258-1328)[2] and Jean de Gerson (1363-1429)[3] discussed biblical instruments as if they were identical with those of Gothic Europe.

It is tempting to conclude that medieval artists and writers had no conception of the fact that musical instruments had evolved and developed since Antiquity, and to relate this ignorance to the lack of period-sense noted by C. S. Lewis. However, this would be rash. A number of medieval writers discuss instruments in evolutionary terms and acknowledge that their ancient forms were different from their later, or present forms. Isidore of Seville (c560-c636), a major authority on musical instruments throughout the Middle Ages, has a firm grasp of these concepts:

According to [Greek] tradition, the form of the cithara was originally like that of the human chest.... Gradually numerous species were invented ... some of square and others of triangular form. The number of strings was also increased and the type altered.[4]

So has a 12th-century copyist of Notker's hymns in a manuscript at St. Gall:

Be it known that the ancient psaltery, I mean a ten-stringed instrument, was in the shape of a letter delta, which is very mystical. But when the musicians and minstrels adopted it for their own purposes, as one authority affirms, they made its shape and form suitable to their convenience, applying additional strings and calling it by the vernacular name *rotta*, thus altering its mystical form of the Trinity.[5]

These two explicit passages are by no means unique. Nicholas Trivet, for example, distinguishes the psaltery as it was 'from ancient times' (*antiquitus*) from the psaltery 'of modern form' (*moderne forme*),[6] and Aegidius of Zamora (13c) distinguishes biblical instruments such as the *cithara* from those of 13th-century Spain—*canon, medius canon, guitarra* and *rabr*—on the grounds that the latter were 'invented finally' (*postremo inventa*).[7] Such an evolutionary theory of instrument-history is outlined in general terms by the author of the *Summa Musicae* (13c).[8]

As we consider these passages we are naturally inclined to ask: where would a medieval artist have turned for models had he wished to represent King David with an 'historical' instrument? While it is true that copying and recopying of manuscripts occasionally bequeathed to the Middle Ages surprisingly accurate representations of ancient instruments (plate 2), there is no evidence that these were studied from an organological point of view, nor that medieval artists

Plate 1 *Musical Instruments of the Levites. Farhi Bible. Completed 1382. From J. Leveen,* The Hebrew Bible in Art *(London, 1944), p. XXXVb.*

Plate 2 *The constellation* fides (lyra) *from an astrological treatise in the British Library, MS Cotton Tib. C.I. c1122, from Peterborough Abbey. This manuscript was copied from a 9th-century manuscript (now Harley 647), itself a copy of a late-classical model. Reproduced by permission of the British Library Board.*

or scholars ever undertook a survey of the musical iconography of antiquity.[9] Biblical archaeology was not an unknown subject in the later Middle Ages, but the remains of instruments that have now been uncovered from sites in the Ancient World were destined to lie hidden for many more centuries.

There was, however, one document, widely circulated and copied in the Middle Ages that purported to describe, with appended illustrations, some of the musical instruments mentioned in the Old Testament. It is the purpose of this article to show that the artists responsible for some musical illustrations in a few medieval manuscripts turned to copies of this work for models of ancient instruments in their belief that the instruments of the past were not, by any means, the same as those of the present. The evidence speaks for itself, and there will be no need to issue explicit warnings to musical iconographers.

Jerome's *Epistle to Dardanus*

One of the most baffling documents that the Middle Ages has left us purports to be a letter from one Hieronymous to one Dardanus, entitled *De Diversis Generibus Musicorum* ('concerning diverse kinds of musical instruments').[10] The letter describes, in most manuscripts with illustrations,[11] some of the instruments mentioned in the Old Testament (*organum, tuba, fistula, cithara, sambuca, psalterium, tympanum* and *chorus*—the last an instrument for the author of the text),[12] and one non-biblical instrument, the *bombulum* (the list varies from MS to MS). The earliest known manuscript dates from the 9th century (plate 3), and the latest from the 14th century.[13] Thereafter we lose track of it until the early 16th century, when parts of it appear in Virdung's *Musica getutscht* of 1511, occupying 'nearly forty per cent of the space Virdung devotes to his introductory survey of instruments'.[14] It has appeared in printed works on musical instruments ever since.

The letter was frequently copied during the Middle Ages. Hammerstein lists eight manuscripts,[15] to which may now be added another two (plates 4-6), and one text without illustrations.[16] It was also widely distributed, copies having been found in English, French, German and Italian manuscripts. The author was generally assumed to be St Jerome (*c*347-420), and given the materials then available, this was a perfectly reasonable supposition. The nature of the epistle—a study guide, in effect, for readers of the Old Testament—recalls Jerome's similar works on Hebrew

Plate 3 *Part of pseudo-Jerome's epistle. Angers, Bibliothèque municipale MS 18, fol. 13r. Chorus, psalterium, two tympana, psalterium and chorus. Between 840 and 850. Northern France. St Rémis de Sens? This is part of the earliest known manuscript of the epistle. Reproduced by permission.*

Plate 4 *Part of pseudo-Jerome's epistle. Rome, Vallicelliana, cod. E.24, fol. 26v. Psalterium and chorus. Late 11th century or early 12th. Umbro-Roman. Reproduced by permission.*

Plate 5 *Part of pseudo-Jerome's epistle. Rome, Vallicelliana, cod. E.24, fol. 27. Psalterium and chorus. Late 11th century or early 12th. Reproduced by permission.*

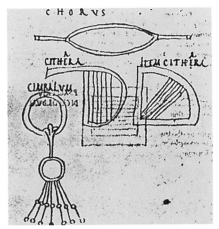

Plate 6 *Part of pseudo-Jerome's epistle. Oxford, Bodleian Library, MS D'Orville 77, fol. 113v. Reproduced by permission.*

names and places mentioned in the Bible, and his collected works do contain another didactic letter addressed to Dardanus. However, historians of musical instruments have long been suspicious of this attribution, and it is not now believed that the epistle is much older than the earliest manuscript[17] (plate 3) which was illustrated in Northern France between c 840 and c 850.[18] Considering the date and provenance of this, the earliest known copy, it is tempting to conclude that the epistle originated among Carolingian scholars, who are known to have compiled 'handy textbooks or chains of select extracts from the Fathers'[19]. There is no doubt that Hrabanus Maurus (780-856), one of the most illustrious of their number, knew the Epistle in the early decades of the 9th century, for he quotes it almost verbatim in his *De Universo*, completed in 844.[20]

The illustrations of the manuscripts have been described as 'fantastic' and even 'a hoax'.[21] How far these statements are dependent upon their authors' ignorance of the fact that in the Middle Ages forgery was by no means irreconcilable with the most serious endeavour is not clear. Certainly it is very tempting for modern organologists who are more interested in accurate depictions of instruments than obscure biblical symbolism to dismiss these pictures outright. But let us imagine how the document first appeared to its medieval readers.

Firstly, it was not considered to be a forgery. It was assumed to be an authentic writing of St Jerome. This most learned doctor of the Church stood in the highest regard during the Middle Ages for his authoritative translation of the Hebrew, Greek and Aramaic texts of the Bible into Latin (the *Vulgate*) and for his many authoritative commentaries upon them. His letters, a large corpus containing a number of didactic items, were also prized. It is difficult to imagine how a document could present better credentials to a medieval reader and be more likely to command his respect than one coming from the pen of St Jerome.

Secondly, the illustrations of the document, generally labelled 'as Hieronymous affirms' or something similar, provided information on a subject that medieval scholars held to be of considerable importance for a true understanding of the Bible: the structure of the musical instruments mentioned in the scriptures. We must recall that the early Latin Fathers of the Church inherited from the Christian scholars of Alexandria the belief that acquaintance with the arts—and indeed with all subjects of worldly learning—was essential for the full study of the Bible.[22] Music, of

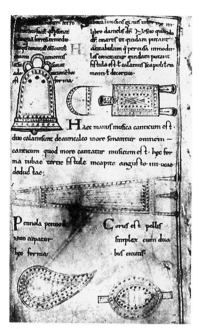

Plate 7 *Part of pseudo-Jerome's epistle. British Library MS Cotton Tib. C.VI fol. 17r. Tintinnabulum, sabuca (sic), tuba, pennola, corus (sic). English. Between 1041 and 1066. Reproduced by permission of British Library Board.*

Plate 8 *Part of pseudo-Jerome's epistle. British Library MS Cotton Tib. C.VI fol. 17v. David with psalterium. English. Winchester School. Between 1041 and 1066.*

course, had its place among the liberal arts, and the nature of musical instruments was a recognized area of musical studies. In his influential treatise *De Doctrina Christiana* St Augustine (354-430) stresses that a biblical scholar requires some knowledge of musical instruments, particularly their structure,[23] and the *Institutiones* of Cassiodorus (*c*485-*c*580), a liberal arts syllabus for biblical students, contains a section on musical instruments.[24] Theologians continued to stress the importance of organological knowledge to biblical studies throughout the Middle Ages.

We cannot avoid the conclusion that pseudo-Jerome's epistle was treated as a serious and authoritative document. Thus it is no surprise to find a copy of the work forming part of the prefatory material gathered for study of the psalms in an 11th-century Anglo-Saxon manuscript at the British Library (plates 7, 8), or taking its place with such major musical authorities as Isidore of Seville and Cassiodorus in a 12th-century musical compendium at Balliol College, Oxford (plates 9-11).[25] We can also see how the epistle would have been useful to artists and writers. Musical theorists, scholars, and also very many artists were doubtless aware that instruments had changed since Antiquity—the mutability of worldly things was too much a favourite theme of the age for them to be entirely ignorant of that—they simply possessed very little information as to what changes had taken place, and how the instruments appeared when they were first used. The epistle appeared to provide historical information pertaining to the instruments of scripture, and the fantastic character of the illustrations probably impressed many medieval readers: what clearly did not represent the instruments of the present could be taken, in a work of such great authority, to represent the instruments of the past.

The epistle and medieval musical iconography

When we turn to medieval musical iconography to look for traces of pseudo-Jerome illustrations, we may distinguish three categories of representations:

(1) Illustrations in manuscripts of pseudo-Jerome generally reproduced in modern works out of context and taken to be actual instruments.

(2) Illustrations that seem to echo features of the pseudo-Jerome manuscripts though actual copying cannot be proved.

(3) Illustrations deliberately copied from manuscripts of pseudo-Jerome's epistle.

303

Plate 9 *Part of pseudo-Jerome's epistle. Oxford, Balliol College MS 173a, fol. 75v. Organum and tuba. Early 12th-century. Reproduced by permission of the Master and Fellows of Balliol College.*

Plate 10 *Part of pseudo-Jerome's epistle. Oxford, Balliol College MS 173a, fol. 76. Bunibula, two citharae. Early 12th century.*

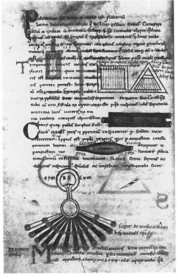

Plate 11 *Part of pseudo Jerome's epistle. Oxford, Balliol College MS 173a, fol. 76v. Two psalteria, tympanum, chorus and cymbalum. Early 12th century.*

Plate 12 *The same illustration as Plate 8 as it appears in the 4th edition of Galpin's* Old English Instruments of Music *(Methuen, London) with confusion of string band removed.*

Illustrations of the first category

A striking example of an illustration of the first category is the representation of a *psalterium* in an 11th-century Anglo-Saxon psalter in the British Library (plate 8). In the fourth edition of Galpin's *Old English Instruments of Music* (revised by Thurston Dart)[26] this illustration is reproduced as an example of an 11th-century English psaltery. To add conviction to the illustration, the confusion in the string-band clearly visible in the original manuscript (plate 8) has been tacitly removed and the string-lines redrawn (plate 12). It is only necessary to turn the pages of the manuscript to discover that the illustration is actually part of a copy of pseudo-Jerome's letter, and in fact does not show an 11th-century English instrument. It should be pointed out that with the disqualification of this illustration, there is no longer evidence that zithers of any kind existed in England during the Anglo-Saxon period.

Illustrations of the second category

Turning from actual manuscripts of the epistle to musical iconography in general, two illustrations from different periods may be cited that are reminiscent in certain details of the epistle illustrations: a representation of a musician with a stringed instrument from the 9th-century Stuttgart Psalter (plate 13),[27] and a similar representation from an 11th/12th-century troper now in the Bibliothèque Nationale (plate 14).[28]

In her book *Stringed Instruments of the Middle Ages*[29] Hortense Panum noted a resemblance between the instrument reproduced here from the Stuttgart Psalter and the quadrangular *psalterium* from the Boulogne pseudo-Jerome (plate 15). Whatever the resemblances (and they are surely not remarkable) it must be admitted that the Stuttgart instrument has a suspicious look. The large decorative protuberances seem most unreal (*pace* Winternitz, who reproduces this illustration in his study of the cithara and cittern).[30] Furthermore the instrument has ten strings, always a danger sign on instruments of the zither class, for very often it signalizes the artist's attempt to illustrate the ten-stringed psaltery of Psalm 33 (which psalm, it should be noted, this picture illustrates). A further feature, which may well connect this illustration with the pseudo-Jerome tradition, is the triangular frame at the top of the instrument enclosing three keyhole shapes. These may be an echo of the similar shapes, often three in number, found in triangular frames on the top of some pseudo-Jerome illustrations (plates 10, 16, 17).

Plate 13 *Stuttgart, Öffentliche Landesbibliothek Bibl. Fol. 23. (The Stuttgart Psalter). Fol. 40, illustration for psalm 33. Third quarter of 9th century, N.E. France.*

Plate 14 *Paris, Bibliothèque Nationale, Cod. Lat. 1118, fol. 110. 11th or early 12th century. Reproduced by permission.*

I

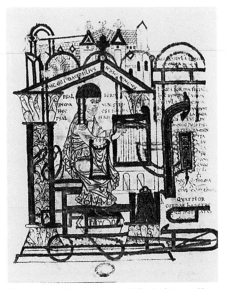

Plate 15 *Part of pseudo-Jerome's epistle. Boulogne-sur-Mer, Bibliothèque municipale MS 20, fol. 2v, Psalterium, fistula, chorus. c1000. ?999, ?1003. Illustrated by Odbert of St Bertin. Reproduced by permission.*

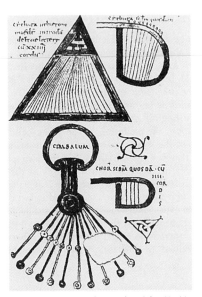

Plate 16 *Part of pseudo-Jerome's epistle. Munich. Staatsbibliothek, cod. lat. 14523, fol. 52r. Two citharae, cimbalum and chorus. 10th century. St Emmeran.*

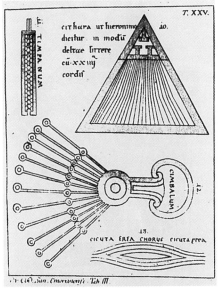

Plate 17 *Part of pseudo-Jerome's epistle, from a 13th-century manuscript found by Gerbert and published in the second volume of De Cantu et Musica Sacra, St Blasien, 1774, T. xxv. Timpanum, cithara, cimbalum, chorus.*

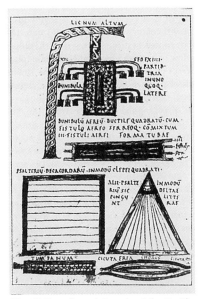

Plate 19 *Part of pseudo-Jerome's epistle. Munich. Staatsbibliothek, cod. lat. 14523, fol. 51v. Fistula, tuba, two psalteria, tympanum, and chorus. 10th century. St Emmeran.*

The second example (plate 14), is well known and has often been reproduced. I suggest that it has at least been influenced by the pseudo-Jerome illustrations. The instrument has the same form and proportions as those in plates 3 and 15, and if the light-coloured bands are the strings (and elsewhere in this manuscript the dark shade is used for wood) then they number ten. Harrison and Rimmer suggest that this illustration represents the ten-stringed psaltery of the psalms, and I agree.[31] See postscript.

Plate 18 *Paris, Bibliothèque nationale MS lat. 11907. Model book illustrated in the Champagne. Late 13th century. From R. W. Scheller, A Survey of Medieval Model Books (Haarlem, 1963), fig. 52 (detail).*

Illustrations of the third category

The first case of actual copying from a manuscript of pseudo-Jerome comes, appropriately and significantly, from a model book: a collection of subjects compiled by a workshop in order that potential patrons might choose the illustrative materials for their manuscripts before work actually commenced. The book from which our illustration is taken (plate 18) was illustrated in the Champagne in the late 13th century.[32] In the top two bands of the right-hand page an artist has drawn subjects derived from the Book of Revelation, including six elders of the Apocalypse with their stringed instruments and flasks (Rev 5:8). The third elder from the left holds a square object that is most likely intended to be a stringed instrument, as there is no basis in the text of Revelation (there is medieval iconographic tradition) for showing the elders with any other kind, though it is certainly not one of the standard medieval types. Outside of Spain the square psaltery does not appear to have been very much used in the later Middle Ages. Indeed, the artist seems to have been very uncertain about the appearance and mechanics of this instrument: it is undecorated and has no strings. It seems likely that it has been copied from a pseudo-Jerome manuscript (cf. plates 11, 19, 20).

The second example, this time a case of extended and most careful copying from the epistle, is taken from the Polirone Psalter (plates 21, 22), illustrated in Polirone under strong Roman influence, perhaps by Romans, *c* 1125.[33] Plate 21, taken from folio 1v of the manuscript, shows David and his four musicians. It is a familiar illustration, having been recently reproduced by Werner Bachmann among others.[34] Bachmann calls the fiddle at the top right-hand corner of the manuscript a 'typical example' of the spade-shaped fiddle,[35] and indeed there is no reason to doubt that the stringed instruments, the horn and the hand bell are

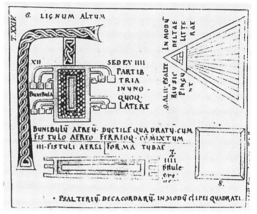

Plate 20 *Part of pseudo-Jerome's epistle, from a 13th-century manuscript found by Gerbert and published in the second volume of* De Cantu et Musica Sacra, *St Blasien, 1774, T.xxiv. Fistula, tuba, two psalteria.*

Plate 22 *Mantua, Biblioteca Comunale, C.III.20, fol. 2 (The Polirone Psalter). Illustrated in Polirone c 1125. Reproduced by permission.*

I

Plate 21 *Mantua, Biblioteca Comunale, C.III.20, fol. 1v (The Polirone Psalter). Illustrated in Polirone c 1125.*

about the time of the Polirone Psalter is not in doubt, for a copy of the letter is included in the Vallicelliana Psalter (plates 4, 5), an Umbro-Roman manuscript of the late 11th or early 12th century[37] (I do not suggest that the Polirone instruments were copied from this source).

In the manuscripts we have been examining, the influence of pseudo-Jerome illustrations, whether merely an echo of a striking feature or a direct copy, is part of an attempt by the artists to recapture the ancient forms of certain musical instruments. It was not thoroughly done—'biblical' instruments are sometimes mixed with modern ones—and we must avoid the temptation to over-intellectualize the artists' procedure. Suffice it to say that complete consistency of approach is rarely to be discerned in any medieval artistic procedures; we encounter instead 'chequerboards of styles and approaches'.[38] We must regard these manuscripts as vivid expressions of certain medieval attitudes to musical instruments.

I am grateful to my wife, Régine Page of the Département d'Histoire de l'Art, University of Toulouse, who first brought some of the manuscript materials in this article to my notice, and to Professor Howard Mayer Brown, who read the first draft and made a number of helpful suggestions.

Abbreviations used in the notes
GS Martin Gerbert, *Scriptores Ecclesiastici de Musica*, 3 vols. (St. Blasien, 1784).
PL J. P. Migne, *Patrologiae Cursus Completus: Patrologia Latina*, 221 vols. (Paris, 1844-1864).

Bibliography
In addition to the studies mentioned in the notes the following works bear upon some of the issues discussed here:
Gelineau, S. J., *Voices and Instruments in Christian Worship*, trans. Howell, (London, 1964).
Gerbert, M., *De Cantu et Musica Sacra*, 2 vols. (St Blasien, 1774), 2, p.137ff.
Gérold, Th., *Les Pères de l'Église et la Musique* (Strasbourg, 1931), 180ff.
Hirsch-Reich, B., 'The Symbolism of Musical Instruments in the *Psalterium X Chordarum* of Joachim of Fiore and its Patristic Sources, *Studia Patristica*, IX (1966), pp. 540-51.
Lemarchand, A., 'Notes sur quelques instruments de la musique des Hébreux d'après un manuscrit du IXe siècle', *Mém. de la Soc. d'agr., sciences et arts d'Angers* (1953).

drawn from life. But what of the wind instrument at the bottom of the picture? According to Sybil Marcuse it is a 'primitive form of bagpipe with short blowpipe, out-sized bag, short chanter—in all probability a double chanter, judging by its sausage shape',[36] and as a rationalization of the illustration this is reasonable enough. It is the underlying assumption that the illustration shows a 'real' instrument that is, I believe, at fault, for this is surely a *chorus* copied from a manuscript of pseudo-Jerome (*cf* plates 11 and 19).

Any doubt as to whether this 'bagpipe' is actually pseudo-Jerome's *chorus* is dispelled when we turn the page of the psalter, for here we find definite evidence that the artists had a copy of the epistle at hand (plate 22). The musician to the left of David holds what is undoubtedly a *cithara* from a pseudo-Jerome manuscript (*cf* plates 10 and 16), and the square instrument held by David has certainly been taken from the same source (*cf* plates 3 and 4). It is worthwhile to point out that the existence of the epistle in the area of Rome at

McKinnon, J., *The Church Fathers and Musical Instruments*, Unpublished Ph.D. dissertation, Columbia University (1965).

McKinnon, J., 'The Meaning of Patristic Polemic against Musical Instruments', *Current Musicology,* 1 (1965), 69-82.

McKinnon, J., 'Musical Instruments in Medieval Psalm Commentaries and Psalters', *Journal of the American Musicological Society,* xxi (1968), 1, 3-30.

Reeves, M., and Beatrice Hirsch-Reich, *The Figurae of Joachim of Fiore,* Oxford, 1972, p. 199f.

Francisci Blanchini Veronensis, *De Tribus Generibus Instrumentorum Musicae Veterum Organicae* (with illustrations), British Library, Add. MS 24110: an 18th-century antiquarian essay that draws deeply on medieval traditions.

Notes

[1] C. S. Lewis, *The Discarded Image* (Cambridge, 1964) p.183.

[2] Nicholas Trivet's commentary upon Psalm 150, with illustrations of musical instruments in Oxford, MS Bodley 738, fols. 250r-250v. But see below for Trivet on the psaltery.

[3] Jean de Gerson, *Tractatus de Canticis.* Text and translation in Christopher Page, 'An Early Fifteenth-century Treatise on Musical Instruments' (forthcoming).

[4] Translation from Oliver Strunk, *Source Readings in Music History: Antiquity and the Middle Ages* (New York, 1965), p. 98. Original text in PL 82 col. 167.

[5] Original text in Hortense Panum, *Stringed Instruments of the Middle Ages* (London, 1940), p. 168.

[6] MS Bodley 738 fol. 250r.

[7] Aegidius of Zamora, *Ars Musica,* in GS, II, p. 388.

[8] *Summa Musicae* in GS, III, p. 193-4.

[9] For the earliest studies of the musical iconography of Antiquity see E. Winternitz, *Musical Instruments and their Symbolism in Western Art* (London, 1967), p. 26ff.

[10] A convenient text is in PL 30 cols. 213-215. For a text with commentary see R. Hammerstein 'Instrumenta Hieronymi', in *Archiv für Musikwissenschaft,* 16 (1959), p. 117-34, with four plates. For a text with German translation and notes on sources see H. Avenary, 'Hieronymus' Epistel über die Musikinstrumente und ihre altöstlichen Quellen', in *Anuario Musical,* 16 (1961) p. 55-80. The title of the epistle alludes to Daniel 3:5.

[11] One manuscript without illustrations that has come to my notice is London, British Library, MS Royal 8.C.III, fol. 2r-6v.

[12] These are mostly the instruments in Daniel 3: 5, 7, 10, 15.

[13] Cambridge, Peterhouse 198, fols. 133r-133v, dating from the 14c, is apparently the latest known manuscript copy. See Hammerstein, *op. cit.,* plates 2, 3 and 4.

[14] E. M. Ripin, 'A Re-evaluation of Virdung's *Musica getutscht*', *Journal of the American Musicological Society,* xxix (1976), p. 216. The illustrations appear on fols. Cijv to Diij of the 1511 edition.

[15] Hammerstein, *op. cit.,* p. 118-19.

[16] See note 11.

[17] For a review of scholarly opinion concerning pseudo-Jerome's letter see Hammerstein, *op. cit.,* p. 119. The view that the document is a forgery dating from the 9th century is generally associated with Curt Sachs (see *The History of Musical Instruments,* London, 1942, p. 281), but F. M. Padelford held this opinion at the end of the 19th century (see *Old English Musical Terms,* Bonn, 1899, p. 33).

[18] An exhaustive description is given in Hugo Steger, *David Rex et Propheta* (Nuremberg, 1961), Dkm. 6.

[19] Beryl Smalley, *The Study of the Bible in the Middle Ages* (second edition, Oxford, 1952), p. 37.

[20] Text in PL III, cols. 495-500.

[21] See Hammerstein, *op. cit.,* p. 119.

[22] See Beryl Smalley, *op. cit.,* p. 12.

[23] For original text see PL 34, cols. 48-9. English translation by D. W. Robertson Jr., *On Christian Doctrine* (New York, 1958), p. 53.

[24] For original text see PL 70 cols. 1208-1209.

[25] For the contents of this manuscript see R. A. B. Mynors, *Catalogue of the Manuscripts of Balliol College Oxford* (Oxford, 1963), no. 173a.

[26] F. W. Galpin, *Old English Instruments of Music,* 4th edn., rev. Dart (London, 1965), plate 12, commentary page 45. For a description of the manuscript see Steger, *op. cit.,* Dkm. 27, 27a and 27b.

[27] Steger, *op. cit.,* Dkm. 16.

[28] Steger, *op. cit.,* plate 18 shows the other illustrations of instruments in this manuscript. See also Dkm. 33.

[29] Panum, *op. cit.,* p. 166.

[30] Winternitz, *op. cit.,* plate 15b.

[31] Frank Harrison and Joan Rimmer, *European Musical Instruments* (London, 1964), pl. 39a.

[32] See R. W. Scheller, *A Survey of Medieval Model Books* (Haarlem, 1963), fig. 52.

[33] For an account of the manuscript see E. B. Garrison, *Studies in the History of Medieval Italian Painting,* III, numbers 3 and 4, 1958, p. 216.

[34] Werner Bachmann, *The Origins of Bowing,* trans. Norma Deane (London, 1969), plate 26.

[35] Bachmann, *op. cit.,* p. 62.

[36] Sibyl Marcuse, *A Survey of Musical Instruments* (London, 1975), p. 674.

[37] Details of the manuscript may be found in Garrison, *op. cit.,* II, 2 (1955), p. 86-91.

[38] Elizabeth Salter, 'Medieval Poetry and the Visual Arts', *Essays and Studies 22* (1969), p. 20.

Ten-stringed psaltery with allegorical captions, from the Praemissiones, Brit. Lib. MS Add. 11439, f.102v⁰, 14c.—a collection of genuine and spurious Joachimist works.

Machaut's 'Pupil' Deschamps on the Performance of Music

Voices or instruments in the 14th-century chanson

1 *Deschamps presents his* Livret de la fragilité d'humaine nature *to Charles VI, from the dedicatory copy sent to the king in 1383. Paris, Bib. nat., f.fr. 20028, f.4v.*

The modern performer of Machaut's music is encouraged to believe by almost all authorities that the untexted tenor and contratenor lines of the polyphonic chansons were rendered instrumentally.[1] Recordings and concert performances show that this view commands complete acceptance.

The 'authenticity' of the instruments generally used in modern performances of Machaut's music is a subject that invites comment,[2] but more important is the general question of how far these performances correspond to medieval practice. It is not the purpose of this article to survey all the evidence bearing upon this question, but to give text and translation of some hitherto little-noticed remarks on the subject by Machaut's 'pupil', Eustache Deschamps (*Art de Dictier et de Fere Chançons*, 1392).[3]

Deschamps, a Champenois like Guillaume de Machaut and Philippe de Vitry, was born *c* 1346. The author of the *Règles de la Seconde Rhétorique* states that he was Machaut's nephew (*nepveux de maistre Guillaume de Machault*),[4] and though we have no proof of this, it is clear that the two poets were on intimate terms. In a poem sent to Péronne d'Armentières (inspiratrice of Machaut's *Voir Dit*) Deschamps claims that Machaut 'brought me up and did me many kindnesses',[5] and in the second of his two ballades on the death of the older poet, Deschamps refers to him as 'very sweet master'.[6] Machaut settled into the relatively peaceful life of a canon in the 1340s[7] and would thus have been in a position to educate the young Deschamps. It is pleasing, if fanciful, to suppose that some of the references to music lessons in Deschamps's poetry derive ultimately from his early experiences as Machaut's pupil at Rheims:[8]

Aprenez le fa et le mi,
Bien vous monstreray l'escripture
Tant que vous n'arez jamais cure
D'autre art sçavoir, fors de compter
Une, deux, les temps mesurer
Et fleureter plus que le cours.[9]

Deschamps was undoubtedly familiar with his master's music, just as he knew his literary works. Strictly speaking, there is no solid evidence in the poems (and there is no external evidence) that Deschamps was a musician with performing skills, but we may assume that he was at least a keen and discriminating listener.[10]

In the *Art de Dictier* Deschamps is primarily concerned with poetic forms and other aspects of *réthorique*, the *science de parler-droictement*. The treatise opens with an

Reprinted from *Early Music* 5 (1977), pp. 484—491. By permission of Oxford University Press.

account of the seven liberal arts, which he studied at the University of Orleans.[11]

In the section on music Deschamps distinguishes between *musique artificiele* (music of voices and instruments) and *musique naturele* (poetry and verse).[12] Contrasting the two forms of music, he states that both are pleasant to hear alone. Poems that are without a musical setting may be recited or read, and music 'may be sung with the voice in an artistic way without words (*par art, sanz parole*)'. The explicitness of *par art* strongly suggests that Deschamps is thinking of polyphonic chansons (rather than simple monodies such as Machaut's *virelais* which do not appear outside of the composer's own manuscripts and were clearly of limited appeal).[13] The artistic music which is sung but which is *sanz parole* must surely be the generally textless tenors and contratenors of these pieces, which are almost invariably performed instrumentally today?

Deschamps proceeds to make a fuller allusion to the vocalisation of these parts, though his statements present difficulties and must be read with circumspection. Continuing the comparison between the two forms of music, he states that the texts of chansons may be recited before one who is ill, or in the presence of lords and ladies in privacy, where music does not always have a place. This is puzzling, for there is abundant evidence to show that the music of voices and instruments was considered therapeutic[14] (a view to which Deschamps subscribes in the opening lines of his chapter on music), and that the music of small instrumental ensembles was considered an appropriate entertainment for intimate aristocratic gatherings.[15] Even if we accept the theory proposed by some scholars that Deschamps, not a musician, is deliberately underestimating the artistic value and social acceptability of music in the *Art de Dictier*,[16] it must seem unlikely that he would make statements in a manual of this kind bearing no relation to the experience of his readers. It is possible that Deschamps's remarks have reference only to the court of the unknown noble for whom he composed the treatise,[17] but this cannot be confirmed. Taken as they stand, they imply that Deschamps understood the music of chansons to be a special artistic genre not to be rendered in the same informal circumstances as the poems.

Deschamps gives two reasons for this state of affairs. Primarily, there is the *haulteur* of this music. This may be interpreted in three ways: as a reference to the music's courtly and noble character; to its high pitch;

2 *The medicinal effects of music. The text accompanying the illustration in the MS begins:* Organare cantum vel sonare. Natura est quaedam raucha et cantus violentus. *('To play a song with instruments. By nature it is somewhat harsh and the singing violent'),* Tacuinum Sanitatis, *Österreichische Nationalbibliothek Codex Vindobonensis series nova 2644. f.103v. Italian, late 14th century.*

or to its loudness.[18] The first and second interpretations are not indefensible, but neither makes very convincing sense of Deschamps's passage as a whole. Music that is courtly and noble in character would not thereby be excluded from performance in private circumstances, nor necessarily from performance in the sick-room. Music of predominantly high pitch might be somewhat incongenial to a *malade*, but why should *seigneurs et dames* have any aversion to it? A reference to the loudness of the music seems the most plausible interpretation. Unfortunately it is not clear whether Deschamps is making the relatively trivial point that the singing voice may make more noise than the reading voice, or whether he intends a specific reference to a cultivated stylistic feature of artistic singing (cf. illusn. 2).[19]

Deschamps's second reason for the inappropriateness of music to the private chamber and the sick-room is that it requires '*three voices for the tenors and contratenors . . . to perform the said music perfectly with two or three people'.*

A reference to the vocal performance of tenors and contratenors by a 14th-century writer who had undoubtedly heard Machaut's music performed is a valuable document of performance practice. Before we accept Deschamps' testimony we must reassure ourselves that 'three voices' is a just translation of the crucial words *triplicité des voix*.

Certainly this rendering creates a difficulty. How can 'two or three people' render a composition with 'three voices'? The problem would be solved by translating *triplicité des voix* as 'three parts'. Two people can render three parts if one of them both sings and plays an instrument. However, *voix* in the transferred sense 'part of a musical composition' is not recorded in Old French,[20] nor is *vox* used in this way in the Latin musical treatises of the period.[21] This translation is therefore untenable.

A second conceivable translation of *voix* would be 'pitches' or 'notes' both vocally and instrumentally produced (cf. Deschamps' reference to *instrumens des voix*). This is certainly in keeping with the theorists' use of *vox* when they are not referring exclusively to the human voice.[22] However, 'three notes' or 'three pitches' does not make good sense in the full context of Deschamps' passage. One might argue that 'three pitches' is a reference to the registers of *cantus, tenor* and *contratenor*, but in actual fact the latter two parts generally operate within much the same range in the 14th-century chanson. A further objection to this translation is that we must explain why such a straightforward matter of musical architectonics as the different registers of polyphonic parts should render chansons unfit for private performance before aristocrats and convalescents.

The most satisfactory translation for *triplicité des voix*, and the one that strains the sense of Deschamps' passage least, is 'three voices', and we are therefore left with an explicit reference to the vocalization of the generally textless tenors and contratenors of chansons, accompanied by a statement that this must be done for the 'perfection' of the music.

A final ambiguity remains. Can Deschamps' reference to *triplicité des voix* for tenor and contratenor parts be taken to indicate that these lines were sung three to a part? This interpretation does not strain the text, but it is an unlikely one.

Pictorial sources and the internal stylistic evidence of the music itself suggest that the individual lines of

3 *The medicinal effects of vocal music. The text accompanying the illustration in the MS begins:* Cantus. Natura concordari voces ystrumentorum sonis, quorum non sunt usus *('Singing. Its nature consists in making voices harmonize with the sounds of instruments which, however, are not used'). MS as illusn. 2, fol. 103r*

14th-century chansons were sung by soloists occasionally doubled by instruments.[23] Many of Machaut's finely delineated tenor and contratenor parts would be unduly thickened and blurred by 'choral' performance (some modern scholars have taken objection to instrumental doubling for this reason).[24] Deschamps's *triplicité des voix pour les teneurs et contreteneurs* surely implies just three vocal parts like *triplicibus* ('in three [parts]') in the *Quatuor Principalia Musica*,[25] and *cum tribus [scilicet cum tenore carmine et contratenore]* ('with three [that is with tenor and contratenor]') in the anonymous 14th-century treatise *Ars Discantus*?[26]

What then of Deschamps's puzzling reference to the performance of three-part vocal polyphony by 'two or three people'? Deschamps's prose is not a model of clarity, and the syntax of the passage in question is tortuous. In this particular case we cannot avoid forming the impression that the sentence is at least elliptical, if not actually careless in expression. The point Deschamps wishes to make is that the performance of music involves more than the *homme seul* that suffices for the recitation of verse. He notes that the number may be increased from one to include two or three performers, but introduces this thought with a reference to the standard chanson arrangement of his day (cantus, tenor and contratenor) that is only consonant with a group of three performers. The two parts of the sentence are not fully congruent, but the overall implication is not obscured.

Deschamps' references to the vocal performance of tenors and contratenors, problematic though they are, are by no means unsupported. Gace de la Buigne, in his poem *Le Roman des Deduis* (written 1359-77) presents a debate between *Amour de Chiens* and *Amour d'Oyseaulx* in which the spokesman for the hunting dogs describes a pack in full cry in terms of part-singing:[27]

Les plus grans chantent la teneur,
Les autres la contreteneur,
Ceulx qui ont la plus clere gueule
Chantent le tresble sans demeure,
Et les plus petis le quadouble
En faisant la quinte sur double.

The relation of such a reference to actual musical practice may seem somewhat oblique, but it is the essence of this literary genre that animals do as humans do. Birds 'deschant',[28] and in contemporary Gothic art animal musicians play instruments demonstrably drawn from the real world. There is no reason to doubt that Gace de la Buigne's passage derives from his experience of music in performance and reflects actual practice.

The hypothesis that the tenors and contratenors of Machaut's polyphonic chansons were generally performed instrumentally in the 14th-century has strong practical appeal. At this present stage of the early music 'revival', crumhorns, viols, sackbuts and other (anachronistic) instruments that can supply these lines at written pitch are readily available, whereas singers willing (and able) to vocalize them are not. Certainly there is no reason to suppose that the apparently entirely vocal performance envisaged by Deschamps was the *only* way in which Machaut's chansons were performed,[29] but his reference should inspire far more experiment with this method of performance. This would please the growing number of musicologists

who believe that the question of instrumental participation in various forms of medieval music needs to be re-examined.[30]

It is true that some 14th-century tenor and contratenor lines are by no means easy to sing effectively (ex. 1, for instance), but singers should be discouraged from assuming that it is possible to make absolute judgements about what is 'vocal' or 'unvocal'.[31] As Lloyd Hibberd has written in a penetrating analysis of the proposition that certain things in music 'are especially suitable and idiomatic for instruments and awkward or even impossible for voices':[32]

'...the argument that short melodic fragments are "unvocal" *per se*, rests largely on a question of taste. Such parts do not often, it is true, seem very expressive to modern ears, in vocal music, but earlier epochs may have felt quite otherwise about them ... As regards "awkward" leaps, rapidity of movement, continuous activity, short melodic fragments, melodic sequences and coloratura passages—the exclusive "instrumentalness" of all these becomes increasingly dubious on closer examination.'

Contratenor

Ex. 1; Section of the contratenor added in five of a total of eleven sources to Machaut's Ballade 18, *De petit po*, one of the most widely diffused of his works. In the five Machaut manuscripts this part does not appear.[33] Quoted here from the edition of Leo Schrade, *Polyphonic Music of the Fourteenth Century*, vols. II and III (Monaco, 1956).

The text
The text given here is that published by Gaston Raynaud in the seventh volume of the *Oeuvres complètes*. It is reproduced by kind permission of the *Société des Anciens Textes Français*.

The translation
The translation aims to be literal without distorting English idiom. In order that it may read clearly and fluently, Deschamps's long and involved sentences have been generally split into smaller units and punctuated accordingly.

The frequency with which Deschamps uses certain technical terms in a variety of contexts is somewhat confusing. The following translations are used here:

Chant, chans: Apparently music in general (both vocal and instrumental music in the first paragraph). It is rendered 'melody' here, as this word may be put into the plural when the context requires (unlike 'music').

Chant de la musique artificiele: 'Music', Deschamps explains the terms 'natural' music and 'artificial' music in the text.

Chant musicant: 'Music', this usage is related to the above.

Chansons natureles: 'Poems'. Deschamps explains the terminology in the text.

The translations of other musical terms (e.g. *deschanter, doubler*) are explained in the notes.

All instrument names have been left in their original forms. Little would be gained by substituting 'gittern' for *guiterne*, etc.

Extracts from *L'Art de Dictier* of Eustache Deschamps (completed 25 November 1392).

Text

De Musique

Musique est la derreniere science ainsis comme la medicine des .VII. ars; car quant le couraige et l'esperit des creatures ententives aux autres ars dessus declairez sont lassez et ennuyez de leurs labours, musique, par la douçour de sa science et la melodie de sa voix, leur chante par ses .VI. notes tierçoyées,[34] quintes et doublées,[35] ses chans delectables et plaisans, lesquelz elle fait aucunefoiz en orgues et chalumeaux par souflement de bouche et touchement de doiz; autrefoiz en harpe, en rebebe, en vielle, en douçaine, en sons de tabours, en fleuthes et autres instrumens musicans, tant que par sa melodie delectable les cuers et esperis de ceuls qui auxdiz ars, par pensée, ymaginaison et labours de bras estoient traveilliez, pesans et ennuiez, sont medicinez et recreez, et plus habiles après a estudier et labourer aux autres .VI. ars dessus nommez.

Et est a sçavoir que nous avons deux musiques, dont l'une est *artificiele* et l'autre est *naturele*.

L'*artificiele* est celle dont dessus est faicte mencion; et est appellée artificiele de son art, car par ses .VI. notes, qui sont appellées *us, ré, my, fa, sol, la,* l'en puet aprandre[36] a chanter, acorder, doubler, quintoier,[37] tierçoier, tenir,[38] deschanter,[39] par figure de notes, par clefs et par lignes, le plus rude homme du monde, ou au moins tant faire, que, supposé ore qu'il n'eust pas la voix habile pour chanter ou bien acorder, sçaroit il et pourroit congnoistre les accors ou discors avecques tout l'art d'icelle science, par laquelle et les notes dessus dictes l'en acorde et donne l'en son divers aux aciers, aux fers, aux boys et aux metaulx, par diverses infusions interposées d'estain, de plomb, d'arain et de cuivre, si comme il puet apparoir es sons des cloches mises en divers orloges, lesqueles par le touchement des marteaulx donnent sons acordables selon lesdictes .VI. notes, proferans les sequences et autres choses des chans de saincte Eglise. Et ainsi puet estre entendu des autres instrumens des voix comme rebebes, guiternes, vielles et psalterions, par la diversité des tailles, la nature des cordes et le touchement des doiz, et des fleutes et haulx instrumens semblables,[40] avecques le vent de la bouche qui bailliée leur est.

Et aussi ces deux musiques sont si consonans l'une avecques l'autre, que chascune puet bien estre appellée musique, pour la douceur tant du chant comme des paroles qui toutes sont prononcées et pointoyées par douçour de voix et ouverture de bouche; et est de ces deux ainsi comme un mariage en conjunction de science, par les chans qui sont plus anobliz et mieulx seans par la parole et faconde des diz qu'elle ne seroit seule de soy. Et semblablement les chançons natureles sont delectables et embellies par la melodie et les teneurs, trebles et contreteneurs du chant de la musique artificiele. Et neantmoins est chascune de ces deux plaisant a ouir par soy; et se puet l'une chanter par voix et par art, sanz parole; et aussi les diz des chançons se puent souventefoiz recorder en pluseurs lieux ou ilz sont moult voulentiers ois, ou le chant de la musique artificiele n'aroit pas tousjours lieu, comme entre seigneurs et dames estans a leur privé et secretement, ou la musique naturele se puet dire et recorder par un homme seul, de bouche, ou lire aucun livre de ces choses plaisans devant un malade, et autres cas semblables ou le chant musicant n'aroit point lieu pour la haulteur d'icellui, et la triplicité des voix pour les teneurs et contreteneurs necessaires a ycellui chant proferer par deux ou trois personnes pour la perfection dudit chant.

Translation

Concerning Music

Music is the final, and the medicinal science of the seven arts; for when the heart and spirit of those

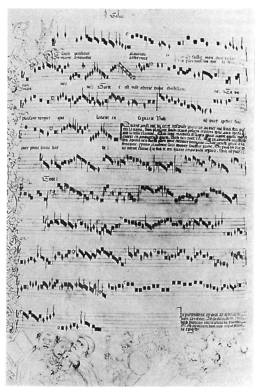

4 *Chantilly, Musée Condé MS 564 (olim 1047), f.37. 3-part Ballade* Le
Sault perilleux *by Jean Galiot (red notation obscured in photograph). Monks
sing in the lower border. Are they singing plainchant or Galiot's Ballade?*

Artificial music is that which is mentioned above. It is
called *artificial* as an art for by its six notes, which are
called *us, ré, my, fa, sol, la*, one may teach the most un-
cultivated man in the world to sing, make harmony
and an octave, fifth and third, make a tenor, and
descant by the form of notes, by clefs and by staves. Or
at least one may do so much, supposing now he did
not have a voice suitable for singing or making
harmony well, that he would know and be able to
recognize accords and discords with all the art of this
science by which, and by the notes mentioned above,
one tunes and gives diverse sound to steels, irons,
woods and metals, by various additives of tin, lead,
bronze, and copper, as may be evident in the sounds of
bells enclosed in various clocks. These, by the touch of
hammers, give harmonious sounds according to the
said six notes, uttering sequences and other things of
the melodies of Holy Church. This harmony may be
heard on other musical instruments such as *rebebes,
guiternes, vielles,* and *psalterions* by the variety of their
size, the nature of the strings and the action of the
fingers. Also on *fleutes* and on similar loud instruments,[40] with the breath that is introduced into them.

Also these two musics are só consonant with one
another that each may well be called 'music', as much
for the sweetness of both the melody and of the words
which are all pronounced and articulated by the
pleasantness of the voice and opening of the mouth. It
is with these two as a marriage, that is, a conjunction
of science, through the melodies which are more
ennobled and are more seemly with the words and the
fluency of the texts than they [lit. *it*] would be alone.
Similarly, poems are made more delightful and embel-
lished by the melody and the tenors, trebles and
contratenors of music. However, each of these two
[i.e., music and poetry] is pleasant to hear by itself.
One may be sung with the voice in an artistic way
without words; also the texts of chansons may often be
recited in many places where they are very willingly
heard, and where their music would not always be
appropriate as among lords and ladies remaining in
private, where poetry may be recited by a single
person, or where some book of these pleasant things
may be read before one who is ill. There are other
similar cases where music would have no place because
of its loudness, and because of the three voices for the
tenors and contratenors that are necessary to perform
the said music perfectly with two or three people.

applied to the other arts treated above are wearied
and vexed with their labours, Music, by the sweetness
of her science and the melodiousness of her voice,
sings them her delectable and pleasant melodies with
her six notes in thirds, fifths, and octaves. These she
performs sometimes with *orgues* and *chalumeaux* by
blowing with the mouth and touching with the fingers;
otherwise with the *harpe, rebebe, vielle, douçaine,* with
noise of *tabours,* with *fleuthes,* and other musical instruments, so much so that by her delectable melody the
hearts and minds of those who were fatigued, weighed
down, and troubled with the said arts by thought,
imagination or labour are revived and restored. Thus
they are afterwards more able to study and labour with
the other six arts named above.

It must be understood that we have two kinds of
music: one is *artificial* and the other is *natural.*

Abbreviations

CS E. de Coussemaker. *Scriptorum de Musica Medii Aevi Nova Series*, 4 vols., Paris, 1864-76.

GS Martin Gerbert, *Scriptores Ecclesiastici de Musica*, 3 vols., Typis San-Blasianis, 1784.

PL J. P. Migne, *Patrologiae cursus Completus: Series Latina*, 221 vols., Paris, 1844-64.

Notes

[1] See, for example, G. Reese, *Music in the Middle Ages*, London, 1941, p. 383; P. H. Lang, *Music in Western Civilisation*, London, 1942, p. 153; Gilbert Reaney, 'Ars Nova in France', in *New Oxford History of Music, III, Ars Nova and the Renaissance*, 1300-1540, ed. Dom A. Hughes and G. Abraham, London, 1960, p. 25; W. Smoldon, *A History of Music*, London, 1965, p. 76; D. J. Grout, *A History of Western Music*, revised ed., London, 1973, p. 124. This view is often argued on the basis of the purely hypothetical notion that the tenors of 13th-century motets were performed upon instruments.

[2] See, for example, Jeremy Montagu, 'The "Authentic" sound of early music', *Early Music*, 3 (1975), 3, pp. 242-243.

[3] Text in *Oeuvres complètes d'Eustache Deschamps*, ed. Le Marquis de Queux de Saint-Hilaire and Gaston Raynaud, Société des Anciens Textes Français, pubs. 9, Paris, 1878-1903, VII, pp. 266-92. The work is mentioned briefly in Gilbert Reaney, 'Voices and Instruments in the music of Guillaume de Machaut', *Revue Belge de Musicologie*, X (1956), fasc. 1-2, p. 3 (note 2) and p. 8.

[4] *Oeuvres*, XI, p. 11, n. 4.

[5] Ballade 447 (Oeuvres, III, p. 259-60) *"Machaut ... Qui m'a nourry et fait maintes douçours"*. In this poem, written after Machaut's death, Deschamps asks to be Péronne's *loyal ami* for *l'onneur* of Machaut.

[6] *Oeuvres*, 1, p. 245.

[7] A. Machabey, *Guillaume de Machault*, Paris, 1955, 1, p. 34f.

[8] Cf. Nan Cooke Carpenter, *Music in the Medieval and Renaissance Universities*, University of Oklahoma Press, 1958 (reprinted Da Capo Press, New York, 1972), p. 75.

[9] Ballade 1169 (Oeuvres, VI, p. 113).

[10] Concerning a possible reference by Deschamps to composition of his own music see the *Oeuvres*, XI, p. 156. Nigel Wilkins ('The post-Machaut Generation of Poet-Musicians', *Nottingham Mediaeval Studies*, XII (1968), p. 83) states that 'Deschamps ... was not a musician ...' For discussion of the view that Deschamps, unlike previous poets, was unable to compose music, and that he wrote the *Art de Dictier* in an attempt to have 'spoken verse accorded the same recognition as the best known poetry before him' see Glending Olson, 'Deschamps' *Art de Dictier* and Chaucer's Literary Environment', *Speculum*, XLVIII (1973), 4, pp. 714-723; Kenneth Varty, 'Deschamps' *Art de Dictier*', *French Studies*, XIX (1965), pp. 164-68; I. S. Laurie, 'Deschamps and the Lyric as Natural Music', *Modern Language Review*, LIX (1964), pp. 561-70.

[11] For the view that this account concentrates more on the practical application of the seven arts than former treatments, see R. Dragonetti, ' "La Poesie ... ceste musique naturele": Essai d'exégèse d'un passage de l'*Art de Dictier* d'Eustache Deschamps', *Fin du Moyen Age et Renaissance; Mélanges de philologie française offerts à Robert Guiette*, Anvers, 1961, p. 53. For a discussion of music and the liberal arts at the University of Orléans in the Middle Ages with special reference to Deschamps and the *Art de Dictier* see Nan Cooke Carpenter, op cit, pp. 69-76.

[12] The inclusion of poetry under the heading of *Musica* may be found in the *Poetria* of Johannes de Garlandia (text and translation in T. Lawler, *The 'Parisiana Poetria' of John of Garland*, Yale University Press, 1974, ch. I, lines 54-5, and 7, lines 469-70), and to some extent in the *De Musica* of Boethius (PL, LXIII, col. 1196). In the musical theorists the terms *naturalis* and *artificialis* are used in a variety of ways. See, for example, the writings of Regino of Prüm (GS, I, p. 236), Aribo

Scholasticus (GS, II, p. 225), John of Affligem (GS, II, p. 232), Marchettus de Padua (GS, IV, pp. 68 and 152), Adam of Fulda (GS, IV, p. 333) and the treatises *Summa Musicae* (GS, IV, p. 199), and *Ars Discantus* (CS, III, p. 103). The author of the *Quatuor Principalia Musica* distinguishes between 'natural' and 'artificial' instruments of practical music. The 'natural' instruments are the lungs and teeth, etc., and the 'artificial' are 'organa, viella, cithara, cistolla, psalterium et cetera' (CS, IV, p. 205).

[13] Gilbert Reaney, 'Machaut's Influence on Late Medieval Music', *The Monthly Music Record*, 88 (1958), p. 51.

[14] For an elaborate account of the medicinal and therapeutic qualities of music see Tinctoris's treatises *Complexus Effectuum Musices* (CS, IV, p. 191f) and *Complexus Viginti Effectuum Nobilis Artis Musices* (ibid 195f) (both versions of the same work). See also plates 2 and 3.

[15] See, for example, the quotations from 14th-century and 15th-century texts gathered in E. A. Bowles, 'Musical Instruments at the Medieval Banquet', *Revue Belge de Musicologie*, 12 (1958), p. 41-51.

[16] See note 10.

[17] Raynaud (*Oeuvres*, XI, p. 155) suggests that the work was composed for the Duke of Burgundy.

[18] See Tobler-Lommatzsch, *Altfranzösisches Wörterbuch* (Berlin, 1925; Wiesbaden, 1954-), 4 (1960), *haut*.

[19] For references to voices as *haut* see Tobler-Lommatzsch, *op. cit.*, 4, *haut*. For related references in Latin see Yvonne Rokseth, *Polyphonies du XIIIe siècle; le manuscrit H 196 de la Faculté de Médecine de Montpellier*, Paris, 4 vols., 1935-39, vol. IV, p. 220f.

[20] See W. v. Wartburg, *Französisches Etymologisches Wörterbuch*, Basel, vol. 14, 1961, p. 638, where the earliest recorded use of *voix* in this sense is dated 1765. The transferred meaning is not given in Antoine Furetière's *Dictionnaire Universel* (3 vols., The Hague and Rotterdam, 1690 (reprinted by Slatkine Reprints, Geneva, 1970) *voix*), although the author lists several specialized musical senses of the word. Ralph de Gorog (*Lexique Français Moderne—Ancien Français*, University of Georgia Press, 1973, p. 328) gives *parçon* as the Old French equivalent of Modern French *partie* in the musical sense (see F. Godefroy, *Dictionnaire de l'Ancienne Langue Française* (Paris, 1880-1902), 5 (1888), *parçon*).

[21] The primary transferred sense of *vox* in the musical theorists is 'note' or 'pitch'; see, for example, Marchettus of Padua, *Lucidarium* (GS, IV, p. 85); *Summa Musicae* (GS, IV, p. 201), *Ars Discantus* (CS, III, p. 110), Johannis Veruli de Anagnia, *Liber de Musica* (CS, III, p. 131), Prosdocimus de Beldemandis, *Tractatus de Contrapuncto* (CS, III, p. 194) and Anon., *Quatuor Principalia Musica* (CS, IV, p. 226). When discussing counterpoint, the theorists either refer to parts by their names (tenor, contratenor, discantus, etc.), use the term *pars*, or employ *cum* followed by a numerical adjective with implied noun, e.g. *cum tribus* ('with three [parts]'). See the discussions of part-writing in the *Ars Discantus* (CS, III, p. 93), and in the *Tractatus de Cantus Mensurabilis* of Aegidius de Murino (CS, III, p. 124f).

[22] See previous note.

[23] See Reaney, op cit, pp. 5 and 94.

[24] See Joscelyn Godwin, 'Mains Divers Acors', *Early Music*, 5 (1977), 2, p. 159.

[25] *Quatuor Principalia Musica* (CS, IV, p. 295).

[26] CS, III, p. 93.

[27] *Gace de la Buigne Le Roman des Deduis*, Ed. Åke Blomqvist, Studia Romanica Holmiensia, III, Karlshamn, 1951, line 8083f.

[28] Godefroy, op cit, 2 (1882), *deschanter*.

[29] There is, for example, an explicit reference to the performance of *teneur* and *contreteneur* on the *psalterium* in the *Pratique du Psalterium Mystique* of Jean de Gerson (d 1429), see Mgr. Glorieux, ed., *Jean de Gerson Oeuvres Complètes*, 10 vols. in 11, Tournai, 1960-73, 7(1), p. 421.

[30] See, for example, with regard to the music of the troubadours, H. van der Werf, *The Chansons of the troubadours and trouvères: A study of the melodies and their relation to the poems*, Utrecht, 1972, and on the

textless parts of the Old Hall manuscript, Margaret Bent's note to the music supplement of *Early Music*, January 1974; 'Vocalization is a likely solution, and one to which modern singers of early music may have to grow more accustomed.'

[31] Cf. Reaney, op cit, p. 8: 'Although certain tenors and contratenors may have been performed vocally, the great majority of those employed in Machaut's polyphonic songs are undoubtedly instrumental. They look so unvocal with their passagework and leaps that we can hardly apply to them Deschamps' important statement that three voices are necessary when a song is properly performed with tenors and contratenors by two or three people.'

[32] Lloyd Hibberd, 'On "Instrumental Style" in Early Melody', *Musical Quarterly*, 32 (1946), pp. 107-130.

[33] See Sarah Jane Williams, 'Vocal Scoring in the Chansons of Machaut', *Journal of the American Musicological Society*, 21 (1968), 3, p. 252.

[34] Deschamps apparently puns on the musical meaning of this word in his Ballade 300 (see the Oeuvres, II, p. 161).

[35] The translation 'in octaves' for *doublées* is supported by (1), the earliest French vernacular musical treatise *Quiconques veut deschanter* (MS 13c) where *doubles* is defined as the *Witisme* ('eighth') note above unison (quoted here from the facsimile of the original MS in *The Music in the St. Victor Manuscript Paris lat. 15139*, Introduction and facsimiles by Ethel Thurston, Toronto, 1959, p. 21 fol. 269); (2), by the French vernacular treatise of Anonymous XIII (end of 13c) in CS, III, p. 497: *Qui veult faire bon deschant il doilt commenchier et finir par acort parfait, c'est à scavoir par unisson, quinte ou double*. ... (3), by Gace de la Buigne's reference (*Le Roman des Deduis*, in Blomqvist, *op. cit.*, lines 8087-8088) to the *quadouble* part being sung '*la quinte sur double*', i.e., a fifth above the octave above the tenor.

[36] Deschamps is presumably thinking of the rules for composing polyphonic music such as are given in the *Ars Discantus* (CS, III, p. 93), in the *Tractatus Cantus Mensurabilis* of Aegidius de Murino (CS, III, p. 124f), and in the *Tractatus de Musica Figurata et de Contrapuncto* (CS, IV, 446f).

[37] The verb *quintoier* simply means 'to sound a fifth', but it appears in several Old French texts where its actual technical meaning is far from clear (see, for example, Gautier de Coinci, *Les Miracles de la*

Sainte Vierge, ed. A. E. Poquet, Paris, 1862, col. 320, line 262). If Deschamps is referring to the rules for composing polyphonic music in this passage (see previous note) then all the verbs he uses derived from the names of intervals must denote the process of putting parts together as described in the treatises (cf. for example, CS, IV, p. 448-9).

[38] Apparently only in Deschamps (see Tobler-Lommatzsch, *op. cit.* (Zweite Lieferung des X bandes, Wiesbaden, 1974) *tenir*, col. 218). My translation is based upon the assumption that Deschamps is referring to composition. However, all the verbs used here may also imply aspects of performance, and one might therefore translate 'perform a tenor'. For a treatise on the composition of motet tenors see Aegidius de Murino, *Tractatus Cantus Mensurabilis* (CS, III, p. 124f).

[39] The *discantus* was the top line in a chanson (also called *superius, cantus, treble*). Again, Deschamps may be referring to performance, or to the composition of a part above a tenor (see Godefroy, op cit, 2 (1883), *Deschant, Deschanter*, and Tobler Lommatzsch, 2 (n.d.), *deschant, deschanter*). The word is used somewhat loosely in vernacular texts, and it is difficult to know how precise in reference Deschamps wishes to be.

[40] Deschamps appears to be implicitly distinguishing the stringed (*bas*) instruments from the winds, predominantly loud (*haulx*). However, the explicit mention of *fleutes* as representative of the *haulx* instruments is puzzling (see E. A. Bowles, ' "Haut et Bas": the grouping of musical instruments in the Middle Ages', *Musica Disciplina*, 8 (1954), pp. 120-1, 126-7).

Acknowledgements

I am most grateful to David Fallows of the University of Manchester and Professor Elizabeth Salter of the Centre for Medieval Studies, University of York, who read the first draft of this article and made many valuable suggestions. I would also like to thank Stephen Minta of the Department of English and Related Literature at York, who examined my translation and use of Old French materials.

Nature *presents her daughters* Sens, Retorique *and* Musique *to Machaut.*
Bibl. natl., f.fr. 9221 f. 1r. By courtesy of Scottish Academic Press

String-Instrument making in Medieval England and some Oxford Harpmakers 1380-1466

ALMOST nothing is known about the stringed-instrument makers of medieval England. Even the few names that can be recovered from documentary sources are largely unknown to musicological literature.[1] How many makers were there, and what was their status? In what cities did they congregate and how was their presence there related to the musical life and economic characteristics of the town? When did professional makers first emerge as specialised craftsmen and why? This article attempts to shed light upon some of these questions, with special reference to the harpmakers of the city of Oxford, whose medieval documents have been readily accessible to me.[2]

TABLE 1 (for material covered see note 2)
STRINGED-INSTRUMENT MAKERS IN LATE-MEDIEVAL ENGLISH DOCUMENTS

	Date of reference	Name	City where listed	
1	1366	John de Toppclyf	York	harpmaker
2	1380/1	William Morton	Oxford	harpmaker
3a	1380/1	Roger	Oxford	le Harpemaker
3b	1384	Roger	Oxford	Harpmaker
4	1416	Robert Somerton	London	harpmaker de London
5	1416	John Scot	London	(Somerton's apprentice)
6a	1416	John Bore	London	harpmaker
6b	1422	John Bore	London	Harpmaker
6c	1435	John Boor	London	Harpmaker
7	1433/4	John Thomas	London	lut maker
8	1434	Lodowycus	London	lute maker
9a	1446	Robert	Oxford	Harpmaker

9b	1451	Robert	Oxford	Harpemaker
9c	1452	Robert	Oxford	Harpemaker
9d	1452	Robert Smyth	Oxford	alias Harpmaker de Candich
10a	1462	John Harryes	Oxford	harpmaker
10b	1466	John Harryes	Oxford	harpmaker
11	1467	Thomas Briker	—	harpemaker

1   F. Collins, ed., *Register of the Freemen of the City of York*, vol. I, Surtees Society, 96 (1896), p. 62. Collins's date is corrected here.

2   J. E. Thorold Rogers, ed., *Oxford City Documents 1268–1665*, Oxford Historical Society, 18 (1891), p. 38. (See Appendix 1.)

3a   Ibid. p. 14. (See Appendix 2.)

3b   H. E. Salter, ed., *A Cartulary of the Hospital of St. John the Baptist*, III, Oxford Historical Society, 69 (1916), p. 202. (See Appendix 3.)

4   Guildhall Library MS. 9171/2 fol. 354. Will of Robert Somerton.

5   Ibid. Somerton leaves John Scot 13ˢ and 4ᵈ.

6a   Ibid. Somerton leaves John Bore 40ˢ.

6b   F. Devon, ed., *Extracts from the Issue Rolls of the Exchequer Hen. III–Hen. VI*, London, 1837, p. 367 (payment for a harp, an unspecified number of strings, and a harp-case supplied by John Bore).

6c   *Calendar of the Close Rolls Hen. VI*, II, 1429–35, London, HMSO, 1933, p. 349 (John Bore as beneficiary in will of Robert Delowe, draper).

7   Guildhall Library MS. 9171/3, fol. 374v. (Nuncupative will of John Thomas).

8   Ibid. fol. 390v. (record of the granting of letters of administration to Matilda, widow and relict of 'Lodowycus').

9a   H. E. Salter, ed., *Registrum Cancellarii*, I, Oxford Historical Society, 93 (1932), p. 128. (See Appendix 4.)

9b   Ibid. p. 255. (See Appendix 5.)

9c   Ibid. p. 267. (See Appendix 6.)

9d   Ibid. p. 271. (See Appendix 7.)

10a   H. E. Salter, ed., *Cartulary of Oseney Abbey*, III, Oxford Historical Society, 91 (1931), p. 250. (See Appendix 8.)

10b   H. E. Salter, ed., *Registrum Cancellarii*, II, Oxford Historical Society, 94 (1932), p. 214. (See Appendix 9.)

11   *Calendar of the Patent Rolls Ed. IV–Hen. VI, 1467–1477*, London, HMSO, 1900, p. 53 (commission to arrest Thomas Briker for counterfeiting money).

A list of all the stringed-instrument makers known to me from medieval English sources is given in Table 1.[3] Three things are immediately clear from the information given there. Firstly, there are very few individuals explicitly named as instrument makers in the published Poll Tax returns and Lay Subsidies of the 12th–15th centuries (about 160,000 names); in the published Freemen's rolls; and in standard works of reference. Secondly, four of the known makers are listed in Oxford documents, all the others (save John de Toppclyf) being mentioned in London sources. Thirdly, all the makers are listed as harpmakers, save two London craftsmen (John Thomas and 'Lodowycus') who are said to be lutemakers.

It is puzzling that there are so few craftsmen with occupational surnames formed from the name of an instrument plus the simple suffix -*maker*. Compounds of this kind were very freely formed in Middle English.[4] The popularity of surnames such as *harpour*, *le harpour*, *fytheler* and *rotour* shows that instrument terms were wholly congenial to the easy colloquial usages that tend to govern naming habits.[5] The Poll Tax and Lay Subsidy returns can not be regarded as complete records of tradesmen,[6] yet it is nonetheless surprising that no occupational surnames for instrument makers are found for the whole of Kent for 1334/5,[7] Somerset for 1327,[8] Gloucestershire for 1327[9]—to name only some southern counties—and that none are listed for the major cities of London for 1319, 1332 and 1412,[10] York for 1301, 1327, and 1380/1,[11] and for prosperous market towns such as Shrewsbury for 1445/6.[12] Even allowing for omissions in the returns and for a reasonably high incidence of tax evasion, there is no good reason to assume that the number of persons with 'instrument-maker' surnames in the English Middle Ages formed a higher proportion of the total population than my discovery of two among the *c*.160,000 names on the printed lists suggests.

Even though the total of individuals with such names is small, the number of practising instrument makers may have been smaller still. By the mid-fourteenth century purely hereditary surnames were extremely common, and nicknames were widely employed.[13] There are also documented cases of surname variation.[14] Clearly the occupational surnames of late medieval England are by no means a sure guide to the professions of their holders. With this in mind, the makers listed in table 1 must be divided into two groups: those whose names take the same form as *Roger Harpmaker* (group 1), and those whose names take the same form as *William Morton, harpmaker* (group 2):

Group 1 Roger Harpmaker; le Harpemaker.

'Lodowycus' lute maker.

Robert Harpmaker; Smyth alias Harpmaker de Candich.

Group 2 John de Toppclyf, harpmaker.

William Morton, harpmaker.

Robert Somerton, harpmaker de London.

46

John Scot (Somerton's apprentice).
John Bore, Harpmaker.
John Thomas, lut maker.
John Harryes, harpemaker.
Thomas Briker, harpemaker.

A man was adequately identified for official purposes by his christian name and surname, the latter quite possibly having no relation to his actual trade (cf. group 1). Any further occupational terms can therefore be assumed to establish another category of reference and indicate genuine trade (cf. group 2). The crucial distinction between the two groups derives from this.

Group 1 therefore presents considerable difficulties. The actual occupation of each member can only be more or less a matter of conjecture. One might argue on *Roger* of Oxford's behalf that, as names with *le-* were becoming increasingly rare in the second half of the 14th century,[15] then such names are more likely to denote actual occupation than those without during this period, but this is very uncertain. '*Lodowycus*' of London is known to me from only one document which contains no other information than that he lived in the parish of St. Edmund, Gracechurch street. However, there is reason to believe that he was actually a maker of lutes as his surname suggests, for another craftsman, *John Thomas, Lut maker*, is known to have been active in London at about the same time as 'Lodowycus', and possibly in the same area of the city.[16] Perhaps the two men were associates, like John Bore and Robert Somerton.[17] *Robert* of Oxford is listed as *Robert Harpmaker* in three documents, but a fourth reveals that his surname was the very common *Smyth*, while *Harpmaker* was his alias or nickname. It seems very likely therefore that he was, or had been at some time, engaged in the manufacture of harps.

With *Group 2* we move onto safer ground. John Bore supplied a harp to Henry V,[18] and Robert Somerton mentions in his will of 1416 'two chests, one long and one small' in which he is accustomed to put his finished harps for safe-keeping.[19] There is no reason to doubt that the other members of *Group 2* were also professional instrument makers, even though their activities cannot be proved from other documents in this way.

The known makers have been briefly considered. Although we can only conjecture how many may have existed who are not mentioned in the surviving records, three points are worth considering:

(1) Some makers may be concealed in the records by misleading names. This follows from what has been said above about the high incidence of hereditary surnames in late medieval England. Robert

presumably took the alias *Harpmaker* to be better distinguished from the great number with whom he shared the name *Smyth*, but there is no reason why every *Smyth* engaged in this craft should have so chosen, thus abandoning their inherited surname.

(2) It is possible that some makers have been obscured by the standard contractions of medieval cursive handwriting. In the Shropshire Lay Subsidy Roll of 1327 for example one *Joh'e le Harp'e* is listed.[20] The full form should perhaps be Joh*anne* le Harpere. However, instances of this surname with final *-e* are extremely rare. Of the thirty-seven forms of it listed by Thuresson, only four are spelled *Harpere*, the remaining thirty-three are written *Harpour*.[21] Further, this surname appears five other times in the Shropshire Roll, and each time it is spelled *Harpour*.[22] It seems therefore that *le Harp'e* is intended to indicate a different word. It has final *-e*, and no other instance of *Harpour* in the Roll is contracted. Perhaps it should be Harp*makere*?

(3) It is plausible that names such as *harpour* denoted makers in addition to players of instruments. If a *chandeler* made candles and a *pinnour* made pins, why should some *harpours* not have made harps?[23] Unfortunately this pleasing hypothesis can only be proved correct in any given case when supporting documents are available to determine the truth of the matter. As yet no such conclusive materials have come to my notice other than a reference in the York Freemen's Register to one Moras Binan, known to have been an organmaker, but described in the Register as *organer*.[24] The philologists' view that such names are merely nicknames must therefore prevail.[25] Nonetheless the tax returns provide a few scraps of evidence so tantalising that speculation becomes irresistable. One John 'le luter' (London, 1319), most probably a merchant, is styled *de Aconia* in a document of 1344/5.[26] This is almost certainly a reference to the famous Crusading port of Acre in the Holy Land. In view of the fact that most lutes of the 14th century look like an imported Oriental *'ūd* we may wonder why this John, perhaps a maker or importer of lutes, was so named.[27]

Some makers may be obscured in these ways, but one cannot long avoid the obvious conclusion that there were very few craftsmen engaged in the full-time manufacture of stringed instruments in medieval England. This warrants the further, important conclusion that so many instruments were built by craftsmen working primarily in other trades, and by private individuals of all kinds, that professional manufacture could only in exceptional circumstances be made to pay. A craftsman establishing himself in this business might have to compete with carpenters producing a wide range of wooden goods,[28] with *mazerers* working in maple (a material known to have been used for

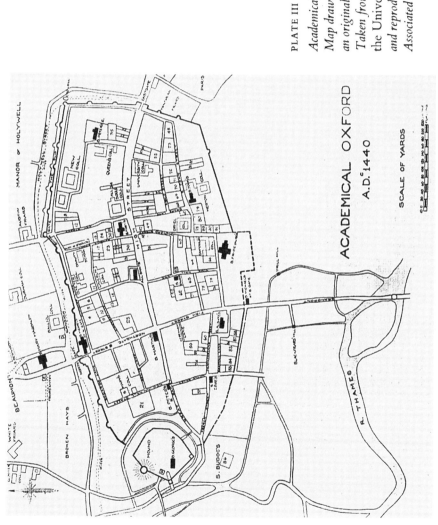

PLATE III

Academical Oxford A.D. c. 1440.
Map drawn by Raymond Morgan from
an original by Hurst.
Taken from Mallet's A History of
the University of Oxford,
and reproduced by permission of
Associated Book Publishers Ltd.

ACADEMICAL OXFORD
A.D.c 1440

SCALE OF YARDS

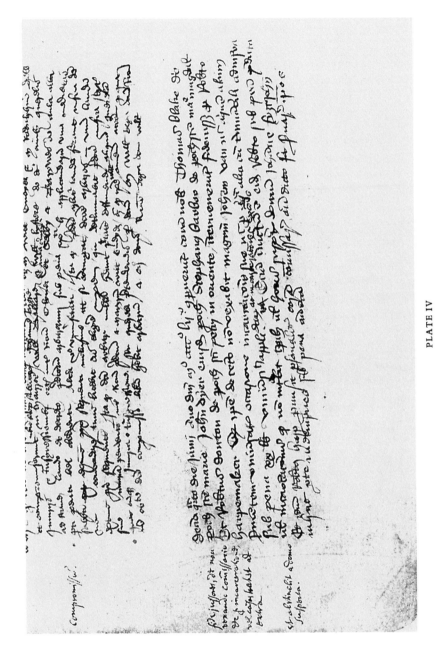

PLATE IV

*Oxford University Archives Reg Aaa fol. 105v (lower). See Appendix 6, p. 67
Reproduced by permission of the Keeper of the Archives*

harps in late medieval England),[29] and with *turnours* (lathe-workers)— to name only some of those who worked with wood for their major source of income.

Naturally the manufacture of instruments by these and other craftsmen is very difficult to document; so few signed instruments survive from the middle ages, and there appear to be no contracts or bills of sale. Nonetheless certain general conclusions can be drawn from the available continental evidence that fills out the picture.

Clock and machine makers. Edmund Bowles's suggestion[30] that the invention of the keyboard in the High Middle Ages is connected with the technology of clocks and machines is strikingly confirmed by several 15th-century sources, and it is tempting to extend it to other musical instruments. Certainly we are encouraged in this by the treatise of Arnault de Zwolle (d.1466).[31] Arnault is well known to modern scholars for his fine working drawings of stringed instruments, yet in 15th-century documents he is described as a builder of clocks and astronomical devices.[32] A glance at the manuscript he compiled serves to place these celebrated drawings in their context, and shows why Jean le Fèvre in the 16th century called him *clarus scientia horologiorum*.[33] In addition to a number of astronomical tables there is a section on an astronomical device built by Johannes Fusoris, Arnault's teacher, several short treatises on *horologia* and an account of some machines.

Two further 15th-century treatises on building keyboard instruments indicate that Arnault's combination of interests was by no means a unique one, and argue strongly for a connection between certain forms of machine technology and musical instrument building. Geneva MS. Lat. 80 contains instructions for building a clavichord, but is essentially a manuscript for an astronomer. Indeed, some material on an astronomical instrument that appears here is also to be found in Arnault's manuscript.[34] Similarly, Yale Medical Library MS. Goff. E.–113, which contains the treatise *De compositione clavichordi*, also includes 'instructions for the fabrication of a celestial globe, sundial and astrolabe'.[35]

Creative designers and organmakers. The case of the architect Giovanni Cellini (d.1527/8) widens the range of instrument makers to include skilled creative designers. His son reports that he made 'wonderful organs with wooden pipes, and harpsichords the best and finest that had ever been seen, as well as viols, lutes and harps, all of them beautifully and excellently fashioned'.[36] Other 15th-century craftsmen built both organs and stringed keyboard instruments.[37] Perhaps some of the English organmakers (who are not lacking in 15th-century documents) were as versatile as this, extending their activities to the manufacture of a range of stringed instruments. It is certainly true that many areas where there were no makers of stringed instruments according to the tax returns, are shown by those same documents to have been supplied with organmakers.

Manufacture by players. Players may have often made instruments, but unfortunately there is little documentary evidence available to show whether this was customary. References in English account books show that minstrels were sometimes given money to *buy* instruments, and although these generally refer to wind instruments (where large-scale amateur manufacture by minstrels seems unlikely because of the technical problems involved), there are occasional references to strings. Durham Priory paid 3ˢ to buy a new harp for Thomas Harpour in 1335–6,[39] and the English wool merchant George Cely lent Thomas Rede, harper of Calais, 9ˢ to buy a harp in 1474.[40] This case is a particularly interesting one, for Rede was a versatile professional able to teach dancing, the lute and the harp (supplying his students with written materials to help them in their study of the first two) and able to maintain his pupils' harps by stringing them and adjusting brays.[41] Nonetheless, when he wanted a new instrument, he purchased it. A few scattered references to repairs of instruments suggest that the average minstrels' talents went little further than basic maintenance. Martinettus the taborer was given 11ᵈ for repairing the drums of Edward the First's sons in 1306, but these instruments were quite possibly toys.[42] The professional examples owned by Janinus the nakerer appear to have been sent away for covering and repair, as the sum of 3ˢ granted to him seems too high just for materials purchased for his own use.[43]

Clearly these scattered fragments of evidence are meagre and of uncertain value. One can only speculate whether the average English itinerant minstrel of the Later Middle Ages, who needed to travel regularly and (one imagines) lightly, had the time or the resources to bend the ribs of a lute or fabricate the parts of a harp. It is difficult to imagine how a musician living in this way would exceed simple bowed and plucked instruments of excavated construction. Whatever the truth of this matter, Werner Bachmann certainly exaggerates when he states that 'the craft of instrument making . . . was the exclusive province of the players themselves'.[44] Instruments must have been produced by a wide range of craftsmen on a more or less casual basis, according to how the maker wished to organise his activities.[45] If this is an accurate picture of medieval instrument making, one can only marvel at the consistency of design achieved virtually throughout

Europe. The wide currency of vigorous and coherent traditions governing design factors cannot be doubted.

Amidst this diversity of manufacture the individuals listed as specialist instrument makers naturally arouse interest. As will be seen from the table, there are four individuals listed as harpmakers in a total of nine Oxford documents covering the period 1380–1466. Two of these, William Morton and Roger Harpmaker, were both active in the city at the same time, for their names appear on the Poll Tax returns of the town for 1380/1 (Appendix 1 and 2). This fact, and the recorded presence of two further individuals named *harpmaker* in the city between 1446 and 1466 suggests a high demand for stringed instruments in the town which is fully in accordance with the indication of literary and documentary sources. The implication of Chaucer's description of the Clerk of Oxenford, with his 'fithele or gay sautrie',[46] is clearly that string playing was one of the most characteristic student frivolities, disdained only by those wholly dedicated to scholarship. In contrast the possessions of *hende Nicholas*, Chaucer's more worldly Oxford scholar, include a *gay sautrie* which is placed on shelves at the head of the bed:

> His Almageste, and bookes grete and smale,
> His astrelabie, longynge for his art,
> His augrym stones layen faire apart,
> On shelves couched at his beddes heed;
> His presse ycovered with a faldyng reed;
> And al above ther lay a gay sautrie,
> On which he made a-nyghtes melodie
> So swetely that all the chambre rong;
> And *Angelus ad Virginem* he song.[47]

(*Almageste*: Ptolemy's astrological treatise, or any astronomical work; *longynge for*: pertaining to; *augrym stones*: abacus counters; *presse*: clothes press; *faldyng*: woollen cloth.)

The same impression of student musical life may be derived from the anonymous Middle English poem *The Mirror of the Periods of Man's Life* (*c*.1450). Here the author thinks of *harpe and giterne* when he reflects upon the frivolities of Oxford students, extending his rebuke to the Inns of Court at London:

> Quod Resoun: "In age of .xx. ȝeer
> Goo to oxenford, or lerne lawe".
> Quod Lust: "harpe and giterne þere may y leere,
> And pickid staffe þerewiþ to plawe,
> At tauerne to make wommen myrie cheere,
> And wilde felawis to-gidere drawe".[48]

(*Lust*: worldly pleasure; *leere*: learn; *pickid*: pointed; *plawe*: play.)

The available documentary sources, lacking the exaggeration of the satirist and moralist, confirm this general picture of instrumental playing in medieval Oxford. The statutes of The Queen's College (1340) explicitly restrict the use of instruments to certain occasions since:

... solet frequentia instrumentorum musicorum levitatem et insolentiam quam pluries provocare occasionemque afferre distractionis a studio et profectu ...[49]
(... it is the custom to provoke levity and insolence as often as possible by an assembly of musical instruments, and thus to make an occaions for distraction from study and progress ...)

Stringed instruments are frequently mentioned among the para-phernalia of books, gowns, coffers and bedsheets listed in the invent-ories of personal effects entered on the Chancellor's register.[50] 'Syre W. Lydbery' (not apparently an Oxford *alumnus*) had 'a lewt price vi^d' among his possessions in 1462/3;[51] William Braggs M.A. owned a lute price x^d in 1468.[52] The goods of John Hosear (apparently not a member of the University) included 'an harpe' valued at fourpence in 1463/4;[53] Reginald Stone, Bachelor of Canon and Civil Law, left 'I harpe [price] 11^s' among his effects at Vine Hall in 1468.[54] Thomas Cooper M.A. owned two instruments, but they were in poor con-dition. The authorities carrying out the inventory at Brasenose Hall in 1438 listed them as 'one old harp and a broken lute' (*1 antiqua cithara ... 1 lute fracta*).[55] Only one wind instrument is mentioned in the inventories on the Chancellor's Register: Simon Berynton M.A., one-time keeper of the Ancient University Chest and Confessor of the King's Household in 1466, owned, oddly enough, 'I hornpipe price I^d'.[56] The only other wind instruments I have encountered in University inventories are two 'pairs' of organs at Canterbury College in 1443 and 1459, said to be in poor condition.[57]

The friars were doubtless also among the string players of the city. Their musical indulgences called forth bitter rebukes from John Wyclif (Master of Balliol in 1360) and his Oxford followers. *Of the Leaven of Pharisees* (c.1383), a lollard tract once attributed to Wyclif himself but now believed to be the work of one of his followers[58] attacks their custom of playing musical instruments on the holy days:
[they indulge in] veyn songis and knackynge and harpynge, gyternynge and daunsynge and oþere veyn triflis to geten þe stynkyng loue of damyselis.[49]
(*knackynge*: singing rapid, articulated, decorative notes.)

Two further documents connected with the regular clergy of Oxford may indicate that stringed instruments were used in academic lectures on *Musica*, one of the liberal arts studied at the University. An unpublished discourse on tuning a harp which Pierre of Peckham incorporated into his poem *La Lumiere as Lais* (completed in Oxford,

1267) is laden with definitions of intervals and technical terms probably taken from the *De Musica* of Boethius, a standard music textbook in medieval Oxford:

> La quarte corde deyt soner
> A la quarte de suz com a per,
> En acord de diatessaron,
> E le vtime sune diapason.
> E[n] diapente deit suner
> La quinte corde en regar [de] sun per.
> . . .
> Dyatessaron deus tuens cuntient,
> Od vn semytoen k'yl sustyent.
> En treis tuens diapente
> E vn semitoen ad aplente.[60]

(The fourth string must sound / In companionship with the fourth below, / In the harmony of a fourth, / And the eighth [string] sounds an octave. / The fifth string must sound / A fifth in relation to its companion / . . . A fourth contains two tones, / With a semitone which it sustains. / A fifth is composed of three tones / And a semitone abundantly.)

The text continues in this manner for over sixty lines with the dull, dry thoroughness of an academic lecture. It is far more exhaustive in its musical reference than Pierre's original comparison between men living in harmony and the strings of a tuned harp requires. The intervals are described and analysed with constant references to the strings of a diatonic harp, and one can easily see how this instrument would suit the lecturer on *Musica* far better than the traditional monochord. On the harp two notes may be sounded simultaneously, which is quite impossible on the ordinary monochord.[61] Further, the presence of a string for each note of the diatonic series on the harp renders the instrument a highly efficient visual/acoustic mnemonic for those wishing to learn the composition and sound-quality of the various intervals. Pierre's text seems to envisage all these factors, and it is possible therefore that it preserves the content of a University lecture on music theory taking the harp as a point of departure.[62] Some support for the hypothesis that everyday stringed instruments were drawn into this aspect of music teaching in medieval Oxford is suggested by a brief passage in the *Quatuor Principalia Musica* (1351). The compiler of this treatise, an anonymous Franciscan apparently working in Oxford,[63] recommends that those who wish to build a monochord to further their musical studies should adapt *viellae*, *cistollae* or similar instruments.[64]

Any account of string playing in medieval Oxford would be incomplete without some reference to Absolon, the parish clerk of

Chaucer's *Miller's Tale*. Musically speaking the demands made upon a parish clerk could be very small in the 14th century, and someone in Absolon's position, pursuing a trade in addition to his obviously light clerical duties, would need little more than an elementary knowledge of certain chants such as might be gained in a song school or grammar hall.[65] His instrumental playing however belongs entirely to the secular world and is a part of his fashionable, even foppish youthfulness. His instruments, the *giterne* and the *rubible*, were widely current as those of the brewhouse, tavern, and the city streets after curfew.[66] They are also the instruments of the rakish young London apprentice Perkyn Revelour of the *Cook's Tale*. Absolon could

> . . . pleyen songes on a smal rubible;
> Therto he song som tyme aloud quynyble;
> And as wel koude he play on a giterne.
> In al the toun nas brewhouse ne taverne
> That he ne visited with his solas.[67]

The music of the common townspeople can rarely be glimpsed in the works of poets and officials. A striking exception is provided by an account of the inquest on Gilbert de Foxlee (1306), where stringed instruments figure in a vivid scene of town life:

. . . die Jouis in vigilia nativitatis S. Johannis Baptiste proxime praecedentis Cissores Oxoñ et alij de villa qui fuerant cum eis vigilabant in Shoppis suis per totam noctem cantantes et facientes solatia sua cum Cytharis, Viellis et alijs diuersis instrumentis . . .[68]

(On Thursday last, the vigil of the nativity of St. John the Baptist, the tailors of Oxford and others of the town with them were keeping the vigil in their shops, singing and making merry all night with harps, fiddles, and other kinds of instruments.)

This then is the context in which the four harpmakers of Oxford are to be placed. During the 14th and 15th centuries there appear to have been string players in abundance at Oxford. In addition to the professional minstrels of the day there was a wide range of amateur players: tradesmen, high-ranking townsmen, students in college halls, friars, University Officials, and high-spirited young men of all sorts such as Chaucer's Absolon and Perkyn Revelour. Clearly this was a town capable of supporting professional stringed-instrument makers.

Roger Harpmaker (1380/1; 1384)

In the 1380/1 Poll Tax returns for the city of Oxford the following entry appears in the list for the South-East Ward (the district on the south side of High Street from St. Martin's to the East Gate): 'From Roger the harpmaker and Alice his wife: xij^d, (Appendix 2). According to the *Rotuli Parliamentorum* (1380)[69] the Poll Tax of 1380/1 was levied from all lay persons over fifteen (excepting beggars) at the rate of one shilling a head. The collectors were instructed to levy the subsidy according to the individual's ability to pay, and the average payment for a man and his wife was 2^s. It therefore follows that Roger falls somewhere below the middle; a man of modest substance purveying an everyday, non-luxury trade. He is far removed from the important London makers John Bore and Robert Somerton. There is no mention of an apprentice but there is proven tax-evasion among the servant and apprentice class at this time so this is not significant.[70]

Among the rentals that appear in the cartulary of the Hospital of St. John the Baptist an entry dated 21 December, 1384, records the amount of 3^s and 4^d for 'the *Boltras* house that Roger Harpmaker holds' (Appendix 3). The property of St. John's Hospital lay on the east side of St. Aldates, and the *Domus Boltras* was Nos. 17 and 18 (one tenement in early times).[71] Here Roger would most probably have had his workshop, shop and lodgings combined.[72]

William Morton, harpmaker (1380/1)

In the 1380/1 Poll Tax returns an entry in the list drawn up for the parish of St. Mary Magdalen (a suburb outside the city walls in the North West) records that William Morton, harpmaker, paid 12^d (Appendix 1). There were therefore two makers of roughly equivalent social standing active in the town at this time, or so the surnames suggest.

Robert Smyth alias Harpemaker de Candich (1446; 1451; 1452)

Robert Smyth appears to have been unable to keep out of trouble with the University authorities. All the references pertaining to him are found on the Chancellor's register, where the Chancellor and his commissaries noted down what they considered worthy of record. The entries appear to have been generally made rapidly, and at the moment (see plate accompanying Appendix 6). The Chancellor had certain powers over townsmen, not altogether clearly defined,[73] and on 25 July, 1446, Robert Smyth appeared in the court with one Roger Carpenter giving assurances that the same Robert would keep the peace with William Barkham, Fuller, and Katherine Ylkins on pain of a twenty pound fine (Appendix 4). It is not known why Robert was bound over to keep the peace with Barkham, or with Katherine Ylkins, the wife of Thomas Ylkins, one of the architects of the Divinity School. Anything from shouting abuse in the street to physical assault may be implied here. Twenty pounds is a heavy fine, but Roger must have become rather indifferent to it over the years. According to an entry in the register dated 30 July, 1451, he was threatened with it again in connection with a legal case pending between himself and one John Bracley (Appendix 5).

Yet a third occasion when Robert was threatened with this fine (and with imprisonment and excommunication) introduces two documents spanning two weeks in June, 1452. Here we find the Chancellor exercising his traditional powers for keeping the peace of the King by punishing sexual offenders. It appears from the first of these that Robert had been in trouble with the University authorities and had caused such annoyance that four tradesmen were called upon to give assurances that he would not

. . . harass master John Van [the Chancellor's commissary] nor any other servant of the University by the occasion of his imprisonment, or in connection with any other legal proceedings against him on pain of a twenty pound fine to be paid to the University and imprisonment and excommunication. (Appendix 6.)

Robert had been leaving his lodgings (which the document tells us were in Candich) and stealing down Catte Street near Smithgate where he visited a serving woman named Johanna Fyzt-John 'in suspicious hours'. An entry in the register dated 28 June gives the following assurance:

Robert Smyth, alias Harpmaker of Candich, suspected of having committed adultery with Johanna Fyzt-John, serving woman, living in the cornerhouse on the east-side of Catte Street . . . has sworn to abjure the society of the same Johanna, and not to come in any place where she will be unless it is a public street, market, church or chapel on the pain of a two pound fine to be paid to the University without remission. (Appendix 7.)

Certain facts emerge from these amusing if peripheral details. The fourfold appearance of the surname *Harpmaker* shows that Robert was generally known by this name during the six years that the documents cover, and the final document indicates that it was an alias, doubtless deriving from his full-time or occasional occupation (see above pp. 44-5). He was clearly a layman, living (and presumably working) just outside the city walls.

John Harryes, Harpmaker (1462; 1466)

The final Oxford harpmaker can also be placed on the map and be shown to have been working in the city in 1462. According to an entry in the Cartulary of Oseney Abbey for this year he occupied the fifth tenement *Raymundi* (Appendix 8), which may be identified with a property about half-way up the north side of Cheyney Lane (now Market Street).[74] Here he probably worked and sold, perhaps living in a solar above the shop.[75] The property was sold to Jesus College in 1675, and college buildings now stand upon it.

John Harryes also appears in an entry in the register dated 14 November, 1466. This states that he had become a scholar's servant receiving the standard six shillings and eightpence a year or a livery of that price (Appendix 9). This is not a living wage, and there is no reason why he should have stopped building harps when he entered the service of Robert Passlew.[76] From these two documents it is clear that he was a layman resident in Oxford.

We must now attempt to use the Oxford evidence, supplemented by material from York and London, to draw together our knowledge of stringed-instrument making in medieval England. The fundamental question is: does the appearance of individuals named as instrument-makers in the 14th century indicate that a specialised craft was emerging at this time, or are there circumstances which limit the significance of the evidence sufficiently to preclude such a conclusion? We consider the limiting factors first.

A craft took its name 'from some one commodity or class of commodities or some skill with which its members were associated',[77] and craftsmen with a particular skill 'could and did make use of it in a number of different contexts'.[78] It is possible therefore that many tradesmen listed as 'carpenters', 'turnours' etc. in official documents may have been able to produce musical instruments to order, thus engaging in professional but not specialised manufacture long before the period of the recorded makers. There may also have been many craftsmen who turned to the trade late in life, preferring to retain their old trade name for convenience; and some who pursued it as a lucrative sideline but did not choose to take their occupational surname from it. These hypotheses, which seem to argue against the possibility of making any certain statements about the emergence of instrument-making as a specialised trade, have obvious commonsense appeal. It is naive to imagine a specialised trade emerging in the 14th century from an activity formerly unconnected with organised manufacture and trading of any kind. However, the evidence does support the view that in the 14th and 15th centuries stringed-instrument making was emerging as a profession in its own right.

All the makers (save Thomas Briker of whom nothing is known)* were active in a few major cities. Far from being scattered over a wide area (as we might expect practitioners of an old, specialised trade to

* See 'note added in proof', p. 60.

be when documentary sources first uncover them), they are concentrated in certain urban communities where special reasons for their presence can be adduced. In the case of the Oxford makers the evidence is sufficient to determine that all were living either in the city (where the sites of their houses can be traced) or just beyond the city walls. All the London makers were active in the city (as far as the periods covered by the documents is concerned) and John de Toppclyf took up the freedom of York in 1366. While there is no reason to assume that urban centralisation of instrument-making was a 14th-century phenomenon—there is evidence for it earlier than that[79]—nonetheless the distribution of the makers suggests a newly emerging specialisation, as yet closely dependent upon a few major cities where it was sure to be supported and sustained.

No simple formula will suffice to explain the location of all the makers. The general observation may be made that all of them, save one, were active in the increasingly important South, but beyond this each case must be examined individually. As for Oxford, the presence of makers there is doubtless closely related to the needs and interests of the University community. Here was a population with a relatively high proportion of individuals with artistic interests. As I have endeavoured to show, literary and documentary sources of the 14th and 15th centuries testify to the enthusiastic cultivation of stringed instruments in many classes of Oxford society. The appearance of makers there in the late 14th century is perhaps related to the increasing financial stability of the University community. Of the many complex interactions between the University and medieval English society, Guy Fitch Lytle distinguishes patronage as the most important single factor.[80] He argues that insufficient funds for study and uncertain prospects for graduates, leading to a decline in student numbers in the 14th century, amounted to a 'patronage crisis'. A remedy was provided by the establishment of colleges in the fourteenth and fifteenth century which 'offered a solution to the problem of financing an education in a period of economic depression'.[81] During this period the colleges were 'far outstripping the University as a corporate body both in wealth and buildings',[82] and it is tempting to connect the rise of professional harpmakers there with this growth.

The presence of makers in London, including two wealthy men, need cause no surprise. During the 14th century substantial migrations to the city had taken place from the East Midlands and elsewhere,[83] swelling the ranks of the merchant class, and changing the character of the London dialect. Although it is easy to imagine a market for high quality instruments in such a 'great port and distributive centre'.[84]

the London makers appear too late to be readily accounted for by the commercial growth of the city. The earliest known, Robert Somerton and John Bore, were both active in the city *c*.1416; yet by 1300 'all the currents of European trade were flowing into London harbour. Anything could be bought there . . .'.[85] It seems likely that Bore and Somerton were catering for a luxury trade in the city itself, owing a great deal to the presence of the court (Bore supplied harps to Henry V) and the wealthy merchant classes. George Cely would certainly not have been the only 15th-century London merchant occupying his spare hours with harp and lute.[86] The cultivation of stringed instruments had always been an aristocratic pursuit in the Middle Ages, and its adoption by the merchant class doubtless owes much to the interpenetration of culture between London merchants and gentry.[87]

Close dependence upon urban support is also clearly evinced in the case of John de Toppclyf. The only known maker active in the North, we find him exactly where we would expect to do so: in York, greatest city of the north of England. His trade is one of several that first makes its appearance in the Freemen's Rolls in the mid-14th century after the Black Death.[88] It is interesting to note that York was able to support several specialised artistic trades during this period, including clock- and colour-making.[89] In the 15th century the town appears to have been something of a centre for organmaking, and this activity was possibly extended to the manufacture of harpsichords and clavichords.[90]

However the fragments of evidence are pieced together to form a coherent picture, certain indications are provided by the reticence of the sources as well as their testimony. The paucity of specialist makers tells its own story. Whereas modern instrument-making is a highly specialised craft whose trade secrets are known for the most part only in well defined professional circles, in the Middle Ages such knowledge was shared by craftsmen of many kinds. Stringed instruments could doubtless be found on a far wider range of market stalls and in many more tradesmen's shop displays than we imagine.

ACKNOWLEDGEMENT

My thanks are due to C. R. H. Cooper, Keeper of manuscripts at the Guildhall Library, Professor B. Dobson of the Dept. of History, University of York, Dr Janet Cooper of the *Victoria History of Oxfordshire*, and Dr Janet Burton, of the Borthwick Institute of Historical Research, York, for practical help and advice.

NOTE ADDED IN PROOF

After this article had gone to press Mr Brian Durham of the Oxfordshire Archaeological Unit drew my attention to the fact that a Thomas Brikar is recorded as having lived in a tenement in St. Aldate's, Oxford, in 1453 (Salter, *Survey of Oxford*, II, p. 22). Mr Durham excavated the site of this tenement with the Unit in 1970 and found substantial remains of bone instrument pegs, some completed, some merely begun, and concluded that the premises had been occupied by a stringed-instrument maker at some time during the 15th century. Mr Durham was unaware of the reference to 'Thomas Briker, harpemaker' in the Patent Rolls included in this article. 'Briker' was an exceptionally rare surname in the 15th century, and it seems very likely that these two instances of the name pertain to the same craftsman. Thomas Briker can therefore be added to the list of Oxford makers, and full details of all the finds from the site of his tenement will be available in Mr Durham's forthcoming study 'Archaeological Investigations in St. Aldate's, Oxford', *Oxoniensia*, xlii (1977). This will include drawings of the pegs and a preliminary report on a coil of wire, possibly music wire, found upon the site.

I am grateful to Dr Janet Cooper for drawing my attention to one 'Radulphus Harpmaker' listed among privileged persons of Oxford for 1384 (Bodleian Library, MS Twyne 4, p. 199). This Ralph, of whom I found no trace while researching this article, may also be added to the Oxford list, bringing the total number of makers active in the city between 1380 and 1466 up to six. Like John Harryes (see above), Ralph was a scholar's servant, which is further evidence of a connection between stringed-instrument making in the city and the University.

NOTES

1 The only discussions of the subject I have encountered are in: Richard Rastall, 'Secular Musicians in Late Medieval England', 2 vols., (unpublished dissertation, Manchester University, 1968), II, App. F (p. 192–3); John Harvey, *Medieval Craftsmen*, 1975, p. 89–91 and 187; Bertil Thuresson, 'Middle English Occupational Terms', *Lund Studies in English*, XIX (1950), pp. 183–191 (collection of terms denoting professional entertainers and musicians with commentary). The London harpmaker John Bore was known to Galpin (*Old English Instruments of Music*, 4th ed., 1965, p. 13). I have not found evidence of any individuals known to have been professional stringed-instrument makers earlier than the period of the makers discussed here.

2 The following Oxford sources were checked: all printed indices of wills proved in the Chancellor's court and Oxfordshire peculiars (no wills were traced for any of the Oxford makers); the indices to the University Archives; the indices to MS. materials in the Dept. of Western MSS; the published college archives; all volumes of the *Oxford Historical Society* publications. I am most grateful to Ruth Vyse, Assistant Archivist at the University Archives for help. This study also draws upon all the published English Lay Subsidies and Poll Tax returns from the 12th to the 15th centuries (listed in E. B. Graves, *A Bibliography of English History to 1485*, 1975, pp. 483–491), a total of some

ninety printed sources containing some 160,000 names. (Graves numbers 3144, 3145, 3182 and 3196 were not available to me.) In addition, all the published Freemen's registers listed by Graves (*ibid.* pp. 700–732) were checked, save 5120 which was unobtainable. W. H. Grattan Flood's collection of materials from the 15th-century Patent Rolls (*Mus. Antiquary*, IV, 1912–13, p. 225 f) was also checked. Sampling of the London sources has been far less systematic than in the case of Oxford, and the list of documents in Table 1 makes no claim to completeness. All the standard lexical records of Middle English and works on the history of personal names have been searched, too numerous to list here.

3 John de Toppclyf is the only stringed-instrument maker listed in the York Freemens' Roll for the medieval period (on the completeness of the Roll see R. B. Dobson, 'Admissions to the Freedom of the City of York in the Later Middle Ages', *Economic History Review*, 2nd series, xxvi, I (1973), pp. 1–22). I know of no further documents pertaining to him, but my search has not been exhaustive.

4 Thuresson, *op. cit.*, p. 277, lists fifty-eight -*maker* compounds from documentary sources (*lutemaker* is not listed). These compounds are outnumbered only by -*man* compounds. A further forty-two examples are listed in G. Fransson, 'Middle English Surnames of Occupation 1100–1350', *Lund Studies in English*, 3 (1935), p. 209.

5 For a list of examples see Thuresson, *op. cit.*, p. 183–188, where eighteen different surnames of this type are assembled. The very frequent *roter* is perhaps often meant for *rotarius*, 'wheelmaker', while *fycheler*, which appears in a number of the published Lay Subsidies, is doubtless an editorial misreading for *fytheler*. I can find no trace of *fycheler* as a personal name in the standard works on the subject. Thuresson, *op. cit.*, p. 186, places instances of this word under *Fitheler*.

6 See M. W. Beresford, *Lay Subsidies and Poll Taxes*, Canterbury, 1963, p. 2, and J. C. L. Stahlschmidt, ed., 'Lay Subsidy Temp. Henry IV', *Archaeological Journal*, xliv (1887), p. 57.

7 H. A. Hanley and C. W. Chalklin, eds., 'The Kent Lay Subsidy Roll of 1334/5', in F. R. H. Du Boulay, ed., 'Medieval Kentish Society', *Kent Archaeological Society Records Branch*, xviii (1964), pp. 71–172.

8 F. H. Dickinson, ed., 'Exchequer Lay Subsidies' in 'Kirby's Quest for Somerset', *Somerset Record Society*, 3 (1889), p. 79–281.

9 *Gloucestershire Subsidy Roll I Ed. III, 1327*, Middle Hill Press, n.d.

10 For the 1319 Roll (on which only one ward is missing) see E. Ekwall, *Two Early London Subsidy Rolls*, Lund, 1951; for 1332 see M. Curtis, 'The London Lay Subsidy of 1332' in G. Unwin, ed., *Finance and Trade under Edward III*, Manchester, 1918, pp. 35–60; for the 1412 Subsidy see Stahlschmidt, *op. cit.*

11 For the 1301 Subsidy see W. Brown, 'Yorkshire Lay Subsidy [1301]', *The Yorkshire Archaeological Society Record Series*, xxi (1896), pp. 117–121; for 1327 see Col. Parker, 'Lay Subsidy Rolls I Edward III, N. R. York and the City of York', *The Yorkshire Archaeological Record Series, Miscellanea*, II (1929),

p. 160–171; for 1381 see Neville Bartlett, 'The Lay Poll Tax Returns for the City of York in 1381', *Transactions of the East Riding Antiquarian Society*, xxx (1953), pp. 1–91.

12 See J. L. Hobbs, 'A Shrewsbury Subsidy Roll, 1445–6', *Shropshire Archaeological Society*, liii (1949–50), pp. 68–77.

13 See Fransson, *op. cit.*, p. 29f, and Thuresson, *op. cit.*, p. 24.

14 For a detailed survey of surname variation based on London documents see E. Ekwall, *Variation in Surnames in Medieval London*, Lund, 1945, p. 207–62.

15 See Fransson, *op. cit.*, p. 25.

16 'Lodowycus' was of the parish of St. Edmund, Gracechurch Street, and John Thomas provided that he should be buried in the church of St. Benet Fink. See map in *The Victoria History of London*, I, ed. William Page, 1909, facing p. 339.

17 See caption 6a to table 1.

18 See caption 6b to table 1.

19 *in cithere mee solomodo ponant[ur] adsalvo custodiend[o]*. See caption 4 to table 1.

20 W. G. D. Fletcher, ed., *A Shropshire Lay Subsidy Roll of 1327*, Oswestry, 1907, p. 114 (NB: pagination discontinuous).

21 Thuresson, *op. cit.*, p. 185.

22 Fletcher, *op. cit.*, pp. 13, 76, 82, 167, 180.

23 The existence of a form *harpmaker* by no means negates this possibility for variation of this kind is recorded. See Thuresson, *op. cit.*, *passim* (examples include *Qwsshynmaker/Quisshoner, Patynmaker/Patoner*, etc.). Fransson, *op. cit.*, p. 165, glosses two instances of *orgoner* as probably equivalent to *organ-maker*, but this is merely a supposition as far as one can tell from the evidence presented.

24 Collins, *op. cit.*, p. 210. For the will in which he is described as an organ-maker see J. Raine, ed., *Testamenta Eboracensia*, v, Surtees Society 79 (1884), p. 22–3.

25 Thuresson, *op. cit.*, p. 24.

26 Ekwall, *Subsidy Rolls*, p. 301.

27 One must exercise extreme caution drawing conclusions from personal names, especially toponymics. Perhaps John was connected with the military religious order called the Knights of St. Thomas of Acre? (I am grateful to Professor B. Dobson for this suggestion).

28 On the activities of carpenters see Harvey, *op. cit.*, p. 147f.

29 See A. Kurvinen, ed., *Sir Gawain and the Carl of Carlisle* [*c.*1400], Helsinki, 1951, (A) line 433: 'The harpe was of a maser fyne'.

30 E. A. Bowles, 'On the Origin of the Keyboard Mechanism in the late Middle Ages', *Technology and Culture*, 7 (1966), p. 152–62.

31 See G. le Cerf and E.-R. Labande, *Instruments de Musique du XVe Siecle*, Paris, 1932, xif.

32 *Ibid.*

33 *Ibid.*

34 For text and discussion see J. Handschin, 'Aus der alten Musiktheorie, V. Zur Instrumentenkunde', *Acta Musicologica*, xvi–xvii (1944–5), p. 4f: '. . . Ihr Inhalt ist hauptsächlich astronomisch. So steht am Schluss ein Traktat über das Astrolabium in einer Übersetzung aus dem Lateinischen in das Französische, die von Johannes Fusoris angefertigt wurde . . .'.

35 Bowles, *op. cit.*, p. 161.

36 D. H. Boalch, *Makers of the Harpsichord and Clavichord 1440–1840*, 2nd ed., 1974, p. 23.

37 Boalch, *op. cit.*, entries for Meister Johann. of Werden (fl.1437), p. 79; Alessandro Pasi of Modena, p. 118 etc.

38 See Rastall, *op. cit.*, II, p. 17, 38, 41, 46, 144. (Two interesting documents in which a harper is paid for repairing a ?doorway, and another harper is mentioned among four companions who are carpenters are translated on pp. 143 and 148.) For references to the purchase of very elaborate wind instruments for minstrels see *Black Prince's Register*, 4 vols. 1930–3, I, p. 30 (two silver trumpets), and IV, p. 73 ('four pipes, silver-gilt and enamelled') and p. 157 (a cornemuse, a pipe and tabor, 'silver gilt an enamelled').

39 E. K. Chambers, *The Medieval Stage*, 1903, II, Appendix E, p. 241: *In I Cythara empta pro Thom. Harpour 3*[s].

40 Alison Hanham, 'The Musical Studies of a Fifteenth Century Wool Merchant', *Review of English Studies*, ns 8 (1957), p. 271: 'Item lent to the sayd Thomas appon an harpe, IX*[s]*'.

41 *Ibid.*

42 Rastall, *op. cit.*, II, p. 52. For a late fifteenth-century payment to minstrels for repairing a lute see J. P. Collier, *Household Books of John Duke of Norfolk and Thomas Earl of Surrey, Temp. 1481–90*, Roxburghe Club, 1844, p. 218.

43 *Ibid.*, p. 38.

44 Werner Bachmann, *The Origins of Bowing*, trans. N. Deane, 1969, p. 71.

45 The very luxurious instruments mentioned in some medieval literary sources—which doubtless had their counterparts in reality; witness the wind instruments given by the Black Prince (note 38)—would often have combined the work of a variety of craftsmen. The maple harp mentioned in *Sir Gawain and the Carl of Carlisle* (see note 29) has pins of gold, and goldsmiths and wiredrawers would also be needed to prepare the strings of gold and silver not infrequently mentioned in a variety of sources (see Christopher Page, 'Fifteenth Century Instruments in Jean de Gerson's *Tractatus de Canticis*', *Early Music*, 6 (1978). There are occasional references to harps with bodies of silver or gold, presumably silver-plated and gilded (see Page, *op. cit.*, and Jean Maillard, 'Coutumes musicales au moyen âge d'après le *Tristan* en prose', *Cahiers de Civilisation Médiévale*, II, Poitiers, 1959, p. 345, 'La damoisele prent la harpe qui de fin or estoit'). The most luxurious instruments are mentioned—as one would expect—in the French romances, though the Middle English *Sir Tristrem* mentions a *rote of yvere* (and a harp said to be made *richelich*). See W. Scott, ed., *Sir Tristrem; a Metrical Romance of the Thirteenth Century*, 1811, Fytte Second, LXIV and LXX.

46 *The General Prologue to the Canterbury Tales*, in F. N. Robinson, ed.,

The Works of Geoffrey Chaucer, 2nd ed., 1957, lines 293–6.

47 *The Miller's Tale*, lines 3208–3216 in Robinson, *op. cit.* On the presentation of the two clerks see James D. Simmonds, 'Hende Nicholas', *Notes and Queries*, 207, ns. 9 (1962), p. 446 and Paul E. Beichner, 'Chaucer's 'Hende Nicholas' ', *Medieval Studies*, xiv 1952), p. 151–3. There is also valuable material on the musical aspects of the Tale in J. A. W. Bennett, *Chaucer at Oxford and Cambridge*, Oxford, 1974, *passim*, and Jesse M. Gellrich, 'The Parody of Medieval Music in the *Miller's Tale*', *Journal of English and Germanic Philology*, lxxiii (1974), 176–188.

48 Text in F. J. Furnivall, ed., *Hymns to the Virgin and Christ*, Early English Text Society Original Series, 24 (1867), pp. 58–78, lines 89–94. (The fourth line as it appears in Furnivall's edition—'And pickid staffe and buckelere, þerewiþ to plawe'—is hypermetrical, and there can be little doubt that 'and buckelere' was inserted to complete the conventional name of the sport, perhaps under the influence of the rhyme *leere/buckelere*.) I assume that the phrase *lerne lawe* (presented as an alternative to Oxenford) refers to the Inns of Court where, at least in the 15th century, students could receive an education beyond the grammar school stage that included musical instruction (see D. S. Bland, 'Chaucer and the Inns of Court: A Reexamination', *English Studies*, xxxiii (1952), p. 145–55.

49 *Statutes of the Colleges of Oxford*, Oxford, 1853, I, *Statutes of Queen's College*, p. 18.

50 H. E. Salter, ed., *Registrum Cancellarii*, Oxford Historical Society 93 (1932) and 94 (1932).

51 Salter, *op. cit.*, II, p. 101. There is no entry for Lydbery in A. B. Emden, *A Biographical Register of the University of Oxford to A.D. 1500*, Oxford University Press, 1957.

52 Salter, *op. cit.*, II, p. 326. For William Braggs see Emden, *op. cit.*, p. 247. The inventory was taken by the Chancellor's commissary for arrears in rent.

53 Salter, *op. cit.*, II, p. 129. There is no entry for Hosear in Emden's *Register*.

54 Salter, *op. cit.*, II, p. 327. For Reginald Stone see Emden, *op. cit.*, p. 1788.

55 Salter, *op. cit.*, I, p. 37. For Thomas Cooper see Emden, *op. cit.*, p. 482.

56 Salter, *op. cit.*, I, p. 160. For Simon Berynton see Emden, *op. cit.*, p. 181.

57 W. A. Pantin, *Canterbury College Oxford*, Oxford Historical Society New Series, VI, VII (1946), VIII (1950), vol. I, p. 3 (Inventory of Warden Robert Lynton on entering office), and p. 11 (Inventory of Warden William Thorndon, on leaving office). Probably the *par organorum* was a College property, and is the same one in each case.

58 For a discussion of authorship see J. Burke Severs, *A Manual of the Writings in Middle English 1050–1500*, 2, Connecticut, 1970, p. 374.

59 F. D. Matthew, ed., *The English Works of Wyclif, Hitherto Unprinted*, Early English Text Society Original Series, 74 (1880), p. 9.

60 Quoted here diplomatically with only punctuation added from York Chapter Library MS. 16.N.3, fol. 112v, the best of the surviving MSS. according to M. Dominica Legge, 'Pierre of Peckham and his "Lumiere as Lais" ', *Modern Language Review*, xxiv (1929), pp. 37–47 and 153–71 (see also *idem*,

'La Lumiere as Lais': a Postscript', *Modern Language Review*, xlvi (1951), p. 191–5). This text was brought to my notice by Michael Morrow. It will be published by Stephen Minta and myself in due course.

61 On the monochord as adapted for teaching purposes by a 15th-century music teacher; see Karl-Werner Gümpel, 'Das Tasten-monochord Conrads von Zabern', *Archiv für Musikwissenschaft*, xii (1955), p. 143–166.

62 On this subject see L. Ellinwood, 'Ars Musica', *Speculum*, 20 (1945), pp. 290–299.

63 The text is printed in E. de Coussemaker, *Scriptorum de Musica Medii Aevi*, IV, p. 200–298, where it is attributed to Simon Tunstede on the basis of the final lines of text as they stand in Oxford, Bodleian Library MS. Digby 90, fol. 63v (translated, with another important note from the same MS. in Andrew G. Little, *The Grey Friars in Oxford*, Oxford Historical Society, xx (1891), p. 60). Gilbert Reaney rightly points out ('The question of authorship in the medieval treatises on music', *Musica Disciplina*, xviii (1964), p. 10) that the treatise must be rather attributed to the *Oxon. quidam frater minor de custodia Brustolis* mentioned on fol. 63v. Andrew G. Little dismissed Tunstede's authorship in 1891 (*op. cit.*, p. 241).

64 Coussemaker, *op. cit.*, p. 208: '*Accipiatur aliquod instrumentum sonum emittens, ut pote viellae, cistollae et hujusmodi . . .*'.

65 Frank Harrison, *Music in Medieval Britain*, 1958, p. 197, points out that 'there is little evidence that polyphonic music was sung or played in parish churches before the second half of the fifteenth century'. On musical education in the grammar and song schools see Carleton Brown, 'Chaucer's "Litel Clergeon" ', *Modern Philology*, 3 (1905/6), p. 467–491.

66 On the low life associations of the gittern as revealed in literary and documentary sources see Lawrence Wright, *GSJ* **XXX**, 1977. For the *rubible* see H. Carter, *A Dictionary of Middle English Musical Terms*, 1961, Ribibe, Ribiben, Ribible, Ribibor.

67 See Robinson, *op. cit.*, p. 61 (*Cook's Tale*) and *Miller's Tale*, lines 3331–3335.

68 J. E. Thorold Rogers, *Oxford City Documents 1268–1665*, Oxford Historical Society, 18 (1891), p. 165–6. I owe this reference to the kindness of the staff of the *Dictionary of Medieval Latin from British Sources*, who allowed me to examine as yet unpublished materials gathered for the Dictionary.

69 *Rotuli Parliamentorum*, III, 1783, p. 90.

70 Harvey, *op. cit.*, p. 22.

71 H. E. Salter, *A Cartulary of the Hospital of St. John the Baptist*, II, Oxford Historical Society 68 (1915), p. 191, and *idem*, *Survey of Oxford*, I, Oxford Historical Society, new series xiv (1960), p. 238.

72 On the shops of medieval craftsmen see Harvey, *op. cit.*, p. 71f.

73 On the Chancellor's powers over townsmen see Salter, *Registrum*, I, xiiif.

74 Salter, *Survey of Oxford*, I, p. 37–8.

75 See H. E. Salter, *Medieval Oxford*, Oxford Historical Society, c (1936), 81f.

76 On Passlew see Emden, *op. cit.*, p. 1432–3.

77 Sylvia L. Thrupp, *The Merchant Class of Medieval London* (1300–1500), Chicago, 1948, p. 4.

78 Elspeth M. Veale, 'Craftsmen and the Economy of London in the Fourteenth Century', in A. E. J. Hollaender and W. Kellaway, eds., *Studies in London History*, London, 1969, p. 144.

79 In the Middle English romance *Sir Beues of Hamtoun* (*c.*1300) it is made quite clear that in order to buy a fiddle it is necessary to go *in to þe bourȝ* (E. Kölbing, *The Romance of Sir Beues of Hamtoun*, Early English Text Society Extra Series xlvi (1885), xlviii (1886) and lxv (1894), line 3910). This detail is lacking in the French original (A. Stimmung, ed., *Der Anglo-normannische Boeve de Haumtone*, Halle, 1899, 2782f). The purchase of the instrument from a minstrel for forty pence is a further detail unique to the Middle English poem.

80 Guy Fitch Lytle, 'Patronage patterns and Oxford Colleges, *c.*1300–*c.*1530', in *The University in Society*, ed. L. Stone, 2 vols., 1975, I, pp. 111–149.

81 *Ibid.*, p. 135.

82 *The History of the University of Oxford*, The Bodleian Library, 1953, p. 10.

83 See E. Ekwall, *Studies on the Population of Medieval London*, Stockholm, 1956.

84 Veale, *op. cit.*, p. 133.

85 Gwyn A. Williams, *Medieval London*, London, 1963, p. 107.

86 Hanham, *op. cit.*

87 Thrupp, *op. cit.*, p. 247f.

88 Harvey, *op. cit.*, p. 26.

89 *Ibid.*

90 See Christopher Page and Lewis Jones, 'Four more 15th-century representations of stringed keyboard instruments' in this issue (Notes & Queries).

APPENDIX 1 to 9
Original documents pertaining to the Oxford harpmakers

1   *Poll Tax and Civil Population of Oxford* 1380: De Willelmo Morton harpmaker xij^d. (J. E. Thorold Rogers, *Oxford City Documents 1268–1665*, Oxford Historical Society, 18 (1891), p. 38.)

2   *Poll Tax and Civil Population of Oxford* 1380: De Rogero le Harpemaker et Alicia vxore eius xij^d. (J. E. Thorold Rogers, op. cit., p. 14.)

3   *Rentals of the Hospital of St. John, 21 December, 1384*: Parochia sancti Michaelis Australis xiii^s iiij^d De domo Boltras quam Rogerus Harpmaker tenet. (H. E. Salter, ed., *A Cartulary of the Hospital of St. John the Baptist*, III, Oxford Historical Society, 69 (1916), p. 202.)

4   *Registrum Cancellarii, 25 July, 1446*: Memorandum quod . . . Rogerus Carpentere et Robertus Harpmaker obligauerunt se quod idem Robertus

seruabit pacem penes Willelmum Barkham fuller et Katerinam Ylkyns sub pena xx librarum. (H. E. Salter, ed., *Registrum Cancellarii*, I, Oxford Historical Society, 93 (1932), p. 128.)

5 *Registrum Cancellarii*, 30 July, 1451: . . . Iohannes Martin sutor interuenit fideiussor pro Roberto Harpemaker de iudicio cisti et iudicato soluendo, sub pena xx librarum, pro quadam lite pendente inter dictum Robertum et Iohannem Bracley. (Salter, *op. cit.*, p. 255.)

6 *Registrum Cancellarii* (see Plate IV), 14 June, 1452: . . . comparuerunt coram nobis Thomas Blake de parochia sancte Marie, Iohannes Dyer eiusdem parochie, Stephanus Barbor de parochia sancte Marie Magdalene, et Robertus Denton de parochia sancti Petri in oriente; interuenerunt fideiussores pro Roberto Harpemaker quod ipse de cetero non vexabit magistrum Iohannem Van nec aliquem alium seruientem Universitatis occasione incarceracionis sue nec pro aliqua alia causa terminabili adinfra sub pena xx librarum Uniuersitati applicandarum [ac incarceracionis et excommunicacionis]; eciam iniunctum est eidem Roberto sub pena predicta, vel incarceracionis, quod non intrabit temporibus uel horis suspectis domum Iohanne Fyzt-John; et idem Robertus Harpe*maker* promisit personaliter coram commissario antedicto seruare ipsos in hac parte indempnes sub pena antedicta. (Salter, *op. cit.*, p. 267.)

7 *Registrum Cancellarii*, 28 June, 1452: . . . Robertus Smyth alias Harpmaker de Candich suspectus de adulterio commisso cum Iohanna Fyzt-Iohn, tap-setrice, morante in domo angulari lateris orientalis de Catstrete, e regione capelle beate Marie virginis in Smythyate, abiurauit societatem eiusdem Iohanne et quod non veniet in aliquem locum ubi ipsa fuerit nisi in strato publico, mercato, aut ecclesia, seu capella sub pena quadraginta solidorum sine contradictione Uniuersitati soluendorum. (Salter, *op.cit.*, p. 271.)

8 *Cartulary of Oseney Abbey. Rentals*: An[ualis redditus] Ten[ementum] quintum eiusdem [Raymundi] xiiis, iiid. . . . . relicta Thome Aas et Ioh. Harryes harpmaker (1462). (H. E. Salter, *Cartulary of Oseney Abbey*, III, Oxford Historical Society, 91 (1931), p. 250.)

9 *Registrum Cancellarii*, 1466: Magister Robertus Passlew conduxit in seruum suum Iohannem Harrys, harpemaker, pro toga vel precio vi^s viii^d et idem Iohannes iuratus est ad priuilegiorum Uniuersitatis obseruanciam etc. (Salter, *op. cit.*, II, p. 214.)

Early 15th-century instruments in Jean de Gerson's 'Tractatus de Canticis'

Jean de Gerson of the French nation, Chancellor of the University of Paris, [was] a man most erudite in the divine scriptures, and not ignorant of worldly learning . . .
Trithème, *De Scriptoribus Ecclesiasticis*, 1494[1]

It need cause no surprise that the earliest medieval technical treatise on a group of secular instruments forms part of a theological work,[2] nor that the material is introduced by its author, Jean de Gerson (1363-1429), 'on account of reverence for holy scripture'. Within the sphere of medieval European culture organology did not emancipate itself from theology until the mid-15th century. Certainly, by the 13th century, academics and musical theorists had begun to interest themselves in instruments (see below), but theologians had always considered the study of them to be part of their discipline. They aimed to be 'most erudite in the divine scriptures, and not ignorant of worldly learning'.

The *Tractatus de Canticis*[3] gives selectively detailed descriptions of four stringed instruments, two types of *tuba*, the organ, tabor and nakers, and two types of bells (the list being dictated by Psalm 150:3-5, to which Gerson makes additions). In some cases these accounts furnish evidence of the first importance to modern instrument makers, while a number of Gerson's remarks throw light upon early 15th-century musical life. In view of the importance of this text, it is rather surprising that no study has been made of the section on instruments.[4] In order that this material may become better known, the present article offers a text of the relevant passages accompanied by a translation and introduction.

Introduction

Gerson and the *Tractatus de Canticis*

Jean de Gerson was educated at the University of Paris, and became its chancellor in 1395.[5] He was a prolific writer (using both French and Latin), and made important contributions to many of the theological debates of his day.

During the troubled years from 1424 to 1426, Gerson appears to have become particularly interested in using musical subject matter for his theological works. It was probably in 1424—the year the English defeated the French at Verneuil in 'un autre Azincourt'—that he composed the *Canticordum du pélerin*, a work which contains a number of informative references to early 15th-century instruments.[6] Among other works with musical subject matter that Gerson probably composed at this time are the *Monocordum Jesu Christi*,[7] the *Psalterium mysticum*,[8] and the *Canon pro scacordo mystico* (a work bearing upon the identity of the mysterious *chekker*).[9] Somewhat later (certainly before 1426) he expanded the material on instruments in the *Canticordum du pélerin* and reworked it into a Latin treatise entitled *De canticorum originali ratione*.[10] This he incorporated into the *Tractatus de Canticis*.

The *Tractatus* is a substantial work treating music and related aspects of theology and philosophy in nine books divided into three volumes. In the first book of volume I, Gerson gives a learned account of *canticum sensuale* (music perceived by the senses) that includes descriptions of the instruments mentioned in Psalm 150:3-5 (*tuba, psalterium, cithara, tympanum, chorus, organum, cymbala*). Gerson also describes the *symphonia* (Daniel 3:5, 7, 10, 15), and the *tympanula* (a non-biblical term). In the manner so dear to the church fathers, he concludes each description with an

1 *Jean de Gerson in his study (presumed portrait), from a 15th-century miniature. Paris, Bib. Nat., Nouv. acq. lat. 3024 f.2v*

Reprinted from *Early Music* 6 (1978), pp. 339—349. By permission of Oxford University Press.

allegorical interpretation of the instrument (these allegories have been omitted in the present text and translation).[11] This part of the *Tractatus* is therefore cast in one of the standard forms of medieval biblical scholarship: the *gloss* or commentary upon a biblical text, in this case Psalm 150:3-5:[12]

3 Laudate eum in sono *tubae*;
  Laudate eum in *psalterio* et *cithara*
4 Laudate eum in *tympano* et *choro*;
  Laudate eum in *chordis* et *organo*.
5 Laudate eum in *cymbalis* benesonantibus.

Medieval glosses on these verses (Gerson mentions the *glossae* twice) generally give brief descriptions of the instruments listed, but these usually derive from early fathers such as St Augustine,[13] from the *Etymologiarum* of Isidore of Seville,[14] or (more rarely) from the *Epistle to Dardanus* of Pseudo-Jerome.[15] Fortunately, Gerson was interested in the instruments of his day and makes little use of the works of these authors.

Gerson's interest in 'contemporary' instruments reflects an intellectual development with its beginnings in the 13th century. Among the musical theorists of this period who show a welcome—if passing—interest in the instruments of their day are Elias of Salomon,[16] Aegidius of Zamora,[17] Johannes de Grocheo,[18] and Jerome of Moravia,[19] while scholars such as Bartholomaeus Anglicus,[20] Albertus Magnus,[21] Nicholas de Lyra,[22] Nicholas Trivet (illus. 2 and 3) and Roger Bacon[23] also gives instruments some consideration within the wider context of their biblical and philosophical studies. Little writing has survived on this subject from the 14th century, but from the 15th century we have, among others, the works of Gerson, Arnaut de Zwolle and others,[24] Paulus Paulirinus of Prague[25] and Tinctoris.[26]

Sources of Gerson's descriptions of the instruments

A book that Gerson may have used in writing his account is the *De Proprietatibus Rerum* ('On the Properties of Things') by Bartholomaeus Anglicus (completed, or a revised version edited, *c* 1250).[27] This encyclopedia enjoyed immense popularity in the late Middle Ages, and was widely read in France both in the original Latin and in a French version by Jean Corbechon (completed 1372).[28] Gerson may well have first read it as a student.[29] The final book of this work contains a chapter on musical instruments incorporating three observations also found in the *Tractatus*: (1) that the organ is the only instrument customarily used in church, (2) that the strings of the *psalterium* are made of wire, and (3) that the drum (*tympanum*) is generally used with a pipe (*fistula*).[30]

Certainly, there is nothing here that Gerson could not have learned from observation. It is quite possible that he possessed enough technical knowledge to write his account of instruments without leaving his study or taking down a book. He was certainly interested in them—referring to them in one place as 'delectable for their variety'[31]—and some

knowledge of musical instruments had been a recognized requirement for the theologian since the days of St Augustine.[32] Several of his works (such as the *Ad Intelligentiam Canticordi*) leave us in no doubt that he had received a musical training.

As a student at the University of Paris, Gerson would have been required to study the liberal arts, *Musica* among them. There is reason to believe that the practical study of musical instruments was integrated into the academic study of *Musica* in some universities, and there is also evidence that the *clercs* of Paris cultivated instruments with great keenness in their leisure hours.[33] Gerson may well have shared in this enthusiasm and learned some instruments himself.

As for his mature years, Gerson must be counted among such important medieval men of letters as Chaucer, Froissart and Deschamps whose musical abilities can only be conjectured. Certainly the details of his biography do not encourage us to believe that he enjoyed much leisure to cultivate practical talents.

The instruments

Tuba

In medieval Latin *tuba* was generally employed to denote a straight trumpet. The Bible mentions *tubae* made from horn and from ductile metal (see plate 2).[34] Gerson's account of the materials and uses of *tubae* derives for the most part from various biblical passages interspersed with snippets from Isidore of Seville and Bartholomaeus Anglicus.

Psalterium

The *psalterium* is shown as an incurved trapezoidal zither in the Bodley manuscript of Nicholas Trivet's commentary on the psalms (plate 2). The same instrument represents the *psalterion* (forms vary) and *psalterium* in a 14th-century French manuscript now in the Pierpont Morgan Library (plate 4), in British Library Manuscript Sloane 3983 (14th century) and in various other sources of the period. It is probably an instrument of this type (not unlike 'the shape of a heart') that Gerson describes in his account of the psalterium.

The rather puzzling statement that the *psalterium* 'sounds from above, proceeding from lower pitches running down to higher pitches' echoes a standard patristic gloss.[35] According to this the *psalterium* was an instrument with its resonating cavity *above* and strings plucked from *below*. This may have been originally a description of a vertical angular harp.[36] Gerson imagines a trapezoidal psaltery held against the breast and reinterprets the above/below gloss in terms of the pitch-direction of the strings:

Psalterium

low pitch (above)

high pitch (below)

2 Tuba cornea, tuba ductilis, psalterium, cithara and tympanum in *Nicholas Trivet's commentary upon psalm 150. Oxford, MS Bodley, 738, fol. 250r. English, early 14th century*

3 Chorus, organum and cymbala. *MS as plate 2, fol. 250v*

The reference that both Gerson and Bartholomaeus Anglicus make to the wire strings of the *psalterium* are of considerable interest. With the exception of a late 12th-century mention of the brass strings for Irish *citharae* made by Giraldus Cambrensis[37] (and often repeated by later medieval writers), there is no evidence to connect any medieval chordophone other than the *psalterium* with the use of wire strings until the mid-15th century, the approximate date of the earliest known technical descriptions of keyboard chordophones. The *clavicordium, clavicimbalum,* and *virginale* described by Paulus Paulirinus of Prague (*c* 1460) all have wire strings.[38]

As for string materials of the *psalterium*, both Gerson and Bartholomaeus mention silver, giving respectively bronze

and brass as alternatives. In his *Collectorium super Magnificat* (1427-8) Gerson mentions both brass and gold strings in connection with the *psalterium*,[39] and it is interesting to note in this connection that in the Middle English poem 'Cleanness' (last quarter of the 14th century) the lids of cups made from precious metals crashing down as they are thrown about, are said to sound 'as merry as the music from a psaltery'.[40]

Cithara

The customary translation of *cithara* in the major vernaculars of medieval Europe was 'harp' (forms vary according to language). The *cithara* is shown as a pillar-harp in many

341

4 Orgues et . . . psalterion *in Guillaume de Deguilleville,* Pilgrimage of the life of Man. *Pierpont Morgan Library, MS 772, f. 93. French, 14th century*

medieval sources, including the Bodley manuscript of Nicholas Trivet's commentary (see illus. 2).

Gerson's statement that the 'sound' of the *cithara* 'extends from lower [notes] below to higher notes above' echoes, as in the case of the description of the *psalterium*, a standard patristic gloss.[41] According to this, the *cithara* was an instrument with its resonating cavity *below* and strings plucked from *above* (the opposite of the *psalterium*). Gerson again re-interprets the above/below gloss in terms of the pitch-direction of the strings:

Cithara

high pitch

low pitch

The statement that the strings of the *cithara* 'are made from the intestines of animals dried, made fine and twisted'[42] agrees with all the medieval accounts of the harp that I have encountered[43] (with the exception of texts relating to the Irish harp), and in the *Collectorium super Magnificat* men-

tioned above, Gerson states that the *cithara* is equipped with 'twisted strings of sinew' (*chordulis nervorum tortis*).[44] A reference in the Old French *Merlin*[45] to a *harpe* with strings of gold and a silver body (played by the magician himself in disguise) can be dismissed as unrepresentative of all but the most luxurious medieval manufacture. In view of this evidence, it can be said that the statements of Curt Sachs[46] and Sybil Marcuse[47] to the effect that medieval harps had wire strings are without foundation. All the available evidence indicates that, with the exception of the Irish harps, medieval harps were generally strung with gut.

In his sermon *Puer natus est nobis*, Gerson notes that the *harpe* has twenty strings.[48]

Tympanum and tympanula

Gerson states that the word *tympanum* (for which he gives the vernacular equivalents *tambour* and *bedon*) is a generic term denoting a variety of percussion instruments put to different uses. His account of one variety, the *tympanula* (for which he gives the vernacular equivalent *naquaires*), is of the greatest interest, for he refers unequivocally to the different pitches of the two drums, thus providing the earliest evidence we have of nakers built in this way.[49] The terms he uses are *obtusus* ('blunt', 'dull', 'enfeebled') and *peracutus* ('acute', 'clear', 'keen') which, at first, suggest difference of tone. However, the allegorical interpretation relates *obtusus* to 'lowly veneration' and *peracutus* to 'hope raised above' which clearly indicate that the terms relate to difference of pitch.

The contrast Gerson establishes between *naquaires* and 'other forms of *tympana* more common among the people because they are easier to play and are louder for uncouth leaping and other dancing', clearly shows that he regards the *naquaires* as refined instruments with a more sophisticated technique (two hands on differently pitched drums), than the popular *tambours* and *bedons*. Literary and documentary sources show that *naquaires* were much used in aristocratic households and military bands;[50] Gerson doubtless associated them with these prestigious uses. His feeling towards the *tambours* and *bedons* probably owes something to the general odium in which theologians of the Middle Ages held the dance and all that was associated with it, but it is also clear that Gerson regarded these instruments as simply inartistic. In a section of the *Tractatus* (not given here), he recalls the story of Midas who chose the pipes of Pan in preference to the lyre of Apollo, and comments somewhat ruefully: 'how many are there today who prefer to listen to the music of pipe and tabor rather than of harp and psaltery?'[51]

Chorus

During the Middle Ages, the Latin word *chorus* (from the Greek) was associated with a number of different instruments including the *bagpipe* and *croud*. Gerson probably refers to a string-drum (plate 5), though beam-shaped dulcimers with few strings are not uncommon in 14th- and

15th-century iconographical sources (plate 6). Perhaps the kind of *dulce melos* used in the villages (according to Arnaut de Zwolle) was a similar instrument?[52]

Symphonia

Symphonia, also derived from the Greek, was another poly-semous word in the Middle Ages. Fortunately, Gerson's *symphonia* is clearly the instrument inelegantly called the *hurdy-gurdy* in many modern organological works. From the 14th century we have the testimony of Jean Corbechon, among others, that the French vernacular word *simphonie* (forms vary) could be used with the same meaning.[53]

Gerson appears to have misunderstood the mechanics of the *symphonia*. His Latin implies that the 'fixed keys' (i.e. the tangents), bring the string into contact with the wheel, whereas the tangents serve only to produce the stopped notes. His account of the instrument is nonetheless of interest as he mentions the kind of resin used on the wheel,[54] and states that the melody string (he uses the singular and does not mention drone strings) is like the strings of a cithara. Paulus Paulirinus of Prague states that 'thick and strong' gut strings are used on the same instrument (his term is *Ysis*),[55] and these two descriptions—separated only by some thirty-five years—are a warning against the easy assumption that medieval instruments of a certain type must have sounded alike.

Organum

As medieval writers were keen to point out (Gerson continuing the long tradition), the word *organum* was a general name for all musical instruments, but specially appropriate to the one that sounds with pipes and bellows. The 'special appropriateness' presumably derived, at least during the later Middle Ages, from the fact that the organ was regarded, in Machaut's phrase, as the 'king' of instruments.[56]

Cymbala

The various meanings of *cymbala* in medieval Latin have been discussed with abundant documentation by Joseph Smits van Waesberghe.[57] His survey of texts demonstrates that this term could be applied to bells as well as to cymbals in the modern sense. Gerson refers to *cymbala* 'which sound when struck together' and *cymbala* 'which we have called bells' (*campanas*).

Gerson distinguishes between *campanae* (i.e. tower bells) and *campanulae pro melodia* (smaller bells to make music). He refers to this latter variety as they are arranged in chiming clocks (*horologia*). In Old French literature, reference is made to *orloges* in the rooms of noble houses and in belfrys, where

5 *Book of Hours, Malvern, from the collection of Dyson Perrins, unnumbered MS f38. Tours, c1450 (above)*

6 *Beam-shaped dulcimer in a manuscript dated 1448 (Coburg, library of the Casimir School). After Alexander Buchner,* 'Musical Instruments: An Illustrated History' *(Prague, 1973)*

they were maintained by *orlogeurs*, often in the employ of the town.[58]

There is ample evidence that at least the domestic *orloges* were regarded as a kind of musical instrument,[59] and there are indications that at least some of them were tuned to play pieces of monophonic church music such as sequences and proses. The poet Deschamps writes in his *Art de Dictier* (1392), that those who are not gifted with a fine singing voice may at least learn to recognize the various notes produced by 'bells enclosed in various *orloges*' which 'give harmonious sounds uttering sequences and other things from the music of Holy Church' (*chans de saincte Eglise*).[60] Gerson, in his *Canticordum du Pèlerin* associates the bells of *horloges* with the singing of *proses*,[61] while in our section of the *Tractatus*, he states that the sound of *orloges* reminds the troubled listener of the seraphic song 'heaven and earth full of thy glory'. This line is based on *Isaiah* 6:3, but Gerson quotes it from the most popular of all medieval hymns, the *Te Deum*, which was certainly associated with the ringing of bells.[62]

Gerson's classification system for the 'variety' of instruments that he admires is an interesting example of his readiness to adapt conventional materials to give a fuller account of the instruments of his day. He groups percussion and strings together and distinguishes between instruments that sound by striking (*pulsu*) and by movement of air (*flatu*). He then expands on this conventional classification by distinguishing three varieties of *pulsu* in order to accommodate the actions of the bow and hurdy-gurdy wheel:

Music with 'striking' may be made in three ways: by rotation as in the *symphonia*; by drawing back and forth [i.e. bowing] as on the *viella* or *rebella*; by beating or striking with the nails or a plectrum, or with a stick as on the *cythara* and *guiterna*, *lituus* [sic], the *psalterium* and *tympanum*, and *campanula*. *Cymbala* sound by being struck together.[63]

[1] Translated from Mgr Glorieux, ed. *Jean de Gerson Oeuvres complètes* (Tournai, 1960-73), vol. 1, p. 146. For other references to music and instruments in Gerson's works, see Glorieux, op cit, 4, pp. 1, 2, 10, 19, 29, 33, 39, 135-7, 150; 7/1, pp. 122f, 297, 421-3; 7/2, p. 966; 8, pp. 26, 36, 81, 166f, 266, 337, 520-3; 9, pp. 21-3, 158, 714-8.

[2] I do not count the 14th-century Berkeley Theory MS here, as it is only concerned with a single aspect of a few instruments and says nothing about construction (Library of the University of California, Berkeley, formerly Phillipps MS 4450. Text, translation, and full discussion in O. Ellsworth, 'The Berkeley Theory MS olim Phillips 4450; A Compendium of 14c Music Theory' (Ph.D. Diss., University of California at Berkeley, 1969, *passim*)). Concerning the ecclesiastical instruments and the treatises upon them, see J. Perrot, *The organ from its invention in the Hellenistic period to the end of the thirteenth century* (London, 1971), *passim*; C. Adkins, 'The technique of the monochord', *Acta musicologica*, 39 (1967), pp. 34-43; J. Smits van Waesberghe, *Cymbala* (American Institute of Musicology, Musicological Studies and Documents, 1 (Rome, 1951), *passim*.

[3] Text in Glorieux, op cit, 9, pp. 524-602. The passages translated here are taken from pp. 532-5.

[4] For a general study of musical terminology in the *Tractatus de canticis* see A. Machabey, 'Remarques sur le lexique musical du *De canticis* de Gerson', *Romania*, 79 (1958), pp. 175-236. Extracts from the text with and without translation may be found in a number of recent books and articles, e.g. Sybil

[5] Marcuse, *A survey of musical instruments* (Newton Abbot, 1975), pp. 61 and 200; Edwin Ripin, 'Towards an Identification of the Chekker', *Galpin Society Journal*, 28 (1975), p. 14ff. Martin Gerbert quoted substantial sections of the original Latin in his *De cantu et musica sacra* (1774), 2/3, pp. 145, 154, etc.

[5] For a compact survey of Gerson's life and a chronology of his works see Glorieux, op cit, 1, pp. 105-39.

[6] For the relevant passages of the text, see Glorieux, op cit, 7/1 pp. 127-32.

[7] Text in Glorieux, op cit, 9, pp. 704-5.

[8] ibid, p. 706 (*Psalterion mysticum*, p. 707). See also 4, pp. 1-2.

[9] Text in Glorieux, op cit, 9, pp. 708-10. For discussion and illustrations from a manuscript in the Bibliothèque nationale, Paris, see Ripin, op cit, p. 14 and plates 3, 4 and 5. On the basis of Gerson's evidence Ripin concludes that the *chekker* was a clavichord. This is a misconstruction as I hope to show in a future study.

[10] Glorieux, op cit, 9, p. 525f.

[11] On these allegories see Th. Gérold, *Les pères de l'église et la musique* (Strasbourg, 1931), p. 180f. Further bibliography is given in Christopher Page, 'Biblical instruments in medieval manuscript illustration', *Early Music*, 5/3 (July 1977).

[12] On the gloss and medieval instruments see Christopher Page, 'Musical Instruments in Medieval Latin Biblical Glosses', *FoMRHI* communication 13 (April 1976).

[13] Augustine's psalm commentary was particularly influential (text in PL 36; see particularly cols. 279-80).

[14] Relevant passage of text in PL 82, cols. 163-79. See also 643-4.

[15] Text in PL 30, cols. 213-15. For modern critical texts, discussion and illustrations from MSS of the *Epistle* see H. Avenary, 'Hieronymus' Epistel über die musikinstrumente und ihre altöstlichen quellen', *Anuario Musical*, 16 (1961), pp. 55-80, and R. Hammerstein, 'Instrumenta Hieronymi', *Archiv für Musikwissenschaft*, 16 (1959), pp. 117-34. For the illustrations and their influence see Christopher Page, op cit, *passim*. See also Tilman Seebass, *Musikdarstellung und Psalterillustration im früheren Mittelalter*, 2 vols., Francke Verlag, Bern, 1973, p. 141ff.

[16] Elias of Salomon, *Scientia Artis Musicae* in GS, 3, pp. 20 and 61; remarks upon the *viella*.

[17] Aegidius of Zamora, *Ars Musica*, ed. Robert Tissot, American Institute of Musicology, *Corpus scriptorum de Musica*, 20 (1974). Aegidius's chapter on instruments reproduces, almost verbatim, that of Bartholomaeus Anglicus on the same subject (see note 20).

[18] Grocheo's treatise is printed in E. Rohloff, ed., *Die Quellenhandschriften zum Musiktraktat des Johannes de Grocheo* (Leipzig, 1972), p. 134-7 (facsimiles p. 76f).

[19] Jerome of Moravia, *Tractatus de Musica*, ed., S. Cserba (Regensburg, 1935); Chapter 28 on the *viella* and the *rubeba*.

[20] Bartholomaeus Anglicus, *De proprietatibus rerum* (c1250). For the text of the chapter on music, see Hermann Müller, 'Der Musiktraktat in dem Werke des Bartholomaeus Anglicus De Proprietatibus Rerum', *Reimann-Festschrift* (Leipzig, 1909), pp. 241-55.

[21] Albertus Magnus, *De animalibus*, ed. H. Stadler, *Beiträge zur Geschichte der Philosophie des Mittelalters*, 15 (Münster, 1916), pp. 1293-4; also *Ethica*, ed. A. Borgnet (Paris, 1891), pp. 4, 30, 165, 404.

[22] Nicholas de Lyra, *Biblia sacra cum glossis*, 5 vols. (Lyon, 1545), glosses on Daniel 3:5 (vol. 4, p. 299). These glosses and others are summarized in Christopher Page, op cit, p. 31.

[23] Roger Bacon, *Opus tertium*, ed. J. S. Brewer in *Roger Bacon opera*, Rolls Series, 15 (1859), p. 228ff. See also *The Opus Majus of Roger Bacon*, ed. J. H. Bridges (Oxford, 1900), 1, pp. 179 and 236-8.

[24] Facsimile of MS edited by G. le Cerf and E.-R. Labande, *Instruments de musique du XVe siècle: Les Traités d'Henri-Arnaut de Zwolle et de Divers Anonymes* (Paris, 1932).

[25] Text in J. Reiss, 'Pauli Paulirini de Praga Tractatus de Musica', *Zeitschrift für Musikwissenschaft*, 7 (1925), pp. 259-64.

[26] Text in A. Baines, 'Fifteenth-century instruments in Tinctoris, *De inventione et usu musicae*', *Galpin Society Journal*, III (1950), pp. 19-26. Other 15th-century materials are given by J. Handschin in 'Aus der alten Musiktheorie: V, Zur Instrumentenkunde', *Acta Musicologica*, 16-17 (1944-5), pp. 1-10.

[27] See note 20.

[28] M. C. Seymour, 'Some medieval French readers of the *De Proprietatibus Rerum*' (*Scriptorium*, 28 (1974), 1, pp. 100-3) stresses the popularity of the work in medieval France.

[29] Seymour points out (op cit, p. 103) that the *De Proprietatibus Rerum* was among the books which the stationers of Paris were required to stock for the use of students in 1286 and 1304.

[30] Müller, op cit, pp. 248, 252, 253.

[31] Glorieux, op cit, IX, p. 530.

[32] Augustine stresses that a theologian requires a knowledge of musical instruments in his influential treatise *De doctrina christiana* (PL 34, cols 48-49).

[33] See L. Ellinwood, 'Ars Musica', in *Speculum*, 20 (1945), pp. 290-9. For a survey of the evidence relating to Paris, see Nan Cooke Carpenter, *Music in the Medieval and Renaissance universities* (Norman, Oklahoma, 1958), pp. 46-69.

[34] Psalm 97:6.

[35] This gloss is given by Bartholomaeus Anglicus in his chapter on instruments. Müller, op cit, p. 252.

[36] See Curt Sachs, *The history of musical instruments* (London, 1940), p. 116. For another opinion see Seebass, op cit, p. 31.

[37] Text, translation and discussion in Lloyd Hibberd, 'Giraldus Cambrensis and Early English "Organ Music" ', *Journal of the American Musicological Society*, 8 (1955), 3, pp. 208-12.

[38] Reiss, op cit, pp. 262-3.

[39] Glorieux, op cit, VIII, p. 521.

[40] I. Gollancz, ed., *Cleanness* (1921), republished with an English translation by D. S. Brewer (1974), ll. 1513-16.

[41] This gloss is also given by Bartholomaeus Anglicus, Müller, op cit, p. 252.

[42] Praetorius in *Syntagma Musicum*, II, *De Organographia* (Wolfenbüttel, 1619), p. 56, gives almost the same sentence as Gerson and attributes it to St Jerome. I have been unable to trace it in Jerome's works.

[43] Relevant texts are quoted and translated in Christopher Page, 'References to string materials in some medieval texts, *c* 1050-*c* 1430. An annotated anthology', *FoMRHI* communication 14 (April 1976).

[44] Glorieux, op cit, 8, p. 521.

[45] H. O. Sommer, ed., *The Vulgate Version of the Arthurian Romances, II, Lestoire de Merlin* (Washington, 1908), pp. 408-9. A similar reference is cited from the Old French romance *Galeran* (*c* 1200) by Yvonne Rokseth in *New Oxford History of Music*, 3 (London, 1960), p. 408.

[46] Sachs, op cit, p. 263.

[47] Marcuse, op cit, p. 389.

[48] Glorieux, op cit, 7/2, p. 966.

[49] For differing views on the procedure to adopt when reconstructing *naquaires* with regards to difference of tone or pitch between the two drums (taking no account of Gerson's crucial evidence) see James Blades and Jeremy Montagu, *Early Percussion Instruments from the Middle Ages to the Baroque* (London, 1976), p. 2; and E. A. Bowles (review of the above), in *FoMRHI* bulletin and communication 14 (April 1976), p. 63: 'Mr Montagu subscribes to the concept

of contrasting tone rather than contrasting pitch ... Since we really have absolutely no way of knowing how the medieval naker sounded, one approach is as good as another.'

[50] On the medieval uses of nakers, see Richard Rastall, 'Some English Consort Groupings of the Late Middle Ages', *Music and Letters*, 55/2 (1974), p. 187ff; E. A. Bowles, 'La hiérarchie des instruments de musique dans l'Europe féodale', *Revue de Musicologie*, 42 (1958), pp. 156-60; H. G. Farmer, 'Crusading Martial Music', *Music and Letters*, 30/3 (1949), pp. 243-9.

[51] Glorieux, op cit, 9, p. 528.

[52] G. le Cerf and E. R. Labande, op cit, p. 19. For further references concerning the *chorus*, see Marcuse, op cit, pp. 200-2.

[53] Jean Corbechon, interpolation in his translation of the *De Proprietatibus Rerum* (see note 20) printed edition of 1485, XIX, chap. 140.

[54] As does Paulus Paulirinus of Prague, who mentions *pix* (pitch). Reiss, op cit, p. 264.

[55] ibid

[56] See Bowles, *Hiérarchie*, p. 160.

[57] Smits van Waesberghe, op cit, pp. 11-12.

[58] See Tobler-Lommatzsch, *Altfranzösisches Wörterbuch*, vol. 6 (Wiesbaden, 1965), cols 1290-1, *orloge*, and F. Godefroy, *Dictionnaire de l'ancienne langue française* (Paris, 1888), *orloguer*.

[59] See for example the reference to *orloiges* in *Le roman de la rose*, ed. F. Lecoy, III (Paris, 1970), lines 21,000-3.

[60] Text and translation in Christopher Page, 'Machaut's "pupil" Deschamps on the Performance of Music', *Early Music* 5/4 (Oct, 1977).

[61] Glorieux, op cit, 7/1, p. 132.

[62] On this question see Richard Rastall, 'Minstrelsy, Church and Clergy in Medieval England', *Proceedings of the Royal Musical Association*, 97 (1971), pp. 83-98; Gilbert Reaney 'The performance of Medieval Music', *Aspects of Medieval and Renaissance Music*, ed. Jan LaRue (London, 1967), pp. 714-15; Tobler-Lommatzsch, op cit, col. 1257. For the text of the *Te Deum*, see F. J. E. Raby, ed., *The Oxford Book of Medieval Latin verse* (Oxford, 1959), pp. 16-17.

[63] Glorieux, op cit, 9, p. 594. In this rendering I have translated the reading *tractu* for Glorieux *tactu*.

[64] ibid.

Instrument terms in the translation

It is still considered legitimate, at least by English organ-ologists, to arrange scholarly discussion of medieval instruments under names such as *rebec, citole*, etc, taken from literary sources. I have the gravest reservations about this procedure; for too long now these words have acted like charms lulling scholars into a greatly simplified view of the typology and terminology of medieval instruments. Consequently, I have not translated Gerson's terms into these ill-considered 'group names'. The preceding section ('The instruments') considers the meaning of each Latin term, which readers may consult in order to clarify their understanding of the text. Terms not discussed there (because Gerson says nothing about those instruments) have also been left untranslated. For information on these, the reader is referred to the already cited works of Sachs, Marcuse, etc.

The text

The text given here is basically that of Glorieux. All deviations from it are indicated at the end of my text. Quotations from, or allusions to, Scriptural texts are indicated in marginal notes, as are other references by Gerson to the instruments mentioned here that are of interest.

Abbreviations

FoMRHI: Fellowship of Makers and Restorers of Historical Instruments, Bulletin and Communications. Issued quarterly to members.
GS: Martin Gerbert, *Scriptores Ecclesiastici de Musica*, 3 vols, Typis San-Blasianis, 1784.
PL: J. P. Migne, *Patrologiae Cursus Completus: Series Latina*, 221 vols, Paris, 1844-64.
Du Pin: Elles Du Pin ed., *Joannis Gersonii Doctoris Theologi et Cancelarii Parisiensis opera omnia*, iii, (Antwerp, 1706), pp. 619-83.

Acknowledgements

I am indebted to Mr Bernard Barr of York Minster Library whose expertise in medieval Latin saved me from a number of errors. I owe a particular debt of gratitude to my wife, Régine Page, who examined the complete works of Gerson for references to music and instruments.

Text

Tractatus de Canticis. I. *De canticorum originali ratione.*
1. *Canticum Sensuale* [Extracts].

. . . ad instrumenta musica pergat sermo noster.

Praeponatur tuba cum sono, vel ut alia translatio habet cum clangore; cujus materia, formaə et usus varius est. Nam est tuba cornea . . . Est tuba ductilis vel argentea, vel aerea, quae metalla suasibilia malleabiliaque sunt . . . tuba clangit nunc ad denuntiationem solemnitatum, nunc ad congressionem bellorum, nunc ad legis promulgationem vel auditum prout in Sinai, nunc ad coetus convocationem, nunc pro neomenia. . . .

Subsequitur: 'laudate eum in psalterio et cithara'.

Differunt haec a tuba vel buccina, quorum pulsu seu tactu non flatu sunt; quorum sonus est capacior atque serenior . . . Haec autem est distantia psalterii cum cithara, quia psalterium sonat a superiori, procedens a gravioribus sonis ad acutiores descendendo. Habet insuper chordulas vel argenteas vel ex electro, quasi tinnientes leviusque tangendas. Citharae vero formam ad psalterium videbis eversam; cujus sonitus a gravioribus deorsum, ad acutiores sursum sonos tendit, cujus fides et chordae de morticinis sunt intestinis animalium desiccatis, subtiliatis et tortis . . . Conveniunt psalterium et cithara quia pectori junguntur et formam cordis habent instar scuti; habent et hanc figuram instrumenta musicalia. Nam trigono vel pyramidi proxima sunt omnia, sive quae pulsu sive quae flatu consonant . . .

Sujungitur: 'laudate eum in tympano et choro'.

Tympanum vulgo gallice dicitur tambourᵇ, vel bedon, compositum ex pelle derasa tensaque, cujusmodi non est una vel magnitudo vel forma vel usus. Sunt tympanula duo, gallice naquaires, unum obtusi supra modum soni, alterum peracuti . . . Sunt alia tympana vulgaribus magis assueta, quia faciliora, quia sonabiliora ad saltus incondites et alia tripudia, quibus solent jungi fistulae biforaminae et triforaminae, tripos insuper non grandis calybeus hinc inde percussus. Cymbala quoque, nonnunquam ex aere, per mutuam collisionem tinnitus acutos reddentia . . .

Chorus vocatur a nonnullis vulgaribus instrumentum quoddam instar trabis oblongum et vacuum, chordas habens grossiores multo plus quam cithara duas aut tres, quae baculis erutis percussae varie variant rudem sonum . . .

Symphoniam putant aliqui viellam, vel rebeccam quae minor est. At vero rectius existimatur esse musicum tale instrumentum quale sibi vendicaverunt specialiter ipsi coeci. Haec sonum reddit dum una manu resolvitur rota parvula thure linita et per alteram applicatur ei cum certis clavibus chordula nervorum prout in cithara, ubi pro diversitate tractuum rotae, varietas harmoniae dulcis amoenaque resultat . . .

Translation

... our discussion proceeds to musical instruments.

The *tuba* 'with its sound' (or as another translation has it, 'with its noise') is put first;[1] its material, shape, and use is [*sic*] various. There is the *tuba* of horn[2] ... There is the ductile *tuba* made of silver,[3] or bronze, metals which are workable and malleable ... the *tuba* sounds now for the announcement of festivals, now for the joining of battles, now for the proclamation or announcement of a law as on Sinai, now for the summoning of an assembly, and now for the new moon[4] ...

'Praise Him on the *psalterium* and *cithara*' follows.

These differ from the *tuba* and *buccina*, as they are sounded by plucking or striking not by blowing; then the sound is smoother and more serene[5] ... This, however, is the distinction between the *psalterium* and the *cithara*, that the *psalterium* sounds from above, proceeding from lower pitches running down to higher pitches. Moreover it has strings of silver or bronze, that must be plucked lightly to produce a ringing sound.[6] You will see that the form of the *cithara* is the reverse; its sound extends from lower [notes] to higher notes above, and its strings are made from the intestines of animals dried, made fine, and twisted ... The *psalterium* and *cithara* come together in that they are held to the breast and have the shape of a heart, like a shield;[7] musical instruments each have this form. All of them, whether they sound aloud by striking or by blowing, are very like a triangle or a pyramid.[8]

'Praise Him on the *tympanum* and *chorus*' is added.

The *tympanum* is called *tambour*, or *bedon* in French,[9] and is made of a scraped and stretched skin, for which there is not a single size, form or use. Two *tympanula*, called *naquaires* in French, comprise one [drum] of very dull sound and another [drum] of very clear sound. ... There are other *tympana* more used among the people, because they are louder for uncouth leaping and other dancing, and to these they customarily join two- and three-holed *fistulae*, and also a moderate sized metal *tripos* [?triangle][10] beaten on both sides. There are *cymbala* also, some made from bronze, giving a high-pitched ringing sound when struck together ...

Chorus is applied by some people to a certain oblong, hollow instrument in the form of a beam, having two or three strings much thicker than those of the *cithara*, which when diversely struck with upturned[11] sticks variously give a crude sound. ...

Some think the *symphonia* to be the *viella* or the *rebecca*[12] (which is smaller). Certainly it is more correctly taken to be such an instrument as the blind have specially appropriated for themselves. This sounds while one hand turns a small wheel smeared with the resin of the incense tree, and the other hand applies a sinew string to it (as used on the harp) with fixed keys; by variously drawing round the wheel a diversity of sweet and delightful music is produced ...

7 Symphonia *from the 15th-century glass of St Denis, Walmgate, York (photograph by Jeremy Haselock)*

[1] The two 'renderings' are the *Hebraicum* and *Gallicanum/Romanum* texts of this passage of the psalter.
[2] Psalm 97:6.
[3] Psalm 97:6. Numbers 10:2.
[4] cf Exodus 19:16-25; Numbers 10:1-10; Psalm 80:4; Leviticus 25:9. Compare *Canticordum du Pélerin* (Glorieux, op cit, 7/1, p. 127 and Bartholomaeus Anglicus on the *tuba* (Müller, op cit, pp. 248-9).
[5] Compare the references to loud and soft instruments in E. A. Bowles, ' "Haut and Bas": The grouping of Musical Instruments in the Middle Ages', *Musica Disciplina*, 8 (1954), pp. 115-40.
[6] In the *Pratique du Psalterium Mystique* (Glorieux, 7/1, pp. 421-3), Gerson refers to the performance of '*teneur et contreteneur*' on the *psalterium*.
[7] These remarks on shapes derive ultimately from Isidore of Seville (loc cit, col. 167) and pseudo-Jerome (loc cit, cols. 214 and 215). Some texts of pseudo-Jerome mention a *psalterium* in the shape of a shield. See Hammerstein, op cit, p. 127).
[8] Gerson is presumably thinking of wind instruments with tapering exterior or a bell.
[9] Compare *Canticordum du Pélerin* (Glorieux, 7/1, p. 128) where Gerson adds the vernacular equivalent *magnaire*.
[10] The translation of *tripos* (lit. 'three-legged stool') is uncertain. See Sybil Marcuse, *Musical Instruments: A Comprehensive Dictionary* (New York, 1964), *Triangle, Trepie, Treppiede*.
[11] 'Upturned' is a guess for *erutis* (from *eruo* 'to pluck, draw out'). *Erutis* might conceivably be (given the standard contractions of medieval handwriting) a misreading for *retortis*, 'bent back'. For a reference to percussion instruments played with *baculis retortis* see Du Cange, *Glossarium ad Scriptores mediae et infimae Latinitatis* (Paris, 1733), under *Tamburlum*.
[12] Compare *Puer natus est nobis* (Glorieux, 7/2, p. 966), where the *reberbe* is said to have three strings, and also the *Canticordum du Pélerin* (Glorieux, 7/1, p. 128) where the *rebebbe* is said to accompany *chansons de gestes*, 'such as those of Roland and Oliver'.

Felix qui magnalia Dei nedum in naturalibus ... sed in artificialibus etiam recognoscit, quemadmodum in perforatione modici ligni in sambuca vel fistulis, aut ex metalli ductione in tubis et cymbalis, aut in nervorum aut intestinorum desiccata tortione prout in citharis tot resonantiae variantur.

Sequitur: 'Laudate eum in chordis et organo'.

Chordae, secundum glossas, positae sunt pro quibuslibet instrumentis aliis a psalterio et cithara quae cordis sonant repercussis, sit viella, sit symphonia, sit lyra, sit rota, sit guiterna, sit lituus, sit nablum, sit sistrum, sit scacarum, sit rebella ...

Ceterum latius adhuc organa recipiuntur a glossis pro musico qualicumque compingatur instrumento. Habet vero modernus usus appropriationem nec irrationabiliter ad organa ex plumbeis vel staneis fistulis, quae cum follibus et cum digitis multiplicem et perfectam habent inter aliud quodlibet instrumentum vocalium resonantiam fistularum, quae fistulae non illiberales appellandae sunt, quia non oris deformatione sed follis inflatione sonant. Hoc solum vel praecipuum retinuit ecclesiastica consuetudo musicum genus instrumenti, cui vidimus aliquam jungi tubam, rarissime vero bombardas seu chalemias seu cornemusas grandes aut parvas, vel alia si qua sint, quae non nominaverimus instrumenta, qualia Danielis liber omnia concludere videtur in adoratione statuae sub omni genere musicorum.

Verumtamen ampliare id quod modo diximus de organorum solo usu per celebrem Ecclesiae ritum commonet id quod propheta subjungit: laudate Dominum in cymbalis bene sonantibus, laudate eum in cymbalis jubilationis. Sunt aerea cymbala ea quae vocavimus campanas quas bene fortiter sonare nullus ambigit. Talibus utitur Ecclesia plus aliis sectis, ad Domini laudes tamquam vice tubarum Legis Veteris, quarum officia metris quidam expressit loquentem inducens campanam: Laudo Deum verum, plebem voco, congrego clerum,/ Defunctos ploro, pestem fugo, festa decoro. Sunt et campanulae pro melodia, velut in horologiis aliquibus ordinatae. Quibus in omnibus nostri possunt interiores affectus erudiri, simul et impelli, qualiter experiebatur ille cujus animus commotus acriter, elevatus, dilatatus, quando fiebat hujusmodi resonantia celebris, jubilabat totus in se recolens illud seraphicum de Deo: pleni sunt coeli et terra gloria tua Or y va tout. Haec est inaestimabilium profusio gaudiorum.

Subinfertur pulchra nimis ad priora conclusio: omnis spiritus laudet Dominum.

Happy is he who recognizes the mighty work of God not only in the things of nature ... but also in the things of craft, how in the piercing of moderate sized pieces of wood as in the *sambuca*[13] and *fistulae*, in beaten out metal as in *tubae* and *cymbala*, or in the dry wringing of sinews and intestines as in the *cithara*, so many sounds are varied.

'Praise Him in strings and the *organum*' follows.

'Strings', according to the glosses, are put for all stringed instruments (other than the *psalterium* and the *cithara*) which sound with vibrating strings, be it *viella, symphonia, lyra, rota, guiterna*,[14] *lituus*,[15] *nablum*,[16] *sistrum*,[17] *scacarum* [or] *rebella*. . . .

In a sense yet more general '*organa*' are taken by the glosses to mean any musical instrument however it is composed. In modern usage the word has been appropriated, and not without reason, for *organa* with pipes of lead or tin, which by means of bellows and the fingers, more than any other instrument, have the various and perfect resonance of the vocal chords, which [organ] pipes are not deemed unworthy because they sound not with contortion of the mouth but with the inflation of bellows. Ecclesiastical custom has retained only or especially this same musical instrument, to which, as we have seen, the *tuba* may be occasionally joined, but very rarely *bombardae, chalemiae, cornemusae* (large or small) or other instruments which we will not name here, all of which the Book of Daniel includes in the adoration of the statue with all kinds of instruments. However, to amplify what we have said about the organ being only used in the most solemn rite of the Church brings to mind what David goes on to say: 'Praise the Lord with sonorous *cymbala*, praise Him in exulting *cymbala*.' Bronze *cymbala* are those which we have called *campanae*, these we rely upon to sound loudly and well. Such as these the Church uses more than any other religion for the praise of God, in the place, as it were, of the *tubae* of the old law. Someone has expressed the offices of these in verses representing a speaking bell: 'I praise the true God, call the people, summon the clergy,/Lament the dead, dispel the plague, and adorn festivities.'

There are also *campanulae* for melody, for example those arranged in certain clocks. By these our inner dispositions of mind may be improved and stimulated, for it has been proved that he whose mind is agitated, weakened or tardy rejoices wholly in himself when this celebrated sound is made, and recalls to himself the seraphic song of God: 'The heavens and earth are full of thy glory *Or y va tout*.'[18] This is the profusion of inestimable joy.

To what has gone before the most beautiful conclusion is added: 'Every spirit praises the Lord.'

[13] Compare *Canticordum du Pèlerin* (Glorieux, 7/1, p. 128) where the *sambuque* is identified with the *doulcaine* (for which see also p. 129). The *sambuca* is mentioned only in Daniel 3:5, 7, 10, 15. In the Middle Ages it was generally taken to be a wind instrument on the authority of Isidore of Seville (loc cit, col. 167). For recent thoughts on the nature of the instrument, see D. Wulstan, 'The Sounding of the Shofar', *Galpin Society Journal*, XXVI (1973), p. 45.

[14] Compare *Puer natus est nobis* (Glorieux, 7/2, p. 966) where Gerson states that the *guiterne* has '*quatre cordes*'.

[15] The *lituus* was a Roman curved wind instrument.

[16] *Nablum* is the Latinized form of the Hebrew word *nével*, well known to the Middle Ages *via* St Jerome's preface to the psalms. It is mentioned in Chronicles 1, 15: 16, 20, 28, and Maccabees 1, 13: 51. See Wulstan, op cit, p. 40.

[17] Another mistake. The *sistrum* belongs to the class of idiophones. See Sachs, op cit, pp. 69-70; 89-90; 121; 456. There was perhaps a tradition in 14th- and 15th-century France that the *sistrum* was a lute (or at least a stringed instrument), for Corbechon takes Isidore of Seville's material on the *sistrum* and applies it to the lute (edition of 1485, XIX, chap. 144).

[18] Presumably a proverb, or some saying with idiomatic force that warrants being included in the vernacular. Perhaps 'Then all [i.e. the malady] goes away'.

Textual notes

(a) *forma*] Glorieux: *finis*. *Forma*, of which *finis* (allowing for contracted forms) is a plausible misreading, makes better sense. Cf. the section on the *tympanum*: 'non est una vel magnitudo *vel forma vel usus*'. (I am grateful to Mr Bernard Barr who proposed this emendation.)

(b) *tambour*] some MSS read *tabour*

(c) *lyra*] Glorieux *myra*. Du Pin *lyra*

(d) *follibus*] Glorieux *fillibus*. Du Pin *follibus*

(e) *chalemias*] Glorieux *thalemias*

8 *Collection of instruments in Guyart Desmoulins*, Bible Historiale, Brussels, Bibliothèque Royale, MS 9002, f. 223. Paris, 1410

Idq; pbat lin. Na que; mese .w. i hypodorio: eade .w. idorio hypate
meson-ab eaque; i quouisin l gue diatessaron consonantia differens.
Ite mese dorii que; η. ab ea que; mese phrigii. id. oι. distat tono .
Na que; mese idorio. η. eade i phrigio licanos meson. Rursi mese phri
gii modi que; oι. ab ea mese que; lidii. id. i distat tono. Na que; e i phrigii
. oι. mese: licanos e. licanos meson. Rursi mese lii modi. ab ea mese que;
mixolidii. id. η. semitonio distat. Et eni is ordo grecoς lidii et uie
mesen: ei ordim grecoς mixolidii mese hic coparat. i pagnula sι iisu
distingue. Ea qq; que; mixolidii. id. η. ad eam mesen que; hipmixolidii.
id. ρ. tom differentia hac. iccirco qui. η. que i mixolidio mese: eade
m hipmixolidio licanos meson. Unde fit. ut mese dorii ab ea mese que;
mixolidii. diatessaron consonantia distat. Id pbat lin. Na mese que; do
rii. id. η. eade; mixolidii. id. η. hipate meson. que ad cui libe modi
mesen diatessaron consonantia seruat. Ite mese dorii. id. η. ad eam mesen
que; hipmixolidii que; ρ. diapente consonantia seruat. Ea eni mese
que; dorii. id ρ. i ordie hipmixolidii licanos hypaton ζ lichanos
aut hypaton ad mesen i diatonico qui i cui libe modo si coparet: dia
pente consonantia distat. Cur aut octauus modus ζ e hipmixolidius adi
iect ζ: hinc patet. Sic bis diapason consonantia hec.

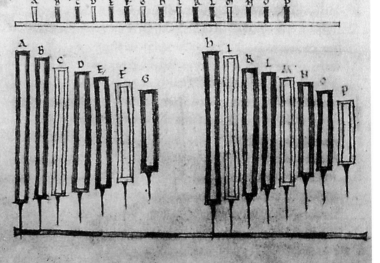

V

The earliest English keyboard

There are three reasons why England occupies an important position in the history of the medieval organ. First, there is evidence that pneumatic organs existed in England at a time when they were still unknown on the Continent. The English scholar Aldhelm (d 709), Bishop of Sherborne, refers to 'organs that breathe with winds produced by bellows' in his metrical treatise *De Virginitate* (c 690);[1] it is not until 756 or 757 that Frankish annals record the gift of an organ 'which was never seen before in *Francia*' to Pepin III from the Byzantine Emperor Constantine Copronymus.[2]

Second, the most spectacular description of an organ in any medieval poem is given in Wulfstan of Winchester's *Narratio Metrica de Sancto Swithuno* (992-4).[3] The dedicatory epistle which opens this text describes the building work carried out at Winchester during the reign of Bishop AElfheah,[4] and among the 'various ornaments' which Wulfstan praises is an organ with four hundred pipes played by two brethren 'of concordant spirit', each governing his own 'alphabet' (*alphabetum suum*) or set of keys with note-letters inscribed upon them.[5]

Third, the earliest known extended source of practical polyphony, the Winchester Troper (dating from 996-1006) now in the library of Corpus Christi College, Cambridge,[6] contains what has a right to be regarded as the earliest example of organ tablature. Several proses in this manuscript appear with the so-called 'organ' or 'Frankish' notation (of which more below) as a supplement to the neumes. This 'organ' notation was a letter system associated with musical instruments, and particularly with the organ.[7]

The earliest known depiction of an organ by an Englishman is close in date to the Winchester Troper mentioned above, but its value for the historian of the organ is almost negligible. This is contained in British Library MS Harley 603, a psalter illustrated at the Cathedral Priory of Christ Church, Canterbury, c 1000-c 1025, and based upon the celebrated Utrecht Psalter (Rheims, c 820) which arrived in Canterbury sometime before the year 1000.[8] On folio 70r of the Harley Psalter (illus. 2) one of the later artists has illustrated the phrase *suspendimus organa nostra* (Psalm 136:2) with an 'organ' hanging in a tree.[9] This comprises seven tapering pipes of

1 *Boethius* De Musica, *Cambridge University Library MS Ii.3.12, f.125v (Christ Church, Canterbury), size of original 10¼" × 7¾". Reproduced by permission of the Syndics of Cambridge University Library*

2 *British Library MS Harley 603, f.70r (the Harley Psalter, Canterbury c 1000-c 1025). Reproduced by permission*

3 *Detail from a Rhineland psalter, Pommersfelden, Gräflich Schönbornsche Bibliothek, Cod. 2777, f.1 (c1070). Reproduced by permission*

4 *Detail from the Bible (dated 1109) of Etienne Harding, Abbot of Citeaux (Dijon, Bibliothèque Municipale MS 14, f.13v). See* Catalogue Général des Manuscrits des Bibliothèques Publiques de France, Départements— Tome V *(Paris, 1889), pp. 4-6. Reproduced by permission*

graduated length joined together by some kind of central brace. It need hardly be stressed that this is far from convincing as a depiction of an organ; doubtless the artist opted for a bundle of pipes without bellows and housing assembly because the whole apparatus would have looked absurd hanging in a tree.

Confronted with this dearth of English pictorial sources, historians of the Anglo-Saxon organ have generally turned to the earliest Continental sources, especially the illustrations in the Pommersfelden Psalter (late 11th century, my illus. 3), the Harding Bible (dated, 1109, illus. 4)[10] and the Rheims Psalter (early 12th century, illus. 5) for information.

Now an English source has come to light which has a strong claim to be representative of certain pre-Conquest English traditions of organ building and playing.

Cambridge University Library MS Ii.3.12 contains a copy of the *De Arithmetica* and the *De Musica* of Boethius, produced *c*1130 at Christ Church, Canterbury.[11] Folio 125v of the *De Musica* (illus. 1) contains the section of the text where Boethius uses a system of pitch notation comprising the letters A–P (without J, which merges with I in the Latin alphabet).[12] In some manuscripts of the *De Musica* (e.g. British Library MS Royal 15.B.IX f.44v) the letters of this series are disposed along the teeth of a comb-like diagram:

A B C D E F G H I K L M N O P

and this is how the letters are shown in our manuscript, but with an additional feature of the first importance: each tooth of the comb has an appropriately lettered organ pipe corresponding to it on the lower half of the page.

There can be little doubt that these 15 shapes are intended to be organ pipes: they are graduated in length (becoming shorter as the pitch rises), each terminates in a tapering foot for insertion into the wind-chest, and each is supplied with a pitch letter. There seems to be no particular significance in their shading; the regular sequence of two dark-rimmed pipes followed by a light one does not correspond to the shading on the teeth of the comb, and is probably just a decorative feature. The eighth pipe (H) has probably been shown the same length as the first—and all the following pipes scaled accordingly—to demonstrate that the eighth note in the series is the same as the first, but an octave higher. On the other hand, it may be that the artist wishes to imply an instrument with two identical ranks; it has been suggested several times that the Winchester organ was a double instrument of some kind, perhaps with each of the *duo . . . fratres* mentioned by Wulfstan operating an octave compass.[13]

If we accept that the shapes on the lower half of our drawing are organ pipes, then the obvious interpretation of the teeth of the comb is that they are the keys. They do not lie adjacently as on a modern keyboard, but this need cause no surprise, for the sliders of medieval organs are often shown arranged in this way (see illus. 3-5). As for the letters represented above the keys, these are an integral part of Boethius' text, but we may imagine them written on or near the keys themselves. Wulfstan mentions the *alphabetum* of each monk at the Winchester organ, and this term is used in a number of

5 *Detail from the Rheims Psalter, early 12th century (Cambridge, St John's College MS B. 18, f.1). See* M. R. James, A Descriptive Catalogue of the MSS in the Library of St. John's College, Cambridge *(Cambridge, 1913), pp. 52-56. Reproduced by permission*

6 *Detail from illus. 1*

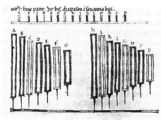

medieval measurement treatises devoted to organ pipes.[14] The Harding Bible (illus. 4) shows the letters C D E F G a b ♮ written just above the keys (though the pipes are shown in reverse order). It was customary to label the keys of *organistra* in this way,[15] and to mark the letters of a monochord upon a strip of parchment glued to the face of the instrument.[16]

The antecedent manuscript which served as a model for this copy of the *De Musica* has not been identified, and may be lost,[17] so we cannot say whether the idea of turning a standard Boethian diagram into a schematic drawing of an organ originated at Canterbury, or was simply copied there from an earlier (and possibly Continental) manuscript. Nonetheless, this drawing may be considered as the earliest English representation of a keyboard so far discovered.

It is particularly revealing that a diagram of the letters A–P has been turned into a schematic organ, for this alphabet (or at least the sequence A–G used twice) was especially associated with musical instruments, and particularly with the organ.[18] Between the 9th and 12th centuries there existed a letter notation variously referred to by modern scholars as the 'organ', 'instrumental', 'Boethian' or 'Frankish' notation.[19] The distinguishing characteristic of this letter system was that it applied to the tone/semitone series TTSTTTS—i.e. a major scale, not the natural minor scale (*A-a'* in Helmholtz notation). There is some doubt as to whether the full alphabet given by Boethius was actually employed (A–P without J); Notker Labeo (*d* 1022) uses only A–G,[20] and this is the series used in the Winchester Troper at Cambridge and in the treatises on pipe measurement.[21] However the full alphabet from A–P makes an important appearance in the *De Institutione Harmonica* by Hucbald of St Amand (*d* 930), a major source for the study of earlier medieval instruments.[22] Hucbald describes the natural minor scale (*A-a'* in Helmholtz notation), then comments that nobody should be surprised to find that the pitches 'of organs and any other kinds of instruments under consideration' (*hydraulia, vel aliud quodlibet musici generis considerans instrumentum*) do not produce this

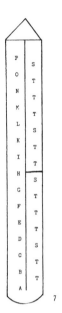

7

7 A clarification of Hucbald's diagram in the Brussels manuscript

scale, but render another 'based upon the arrangement of that most wise man, Boethius'.[23] A diagram of this scale appears in the 11th-century Brussels manuscript (generally accepted as one of the most reliable witnesses to the text).[24] In his commentary on a recently published translation of the *De Institutione Harmonica*, Claude Palisca proposes that the letters A–P in the diagram (my illus. 7) 'are neither explained nor used hereinafter and thus seem a scribal addition'.[25] However, these letters also appear in another 11th-century manuscript of Hucbald's treatise, now in the University Library, Cambridge,[26] and in a (?)14th-century copy of the text now in the Bodleian Library, Oxford.[27] The Oxford copy is too late in date for its evidence to be of very much value, but the testimony of the Cambridge manuscript shows that even if the letters A–P do not have Hucbald's authority, they were disseminated in the manuscript tradition of his treatise at an early date.[28]

We have now to ask whether the A–P series in illus. 1 & 6 was intended by the artist as a two-octave instrumental alphabet denoting a major scale, or as a natural minor scale.

Fortunately we can demonstrate that the instrumental alphabet was studied in Canterbury towards the year 1100, and our evidence comes from the Cambridge manuscript of Hucbald's treatise mentioned above. In this source, from the monastery of St Augustine, Canterbury, Hucbald's work forms part of a diversified compilation of material, generally referred to as the 'Cambridge Songs' manuscript after a famous collection of Latin lyrics which it incorporates. This is a somewhat single-minded custom, for the manuscript contains a great deal of material of the first interest. The two most recent investigators distinguish three separate, but related, class-books from Canterbury within the manuscript, together with the 'Cambridge Songs' (possibly not intended for classroom use).[29] The importance of this conclusion for our purposes lies in the fact that Hucbald's treatise forms part of one of these classbooks, so we may assume that the A–P instrumental notation was being studied—and perhaps being used—at Canterbury around 1100.

There is a second source from which a knowledge of the instrumental alphabet (this time in its A–G form without the letters H–P) may have been disseminated at Canterbury. The A–G alphabet is used to denote a major scale in the *Scolica* (or *Scolia*) *Enchiriadis*,[30] a commentary cast as a colloquy upon the *Enchirias de Musica*, and we may be confident that the *Scolica* was studied at Canterbury. A little-known manuscript, written at Christ Church, Canterbury, in the 10th century and now in the library of Corpus Christi College, Cambridge, contains a complete text of the *Scolica Enchiriadis* together with the *Enchirias de Musica*.[31] Both texts are handsomely copied and attest to the interest of the subject-matter for Canterbury readers.

A continuing Canterbury interest in the *Scolica* can be documented by the 'Cambridge Songs' manuscript mentioned above. Here the text of Hucbald's *De Institutione Harmonica* is followed by material which proves to be a tissue of fragments from the *Scolica Enchiriadis* and the *Enchirias de Musica*.[32]

Where do matters stand at the end of our analysis? The drawing shown in illus. 1 is the earliest known English representation of a keyboard, dating from *c*1130. It shows 15 keys (or 'sliders') represented, in all likelihood, much as they appeared in reality. Since the keys of earlier medieval organs (and various other instruments) were customarily lettered, it seems likely that the artist turned a Boethian diagram of the letters A–P into a schematic representation of an organ because this letter series, or at least part of it, was customarily inscribed on the keys of the organs he knew. Whether the full A–P series was used, or simply A–G, cannot be determined; the Winchester Troper suggests that the A–G system was used in Anglo-Saxon England. As for the progression of intervals that the artist wished to denote by the letters A–P, we know that the so-called 'organ' notation, where A–G defines a major scale, was being studied in late 11th-century Canterbury. Thus it is possible that the keyboard in our manuscript preserves at least a partial likeness of the Winchester organ keyboard, and perhaps of other Anglo-Saxon organs.

I am most grateful to David Fallows, John Caldwell and Régine Page for helpful criticism and advice during the preparation of this article.

The abbreviation *GS* is used throughout for references to Martin Gerbert, *Scriptores Ecclesiastici de Musica*. See note 15.

1 Text in Rudolfus Ehwald ed., *Aldhelmi Opera* (*Monumenta Germaniae Historica [MGH]*, *Auctorum Antiquissimorum Tomi* 15, Berlin, 1913-19) part 2: *De Virginitate* lines 2788-9. Compare also lines 71-3. Aldhelm's riddle *De Barbita id est organo* (ibid, p. 103) is lacking in specific detail. It may be a learned, bookish production based upon earlier references to water organs in authors read by Aldhelm.
    McKinnon ('The Tenth Century Organ at Winchester', *The Organ Yearbook*, 5 (1974), pp. 4-19) is mistaken in his view that there are no pre-10th-century English references to organs other than those contained in the writings of Aldhelm. The organ (and several other instruments) is mentioned in the Old English poem *The Phoenix*, generally dated to the 9th century: see the edition of N. F. Blake (Manchester, 1964), line 136 b. There is also an Old English riddle that has been solved as 'organ', though other solutions have been proposed. See Craig Williamson ed., *The Old English Riddles of the Exeter Book* (Chapel Hill, North Carolina, 1977), p. 115 no. 82. Since this text is brief I append my own translation

of it here: 'A creature came in where men were sitting, a company talking wise in mind. It had one eye, two ears, two feet, and twelve hundred heads, a back and a stomach, and two hands, arms and a shoulder, one neck and two sides. Say what I am called.' The term 'creature' (*wiht*) is frequently applied to inanimate objects in these Old English enigmas, while speaking in terms of body and limbs is a favourite device of the Anglo-Saxon riddlers. It may be significant that the next riddle in the manuscript is almost certainly to be solved as 'bellows' (Williamson, op cit, pp. 115-16 no. 83).
2 For the statement that the organ was 'never before seen in *Francia*' (*quod antea non visum fuerat in Francia*) see the *Annales Mettenses* (sub anno 757) in *MGH, Scriptorum*, 1, p. 333. There is some doubt about the date of the arrival since some annals give 756 and others 757. See the *Annales Blandinienses* (*MGH, Scriptorum*, 5, p. 22) for 756, and the *Annales Laureshamenses, Alamannici*, and *Nazariani* (*MGH, Scriptorum*, 1, pp. 28-9) for 757.
3 Text in A. Campbell ed., *Frithegodi Monachi Breuiloquium Vitae Beati Wilfredi et Wulfstani Cantoris Narratio Metrica de Sancto Swithuno* (Zurich, 1950), lines 141f. The instrument described by Wulfstan is discussed in detail by McKinnon (see note 1) and Holschneider (see note 6). For another reference to the organ—probably by Wulfstan—see G. M. Dreves ed., *Analecta Hymnica*, 48 (Leipzig, 1905), p. 12 (*De Sancto Birino*, lines 27-8). Further material of importance is contained in Konrad Körte, 'Die Orgel von Winchester', *Kirchenmusikalisches Jahrbuch* (1973), pp. 1-24.
4 The name is sometimes given as *AElphege*, but the group *–ph–* is not used in Old English spelling. The element *(h)ege* is an inflected form of *heah* ('high, sublime'), thus the name means 'sublime elf'.
5 Campbell, op cit, line 156.
6 For a full account of this manuscript see A.

Holschneider, *Die Organa von Winchester* (Hildesheim, 1968), passim (on the instrumental notation pp. 89f), and Alejandro Enrique Planchart, *The Repertory of Tropes at Winchester*, 2 vols (Princeton, 1977), 1, pp. 17f (on the instrumental notation pp. 52f).
7 See Holschneider, op cit, plate 1, and the same author's article 'Instrumental Titles to the Sequentiae of the Winchester Tropers', in F. W. Sternfeld ed., *Essays on Opera and English Music in honour of Sir Jack Westrup* (Oxford, 1975), pp. 8-18. For a good account of the history of this notation see Smits van Waesberghe, 'Les origines de la notation alphabétique au moyen âge', *Anuario Musical*, 12 (1957), pp. 3-16. The system survived until the early 15th century, to judge by a diagram in Anselmi's *De Musica* (*Georgii Anselmi Parmensis De Musica*, ed. G. Massera (Florence, 1961), table facing p. 128). Anselmi uses a notation from A–G for the sequence TTSTTTS covering a four-octave range. The diagram he gives is intended to represent his *monochordum*, apparently a clavichord (see W. Nef, 'The Polychord', *Galpin Society Journal*, 4 (1951), p. 23). Thus we have the system still being used for a keyboard instrument as late as the 15th century (though I hesitate to assume a direct continuity of usage from the early to the late Middle Ages without further investigation).
8 For an account of the Harley Psalter see Elźbieta Temple, *Anglo-Saxon Manuscripts 900-1066, A Survey of Manuscripts Illuminated in the British Isles*, 2 (London, 1976), catalogue no. 64. The Utrecht Psalter illustrations may be studied in E. T. De Wald, *The Illustrations of the Utrecht Psalter* (Princeton, London and Leipzig, 1933).
9 There is no organ in the Utrecht Psalter at this point (De Wald, op cit, f.77r). The same literal interpretation of the text is found in the 9th-century Stuttgart Psalter—*Der Stuttgarter Bilderpsalter*, 2 vols (Stuttgart, 1965 and 1968), 1 (*Facsimile-Band*), f.152r.

[10] For a study of this illustration see J. Chailley, 'Un clavier d'orgue à la fin du XIe siècle, *Revue de Musicologie*, 61 (1937), pp. 5-11.

[11] See C. M. Kauffman, *Romanesque Manuscripts 1066-1190, A Survey of Manuscripts Illuminated in the British Isles*, 3 (London, 1975), catalogue no. 41.

[12] G. Friedlein ed., *De institutione arithmetica libri duo. De institutione musica libri quinque* (Leipzig, 1867 *R* Frankfurt, 1966), p. 347. On the presentation of this material by Friedlein see G. Reese, *Music in the Middle Ages* (New York, 1940), p. 135 note 17.

[13] McKinnon, op cit, p. 12. This article should be read in conjunction with John Caldwell's letter in *The Organ Yearbook*, 8 (1977), p. 79.

[14] See Klaus-Jürgen Sachs, *Mensura Fistularum* (Stuttgart, 1970), pp. 58, 112, 113, 122, 124 and 125.

[15] The lettered keys of the *symphonia que dicitur organistrum* are mentioned by the anonymous author of the 13th-century treatise *Summa Musice* (?Paris ?Liège). See Martin Gerbert, *Scriptores Ecclesiastici de Musica*, 3 vols (Typis San-Blasianis, 1784 *R* Milan, 1931), vol 3 p. 216 b; further references to this work are cited *GS* by volume, page and column a/b. The use of such keys with letters seems to be implied by the *mensura* treatises devoted to the *Organistrum*, some of which are printed—extremely badly—in Marianne Bröcker, *Die Drehleier*, 2 vols (Dusseldorf, 1973) 1, pp. 246ff.

[16] On the letters of the monochord see Smits van Waesberghe, *Musikerziehung* (*Musikgeschichte in Bildern*, III/3, Leipzig, 1969), p. 82.

[17] Kauffman op cit, catalogue no. 41, discusses links between our manuscript and certain Continental copies of the *De Musica*, but does not attempt to identify the source of the Cambridge copy.

[18] The system is treated by Hucbald of St Amand (*GS* 1, p. 110 a) and by Notker Labeo (ibid p. 96 a). Hucbald's material can be read in English translation in W. Babb and C. V. Palisca, *Hucbald, Guido and John on Music* (New Haven, 1978), pp. 24f. For further discussion see R. Weakland, 'Hucbald as Musician and Theorist', *Musical Quarterly*, 42 (1956), pp. 66-84, and W. Nef, 'Vom Musiktraktate des Notker Labeo', *Schweizerisch Musikzeitung*, 87 (1947), pp. 323-6.

[19] It is difficult to say when the system first came into use; Hucbald (*d* 930) says that instruments built to supply the major scale sequence had been in use for a very long time (*longevitatis usu*), but makes no specific comment about the instrumental letter-notation itself. (*GS* 1, p. 110 a).

[20] *GS* 1, p. 96 a.

[21] Holschneider, *Die Organa*, p. 90; K-J Sachs, op cit, passim.

[22] *GS* 1, p. 110 a. For a survey of Hucbald's treatise as a source for the historian of instruments see M. Huglo, 'Les Instruments de Musique chez Hucbald', *Hommages à André Boutemy*, ed. Guy Cambier (Brussels, 1976), pp. 178-96.

[23] *GS* 1, p. 110 a.

[24] Brussels, Bibl. Roy. de Belgique MS 10078/95, ff. 84v-92r. See Weakland, op cit, for a discussion of the manuscript and a facsimile of the original diagram. As Weakland points out (p. 79) the letters are slightly misplaced in the manuscript. They have been adjusted here, and a redundant T at the top of the series has been omitted.

[25] In Babb and Palisca, op cit, p. 24 note 11.

[26] Cambridge University Library MS Gg.5.35 (St Augustine's monastery, Canterbury, *c* 1050), f.267v. For a full inventory of the manuscript and a study of its contents and compilation see A. G. Rigg and G. R. Wieland, 'A Canterbury Classbook of the mid-11th century (the "Cambridge Songs" manuscript)', *Anglo-Saxon England*, 4 (1975), pp. 113-30. The authors point out that the manuscript continued to be used until *c* 1100.

[27] MS Canon. Misc. 212, f.34v. In this manuscript however the interval series is given as TSTTSTT/TSTTSTT, i.e. a two-octave natural minor scale.

[28] The promised critical edition of the *De Institutione Harmonica* by Yves Chartier may be expected to elucidate the relationships between the surviving manuscripts of the text.

[29] Rigg and Wieland, op cit, passim.

[30] *GS* 1, p. 209 b.

[31] See M. R. James, *A Descriptive Catalogue of the Manuscripts in the Library of Corpus Christi College Cambridge*, 2 vols (1909-12), 2, p. 10.

[32] The text of Hucbald ends on f.272v with the words *deductus protenditur* corresponding to *GS* 1, p. 121 a, line 5. There is good reason for assuming that the text genuinely ends here, and that the further material printed by Gerbert does not belong to the text. See L. Gushee, 'Questions of Genre in Medieval Treatises on Music', in Wulf Arlt ed., *Gattungen der Musik in Einzeldarstellungen, Gedenkschrift Leo Schrade, Erste Folge* (Berne and Munich, 1973), p. 397. After Hucbald's treatise there is a brief text on the *cithara* (beginning with the rubricated heading *Quinq; gradvs simphoniarvm*) then the material from the *Scolica Enchiriadis* and the *Enchirias de Musica* begins. There is only one extract from the *Enchirias* (corresponding to *GS* 1, p. 172 b: *Nam effectus . . . verborum*), but the extracts from the *Scolica* are substantial (corresponding to *GS* 1, pp. 174 b-183 a, with some omissions), and there were probably more, since several folios are missing from the manuscript. The section with the instrumental notation is not included in the part of the *Scolica* which this manuscript contains.

VI

The myth
of the chekker

1 *Angel with clavicytherium, 1490-7, restored (St Wolfgang's Church, Kefermarkt, Upper Austria). All illustrations here reproduced by permission*

Numerous poems and prose-texts of the late Middle Ages mention an instrument variously named *eschiquier, exaquier, chekker* etc (hereafter I refer to the chekker).[1] Guillaume de Machaut (*d* 1377) writes of an *eschaquier*,[2] and in 1392 the Bishop of London, R. Braybrook, was entertained at Stepney by a musician who played *le chekker*.[3] The French cleric and theologian Jean de Gerson (*d* 1429) mentions the *eschanquier* in his treatise *Canticordum du Pélerin*,[4] and there are many references in the same vein as these.

What was this chekker? The question seems a perfectly proper one, and many scholars have attempted to answer it. Galpin argues for a variant form of Arnault de Zwolle's *dulce melos* (an instrument fitted with an action related to that of the modern piano),[5] while Farmer points to an Arabic instrument *al-shaqira*, which he attempts to identify as a form of virginal.[6] Edmund Bowles opts for a 'small, upright protoharpsichord',[7] while Edwin Ripin, author of the most systematic study of the problem to date, proposes the clavichord.[8] I shall argue here that none of these theories are tenable in the form in which they have been proposed; not only are they based upon slender evidence—they are fundamentally misconceived.

The *al-shaqira*

In medieval Arabic literature there is one reference (and apparently only one) to an instrument named *al-shaqira*; the author in question, Al-Shaqandī (*d* 1231), describes it as belonging amongst the *mazāmīr*, or woodwind instruments.[9] On this somewhat unpromising basis the Arabist H. G. Farmer published an article in 1926 proposing that 'the European instrument known as the *eschaquiel* or *exaquir* was surely derived from the Arabian ... *al-shaqira* ...'[10] Undeterred by the explanation of the term by Al-Shaqandī, Farmer cites a 13th-century Arabic source in which the *mizmār* (singular of *mazāmīr*) is said to be a stringed instrument;[11] thus he surmises that the *al-shaqira* was a chordophone—a singularly leading treatment of the evidence.[12] Next Farmer turns to the question of whether the Arabs knew stringed keyboard instruments at all:

That the principle of a plucked instrument with a keyboard, as in the virginal, might have been known to the Arabs in the 9th-12th century, there are reliable grounds for believing. *Plectra* were already used for their psalteries and beating-rods for their dulcimers, and as they knew of the keyboard system in the organ, all that was necessary was a combination of the two.[13]

There is nothing of any substance in this; the

Reprinted from *Early Music* 7 (1979), pp. 482—489. By permission of Oxford University Press.

argument is specious—and desperate. Even Farmer seems to have recognized the weakness, for the strident claims which characterize so much of his writing are not found here; 'it is tolerably . . . clear', he concludes, 'that the Arabs knew of the keyboard principle of the eschaquiel-virginal in the 9th-12th century'.

> But yet, I say,
> If imputation and strong circumstances
> Which lead directly to the door of truth
> Will give you satisfaction, you might have't.

I shall not press the comparison between Farmer and Iago.

The 'upright harpsichord' theory

Two letters written by King John I of Aragon (d 1396) have given rise to the view that the chekker was an upright harpsichord. The first of these letters, written in 1387, is a request for an *exaquier*:

Lo Rey
En Pere ça Costa. Manamvos quencontinent nos trasmetats 1 sturment appelat exaquier lo qual te en Bartholomeu de Castro cambrer nostre, et que y hayats una atzembla en que sia aportat et trossat, per tal manera que nos puxa trencar ni pendre algun damnatge . . .[14]

[The King
To Pere ça Costa. We order you to send at once an instrument called *exaquier* which our chamberlain Bartholomew de Castro owns, and take a pack-animal such that it can be loaded and arranged in a way that guarantees against breakage and damage . . .]

The second letter, dated 1388, is a request for a mysterious instrument 'seeming like organs which sounds with strings'—perhaps an upright harpsichord, so described because of its resemblance to a portative organ:

Lo Rey
Entes havem que en Devesa ha 1 sturment semblant dorguens que sona ab cordes, manamvos quel comprets et quel nos trasmetats de continent . . . fets lo stibar e plegar al dit Devesa, per tal quel nos puxen portar sens perill de trencar.[15]

[The King
Having heard that Devesa has an instrument seeming like organs which sounds with strings, we order you to buy it and send it to us at once . . . have it packed and wrapped by the said Devesa, so that it can be transported without risk of breakage.]

Various writers print these two letters side by side as I

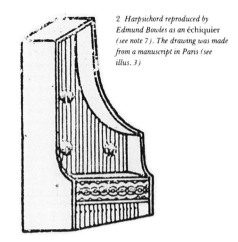

2 *Harpsichord reproduced by Edmund Bowles as an* échiquier *(see note 7). The drawing was made from a manuscript in Paris (see illus. 3)*

do; the reader is generally left to assume that the *exaquier* is the subject of both. Yet although the first letter definitely deals with the *exaquier*, the second letter makes no mention of it. Consequently there is no reason to assume that the instrument 'seeming like organs which sounds with strings' is an *exaquier*, or chekker. The two letters probably relate to different instruments, for they were written as much as ten to twelve months apart, and the king was a keen collector of instruments throughout his reign.[16]

The earliest surviving stringed keyboard instrument is an upright harpsichord, and there are various supposedly 15th-century depictions of such an instrument that have also been drawn into the chekker debate at various times. All of this material can be put aside immediately. The clavicytherium now in the Royal College of Music in London[17] has no special bearing upon our enquiry; we must not confuse the earliest surviving stringed keyboard instrument with the earliest mentioned one, especially as the London example belongs to the last quarter of the 15th century whereas the chekker is first mentioned in 1360.[18] As for the pictorial sources, the famous clavicytherium held by an angel at Kefermarkt in Upper Austria (illus. 1) is said by Van der Meer to be a restoration dating from the 19th century;[19] I have been unable to verify this, but in good photographs of the sculpture a line is visible across the player's right wrist which looks suspiciously like a join in the work. We can be more certain about the illustration reproduced by Bowles as an '*échiquier* . . . a small, upright protoharpsichord' (illus. 2);[20] this is a normal, horizontal instrument

3 *The illus. 2 instrument shown horizontal as in the original manuscript, Paris, Bibliothèque nationale MS fr 331, f.145v (1468)*

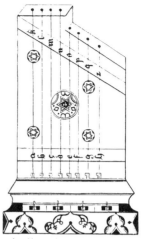

4 *A drawing reproduced by Vander Straeten, and interpreted by Curt Sachs as 'a small upright harpsichord . . . from a manuscript of about 1450' (see note 21)*

which has been unfortunately turned on its end (cf illus. 3). Finally the drawing (illus. 4) interpreted by Sachs as 'a small upright harpsichord . . . from a manuscript of about 1450'[21] derives from a source which actually dates from 1503-4 (illus. 5). Thus the upright harpsichord is represented in the 15th century only by the extant example, now in London, which dates from after *c* 1475.[22] Clearly this type of instrument has no special claim to be identified with the chekker.

The clavichord theory

Chekker studies have been placed on a firm foundation by Edwin Ripin, whose survey of the problem was published posthumously in 1975.[23] Ripin assembles all the known references to the chekker (together with facsimiles of the crucial primary sources), and concludes that the evidence 'points strongly to the identification of the chekker with the clavichord':[24]

Although I cannot deny a certain disappointment in the anticlimactic nature of the conclusion that the chekker was in fact only a clavichord—it certainly would have been more satisfying to have identified the instrument as something exotic—this solution to the problem does have the workaday recommendation of simplicity, and it neither requires one to postulate the existence of any lost or unrecorded instrument nor to invent one to fit the conflicting implications of the literary sources.[25]

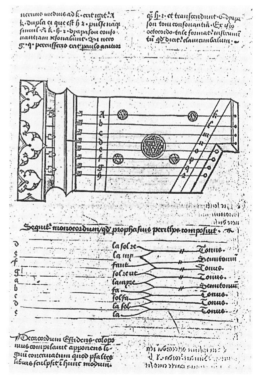

5 *The original from which the instrument in illus. 4 was drawn (Ghent, Universiteitsbibliotheek, MS 70 (71), dating from 1503-4)*

Ripin bases his theory on a note in the account books of the French Court (1488) mentioning an *eschiquier ou manicordion*, partly paid for by one Jehan Ryet *vaulet de chambre du Roy*.[26] The past tenses used in the document suggest that the instrument had already been delivered when the account was drawn up,[27] so Ripin concludes that the two words *eschiquier* and *manicordion* are synonyms 'provided in order to eliminate all possible ambiguity in the record'.[28] Translating *manicordion* as 'clavichord' (without defending this rendering)[29] he produces the neat equation *eschiquier* = *manicordion* = clavichord.

There are a number of flaws in this procedure, not the least of which is Ripin's failure to defend his interpretation of *manicordion*. This is a particularly damaging oversight, for this word was not only applied to the clavichord in the 15th century.[30] A small piece of parchment in the manuscript of Arnault's treatise at Paris mentions a *monocordium* whose keys are equipped with a quill (*pluma*);[31] so Arnault knew at least one type of *monocordium* that was clearly not a clavichord.

This uncertainty surrounding the meaning of *manicordion* casts considerable doubt upon Ripin's hypothesis that the chekker was a clavichord. And there is a further difficulty: why did the scribe use the two terms *eschiquier* and *manicordion*? According to Ripin he did so to eliminate all ambiguity; but why should there have been any ambiguity? Even Ripin cannot escape the powerful suggestion in the document that the scribe was uncertain about something. Perhaps he did not really know what kind of instrument had been delivered, or if he did, perhaps he was ignorant of its proper name? Perhaps the word *eschiquier* meant more than one kind of instrument to the scribe, so that some qualification was necessary? All of these possibilities crowd together until the brief phrase *eschiquier ou manicordion* is almost obscured by uncertainties.

Although we see that the foundation is weak, let us follow Ripin through his argument that the chekker was a clavichord. He begins with the etymology of the name. Most writers have assumed that it is a transference of *chekker, eschiquier* etc in the sense 'chessboard', but Ripin points out that there is another sense to consider. He argues that the name derives from the counting tables used in the English and Norman financial court, the Exchequer.[32] These tables have a special bearing upon Ripin's clavichord hypothesis, as will be clear from the following description of them which Ripin quotes from a medieval Latin source:

The exchequer . . . is an oblong board measuring

about ten feet by five, used as a table by those who sit at it, and with a rim around it about four finger-breadths in height, to prevent anything set on it from falling off. Over the . . . exchequer is spread a cloth, bought in Easter term, of a special pattern, black, ruled with lines a foot, or a full span, apart.[33]

Ripin comments: 'A rectangular board with a raised edge and having parallel lines ruled on its surface sounds very much like the objects we identify as stringed keyboard instruments in the drawings, paintings and sculptures of the 15th century, and this suggests that the chekker may have received its name because it had the shallow rectangular form to be observed in the majority of these 15th-century representations.'[34]

This carries a certain conviction, but it is not as straightforward as it seems. The description of the exchequer table is not taken from a 14th- or 15th-century source as we might expect, but from a 12th-century one, Richard Fitz Nigel's *Dialogus de Scaccario*.[35] In contrast a fine drawing of the exchequer from the reign of Henry VI (*d* 1471) shows a table whose resemblance to a clavichord is strictly limited to its rectangular shape;[36] if such a rudimentary likeness served to motivate the chekker's name, it is hard to imagine why words denoting far more familiar objects such as 'table', 'box' or 'chest' were not chosen, in preference to the special table of the royal financial court. It is also important that the lines which ran over the exchequer cloth formed a criss-cross pattern, and did not only follow the long axis (as do the strings in a clavichord). Thus these lines covering the table would not necessarily have suggested a resemblance to the instrument.[37] In the same way the rim which Fitz Nigel describes, which is only 'about four finger-breadths in height', would produce the effect of a shallow tray rather than a shallow box, for the table itself measured about five feet by ten. It is anyway unnecessary to turn to the exchequer table for this feature, for chessboards were sometimes built with such rims in the Middle Ages; Jacobus de Cessolis refers to these *labia tabularii* in his moral work on chess written *c* 1300.[38]

The final piece of evidence we shall consider brings us again to the medieval chessboard. Seeking to demonstrate that the chekker was rectangular—and thus a clavichord—Ripin[39] points to several drawings which accompany a treatise by the French cleric Jean de Gerson (*d* 1429) entitled *Canon pro scacordo mystico* ('A rule [for interpreting] the mystical chessboard').[40] An example which Ripin does not reproduce is shown in illustration 6. The text is little more than an extended

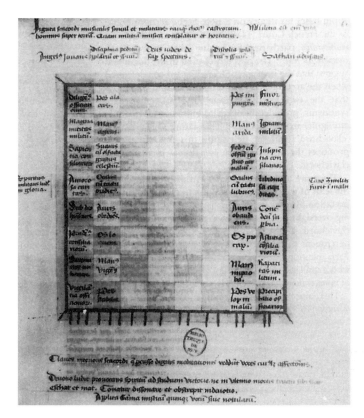

6 *Allegorical chessboard accompanying Jean de Gerson's treatise* Canon pro scacordo mystico *(Tours, Bibliothèque municipale MS 379, f.64r)*

gloss on the drawings, which show chessboards with contrasting virtues and vices written in the squares normally occupied by the pieces,[41] and crude keys projecting from one of the sides.

The drawing (illus. 6) is extremely difficult to interpret. We are clearly looking at a chessboard, so we must either assume that the chekker looked exactly like the boards then in use—down to the square shape and 64 chequered squares—or accept that the drawing does not preserve an exact form of the instrument. Once we entertain this doubt there is no end to the uncertainties that present themselves. It is obvious that the crude keys are schematic; chekker *claves* can hardly have looked like this.[42] Could it be that the chekker body is schematic also? Is it possible that the drawings simply show a chessboard with schematic musical accessories rather than a genuine musical instrument?

The theories we have examined are all based upon an attempt to find *one* solution to the chekker problem, and it is not difficult to account for this. Today we are

accustomed to using our keyboard terms with consistency and precision: each name denotes an instrument with a specific action. Yet perhaps '. . . it is the fault of our age that we proceed in too scientific a manner . . . we certainly expect a word to have a precise meaning, and it is even difficult for us to appreciate that this is to some extent a prejudice. The Middle Ages rarely expected such precision . . .'[43]

The evidence of Arnault de Zwolle

Let us consider the writings of Arnault de Zwolle in the light of these remarks. His treatise (written between 1436 and 1466)[44] is by far the most detailed 15th-century source for the history of stringed keyboard instruments, and if we are to revise our notions we must begin with Arnault.

The treatise does not use any form of the word chekker. Arnault's terms are *clavicordium*, *clavisimbalum* and *dulce melos* (*monocordium* is also used, on a fragment of parchment written by Arnault and inserted into the treatise).[45] What Arnault has to say about these instruments clearly shows that he did not invariably associate a specific name with a specific action in the way we are accustomed to do. Thus he uses the name *clavisimbalum* to denote a harpsichord, or an instrument with a quilled action,[46] and *clavicordium* for a clavichord, or an instrument with a tangent action.[47] Yet this neatness does not last, for we are told that both of these instruments can be fitted with the action of the *dulce melos*, that is, a hammer action akin to that of the modern piano.[48] Thus we have the names *clavisimbalum* and *clavicordium* applied to instruments with two different actions. Later Arnault carries this blending of names and actions still further, for he tells us that a *clavicordium* can be fitted with a quilled action.[49] Thus we have the following terminology in Arnault's treatise:

clavicordium	tangent action
	hammer action
	quilled action
clavisimbalum	quilled action
	hammer action

As for the *dulce melos*, Arnault's words written on the instrument (f.129v) suggest a similar flexibility of terminology: 'this instrument can be called a *dulce melos*'.[50] It is almost as if he had just invented the name himself.

In view of these comments by our best 15th-century witness, I doubt if it is realistic to search for one action behind the name chekker and its variants. If Arnault was prepared to use the word *clavicordium* to cover an instrument with three different actions, there is hardly anything to be gained by seeking a 'chekker' action. Thus the chekker as it has been formerly understood is a myth; it never existed.

If Arnault's choice of names for stringed keyboard instruments was not determined by an association of name and action, then what were the principles governing his usage? Once we dispose of action as a determinent of name the only salient feature left is shape. For Arnault a *clavisimbalum* must have been any stringed keyboard instrument that was wing shaped (e.g. illus. 7), while a *clavicordium* was rectangular.

If, as seems almost certain, the chekker was named after its resemblance to a potent image for the medieval mind, the chessboard, then it was probably rectangular, at least in the earliest years of its existence. It is therefore possible that the drawings accompanying Gerson's treatise (of which illus. 6 is one) are trustworthy in their representation of the instrument's form. Yet at the present time no 15th-century drawing of a stringed keyboard instrument has come to light which shows a specimen in this form.[51] However new illustrations are frequently found; four appeared in 1978,[52] and I am able to add another here (illus. 8) which brings us a little closer to the shallow, tablet shape that might have inspired the name chekker. We must continue the fine work begun by Edmund Bowles and search for new pictorial sources; at present we have too few to proceed. And we must seek new literary references, asking ourselves 'what was this chekker as known to this author at this time?'

[1] All the known references to the instrument are assembled in the Appendix to Edwin M. Ripin, 'Towards an Identification of the Chekker', *GSJ* 28 (1975), pp. 15f.

[2] ibid, no. 2.

[3] ibid, no. 10.

[4] ibid, no. 15.

[5] *Grove* 5, 1, sv *Chekker*.

[6] H. G. Farmer, 'The Origin of the Eschaquiel', *Studies in Oriental Musical Instruments*, First Series (London, 1931), pp. 19-23. See also 'The Canon and Eschaquiel of the Arabs', *Journal of the Royal Asiatic Society* (1926), pp. 239-56. Farmer adequately disposes of the arguments adduced by W. H. Grattan Flood, 'The Eschequier Virginal: An English Invention', *Music & Letters*, 6 (1925), pp. 151-3.

[7] Edmund A. Bowles, 'On the Origin of the Keyboard Mechanism in the Late Middle Ages', *Technology and Culture*, 7 (1966), p. 153.

[8] Ripin, op cit, passim.

[9] Farmer, op cit, p. 21.

[10] ibid, p. 19.

[11] ibid, p. 21.

[12] ibid.

[13] ibid, p. 22.

[14] Quoted in Felipe Pedrell, 'Jean I D'Aragon, Compositeur de Musique', in *Riemann—Festschrift* (Leipzig, 1909), p. 231. Translations throughout the present article are my own.

[15] ibid.

[16] The letter of 1387 was written at Vilafranca de Panades, and the letter of 1388 at Monzon. See Daniel Girona Llagostera, 'Itinerari del Rei en Joan I (1387-1396)', *Estudis Universitaris Catalans*, 13 (1928), pp. 93-134. On John as a collector of instruments see Higini Anglès, 'El músic Jacomí al servei de Joan I i Martí I durant els anys 1372-1404', in *Homenatge a Antoni Rubió i LLuch* (Barcelona, 1936) 1, pp. 613f.

[17] On this instrument see Frederick Crane, *Extant Medieval Musical Instruments* (Iowa, 1972), no. 351.1; J. H. Van der Meer, 'A contribution to the history of the clavicytherium', *EM* 6/2 (April 1978), pp. 247-59; Elizabeth Wells, 'An early stringed keyboard instrument . . .', *EM* 6/4 (October 1978), pp. 568-71; Van der Meer corr., *EM* 7/1 (January 1979), p. 140.

[18] Ripin, op cit, p. 11.

[19] Van der Meer, op cit, p. 249.

[20] Bowles, op cit, p. 153.

[21] Curt Sachs, The History of Musical Instruments (London, 1940), p. 336. The illustration was originally published in E. Vander Straeten, *La Musique aux Pays-Bas avant le XIXᵉ Siècle*, 2 vols (Brussels, 1867 and 1872) 1, facing p. 278.

[22] I pass over the account of a combined upright harpsichord and organ by Paulus Paulrinus of Prague (Josef Reiss, 'Pauli Paulirini de Praga Tractatus de Musica', *Zeitschrift für Musikwissenschaft*, 7 (1925), pp. 263-4).

[23] Ripin, op cit.

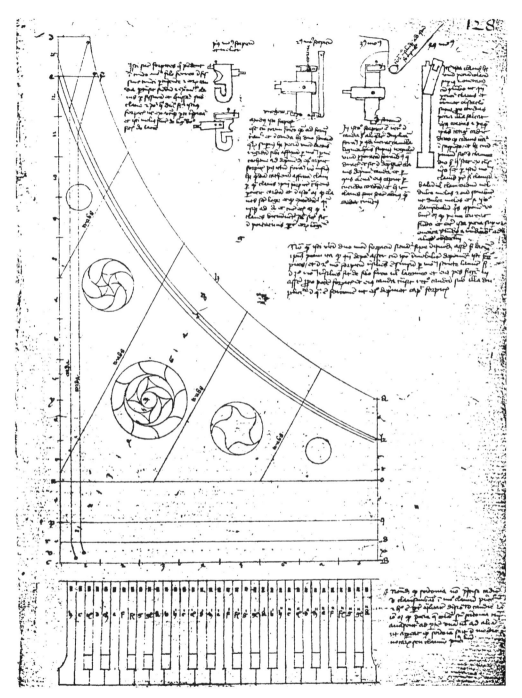

8 *Choirbook illuminated by Juan de Carrión, before 1496 (Vitrina 14 de la Sala de Cantorales, libro 1, f.81). (Avila, Museo de la Catedral)*

7 *Arnault de Zwolle's diagram of the* clavisimbalum *(Paris, Bibliothèque nationale MS lat. 7295, f.128)*

[24] ibid, p. 14.　　　　[25] ibid, pp. 14-15.

[26] ibid, Appendix, no. 25. The reader should note that *emplont* in Ripin's text (line 3) is a misreading for *employee* in the original.

[27] ibid, p. 12.

[28] ibid.

[29] ibid.

[30] For two 15th-century sources in which *monochordum* is used as the name of a clavichord see the treatise of Johannes Keck in Martin Gerbert, *Scriptores Ecclesiastici de Musica*, 3 vols (Typis San-Blasianis, 1784, *R* Milan, 1931) 3, p. 329. The treatise is accompanied by a drawing of the monochord to which Keck refers; it is a single-string clavichord—the drawing is reproduced in Sibyl Marcuse, *A Survey of Musical Instruments* (Newton Abbot & London, 1975), p. 246. For a second 15th-century source see the treatise of Johannes Gallicus in Edmond de Coussemaker, *Scriptorum de Musica Medii Aevi*, 4 vols (Paris, 1864-76) 4, pp. 317f. The treatise is accompanied by a drawing of the *monocordum* in question, reproduced in Jeremy Montagu, *The World of Medieval and Renaissance Musical Instruments* (Newton Abbot, 1976), plate 42; it is also a single string monochord (though Gallicus states in his text that the instrument does not necessarily have a single string and is distinct from the *verum . . . monocordum* or 'true monochord'). For a reconstruction of such a monochord/clavichord see *EM* 6/2 (April 1978), p. 209.

[31] See G. le Cerf and E.-R. Labande eds., *Instruments de Musique du XVᵉ Siècle: Les Traités d'Henri-Arnaut de Zwolle et de Divers Anonymes* (Paris, 1932 *R* Kassel, 1972), p. 22 and Planche XIV (f129 *bis*).

[32] Ripin, op cit, pp. 13f.　　　[33] ibid.

[34] ibid, pp. 13-14.

[35] C. Johnson, ed., *Dialogus de Scaccario* (London, 1950), pp. 6-7.

[36] See G. R. Corner, 'Observations on four illuminations representing the Courts of Chancery . . .', *Archaeologia*, 39 (1863), pp. 357f and plate XIX.

[37] See the drawing in Johnson, op cit, p. xlii.

[38] See H. J. R. Murray, *A History of Chess* (Oxford, 1913), p. 544.

[39] Ripin, op cit, p. 14.

[40] The text is in Mgr Glorieux ed., *Jean Gerson Oeuvres Complètes*, 10 vols in 11 (Paris 1960-73) 9, pp. 708-10. Some of the material also exists in a French version by Gerson (ibid p. 712-13). It should be pointed out that Ripin was not the first to reproduce drawings in this series; two are given by Armand Machabey, 'Remarques sur le lexique musical du *de Canticis* de Gerson', *Romania*, 79 (1958), plates 2 and 3.

[41] For a treatment of such chessboard symbolism in the Middle Ages see F. Tupper, *Types of Society in Medieval Literature* (New York, 1926), pp. 18f, and Murray, op cit, pp. 529f.

[42] Compare the drawings reproduced in Ripin, op cit, and Machabey, op cit.

[43] Gilbert Reaney, 'Terminology and Medieval Music', *Festschrift Heinrich Besseler* (Leipzig, 1961), p. 149.

[44] Full text in le Cerf and Labande, op cit.

[45] See note 31.

[46] ibid, p. 6 (third paragraph), and Planche VI (text at bottom right); this shows that the wing-shaped instrument is called *clavisimbalum*, and three quilled actions (together with one hammered action) are drawn above it.

[47] ibid, Planche IX.

[48] ibid, pp. 5-6 . . . *et per istum modum clavis* [the hammer action] *potest fieri clavisimbalum vel clavicordium vel dulce melos . . .*

[49] ibid, p. 21 . . . *etiam posset fieri quod clavicordium sonaret ut clavisimbalum . . . per secundum vel tercium modum forpicis* [both quilled] . . .

[50] ibid, p. 19, and Planche X.

[51] See Edmund A. Bowles, 'A Checklist of Fifteenth-Century Representations of Stringed Keyboard Instruments', in E. Ripin ed., *Keyboard Instruments*, 2nd edition (New York, 1977), pp. 11f.

[52] See Christopher Page and Lewis Jones, 'Four more 15th-century Representations of Stringed Keyboard Instruments', *GSJ* 31 (1978), pp. 151-5 and plates 11-12.

Jerome of Moravia on the *Rubeba* and *Viella*

JEROME of Moravia's *Tractatus de Musica* is the most important written source for the history of Western stringed instruments before the 15th century. At a time when musical theorists were inclined to say little if anything about instruments Jerome gives three tunings for the *viella* and one for the *rubeba*, specifying the fingering of each and, in the case of the *viella*, describing a virtuoso technique. Hitherto only extracts from this work have been made available in English, many of which incorporate serious errors in translation.[1] It is perhaps because of this that few of the many authors who have quoted the tunings have managed to get them right; the notes of the strings are variously back to front, an octave too high or low, in the wrong order, or simply incorrect. Worse still, they have been tacitly re-arranged to fit various prejudices and preconceptions. The purpose of this article is to provide a text that is closely based upon the original manuscript (Pls. XX–XXII), accompanied by a translation that is as literal as possible in the hope that these errors, once exposed, will evaporate.

JEROME OF MORAVIA AND THE *TRACTATUS DE MUSICA*

The unique manuscript of the *Tractatus de Musica* is preserved in the Bibliothèque Nationale at Paris. It is our only source of information concerning Jerome's life: a note at the end of the treatise refers to him as a Dominican friar from Mähren.[2]

The work was probably composed in the city of Paris, for the manuscript was circulating in university circles there not long after its completion (see below), while certain aspects of its make-up show that it is an official copy made for the inspection of university authorities before the text was released for publication.[3]

The date of the work can not be precisely determined. In the seventh chapter Jerome quotes from a treatise of Thomas Aquinas completed in 1272, and thus a firm *terminus a quo* can be fixed. Yet it is possible that this terminus may be brought forward by at least a decade or so, since Franco's *Ars Cantus Mensurabilis* is one of the treatises that Jerome includes in his compilation; recently a date of *c.* 1280 for this text has gained influential support.[4] A *terminus ad quem* is established by the death of Pierre de Limoges (1306) who bequeathed the manuscript to the Sorbonne.[5] In all probability therefore Jerome's *Tractatus* was composed sometime during the last two decades of the 13th century, and not *c.* 1250 as has so often been stated.

As it stands in the manuscript the text of the *Tractatus de Musica* is a most complicated affair. In addition to the columns of main text there are corrections in various hands for which at least two different readers are responsible (the initials of two names, both correctors, appear in marginal notes in the manuscript[6]). We cannot avoid the questions these corrections and annotations raise since they incorporate material of the highest interest.

In the section on the *rubeba* and the *viella* (see Plates) we may detect three hands: (1) the hand of the main text; (2) the hand who supplies material omitted by the first hand in Pl. XX (far-right margin) and Pl. XXI (same place); (3) the hand responsible for various notes and comments in Pl. XXI (far-right margin top, and bottom margin); also in Pl. XXII (far-left margin and bottom margin). We need not consider the work of the second hand, since he only adds material which should have been in the text but was omitted. The work of the third hand is far more important, since it includes a long note on the use of the *bordunus* at the bottom of Pl. XXII which is one of the most important pieces of evidence in the whole text.

Two crucial questions must be answered: (1) when were the notes by hand 3 added? (2) If they were added at an early date, were they intended as corrections to be incorporated in future copies of the text made from this exemplar? Fortunately new evidence has come to light which removes most of the uncertainty surrounding these additions.

A note in the manuscript at Paris reveals that the *Tractatus* was bequeathed to the Sorbonne by one Pierre de Limoges (*ex legato magistri Petri de Lemovicis*). Pierre was a Master of Arts associated with the Sorbonne. He died in 1306, leaving more than a hundred books to the University of which sixty-seven still rest in Paris at the Bibliothèque Nationale. Madeleine Mabille has shown that Pierre annotated a number of his manuscripts in a small, cramped hand quite unlike the main text hand of each manuscript concerned.[7] At my request François Avril, Conservateur at the Bibliothèque Nationale, compared the manuscripts annotated by Pierre with the notes at the close of the *Tractatus de Musica* (the originals of all the relevant manuscripts were at his disposal). He concluded that, in spite of minor differences in the hands (possibly due to the varying space into which Pierre had to cram his annotations) the notes in all the manuscripts were written by the same person.[8] Thus we may assume that the identity of hand 3 has been established: these notes were written by Pierre de Limoges sometime before 1306, and not in the late 14th century as has often been assumed.[9]

The question remains whether Pierre wrote these notes in some official capacity so that they might be included in future copies from this exemplar. It is actually most unlikely that they are anything more than personal annotations. They are not corrections; they explain and amplify the text. In the far right margin of Pl. XXI, Pierre notes that a string referred to by Jerome as the *secunda* is actually first on the instrument (*que est prima vielle*); similarly he notes at the bottom of the same page that the D string, now running over the fingerboard, produces two stopped pitches which Jerome does not bother to specify. The private character of the notes is fully revealed in Pl. XXII (far-left column): here Pierre comments in the first person that he does not understand how *b acutum* can be produced with the third tuning; *sed non video*, he writes, *quomodo b acutum formetur* ('but I do not see how b♮ may be formed').

Why did Jerome include a section on the *rubeba* and *viella* in his treatise? It is at least clear that the material in the chapter was designed to be used; it is far removed from the purely theoretical treatises on the organistrum and monochord. Jerome's desire that the student should grasp the rudiments of the instruments cannot be mistaken, and several of his remarks bring us as close to the actual business of instrumental tuition in the Middle Ages as we are ever likely to get. An almost intimate, conversational tone prevails. 'Having reviewed these things and committed them to memory', Jerome assures his reader, 'you will be able to encompass all the art of *viella* playing'. To this end he gives variant tunings for the *viella* and specifies the letters of the notes produced by each of the stopping positions used at the time.[10] The reader is clearly intended to work through the tunings as Jerome describes them, familiarising himself with the note names (probably in conjunction with a copy—or at least a good mental picture—of the Guidonian hand). Details of fingering are not overlooked; we are told that the *rubeba* must be held 'in a natural position in the left hand, between the thumb and the first finger', while some fingers must be applied 'bent' and others 'naturally . . . which is to be done with all the other fingers on the *rubeba* and the *viella*'.

Clearly therefore Jerome envisaged a readership of well-educated persons trained to learn by studying pages of Latin and anxious to acquire the rudiments of the *viella* and *rubeba*. We know from his introduction to the *Tractatus* that the work was intended for the 'brothers of our order or another' (*fratres ordinis nostri vel alii*),[11] but if the treatise achieved any success in Paris its circulation was probably wider than this. We do not know whether our manuscript was ever used for the purposes for which it was intended prior to its acquisition by Pierre de Limoges. But assuming the whole project of copying out the exemplar led to something rather than to nothing whatsoever, then the separate sections (*pecia*) of the manuscript would have been hired from the stationers of Paris by masters, pupils, or scribes acting on their behalf.[12] It would therefore have been at large in Paris, at the disposal of anyone who both wished and was able to read it.

There are numerous indications in other sources that a literate class of *viella* players existed, the class for whom Jerome compiled his chapter. In an arresting passage the theorist Lambertus (pseudo-Aristotle), a contemporary of Jerome, states that a good student of *musica mensurabilis* should be able to transcribe musical handwriting in such a way that 'however much any music has been diversified to the limit, it may be made consistently manifest by means of [musical handwriting] in the manner of a *viella*'.[13] This fascinating and enigmatic passage seems to suggest, at the very least, that some *viellatores* performed from notated music, and may even imply the existence of a form of *viella* tablature hitherto unsuspected. That fiddlers existed who practised their art in relation to the rules of *musica* as a literate skill is clear not only from Jerome's text, but also from Albertus Magnus's distinction between fiddlers who play *ex arte* and those who play *ex usu*.[14] It is presumably the type of fiddler playing *ex arte* which Johannes de Grocheio has in mind when her refers to the '*bonus artifex in viella*', while praising the instrument above all others.[15]

Another French theorist, Elias of Salomon, writing his *Scientia Artis Musice* (1274) 'in curia Romana', gives the *viella* a place in the world of the trained *cantor*. He inveighs against the singer who is ignorant of the Guidonian hand (an aid to advanced *viella* playing according to Jerome) and 'does not know how to adjust his voice to singing the kind of song which would best be sung with a wooden instrument, a *viella*'.[16] Elias joins Jerome and Johannes de Grocheio in praising the versatility of the instrument,[17] but he is only concerned with literate players: the singer who plays the *viella* and knows the Guidonian hand is a *cantor* but anyone who does not know the hand is merely a *ioculator seu iauglator*

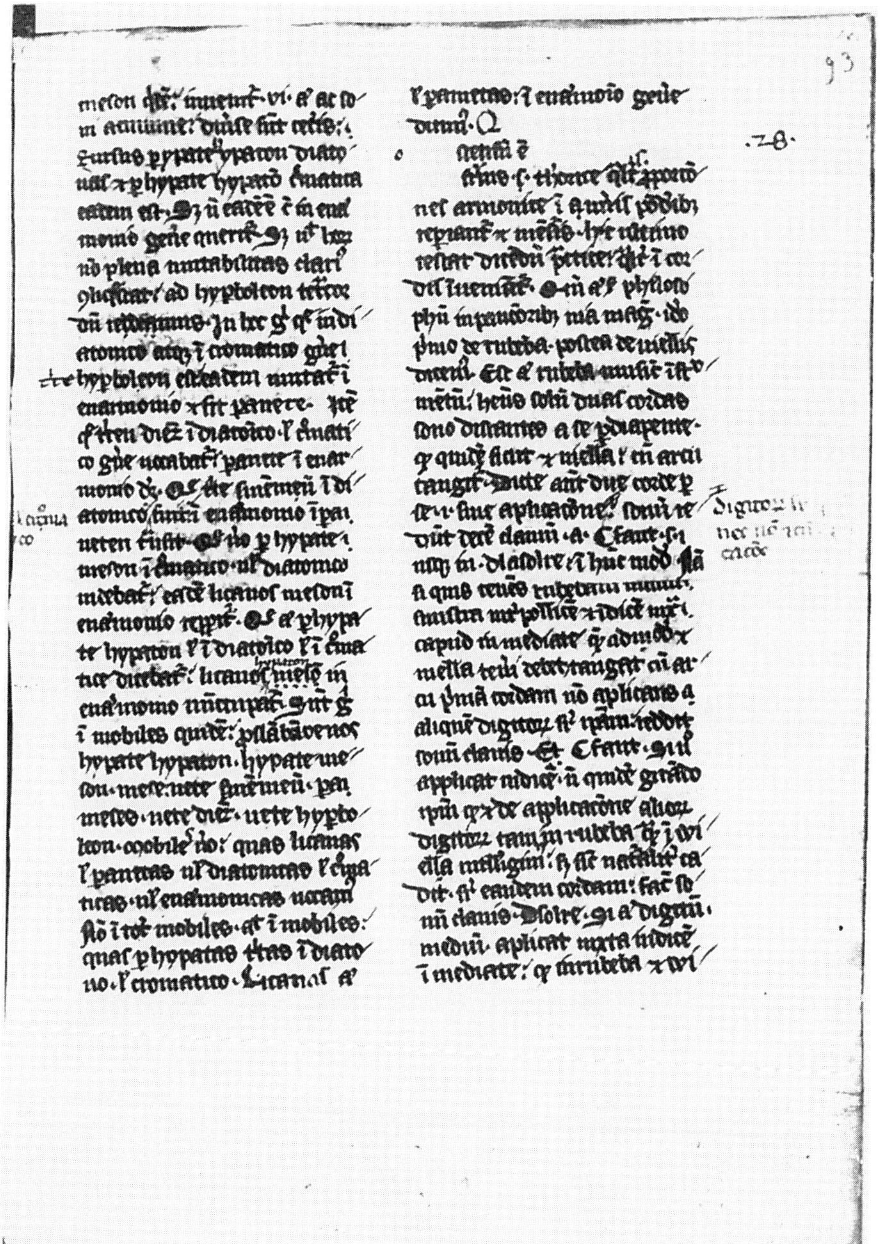

PLATE XX

Paris, Bibliothèque Nationale, MS. Lat. 16663, fol. 93r. Opening of Jerome's chapter on the rubeba *and* viella

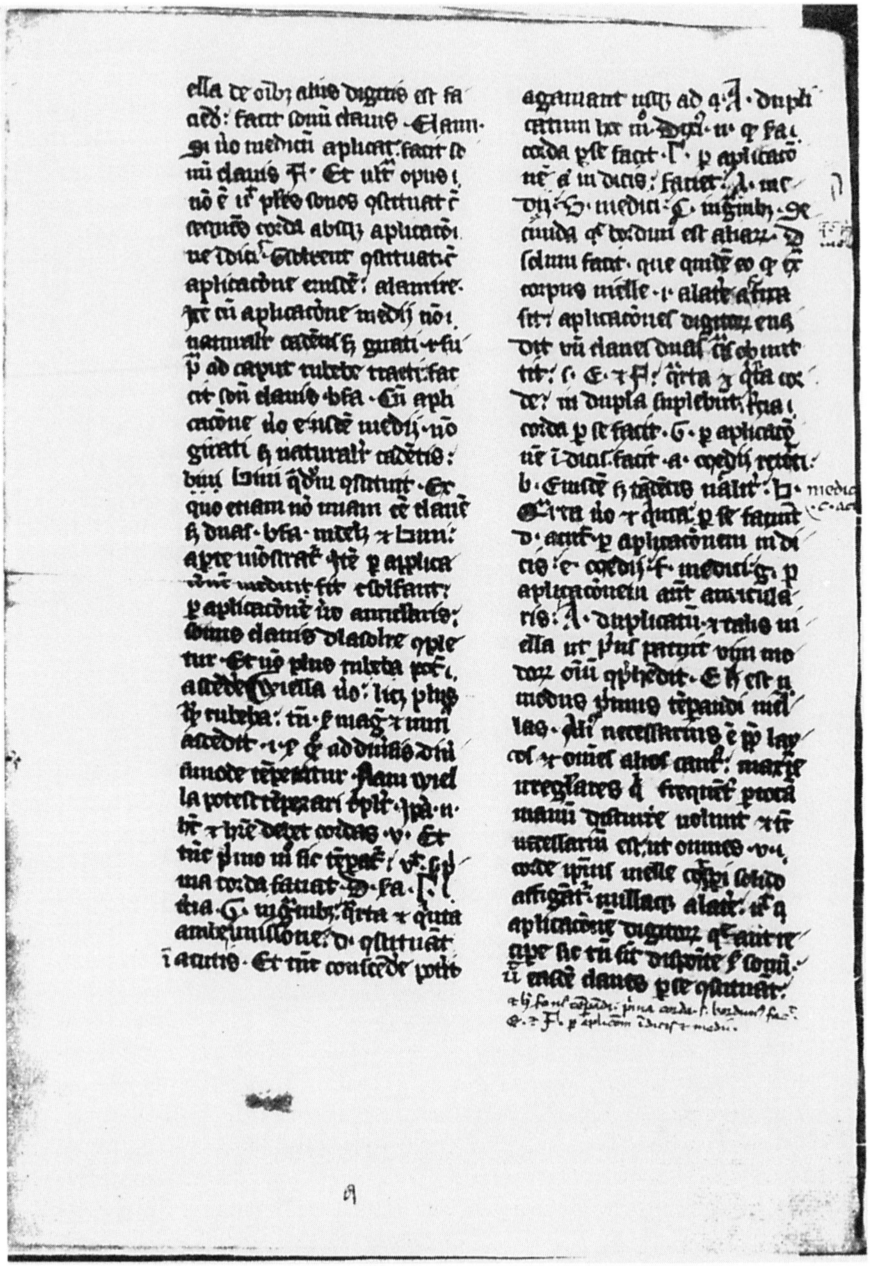

PLATE XXI

Paris, Bibliothèque Nationale, MS. Lat. 16663, fol. 93v.

in his estimation.[18] This distinction between literate musicians and *ioculatores*—found in other treatises including the *De Musica* of John 'Cotton'[19]—should put an end to any suggestion that Jerome is concerned with the world of 'amateurs and minstrels'. This phrase (an inaccurate translation of Jerome's *laycos cantus* which can be traced to Hortense Panum and probably further[20]) has been widely quoted and, given the general vagueness of the term 'minstrel', has served to obscure the fact that the real milieu from which Jerome's chapter is derived is that of well-educated Parisian circles, and primarily that of *cantors* amongst the secular and regular clergy.

Considering this evidence, we must ask whether it is likely that Jerome was the only pedagogue of the Middle Ages who catered for the instrumental needs of this readership. Did he set out upon his chapter as a pioneer without models or precedents of any kind? It is more probable that the aspirations of such musicians were catered for by a now vanished genre of Latin technical writing dealing with the rudiments of stringed instruments. These documents would have been instrumental tutors in effect, probably taking the form of a few folded leaves. Jerome's chapter on the *viella* and *rubeba* may be such a tutor taken over wholesale and inserted into the *Tractatus*; this would be in keeping with the nature of the treatise which is essentially a compilation of pre-existing materials. The fact that other 'tutors' do not survive need cause no surprise; where are the tutors that could be purchased from English minstrels in the late 15th century?[21] It is in the nature of such documents to be literally thumbed out of existence.[22]

However, enthusiasm for this hypothesis must not be allowed to obscure the literary tradition in which Jerome's chapter belongs. His introduction presents the material as a formal, practical demonstration of theoretical points already studied. The guiding principle is the same as that enunciated by Regino Prumensis several centuries earlier: any discussion of music must end with *musica artificialis*, including instruments, so that the invisible may be finally demonstrated by means of the visible;[23] thus Jerome's chapter on instruments stands at the end of his work, so that all may close *practice . . . in cordis*. The practice of referring to current secular instruments (rather than purely pedagogical ones such as the monochord) in order to make theoretical points can be traced to the *De Institutione Harmonica* of Hucbald (d. 930) where remarkable use is made of the six-stringed European lyre.[24] Similar, but briefer references occur in a number of minor works, including a treatise once attributed to Odo of Cluny which refers to the octave range of the *fidula*—perhaps a bowed instrument.[25]

It is certain that by the 13th century the practice of referring to current instruments to make theoretical points was widespread. Lambertus (pseudo-Aristotle) advises the novice to mark the letters ΓABC on the neck of a *'cythara, viella* or *citole'*,[26] and the same injunction may be found in the anonymous *Quatuor Principalia Musica* (1351) where *vielle, cistolle* and similar instruments seem to be recommended as monochord substitutes.[27] In the light of these texts Jerome's chapter appears as a rather less amazing document, and one written within a well-established tradition of theoretical practice.

VIELLA AND RUBEBA

Of the two instruments which Jerome describes the *viella* is the easiest to identify. This five-stringed bowed instrument may be encountered in many French manuscript illustrations and carvings of the 13th century (Pl. XXIII). It is often shown with the lateral bourdon string that Jerome describes.

The *rubeba* presents more serious problems.[28] The source of this word itself is clearly Arabic *rabāb* which today, in various forms, denotes a host of stringed instruments all over the Arabic-speaking world. The *rabāb* of Morocco, shown in very much its modern form in the celebrated *Cantigas* manuscript (Seville?, 1280–3, see *GSJ* XXI, Pl. XVII*d*), is one plausible candidate that has been suggested for Jerome's *rubeba*.[29] This instrument is bi-chordic (a relatively rare phenomenon in medieval Europe), and is tuned to a fifth. In both respects it corresponds to Jerome's *rubeba*, but its pitch is particularly interesting (approximately *c g* like the two bottom strings of a modern viola),[30] for Jerome's *rubeba* is tuned *C fa ut/G sol re ut* (i.e. *c g*) which is a much lower pitch than we are accustomed to associate with medieval names built on an *r-b* stem such as *rebec, rebebe* etc. This Moroccan instrument was widely distributed in the Middle Ages,[31] and there are several representations of it in northern European sources. As far as I am aware no example has been found contemporary with Jerome, though a 12th-century French example has recently come to light.[32]

THE TUNINGS

The tunings given by Jerome have often been misrepresented. They are:

rubeba	viella		
c g	d Γg d′d′	d Γg d′ g′	ΓΓ d c′c′

The arrangements shown here preserve the sequence of the notes exactly as they are given by Jerome, but grouped into probable courses which Jerome does not specify. The most important observation to be made is that the second tuning for the *viella*—the one said by Jerome to be best for secular melodies—is *not* the constantly ascending series it has so often been said to be (i.e. it is not Γ-d-g-d'-g'). It is simply the first tuning with the top string taken up a fourth. Far from being a continuous series it is (1) re-entrant, and (2) the Γ and g form in all probability an octave course. With regard to (1), Jerome's Latin is abundantly clear: '[the strings of the second tuning] should be so arranged in pitch (*sic tamen sint disposite secundum sonum*) that they make the same notes as in the method of the first [*viella*]; this is true of the first, second, third and fourth strings, but not of the fifth, which is not in unison with the fourth but is said to make sesquitertia [4:3, i.e. a fourth]; thus it is placed at *g* among the *superacutae*. The phrase *secundum sonum* might be rendered 'according to pitch' and taken to mean that the strings are rearranged on the fingerboard in ascending order of pitch, but this conflicts with Jerome's unequivocal assertion that strings 1–4 produce exactly the same notes as in tuning 1.

The next important aspect of the tunings is the placement of the lateral bourdon string. Jerome's remarks in this regard have often been muddled with those of the later annotator, Pierre of Limoges. According to Jerome, only *one viella* tuning, the first, uses a lateral bourdon string. He is quite specific that all the strings run over the fingerboard in the second *viella* tuning, and he says nothing at all with respect to the third. It is Pierre de Limoges who, in an extensive note at the close of the chapter (Pl. XXII, bottom), says that there is a gamma *bordunus* in the third tuning.

The fact that Jerome notates the *viella* tunings with gamma as the lowest note has prompted the view that the instruments he knew were actually tuned in the region of modern G at the bottom of the bass clef. There are a number of reasons for rejecting this idea. It is quite clear that in the Middle Ages the gamut was an infinitely moveable framework of pitch nomenclature and musicians put it where it was required.[33] The actual pitch of gamma for example was a matter of indifference to the authors of the monochord treatises who worked by proportion, not by measurement from a standardised quantity.[34] The implication of the passage from the *Quatuor Principalia Musica*, alluded to above, is that the lowest pitch of any *viella* might be labelled gamma by the student using the instrument in place of the traditional monochord. Given the relatively short string-length employed on most medieval bowed instruments it is inconceivable that any but the very largest examples were capable of reaching down to G with the gut of the period.[35]

The danger of drawing conclusions about instrumental pitch from the use of gamut letters can easily be illustrated by the case of medieval chime-bells or *cymbala*. The numerous treatises that survive on the manufacture of these bells frequently employ a series beginning on C *fa ut* (i.e. *c*) to denote the pitches of the bells. Yet as they are shown in medieval art *cymbala* are quite small, and probably sounded at least two octaves higher than *c*.[36]

Jerome had no choice but to notate the *viella* tunings from gamma upwards. We must remember that he specifies the stopped pitches as well as the open ones, and the second *viella* tuning with the especially wide compass covers a range of two octaves and a fifth. Since the complete compass of the gamut in the 13th century did not exceed two octaves and a sixth, Jerome was compelled to begin with the lowest degree; had he started any higher he would simply have exhausted the range of signs available to him. From this it follows that all the *viella* tunings must be notated in this range for, as Jerome is most careful to specify, the tunings are very closely related to one another. The second is simply the first with the top string taken up a fourth, and the last is 'the opposite of the first'. Using a standard pitch notation for all three tunings these relations are apparent; a change in the notational basis would obscure them. Thus the relation between d Γg d′d′ and d Γg d′ g′ is clear; similarly the fact that the third tuning begins with an inversion of the opening intervals of the first is clear from the notation d Γg d′d′ and ΓΓ d c′c′ (dΓg/ΓΓd).

The *Tractatus de Musica* has generally been regarded as the only 13c. source for the tuning of bowed instruments. In fact there is a second, almost exactly contemporary source, which confirms the type of tuning given by Jerome. This anonymous text, the *Summa Musicae*, was written between 1274 and 1307, most probably in France, and possibly in Paris.[37] The author divides stringed instruments into those which have 'no greater continuous [intervals] than tone and semitone', including *citharae* (harps), and *psalteria* (psalteries), and those 'which are tuned in the consonances of octave, fourth and fifth; by variously stopping with the fingers the players of these make tones and semitones for themselves'.[38] These are clearly fingerboard instruments tuned in very much the same way as Jerome's *viella*. Bowed instruments are by far the most common examples of the lute class in French iconography of the period 1274–1307, and the author was undoubtedly thinking of *vielle* among other instruments when he wrote. Thus Jerome of

Moravia's testimony can be safely accepted as a wholly reliable guide to the tuning of the *viella* and the *rubeba* in late 13th-century Paris.

NOTES TO THE ABOVE INTRODUCTION

[1] Jerome of Moravia's treatise on the *viella* and *rubeba* first attracted attention in 1828, when Perne published a French translation and commentary (*Revue Musicale*, II (1828), 457–467, 481–490). The text was first published by Coussemaker (CS, I, p. 152–3). An English paraphrase of the material was published by J. F. R. Stainer in 1900 ('Rebec and Viol', *Musical Times*, September 1, 1900, p. 596–7). A text with Italian translation (but no critical commentary to speak of) was published by Anna Puccianti in 1966 (*Collectanea Historiae Musicae*, IV, p. 227f); Puccianti did not use the complete edition of the *Tractatus de Musica* published by S. Cserba in 1935 (*Hieronymus de Moravia O.P. Tractatus de Musica*, Regensburg, 1935).

Jerome's chapter is mentioned in a host of secondary sources, but many of these have little value because of their inaccuracies. The only modern work which deals with the tunings and is genuinely worth mentioning is Werner Bachmann's *Origins of Bowing*, trans. Norma Deane, 1969, *passim*.

[2] See plate XXII. For an account of the materials pertaining to Jerome's life see Cserba, *op. cit.*, xix f.

[3] That is to say that the manuscript is made up of *pecia*, or free sections, to be hired and copied individually by scribes. This system was used at the university of Paris in Jerome's day. See Jean Destrez, *La Pecia dans les Manuscrits Universitaires du XIIIe et du XIVe siècle*, Paris, 1935, and Cserba, *op. cit.*, lxxxii. See also M. B. Parkes and A. G. Watson, *Medieval Scribes Manuscripts and Libraries*, 1978, p. 145f.

[4] See G. Reaney and A. Gilles, eds., *Franconis de Colonia Ars Cantus Mensurabilis*, American Institute of Musicology, *Corpus Scriptorum de Musica*, 18 (1974), p. 10–11.

[5] For the date of Pierre's death I have followed Madeleine Mabille, ('Pierre de Limoges, copiste de manuscrits', *Scriptorium*, 24 (1970), p. 45–47). Cserba (*op. cit.*, xix) gives the date as 1304, not 1306.

[6] Cserba, *op. cit.*, lxxix, gives the details.

[7] Mabille, *op. cit.*, *passim*.

[8] Private communication, 4 October, 1978.

[9] The date assigned to them by Cserba, *op. cit.*, p. 291.

[10] That is to say he does not go beyond the first position. It is quite certain that some stopping positions were used which Jerome does not specify. See the commentary below.

[11] Cserba, *op. cit.*, xvii.

[12] The operation of the *pecia* system is described in Destrez, *op. cit.*, p. 5f. But cf. Parkes and Watson, *op. cit.*, *passim*.

[13] CS, I, p. 269.

[14] *Ethica*, ed. A. Borgnet, Paris, 1891, p. 165.

[15] E. Rohloff, ed., *Die Quellenhandschriften zum Musiktraktat des Johannes de Grocheio* (Leipzig, 1972), p. 134–7.

[16] GS, III, p. 61.

[17] *Ibid.*, p. 26, 'in viella et similibus in quinque chordis totus cantus potest compleri'.

[18] *Ibid.*, p. 23.

[19] Jos. Smits van Waesberghe, ed., *Johannis Affligemensis De Musica cum Tonario*, American Institute of Musicilogy [AIM], *Corpus Scriptorum de Musica* [CSM], I, Rome, 1950, p. 51. See also *idem, Aribonis de Musica*, AIM, CSM 2, 1951, p. 47.

[20] Hortense Panum, *Stringed Instruments of the Middle Ages*, 1940, p. 388. Panum also gives the title of the treatise incorrectly (p. 385).

[21] See Alison Hanham, 'The Musical Studies of a Fifteenth Century Wool Merchant', *Review of English Studies*, NS viii (1957), p. 271. The merchant George Cely pays a harpist 3s and 6d (a remarkable sum) for a 'byll ffor to lerne to tevne the levt'.

[22] See H. S. Bennet, 'Science and Information in English writings of the Fifteenth Century', *Modern Language Review*, 39 (1944), p. 2, remarks upon treatises upon hawking: '. . . probably manuals were more frequent than the existing number would suggest, for it is most likely that their constant use made it inevitable that they fell to pieces sooner or later, literally thumbed out of existence'.

[23] GS, I, 236.

[24] See M. Huglo, 'Les Instruments de Musique chez Hucbald', *Hommages à André Boutemy*, ed. Guy Cambier, Brussels, 1976, p. 178–96.

[25] GS, I, 271.

[26] CS, I, p. 257–8.

[27] See *GSJ* XXXI, p. 53.

[28] See *GSJ* XXX, p. 10.

[29] Anthony Baines, 'Jerome of Moravia', *FoMRHI Quarterly*, April, 1977, p. 25.

[30] I am grateful to Jean Jenkins for information on this point.

[31] For an excellent collection of illustrations see I. Woodfield, *The Origins of the Viol*, Dissertation, University of London, 1977.

[32] Information provided by Laurence Wright.

[33] I am grateful to Professor Joseph Smits van Waesberghe and Dr. Gaston Allaire for corresponding with me on this subject.

[34] See C. Adkins, 'The Technique of the Monochord', *Acta Musicologica*, xxxix (1967), p. 34f.

[35] I am grateful to Dr. Ephraim Segerman for several long and informative letters on this topic.

[36] This observation was kindly confirmed by Mr. Hughes of the Whitechapel Bell Foundry Ltd., London.

[37] To judge by the forms *flaiota* and *flauta* which the author uses, he was French. Jos. Smits van Waesberghe (*Johannis Affligemensis De Musica*, p. 33) surmises that the treatise was written in Paris or Liège.

[38] GS, III, p. 214.

PREFACE TO THE TEXT

The text follows the manuscript as closely as possible. The absolute minimum of editorial changes have been made, all of which are indicated in the apparatus and explained in the notes which follow. MS. v for w and w for v have been reproduced by w and v respectively (thus *viella* for MS. *wiella*, *ut* for MS. *vt* etc). The MS. punctuation has been discarded in favour of a system following modern practice. The additions (generally corrections in the form of insertions) by hand 2 are contained in round brackets and inserted in the text, as are the annotations of hand 3, Pierre de Limoges. The hand responsible for the material is specified in each case. The contractions in the script— involving well over three quarters of the words in the text—have been expanded without italicising the interpolated letters. Letters introduced for the purposes of emendation are placed in square brackets. The purpose of the apparatus is to account for every stroke in the original manuscript; errors deleted by the scribe and others missed by him and his correctors are noted by line number.

Note: Jerome uses the standard gamut and hexachord notation Γ (gamma) A B C D E F G a b♭ b♮ c d e f g a b♮ c d, with each letter identified by its solmisation syllables. Nominally Γ corresponds to G (at the bottom of the bass clef).

THE TEXT

[In tetracordis et pentacordis musicis instrumentis, puta in viellis et similibus per consonancias cordis distantibus mediis vocum invencionibus]

[fol. 93r col. 2] Ostensum est superius theorice qualiter scilicet proporciones armonice in numeris ponderibus reperiantur et mensuris. Hic ultimo restat dicendum practice qualiter in cordis inveniantur. Quoniam autem secundum philosophum in paucior-
5 ibus via magna, ideo primo de rubeba, postea de viellis dicemus.

Est autem rubeba musicum instrumentum habens solum duas cordas sono distantes a se per diapente. Quod quidem, sicut et viella, cum arcu tangitur. Dicte autem due corde per se, id est sine aplicacione (*hand 2* digitorum super ipsas nec non et cum aplica-
10 cione) sonum redunt decem clavium a C fa ut scilicet usque in d la sol re in hunc modum.
Nam si quis tenens rubebam manu sinistra inter pollicem et indicem iuxta capud immedi[t]ate, quemadmodum et viella teneri debet, tangat cum arcu primam cordam non aplicans aliquem
15 digitorum super ipsam, reddit sonum clavis C fa ut. Si vero applicat indicem non quidem girando ipsum, quod et de applicacione aliorum digitorum tam in rubeba quam in viella intelligimus, sed sicut naturaliter cadit super eandem cordam, facit sonum clavis D sol re. Si autem digitum medium aplicat iuxta
20 indicem immedi[t]ate, quod in rubeba et vi[*fol. 93v col. 1*]ella de omnibus aliis digitis est faciendum, facit sonum clavis E la mi. Si vero medicum aplicat facit sonum clavis F. Et ultra opus non est, ut plures sonos constituat, cum sequens corda absque aplicacione indicis G sol re ut constituat; cum aplicacione eiusdem a la
25 mi re. Item cum aplicacione medij non naturaliter cadentis sed girati, id est supra ad caput rubebe tracti, facit sonum clavis b fa. Cum aplicacione vero eiusdem medij non girati sed naturaliter cadentis, ♮ mi quadrum constituit. Ex quo etiam non unam esse clavem, sed duas, b fa videlicet et ♮ mi, aperte monstratur. Item
30 per applicacionem medici fit c sol fa ut; per applicacionem vero auricularis sonus clavis d la sol re completur. Et non plus rubeba potest ascendere.

TRANSLATION

(*N.B.* '*hand 3*': Pierre de Limoges)
[Concerning four- and five-stringed instruments of music, especially *vielle* and such, for the sake of consonances on strings separated by intervals, with the performance of notes between.[1]]

It has been shown above theoretically how the harmonic proportions may be obtained in harmonious weights and quantities.[2] Here at the end [of the work] something remains to be said of how they may be practically found upon strings. Since, according to the philosopher, 'the true way lies among smaller things',[3] therefore we will speak first of the *rubeba*, and afterwards of *vielle*.[4]

The *rubeba* is a musical instrument having only two strings standing a fifth apart. It is played with a bow just as the *viella*.[5] The said two strings by themselves, that is without the application (*hand 2*: of the fingers upon them as well as with their application) give the sound of ten letters, namely from *C fa ut* up to *d la sol re* in the following manner.

If one holds the *rubeba* next to the peg box, in a natural position[6] in the left hand between the thumb and the first finger in the way that the *viella* must be held, and touches the first string with the bow, not applying any of the fingers to it, it gives the sound of the letter *C fa ut*. If, however, one applies the first finger—but not by twisting it; this is a caveat we so observe for the other fingers as much on the *rubeba* as on the *viella*—but just as it falls naturally over the same string, it makes the sound of the letter *D sol re*. If one applies the second finger naturally next to the first—which is to be done with all the other fingers on the *rubeba* and *viella*—it makes the sound of the letter *E la mi*. If, however, one applies the third finger, it makes the sound of the letter *F*. There is no further need that it produce more notes, since the following string may make *G sol re ut* without the application of the first finger, and with the application of the same [may make] *a la mi re*. Similarly, with the application of the second finger not naturally falling but bent—that is drawn towards the pegbox of the *rubeba* above[7]—it produces the sound of the letter *b fa*. With the application of this same second finger not bent, but naturally falling, it makes ♮ *mi quadrum*. Thus it is clearly shown that there are two letters here, not one, that is *b fa* and ♮ *mi*. Similarly, by the application of the third finger *c sol fa ut* is made, and by the application of the fourth finger the sound of the letter *d la sol re* is accomplished. The *rubeba* may ascend no more.[8]

Viella vero licet plus quam rubeba, tamen secundum magis et
minus ascendit, id est secundum quod a diversis diversimode
35 temperatur. Nam viella potest temperari tripliciter. Ipsa enim
habet, et habere debet, chordas v. Et tunc primo modo sic temperatur: ut scilicet prima corda faciat D; secunda Γ; tertia G in
gravibus; quarta et quinta ambe unissone d constituant in acutis.

Et tunc conscendere poterit [*col. 2*] a gamma ut usque ad $\overset{a}{a}$ dupli-
40 catum hoc modo. Diximus enim quod secunda corda per se facit Γ;
per aplicacionem autem indicis faciet A; medij B; medici C in
gravibus. Secunda, que bordunus est aliarum (*hand 3* que est
prima vielle) D solum facit. Que quidem eo, quod extra corpus
vielle, id est a latere, affixa sit, aplicaciones digitorum evadit. Unde
45 claves duas quas obmittit, scilicet E et F, quarta et quinta corde in
dupla suplebunt. Tertia corda per se facit G; per aplicacionem
indicis facit a; medij retorti b; eiusdem sed cadentis naturaliter ♮;
(*hand 2*: medici c acutum). Quarta vero et quinta per se faciunt d
acutum; per aplicacionem indicis e; medij f; medici g; per

50 aplicacionem autem auricularis $\overset{a}{a}$ duplicatum. Et talis viella, ut
prius patuit, vim modorum omnium comprehendit.

Et hic est modus primus temperandi viellas.
Alius necessarius est propter laycos et omnes alios cantus, maxime
irregulares, qui frequenter per totam manum discurrere volunt. Et
55 tunc necessarium est ut omnes v corde ipsius vielle corpori solido
affigantur nullaque a latere, ut aplicacionem digitorum queant
recipere. Sic tamen sint disposite secundum sonum ut easdem
claves per se constituant (*hand 3*: et hoc secundo modo temperandi
prima corda, scilicet bordunus, facit E et F per aplicacionem
60 indicis et medii) [*fol. 94r col. 1*] quas modo prime, et prima corda,
secunda, tertia et quarta sed non quinta que non unissona cum
quarta sed sesquitertia fieri dicitur, id est in g collocata superacuto.

Et tunc dicta corda quinta per applicacionem indicis faciet $\overset{a}{a}$;
medij retorti $\overset{b}{b}$; eiusdem sed naturaliter cadentis aliud $\overset{♮}{♮}$; per
65 applicacionem medici $\overset{c}{c}$; per applicacionem vero auricularis $\overset{d}{d}$.
De reliquis cordis sicut prius.

The *viella* is more highly valued than the *rubeba*, yet it ascends both more and less completely;[9] that is, according to how it is variously tuned by different players. For the *viella* may be tuned in three ways. It has, and must have, five strings. According to the first manner it is tuned as follows: the first string should make *D*; the second Γ; the third *G*—all among the *graves*,[10] and the fourth and fifth strings should form two unisons at *d* among the *acutae*. Then it will be able to ascend from *gamma ut* up to $\overset{a}{a}$ in the following way. We have said that the second strings makes Γ by itself; however, with the application of the first finger it will make *A*; of the second *B*; of the third *C*—all among the *graves*. The second string,[11] which is the *bordunus*[12] of the others (*hand 3*: which is the first of the *viella*) only makes *D*. This string, because it must be fixed outside the body of the *viella*, that is, to the side, escapes the contact of the fingers. The two notes which it omits, namely *E* and *F*, will be supplied by the fourth and fifth strings in unison.[13] The third string by itself makes *G*; by application of the first finger *a*; of the second finger bent *b*; of the same but naturally falling ♮; (*hand 2*: of the third [finger] high *c*). The fourth and fifth strings by themselves make high *d*; by the application of the first finger *e*; of the second *f*; of the third *g*, and of the little finger $\overset{a}{a}$. Such a *viella* as just described encompasses the material of all the modes.[14]

This is the first manner of tuning *vielle*.

Another [tuning] is necessary for secular songs[15] and for all others—especially irregular ones—which frequently wish to run through the whole hand. Then it is necessary that all the five strings of this *viella* are fixed to the real body of the instrument, not to the side, so that they may be able to receive the application of the fingers. However, they should be so arranged in pitch that they make the same notes as in the method of the first [*viella*] (*hand 3*: and in this second manner of tuning the first string, namely the *bordunus*, makes *E* and *F* by the application of the first and second finger). This is true of the first, second, third and fourth [strings], but not of the fifth, which is not in unison with the fourth but is said to make *sesquitertia* [4 : 3 ie a fourth], thus it is placed at *g* among the *superacutae*. Then the said fifth string will make $\overset{a}{a}$ by the application of the first finger; $\overset{b}{b}$ by the second finger bent; $\overset{♮}{♮}$ by the same naturally falling; by the application of the third finger $\overset{c}{c}$, and by the application of the little finger $\overset{d}{d}$. The remaining strings [produce stopped notes] as before.

Tertius modus oppositus est primo, eo scilicet, quod prima et
secunda corda facit Γ; tertia D; quarta et quinta c. Et in hoc
quoque modo tercio voces medie inveniuntur modo superius
70 prenotato (*hand 2*: sed non video quomodo b acutum formetur).

Quibus visis et memorie commendatis totam artem viellandi
habere poteris arte usui aplicata. Finaliter tamen est notandum
hoc quod in hac facultate est difficilius et solempnius meliusque,
ut scilicet sciatur cum unicuique sono ex quibus unaqueque
75 melodia contexitur cum bordunis primis consonanciis respondere,
quod prorsus facile est scita manu secundaria, que scilicet solum
provectis adhibetur et eius equante que in fine huius operis
habetur (*hand 3*: scilicet in pagina sequenti).

(*hand 3*: Quod D bordunus non debet tangi pollice vel arcu nisi
80 cum cetere corde arcu tactu faciunt sonos cum quibus bordunus
facit aliquam predictarum consonanciarum scilicet diapente,
diapason, diatessaron etc. Prima enim corda, scilicet superior
exterior, que dicitur bordunus, secundum primam temperacionem
facit D in gravibus, secundum terciam facit Γ, id est gamma. Per
85 manum autem sequentem scitur cum quibus litteris hae due
faciunt consonanciam).

APPARATUS CRITICUS

Title: lacking. Supplied from prologue list of chapter headings.
1 Ostensum] o *in margin,* superius] superius .s. *with* .s. *deleted. 2* in numeris]
in a numeris *with* a *deleted. 10* scilicet] scilicet *with following superfluous descender
deleted. 13* iuxta] iuxta *with following superfluous descender deleted.* immedi[t]ate]
in mediate. *14* aplicans] aplicans a *with* a *deleted. 15* clavis C fa ut] clavis El C
fa ut *with* El (E l[a mi]) *deleted. 20* immedi[t]ate] in mediate. *22* opus] opus
with following superfluous descender deleted. 23/4 aplicacione] aplicacoi/ne *with
second* i *deleted. 25* non] nōi *with* i *deleted. 26* facit] fac/cit. *28* cadentis, ♮ mi
quadrum] cadentis bmi ♮ mi quadrum] *with* bmi *deleted. 30* medici] medicit
with t *deleted. 34* a diversis] ad diversis. *37* secunda Γ] secunda Γ *with following
superfluous descender not deleted. 39* ā] a ā *with first* a *deleted. 40* secunda] secunda
with following superfluous descender deleted. 46 Tertia] tertiai *with second* i *deleted.
52* est] est u *with* u *deleted. 55* v] v c *with* c *deleted. 56* ut] ut a *with* a *deleted.*
62 collocata] collaocata *with first* a *deleted.* d *in left margin. 63* ā] ā A *with* A
deleted. 67 est primo] est primus primo *with* primus *deleted. 68* tertia] tertiam
with m *deleted.* hoc] hoc *with following superfluous descender deleted. 79* D] d.
84 D] d.

The third manner [of tuning] is the opposite of the first, by virtue of the fact that the first and second strings make Γ, the third D, and the fourth and fifth c.[16] In this third tuning the [stopped] notes in between are found in the manner discussed above (*hand 3*: but I do not see how b♮ may be formed).

Having reviewed these things and committed them to memory you will be able to encompass all the art of *viella* playing by joining art to practice. However, one thing must be finally noted, namely that which is most difficult, serious[17] and excellent in this art: to know how to accord with the *borduni* in the first harmonies any note from which any melody is woven. This is certainly easily known from the suitable second hand, which is only used by advanced players, and from its equivalent which is to be found at the end of this work (*hand 3*: that is to say on the following page).

(*hand 3*: Because the D *bordunus* must not be touched with the thumb or bow, unless the other strings touched by the bow produce notes with which the *bordunus* makes any of the aforesaid consonances namely fifth, octave and fourth etc.[18] For the first string, namely the upper outer one which is named *bordunus*, according to the first tuning makes D among the *graves*, and according to the third makes Γ, that is, *gamma*. By the following hand it may be known with which letters these two make consonance).[19]

COMMENTARY ON THE TRANSLATION

[1] This reference to *tetracordis . . . instrumentis* ('four-stringed . . . instruments') is puzzling, since this description fits neither the *rubeba* nor the *viella*. It is also noteworthy that Jerome's promise to deal with '*vielle* and such' implies rather more than he actually supplies. Both of these instances in which the chapter heading is not fully consonant with the content of the text suggest that, if this chapter was in circulation before Jerome, then it originally contained more (or at least somewhat different) material. Galpin (*Old English Instruments*, p. 61) seems to have taken the reference to four strings as an indication that the *rubeba* had double courses. Sibyl Marcuse's statement that this *rubeba* tuning is confirmed by Pierre Picard (*A Survey of Musical Instruments*, Newton Abbot and London, 1975, p. 484) is based upon an over-hasty examination of Coussemaker's edition; the twenty-eighth chapter of Jerome's *Tractatus de Musica* is not part of Pierre of Picard's *Ars Motettorum Compilata Breviter* (see the edition of F. Alberto Gallo, *Corpus Scriptorum de Musica*, 15 (1971), p. 11f.

As for the pitch of the tuning Werner Bachmann has notated Jerome's *C fa ut/G sol re ut* (nominally *c g*) as *c' g'* (*Origins of Bowing*, p. 134) This conflicts with his transcription of the *viella* tunings, and has presumably been done because *c g* is a lower pitch than Bachmann associates with instruments whose names are built upon *r–b* stems. Two suggestions may be made: (1) that the *rubeba* known to Jerome was actually tuned low like the two-stringed Moroccan *rabāb* (see Anthony Baines, 'Jerome of Moravia' in *FoMRHI Quarterly*, April, 1977, p. 25); (2) that Jerome wished to designate the *rubeba* pitch as being roughly a fifth above *viella* pitch (which was defined, for Jerome's purposes, by notational consideration—see above).

[2] Jerome's original Latin here alludes to a biblical passage, *Sapientia* II: 21.

[3] The aphorism '*in paucioribus via magna*', which is presumably intended to say something about the relative characteristics of *viella* and *rubeba*, is a mystery. It is not recorded in H. Walther, *Carmina Medii Aevi Posterioris Latina, Proverbia Sententiaeque Latinitatis Medii Aevi*, 5 vols., Göttingen, 1963–67, nor in J. Werner, *Lateinische Sprich-wörter und Sinnsprüche des Mittelalters*, Heidelberg, 1966. The *philosophus* should be Aristotle, but no likely source comes to mind. I am grateful to Dr David Rees for the conjecture that *via* should be *vis* (thus: 'in smaller things great strength'); this might then be an allusion to Plato, *Republic*, Bk. IV, where it is suggested that a small city may gain strength from its cohesion, whereas a large one may be disunited. Jerome would then be making a comparison between the virtues of

the compact, two-stringed *rubeba* which has the advantage of smallness, and those of the *viella*, a larger and more diversified instrument.

⁴ The use of the plural *vielle*, both here and in the chapter heading, clearly indicates that Jerome does not imagine all the *viella* tunings as *scordatura* for a single instrument and a single set of gut strings.

⁵ In view of the fact that *rubebe* seems to have been a new word in the French language when Jerome wrote (see *GSJ* XXX, p. 10) it is striking that he feels compelled to define the *rubeba* as 'a musical instrument' and to assure his readers that it is 'played with a bow'. Generally speaking he discusses the *rubeba* in terms of the obviously more familiar *viella* whenever he can. Thus we are told that the *rubeba* is bowed 'just as the *viella*'; that it must be grasped 'in the way that the *viella* must be held', and that the first finger must be applied naturally 'as much on the *rubeba* as on the *viella*'. Possibly this part of the treatise incorporates material originally written in a country where the *rubeba* was more familiar; Spain perhaps?

⁶ The translation 'in a natural position' is based upon my emendation of the manuscript *in mediate* (for *immediate*, 'immediately, without intermediary') to *immedi[t]ate* 'naturally, unstudied' which gives better sense (compare Jerome's insistence that fingers be placed down *naturaliter*). Since the interval of a tone is not accomplished by placing one finger *immediately* next to another, the emendation to *immedi[t]ate* seems best in line 20 also where the manuscript again has *in mediate*. If Jerome had wished to refer to such 'immediately' adjacent placement of fingers, he would surely have recommended it for the semitone rather than the tone.

⁷ Jerome is compelled to explain what he means here since he has already forbidden that the fingers be twisted when they are applied.

All Jerome's fingerings are diatonic; the index finger stops the first tone after the nut, the second finger stops the minor and major thirds, and the third finger stops the interval of a fourth. The little finger is only used on the highest string. All his stopped notes are *musica vera*; he specifies no stoppings that produce notes not found in the Guidonian hand.

⁸ In no case does Jerome exceed the resources of the first position.

⁹ This statement that the *viella* may sometimes have a more narrow compass than the *rubeba* presumably refers to *viella* tuning 3 (ΓΓ d c'c'), thus indicating that this tuning is a drone block ΓΓd with a melodic facility running from the subdominant of the chord to the tonic (c'–g'), giving it an effective melodic range of a fifth as opposed to the *rubeba*'s ninth.

¹⁰ The *graves* ('*low notes*'), the *acutae* ('high notes') and the *superacutae*

('above the high notes') are the three divisions of the gamut (Γ-G. a–g, $\overset{a}{\mathrm{a}}\overset{e}{\mathrm{e}}$).

[11] Jerome gets into a muddle here by referring to the first string on the fingerboard (Γ) and the lateral *bordunus* (D) as both being the 'second' string. Pierre de Limoges has sorted out the confusion with a marginal note.

[12] *Bordunus* is a word with an extremely complicated history. I have heeded the warning of Anthony Baines (*op. cit.*, p. 25) and resisted the temptation to translate it as 'drones' for this technique is not actually implied in the treatise.

[13] These notes are, of course, actually supplied an octave *higher*. This reflects Jerome's indifference to octave transposition which was certainly a common resource of medieval string players.

[14] This tuning certainly comprehends all the modes, since all the modal material is contained within an octave. However all the modes cannot be played if the instrumentalist restricts himself to the stopping positions which Jerome describes. This point may be simply demonstrated by placing the modal interval sequences below the sequence produced by the tuning:

Γ A B♭ B♮

G a b♭ b♮ c d e f g a

Notes of tuning	T	S	S	S	T	T	S	T	T	
Dorian	T	S	T	–	T	T	S	T		
Hypodorian	T	–	S	T	T	S	T	T		
Phrygian		S	T	–	T	T	S	T	T	
Hypophrygian				S	T	T	S	T	T	[T] beyond range
Lydian			T	–	T	T	S	T	T	[S] beyond range
Hypolydian				T	T	S	T	T	[T S] beyond range
Mixolydian	T	T	–	S	T	T	S	T		
Hypomixolydian	T	S	T	–	T	T	S	T		

[15] Here Jerome's Latin may be construed in two ways, both equally correct: (1) *laycos* may be taken as an adjective ('secular') governing *cantus*, thus the full phrase would be rendered 'another is necessary for secular songs'; (2) *laycos* may be taken as a noun ('laity') thus: 'another is necessary for the laity and all other types of song'. The difference between the two renderings is not, perhaps, as significant as it may first appear; Jerome describes this tuning as specially appropriate for secular music in one, and for secular musicians in the other. The most interesting implication of the Latin, however it is translated, is that secular melodies formed only a part of the *viella* repertory. The

Paris, Bibliothèque Nationale, MS. Lat. 16663, fol. 94.

PLATE XXIII

Fiddle player (the lateral bordunus *is clearly shown). New York, Pierpont Morgan Library, MS. 638, fol. 17r, illustration to Judges 21: 21. French (?Paris), 13c.*

special reference to lay music (or lay musicians) suggests that some of Jerome's material is relevant to the other social group implied by this distinction—the clergy, and to their music.

It is by no means clear what these 'irregular' melodies are that 'frequently wish to run through the whole hand', i.e. two octaves and a sixth in Jerome's day. The monophonic repertories of the period rarely exceed a twelfth and the polyphonic motets rarely exceed two octaves. Possibly Jerome is thinking of certain special performance techniques which involved rendering material in different registers, or to certain conventional preambles in which it was customary to exploit a wide range.

It should be noted that this tuning is reentrant and, given the likelihood that Jerome's Γ and G form an octave course, does not give an unbroken linear ascent throughout its compass. The instrument's sound picture would have been rich in octave ambiguities, concealed by the incorrect way the tuning has been presented in many modern works. This means that when the player ran through the compass of the instrument it sounded not thus:

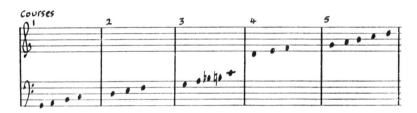

but thus:

courses
I 2 3 4 5
D ΓG d' g'

[16] This tuning is the 'opposite of the first' because it begins with ΓΓd, whereas the first began with dΓg.

[17] *solempnius* might be rendered in a variety of ways in addition to my 'more . . . serious'. 'More established' or 'more customary' would

also be possible, but neither of these convey the clearly superior character of the technique Jerome wishes to describe. 'Serious' implies a keen and studious devotion to the more artistic aspects of fiddling, and I take it that this is what Jerome means. One might also translate 'more eminent', and this suits the context.

[18] A discussion of this technique must, unfortunately, be reserved for treatment elsewhere.

[19] The hand in question is a normal Guidonian hand.

ACKNOWLEDGEMENTS

This article represents some of the results of six years interrupted work on Jerome, and during that time I have incurred many obligations. Nicholas Ostler, Bernard Barr and J. W. Binns read and checked the translation at various stages. I am myself responsible for any errors that remain. François Avril, Conservateur at the Bibliothèque Nationale, Paris, never failed to answer my queries promptly, personally and in detail. Professor Jos. Smits van Waesberghe, Dr Gaston Allaire, Dr Richard Rastall, Dr Ephraim Segerman and Prof. D. Randel answered many of my enquiries with encouraging letters representing a most generous sacrifice of their leisure. Editors of numerous unpublished Latin Dictionaries—too numerous to specify I fear—sent me their citations for *rubeba* and *viella*.

Above all I am grateful to Professor Howard Mayer Brown, with whom I corresponded on this subject during 1977.

Fourteenth-century Instruments and Tunings: a Treatise by Jean Vaillant? (Berkeley, MS 744)

IT has been widely assumed that only one medieval document deals with the tuning of stringed instruments: Jerome of Moravia's *Tractatus de Musica* (see my edition and translation in *GSJ* XXXII). However, there are numerous other sources of information, of which the so-called Berkeley Theory manuscript (hereafter *B*) is the most important.[1] This compendium of 14th-century theory contains drawings of a fiddle, a gittern, two harps and two psalteries with tunings written upon the strings in red (see Pls. II–V). As this article will attempt to show, it is the most comprehensive account of chordophonic tunings in Western medieval sources before the *De Inventione et Usu Musicae* of Tinctoris (? 1487; see *GSJ* III). Since this text has been generally overlooked by historians of instruments[2] a text and translation with commentary is well overdue; this article is an attempt to fill the gap.

THE DATE AND AUTHORSHIP OF THE MATERIAL

B consists of four separate treatises and a fragment of a fifth dealing with such matters as the Guidonian hand and *musica ficta* (1), discant progressions and tables of consonances (2), mensuration and ligatures (3), and intervals, the monochord and related topics (4).[3] The first three of these treatises form 'a cohesive trilogy of *musica practica*' (Ellsworth), but the fourth turns to speculative matters and incorporates a section on the evolution of the decachord *etc.* from the tetrachord (i.e. the addition of strings to the classical *cithara*). This material is partly illustrated by the drawings of Gothic instruments that form the basis of our study.

Treatises 1–3 originally circulated as a separate work. Two manuscripts of the 15th century contain these treatises but *not* treatise 4 and the material on instruments.[4] Further evidence is provided by MS. 70 (71) in the Universiteitsbibliotheek in Ghent, dating from 1503–4;[5] here it is treatise 4 which appears by itself, without treatises 1–3.

This division of material has a direct bearing upon the date of our material, for in *B* it is only treatises 1–3 that are dated. The closing lines of treatise 3 state that 'this book' (i.e. sections 1–3) was 'compiled' (*compilati*) at Paris in 1375,[6] but this has no bearing on the date of treatise 4. In our search for a dating for the material on instruments we must therefore pursue the question of authorship.

THE AUTHOR

The name of the composer Johannes Vaillant has several times been associated with the contents of *B*, apparently only because Vaillant is known to have been a music teacher active in Paris in the 14th century.[7] No evidence has been found which connects him directly with the treatises in the MS. However treatise 4 contains a possible clue to the author's identity which seems to have been hitherto overlooked. This clue takes the form of a puzzle built into verses at the start of treatise 4. In accordance with general medieval practice when verses are embodied in prose texts, these are written out as prose in *B*. Numerous initial letters are rubricated, and it is clear that in attempting to arrange the lines as poetry we must take our cue from these, even though it is possible that they have been muddled or tampered with during transmission of the text. If we follow the indications they provide and avoid enjambement (so that each line is a self-contained unit of sense) we may arrange them (as does Ellsworth) in the following way:

In omnibus requiem quesivi,
omne delectamentum in se habentem.
Hec requies mea in seculum seculi.
Hic habitabo, quoniam elegi eam,
ad quam meditatus sum a iuventute mea,
nomine precioso dicta,
tam novercam viciorum,
[quam]⁸ matrem leticie,
et sanitatis exordium.

O quam dulce commercium,
lucerna benivolencie,
innocencie rivulum,
vernantem rosarium,
concordie pinccrvam,
racionis florem,
irroratricem deliciorum,
ydeo de qua omne bonum possum
       dicere,
quam amplector,
per quam delector,
in deliciis affluens iocunditate.

This is an odd result. Some lines seem to scan roughly (the last four lines of the first column and the opening lines of the second) while others do not scan at all (the opening lines of the first column). I suggest that the first five lines of the first column (*In omnibus . . . iuventute mea*) are not poetry but a prose introduction, and that the verses begin with *nomine precioso dicta*, 'verses on the precious name', in line 6. From here until *racionis florem* in the second column (line 6) the lines seem to fall into an accentual, 4-stress pattern. Here is Ellsworth's translation (1, p. 135):

In everything I have sought rest, / which contains every delight. / May this give me rest forever. / Here I dwell, for I have chosen her, / on whom I have meditated from my youth, / saying her precious name, / as much the step-mother of the sinful / as the mother of joy, / and the source of discretion. /
Oh what sweet fellowship, / lamp of benevolence, / rivulet of innocence, / flourishing rose garden, / servant of reconciliation, / flower of reason, / wanderer in delights, / therefore of whom I can say everything good, / whom I embrace, / through whom I rejoice, / abounding in delights with joy.

Ellsworth construes the lines as a poem of praise addressed to the Virgin, and they are certainly that—at least for the greater part. But what is striking is the number of words in the text which are ambiguous and suggestive of another purpose being pursued at the same time. *Requies,* for example, does mean 'rest', but it may also be translated 'resting place',[9] so the author may be writing about his own 'resting place' as well as about Mary. Then we are told that this *requies* 'contains within itself every amusement' (*omne delectamentum in se habentem*), an assertion that should put us on our guard. The suggestion that some kind of riddling name concealment is involved becomes pronounced when the author claims that 'here I will live' (*Hic habitabo*) and refers to 'verses on the precious name' (*nomine precioso dicta*). Here is a translation which brings out these ambiguities:

> In everything I have sought a resting place,
> having in itself every amusement;
> this is my resting place for ever.
> Here I will live, for I have chosen such a one
> which I have mused upon since my youth:
> verses on the precious name.

Might this be an invitation to treat the lines as a puzzle revealing the name of the author?

It is tempting to look for an acrostic, the most favourite of medieval name-riddles, and whilst it is probably true that anyone who is determined to find an acrostic in a text will always find one, the following result is nonetheless striking:

Prose introduction

I n omnibus requiem quesivi *O* mne delectamentum in se habentem *H* ec requies mea in seculum seculi *H* ic habitabo quoniam elegi eam *A* d quam meditatus sum a iuventute mea (*N* omine precioso dicta) [*IOHHAN*]

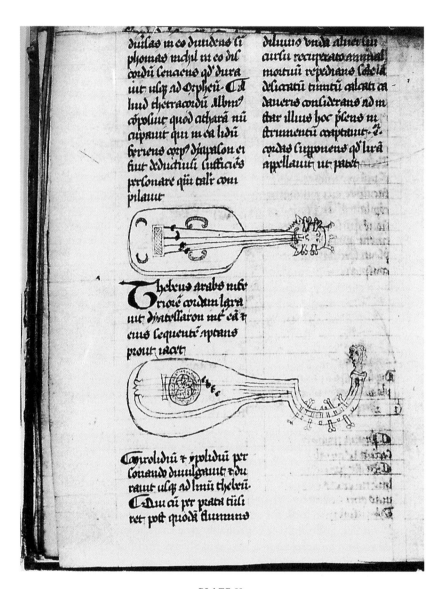

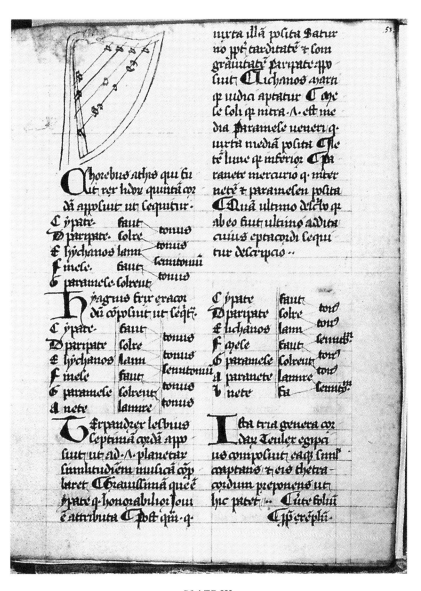

PLATE III

MS. as Pl. II, page 53

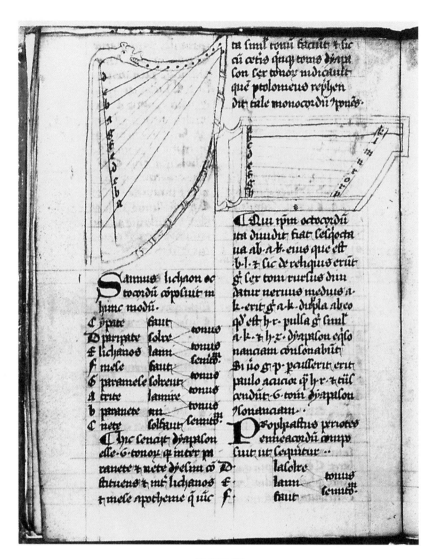

PLATE IV

MS. as Pl. II, page 54

PLATE V

MS. as Pl. II–IV, page 55

Verses (7 lines):

TAM NO	V	ERCAM VICIORUM
QUAM M	A	TREM LETICIE
ET SAN	I	TATIS EXORDIUM
O QUAM		DULCE COMMERCIUM
LUCERN	A	BENIVOLENCIE
INNOCE	N	CIE RIVULUM
VERNAN	T	EM ROSARIUM [*VAIANT*]

Thus we produce the result: IOHHAN VAIANT. In the verse acrostic I have treated the space between words as one unit; if the letters are counted as one unit also and added to the spaces, then the letters which make the name *VAIANT* are always the seventh unit in the line.

This is a remarkable, but not an entirely reassuring result. Firstly, I have been able to find no examples of *internal* acrostics dating from this period,[10] though such acrostics can be found in earlier Latin poetry.[11] Secondly, we have IOHHAN where we would expect IOHANN, and VAIANT without an -l- (but was it the -l- of *dulce* in line 4 which has become misplaced?). These are weighty objections, though I confess that in the final analysis my judgement is swayed by the remarkable coincidence of being able to produce from the lines something extremely close to Vaillant's name by a consistent principle. I do not wish to state that Jean Vaillant was the author of the instrument material in the Berkeley Theory MS., but it seems extremely likely.

We are well informed about the career of Johannes Vaillant. He came from Vendrest, not far from Paris, and was a priest at Pont-sur-Yonne in the diocese of Sens until 1352 when he entered the Papal chapel.[12] He died, possibly a victim of plague, in 1361. He is represented by five compositions in the Chantilly codex where his name is spelled *Vaillant* and *Vayllant*,[13] yet documentary sources from Avignon give his name as *Johannes Valhant* and *Johannes Valentis* with a single 'l'.[14] If Vaillant was the author of the *B* material on instruments, then the treatise must date from before 1361. One further point should be noted. We know that Vaillant ran a music school at Paris; could there be a connection between the studies of the school and the state of the instrument material as we have it in *B*? There are numerous corruptions in the *B* text of treatise 4; perhaps our version derives from a somewhat careless student's copy.

SOURCES OF THE INSTRUMENT MATERIAL IN *B*:
AN ARABIC LINK

In his opening paragraphs the author of treatise 4 claims that he has drawn material from Ignatius, Gregory and Ambrose, together with 'some things from others'; later in the text he refers the reader to Boethius, and a mysterious Jacobus de Montibus.[15]

I can find nothing in Ignatius, Gregory and Ambrose that could have inspired the account of instruments in *B*, and although Boethius is an important source for the treatise, the tunings written on the drawings of Gothic instruments in *B* do not come from the *De Musica*. Jacobus de Montibus is an enigma. If, as Ellsworth proposes (2, p. 199f), he is identical with Jacobus of Liège (the toponymic is not found in any medieval source) then he can be dismissed, for this Jacobus has nothing to say about Gothic stringed instruments that could have served as a source for the material in *B*.

What may the 'some things from others' have been which the author lists among his sources? The only ascertainable source for the material on instruments is the *De Musica* of Boethius; yet when we compare the material in *B* with the treatise of the great Roman theorist we seem to glimpse other sources, and quite exotic ones at that.

Boethius, following Greek authorities, attributes the addition of each *cithara* string to an historical or mythical personage.[16] These include *Hyagnis Phryx* (Íagnis, a mythical musician from Phrygia), *Prophrastus, Histiaeus Colophonius* (Istiéos, 5c-4c BC, a musician from Colophon), and *Timotheus Milesius* (Timótheos, d. *c*.360 BC).[17] Treatise 4 in *B* has all of them, but in addition several others of which three are of the first interest:

Albinus	[fiddle]	
Thebeus Arabs	[gittern]	'Thebeus the Arab'
Linus of Thebes	[harp]	
Teulex Egipcius	[harp]	'Teulex the Egyptian'
Psaltes Libius	[psaltery]	'The Libyan'

Let us briefly consider the Classical figures first, who are relatively unremarkable.

Albinus is probably the Albinus mentioned by Boethius and Cassiodorus.[18] This author (a consul in 335) wrote a treatise on music which has not survived[19] (a circumstance remarkably anticipated by Cassiodorus (d.*c*. 580) who told his monks at Vivarium what they should read were Albinus's work to be carried off by Barbarians.[20]) Boethius has a very brief chapter entitled 'The names with which Albinus referred to the strings [of a *cithara*]' (*Quibus nominibus nervos appella-*

verit Albinus),[21] and the author of the instrument material in *B* may have introduced Albinus from here. Linus of Thebes is mentioned as one of the inventors of music in the extremely influential *Etymologiae* of Isidore of Seville (d. 636).[22]

It is the remaining three persons who deserve our attention: each of them is linked with the Arab world. Thebeus, 'the Theban', is dubbed *Arabs*, 'the Arab'; Teulex is styled *Egipcius*, 'the Egyptian', and Psaltes, 'the player of plucked stringed instruments', is *Libius*, 'the Libyan'. If the Thebes implied by *Thebeus* is the famous city of Egypt, then all three persons are connected with North Africa. They are of the first importance, for three instruments in *B* (the gittern, the second harp and the psaltery) are associated with them. Could it be that our author was working with a Latin translation of an Arabic work on instruments? I know of no evidence that such texts (as distinct from Latin versions of Arabic writings on *music*) circulated in medieval Europe, but I would not care to argue *ex silentio* that such documents never existed.

But we must exercise caution here. The names in *B* are obviously not Arabic. Thebeus is an adjective traceable to Classical Latin and Psaltes is from Classical Latin via Greek. Teulex looks like Greek or pseudo-Greek. All the first names therefore derive from Graeco-Roman tradition and the persons Thebeus, Psaltes and Teulex are 'Arab', 'Libyan' and 'Egyptian' only by virtue of their toponymics.

Yet the Arabic connection of the *B* material cannot be dismissed quite as lightly as this. The fiddle tuning in the MS. is *c-d-g-c'* (relative pitch): a tone followed by two fourths. The gittern tuning is the same, but with the tone step at the bottom widened to a fourth (so *A-d-g-c'*). These tunings are shown in Ex. 1(*a*).

There are two curious points here. Firstly, the tuning of the gittern (three fourths) which is attributed in *B* to 'Thebeus the Arab', is the same as the prevailing tuning of the medieval Arabic lute. Secondly, the way the gittern tuning is derived from the fiddle tuning—by slackening the lower string and thus widening a tone to a fourth—is very similar to a modification of lute tuning carried out by the Arabs under Persian influence, probably in the seventh and eighth centuries A.D. According to Farmer[23] the original Arab accordatura was *c-d-g-a* (compare *B*: fiddle *c-d-g-c'*) with a tone step at the bottom and top. Then, under Persian influence, the Arabs adopted an accordatura of fourths by lowering the bottom course so that it sounded a fourth, not a tone with its neighbour. They also raised the top course. These developments may be set beside the change described in *B* so that the similarity becomes clear:

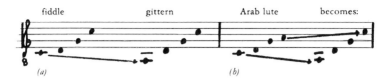

Ex. 1

Indeed the first part of the Islamic procedure can be described in words taken directly from *B*: '. . . the Arab loosened the lower string adjusting a fourth between it and its neighbour'.

A further piece of evidence, also suggestive of an Arabic connection, is the similarity between the drawings in *B* and a page of sketches in a 14th-century manuscript now in the Bibliothèque Nationale (reproduced in *GSJ* XXX, facing p. 32). This source, a compendium of scientific and musical material, was compiled in Paris *c.* 1362.[24] It derives from a background of learning in subjects such as geometry, astronomy, optics and mechanics where Arabic—and Greek *via* Arabic—influence was strong in medieval Europe. Indeed one of the treatises in the MS. (fols. 27v–29), the *Liber de Crepusculis*, is a translation of a work by the Arabic scholar Ibn al Haitam.

The Paris MS. and *B* share several instruments of similar form, as is readily apparent and need not be explained in detail here. However, the large psaltery-type instruments in both must be compared with particular care. They are unlike the majority of medieval zithers, though they are quite similar to one another:

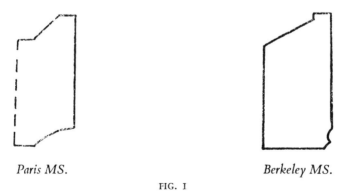

Paris MS.   Berkeley MS.

FIG. 1

The name written beside the instrument in the Paris MS. is particularly interesting: it is *canon*, probably derived from Arabic *qānūn*.

These two manuscripts can be linked on other grounds. The instruments in the Paris MS. appear at the end of the *Musica Speculativa* by Johannes de Muris, and they have surely been put there to illustrate the statement in the text that the monochord contains all instruments within itself (*hoc instrumentum omnia continet in se instrumenta . . . GS*, III, 283). Now I have already mentioned that the material on instruments in *B* is also found in the Ghent MS. of 1503–4, and there it is introduced with the heading *De diversis monocordis*, 'concerning various kinds of monochords'. In other words the rationale behind the instruments in the Ghent MS. is exactly the same as in the Paris copy of Johannes de Muris.

I do not believe that the history of the drawings in *B* can now be disentangled, though I am certain that it is bound up with the drawings in the Paris MS. mentioned above, which seems to derive from a background of study with an Arabic element. My summary of the situation would be roughly as follows. Treatise 4 in *B* with its material on instruments is a document of speculative writing, and its author— very probably the composer Jean Vaillant—may well have known the *Musica Speculativa* of Johannes de Muris. At some stage in the textual transmission of the *Musica Speculativa* (completed 1323) drawings were added at the end of one or more copies to illustrate the statement in the text that the monochord contains all instruments within itself. The author of *B* treatise 4 saw these drawings and based his own upon them.

At this point something fascinating and obscure comes into the story. The author seems to have used a work with fragments of Arab material on instruments embedded in it. This appears to have (a) included the story relating how the Arabs modified the accordatura of their lute under Persian influence (b) possibly contained the tuning of the medieval Islamic lute, and (c) included some, or all of the persons mentioned in *B*: Teulex the Egyptian, Psaltes the Libyan, and Thebeus the Arab. What was this document? Perhaps it was a translation of an Arabic work made in Italy or Spain and circulating amongst the scholars of Paris in the early 14th century.

The relationship of the materials we have been discussing is presented, in simplified form, in Fig. 2 opposite.

THE ARRANGEMENT OF THE TUNINGS IN THE TEXT

At the beginning of his treatise, the author proposes four topics for consideration: (1) the division of the tone; (2) the 'harmonic body' (*corpus armonicum*); (3) tetrachords, pentachords, etc. (the instrument

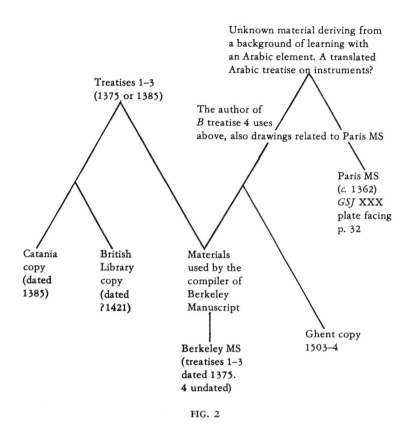

Unknown material deriving from a background of learning with an Arabic element. A translated Arabic treatise on instruments?

Treatises 1–3 (1375 or 1385)

The author of *B* treatise 4 uses above, also drawings related to Paris MS

Paris MS (*c.* 1362) *GSJ* XXX plate facing p. 32

Catania copy (dated 1385)

British Library copy (dated ?1421)

Materials used by the compiler of Berkeley Manuscript

Ghent copy 1503–4

Berkeley MS (treatises 1–3 dated 1375. 4 undated)

FIG. 2

material appears here, and (4) monochords. The first two subjects are dealt with in a summary fashion, and tetrachords etc. receive extended treatment as follows:

Strings	Associated with	Source	Illustration		
tetrachord 1	Mercury	[Boethius]	diagram		
tetrachord 2	Albinus		FIDDLE	}	Pl. II
tetrachord 3	THEBEUS ARABS		GITTERN		
tetrachord 4	Linus of Thebes	[Isidore]	HARP 1		
pentachord	Chorebus Athis	[Boethius]	diagram	}	Pl. III
hexachord	Hyagnis Frix	[Boethius]	diagram		
heptachord	Terpandrex	[Boethius]	diagram		
	TEULEX EGIPCIUS		HARP 2		
octochord	Samius Lichaon	[Boethius]	PSALTERY 1	}	Pl. IV
enneachord	Prophrastus Periotes	[Boethius]	diagram		
decachord	Estieus Colonius and	[Boethius]		}	Pl. V
	PSALTES LIBIUS		PSALTERY 2		

THE TEXT

This is taken from photographs of *B*; the square brackets around a word (e.g. [*lidium*]) indicate that a reading has been taken from the Ghent manuscript. In these cases the rejected *B* reading is indicated at the foot of the text. MS. *u* for consonantal *v* and *v* for vocalic *u* have been normalised (thus *laxavit* not *laxauit*). Punctuation has been introduced according to modern principles but capitalisation has been left as it stands in the manuscript. MS contractions have been expanded silently. *In the text tunings are printed with the letters as they appear in the MS.* For translation see facing page.

[*Pl. II, column a, line 4f*] Aliud thetracordum Albinus composuit quod citharam nuncupavit, qui in ea [lidium] feriens corpus, dyapason ei fuit deductivum sufficiens personare, quam taliter compilavit:

FIDDLE
[*Four strings c d g c in ascending order of pitch.*]

5 Thebeus arabs inferiorem cordam laxavit, dyatessaron inter eam et eius sequentem aptans, prout iacet:

GITTERN
[*Four strings e b f c in ascending order of pitch. This series must either be read in reverse with accidentals (c f b♭ e♭), or emended to a d g c which is the series the text requires. See commentary.*]

Mixolidium et ypolidium personando divulgavit, et duravit usque ad linum thebeum.

    Qui cum per prata transiret, post quodam fluminis [*Plate II, column b*] diluvio (unda alvei sui cursu recuperato), animal mort-
10 uum [reperiens], sole iam desiccatum, [tinnitum] calcati cadaveris considerans, ad instar illius hoc presens instrumentum coaptavit, quattuor cordas superponens, quod liram appellavit, ut patet:

HARP 1 (no tuning)
[*In the following sections there are no drawings of instruments; Chorebus athis adds the fifth string; Hyagnis frix adds the sixth, and Terpandrex lesbius adds the seventh to produce the heptachord C D E F G a b.*]

TRANSLATION

(*In this, pitches of tunings are converted to Helmholtz notation with relative pitch.*)

Albinus put together another tetrachord which he called the *cithara*; striking the Lydian system upon it, it sufficed to play the derived diapason with [the *cithara*] which he had put together in this way:

FIDDLE — Pl. II
[c–d–g–c']

Thebeus the Arab loosened the lower string, adjusting a fourth between it and its neighbour, as here:

GITTERN — Pl. II (lower)
[*written: e b f c* for *A–d–g–c'*. See commentary]

He spread the mixolydian and the hypolydian in his playing, and [the arrangement] lasted until Linus of Thebes.

As he [Linus] was crossing the plains after a certain river had flooded (the tide of its channel having regained its proper course) he found a dead animal now dried by the sun and, pondering upon the ringing sound of the quashed corpse, he immediately put this instrument together as if in the fashion of it, placing four strings upon it and calling it *lyra*:

HARP I — Pl. III
[No tuning]

[*Pl. III, column b, line 16f*] Ista tria genera cordarum Teulex egipcius
15   composuit, eaque simul coaptans, et eis thetracordum preponens
ut hic patet (verte folium propter exemplum):

HARP 2
[*Pl. IV. 11 strings a b c d e f g a b c d in ascending order of pitch.*]

[*No drawings of instruments in the material immediately following.
Samius lichaon adds the eighth string to produce the scale C D E F G
a b c. A diagram of a psaltery-like instrument follows here, but it has no
tunings; it is used to demonstrate Ptolemy's proof that six tones slightly
exceed an octave.*]

PSALTERY 1 (no tuning)
[*Prophrastus periotes adds the ninth string to produce the scale D E F
g a b c d e.*]

[*Pl. V, column a, line 1f*] Decacordum estieus colonius compilavit,
apponens concavatum quod Psaltes libius sculpsit hoc modo:

PSALTERY 2
[*Five quadruple courses with two pairs of like pitch within each course:
aabb ccdd eeff ggaa ♮♮cc in ascending order of pitch. Accidentals indicate
variant tunings leading to almost complete chromaticism. See commentary.*]

[T]himo milesius undecimam, que super hypaten et paripaten
20   sunt addite.

TEXTUAL NOTES   2 *lidium*] B *lidum*   11 *reperiens*] B *repedians*
tinnitum] B *timitum*

Teulex of Egypt put together these three kinds of strings (?), adjusting them together at the same time and putting a tetrachord before them as here (turn the folio for the example):

HARP 2 — Pl. IV
[*A B c d e f g a b c′ d′*]

PSALTERY 1 — Pl. IV
[No tuning[

Estieus colonius produced the decachord, adding the instrument which the Libyan player of plucked string-instruments fashioned in this manner:

PSALTERY 2 — Pl. V
[*AABB ccdd eeff ggaa* ♮♮*c′c′*]

Thimo milesius supplied the eleventh; these are added above at hypate and parhypate.

COMMENTARY ON THE TEXT

Fiddle. The first instrument [Pl. II, top] has characteristics of the medieval fiddle: a roughly rectangular body with rounded corners, C-shaped soundholes (two pairs) arranged symmetrically around the string band, and a relatively short neck. The frontal string-holder is curious, for end-pin attachment with tail-piece or sling is a diagnostic characteristic of medieval Western bowed instruments (though exceptions occur), while the string-holder is a distinctively Byzantine feature. The pegs are intended to be sagittal (since their shafts are not visible beyond the point where they meet the surface of the board), yet the device of the decorative head may be an echo of a lateral peg-box; I have not seen a peg-*board* decorated in this way in any source, though such ornament was a standard feature of peg-*boxes* (see the gittern in Pl. II). On the whole, this is a somewhat 'mixed' instrument with marked Eastern characteristics, for in medieval contexts the combination of string-holder and lateral pegbox is found on Byzantine bowed instruments but not, as far as I am aware, on occidental ones.[25] The descent of the material in *B* thus seems all the more complicated, and involvement at some stage of transmission with materials originating outside the West is likely.

The tuning, which is attributed to Albinus, is written c d g c (see Ex. 1*a*). This is an unlikely tuning for a flat-bridged bowed instrument, but it might well be used on a round-bridged one.

Gittern. This (Pl. II lower) is similar to many instruments in pictorial sources. Four courses seems to have been standard for the 14th-century gittern (*GSJ* XXX, p. 18). Here they are clearly double, for there are eight pegs.

The tuning lettered on the instrument is not consonant with the text, but fortunately the author's intention is clear. Thebeus the Arab loosened the lowest string of the previous fiddle tuning so that it sounded a fourth with its neighbour (see Ex. 1*a*). Since the fiddle tuning is *c-d-g-c'* (Helmholtz notation, relative pitch), we expect a pile of fourths on the gittern: *A-d-g-c'*. Instead we find, as written, *e-b-f-c*. This must be wrong, for the series opens with a fifth, and not a fourth as required by the text. In the Ghent copy (where this tuning is omitted) the instrument corresponding to the gittern (a four-course lute) is shown with the pegbox on the *left* of the picture, not on the right as in *B*. If we leave the tuning as its stands in *B* but rotate the instrument through 180 degrees, then the MS. *e-b-f-c* becomes, in ascending order on pitch, *c-f-b-e*, which gives us the initial fourth we require and, if we assume B♭ and E♭, provides the expected pile of fourths. I suggest that somewhere along the line of textual transmission the conversion of the fiddle tuning to the gittern tuning, which should have followed process (a), followed process (b) [Ex. 2].

(a)   (b)

EX. 2

This tuning in fourths, as noted above, is identical with the prevailing tuning of the medieval Arab ʼ*ūd*, and there can be little doubt that gitterns were disseminated into Northern Europe from Southern areas such as Italy and Spain where Arabic influence was strong (cf. *GSJ* XXX, p. 10). Gitterns are rare in Northern iconographical sources before the later 13th century, but small, piriform plucked instruments with pegboxes can be found in Islamic pictorial sources of an appreciably earlier date.

Harp 1. This first harp (Pl. III, upper) has only four strings, with enigmatic letters written upon them. These are found elsewhere in the manuscript, and I believe that their importance is considerable though they cannot be discussed here (a separate study has been devoted to them).[26]

Harp 2. Fortunately the second harp in the manuscript (Pl. IV, above) is straightforward. Its eleven strings are tuned to a diatonic series MS: *a b c d e f g a b c d*. The number of strings has probably been reduced for ease of drawing; Machaut mentions twenty-five and Gerson (d. 1429) twenty.[27] The design of the harp has a late 14th-century look and is particularly reminiscent of Italian instruments. Pl. VI shows a very similar example from a Lombardy model-book of the late 14th century (note the zoomorphic head and the 'binding' design on the pillar).

Psaltery 1. This (Pl. IV, right) has no tunings; the letters of the alphabet placed at the extremes of the strings are points of reference used in the exposition (written around the drawing) of Ptolemy's proof, repeated by Boethius, that six tones slightly exceed an octave, i.e. $(\frac{9}{8})^6 : 2$, which gives the Pythagorean comma.

By far the most interesting feature of this drawing is the powerful suggestion of a keyboard housing on the left-hand face of the instrument. No keyboard is shown, but nonetheless the form of the instrument looks curiously as though it is designed to accommodate one. It is also noteworthy that the longest strings are on the 'correct' side for a keyboard instrument. In the early-16th century Ghent copy, keys *are* shown, and the instrument is labelled *clavicembalum*. Unfortunately we cannot tell whether the keys are an authentic feature which has been lost in *B*, or whether they were added in the Ghent manuscript (or its model) at a time when keyboard instruments were well known.

Psaltery 2 (Pl. V, left) is a standard pig-snout instrument. The strings are arranged in bands of four—a feature sometimes seen in other pictorial sources—but each band is actually divided into pairs of identical pitch:

FIG. 3

There are therefore five quadruple courses producing ten notes. This is the decachord referred to in the text, and the psaltery has obviously been placed at this point because a ten-stringed psaltery is mentioned in psalm 32: 2 (*AV* 33: 2). The sharps and flats written between the courses are a puzzling feature of the drawing. Each sign appears at the end of a line extending half-way across the body of the instrument. These can hardly be octave strings (which are shown on some psalteries)[28] since they extend too far up the instrument's compass. The sequence of pitches they create, taken together with the course-pitches, is: a b [♯] c d [♭] e f [♯] g a [♭] ♮ c [♯]

The only explanation I can offer is that these accidentals are intended to indicate *scordatura* or changes of tuning. Thus the diatonic series might be extended in the following way:

Basic a b c d e f g a ♮ c
Altered b♮ e♭f♯ b♭ c♯

If we regard the basic series here as a C major octave with two notes below, then we can see how these alterations would be useful. The b♮ (in both octaves) would provide a sharpened leading note, and the e♭ the minor third. F♯ is, of course, the most common chromatic inflection in the music of the 14th century.

SUMMARY OF TUNINGS

Instrument	Notation in MS.	Helmoltz Notation (relative pitch)
Fiddle	*c-d-g-c*	*c-d-g-c'*
Gittern [should be as fiddle with bottom string a fourth from its neighbour]	*e-b-f-c*	read *c-f-b♭-e♭'* [MS. series reversed] or *A-d-g-c'*

PLATE VI

Bergamo, Town Library MS. Δ, VII, 14 (end of 14c) folio 3ᵛ (a model book).
Lombardy. Compare the harp in Pl. IV

Harp 1	no tuning	
Harp 2	a b c d e f g a b c d	*A B c d e f g a b c' d'*
Psaltery 1	no tuning	
Psaltery 2	aabb ccdd eeff ggaa ♮♮cc	*AABB ccdd eeff ggaa ♮♮c'c'*
	with chromatic inflexions:	♭♮ ♭♮♯ ♭♮ ♯ *AABB ccdd eeff ggaa ♮♮c'c'*

ACKNOWLEDGMENTS

I am most grateful to Vincent Duckles of the Music Dept. of the Library at the University of California, Berkeley, for permission to reproduce four pages of MS. 744; to John Emerson, also of the University of California, for checking a point with the original MS. at my request; to John Griffith of Jesus College, Oxford, who examined my explanation of the Latin acrostic, and to David Fallows who, as always, made many helpful suggestions.

Above all I wish to acknowledge my debt to Oliver Ellsworth, whose fine thesis on the Berkeley MS. has been my point of departure throughout.

NOTES

1 Library of the University of California, Berkeley, MS. 744 (*olim* Phillipps 4450).
It was acquired by the 19th-century bibliophile Sir Thomas Phillipps from an unknown source (see A. N. L. Munby, *Phillipps Studies*, 5 vols., Cambridge 1951–60, III, p. 156, and *Catalogus Librorum Manuscriptorum in Bibliotheca Thomae Phillipps Bart AD 1837*, MS. 4450). The MS. was sold by Sotheby's on 30 November 1965 (lot 19), but a copy was deposited in the British Library (*Register of Microfilms and other Photocopies in the Department of Manuscripts British Library*, List and Index Society, Special Series 9 (1976) m/775 (2)). There is a description and inventory of the MS. in R. L. Crocker, 'A new source for medieval music theory', *Acta Musicologica*, 39 (1967), pp. 161–171. See also M. Bent, 'A postscript on the Berkeley theory MS.' *Acta Musicologica*, 40 (1968), p. 175. There is a text and translation of the source in Oliver Bryant Ellsworth, *The Berkeley Manuscript* (olim *Phillipps 4450*): *A Compendium of Fourteenth-Century Music Theory*, D.Phil. dissertation, University of California, 1969 (University Microfilms International order number 7013044).

2 E. van der Straeten (*The History of the Violin*, 2 vols., 1933, I, p. 15) is the only organologist to have used it, as far as I am aware. However he did not know the material from the Berkeley MS. itself; his reference to a '14th-century MS. treatise on stringed instruments in the library of Gand (Belgium)'

shows that he used Ghent Universiteitsbibliotheek MS. 70 (71), written in 1503–4 at the Abbey of St. Bavo in Ghent (RISM, *Theory of Music*, I, p. 65). Folios 63r to 70r of this MS. contain a version of the instrument material in *B*.

3 A detailed inventory of the different sections is given in Crocker, *op. cit.*, and Ellsworth, *op. cit.*, *passim*.

4 These MSS. are: (1) Catania Bibliotheche Riunite Civica e Antonio Ursino Recupero D.39, fols. 24v–30r (see F. Alberto Gallo, 'La Tradizione dei Trattati Musicali di Prosdocimo de Beldemandis', *Quadrivium*, 6 (1964), p. 71f; (2) British Library Reference Division MS. Add. 23220 (see Bent, *op. cit.*).

5 See note 2.

6 I am most grateful to John Emerson of the University of California, Berkeley, for sending me a facsimile of these lines. They run as follows (italicised letters indicate expansion of MS. contractions): . . . *per hoc* sit finis hu*ius* libri com / pilati parisius Anno a / natiuitate do*mini* .M°. ccc° / Septuagesimo quinto / die duodecima mensis / Ianuarij .

7 Ellsworth, *op. cit.*, 2, p. 213.

8 The *quam* (also supplied by Ellsworth) is clearly required by the *tam* in the preceding line; it is an adverbial correlative construction.

9 See Lewis and Short, *A Latin Dictionary*, sv. *requies*.

10 Initial acrostics, of course, are abundant at this date. Let the example of Jacques de Liège suffice (R. Bragard, 'Le Speculum Musicae du Compilateur Jacques de Liège', *Musica Disciplina*, 7 (1953), p. 82).

11 See *Monumenta Germaniae Historica, Poetarum* 5, p. 381 for an example. Here the internal acrostic is formed by letters no. 14, 15, 16, 16, 12, 16 and so on in an irregular manner.

12 See Ursula Günther, 'Johannes Vaillant', in H. Becker and R. Gerlach (eds.), *Speculum Musicae Artis: Festgabe für Heinrich Husmann zum 60 Geburtstag*, Munich, 1970, p. 171f.

13 See Gilbert Reaney, 'The Manuscript Chantilly Musée Condé 1047', *Musica Disciplina* 8 (1954), p. 79.

14 Günther, *op. cit.*, *passim*.

15 Ellsworth, *op. cit.*, 1, p. 77–8. A Iacobus de Monte Iudaico (a Spanish author) was active *c.* 1321 (see M. C. Diaz y Diaz, *Index Scriptorum Latinorum Medii Aevi Hispanorum*, Madrid, 1959, number 1993) but there is nothing to connect him with the Jacobus de Montibus mentioned in *B* so far as I know.

16 Text in G. Friedlein, *A.M.T.S. Boetii De institutione arithmetica libri duo, De institutione musica libri quinque*, Leipzig, 1867 (reprinted Frankfurt, 1966) p. 205ff.

17 On these persons see Solon Michaelides, *The Music of Ancient Greece An Encyclopaedia*, 1978, *passim*.

18 For Boethius's reference see Friedlein, *op. cit.*, p. 199, and for the Cassiodorus passage see R. A. B. Mynors ed., *Cassiodori Senatoris Institutiones*, corrected ed., 1961, p. 149.

19 See Günther Wille, *Musica Romana*, Amsterdam, 1967, p. 599f.

20 Mynors, *op. cit.*, p. 149.

21 Friedlein, *op. cit.*, p. 218.

22 W. M. Lindsay ed., *Isidori Hispalensis Episcopi Etymologiarum*, 2 vols., 1911, I, III: xvi.

23 H. G. Farmer, *An Old Moorish Lute Tutor*, Glasgow, 1933, p. 25f.

24 MS. Lat. 7378a, fol. 45v. For a catalogue and inventory of the MS. see Ulrich Michels, ed., *Johannes de Muris Notitia Artis Musicae*, American Institute of Musicology, *Corpus Scriptorum de Musica*, 17 (1972), pp. 24–31.

25 See Werner Bachmann, The Origins of Bowing, trans. N. Deane, 1969, p. 39f. There is an important discussion of these points in Laurence Picken, *Folk Musical Instruments of Turkey*, 1975, p. 317f.

26 See Christopher Page, 'French lute-tablature in the 14th-century?', *Early Music*, July 1980.

27 See Karl Young, ed., 'The *Dit de la Harpe* of Guillaume de Machaut', in H. M. Peyre ed., *Essays in Honor of Albert Feuillerat*, Yale Romanic Studies, xxii, 1943, p. 1f, and Christopher Page, 'Early 15th-century instruments in Jean de Gerson's Tractatus de Canticis', *Early Music*, 6 (1978), p. 342 (column b).

28 As for example on the instrument shown in Memlinc's famous triptich (see J. Montagu, *The World of Medieval and Renaissance Musical Instruments*, 1976, colour plate 8; and Edward L. Kottick, 'The Memling "Angel Musicians" Psaltery', *FOMRHI Quarterly*, 15 (April, 1979), comm. 203).

The 15th-century lute:
new and neglected sources

1 Lutenist with singers. Oxford, St Hilda's College, MS 1 (Dutch, late 15th-century), f.55v

It was the period of Dufay (*d* 1474) that saw the development of the 'classic' lute: a fretted, finger-plucked instrument, tuned in fourths around a third, used for polyphonic as well as monophonic playing, and associated with its own system of notation. These innovations rested upon some two hundred years of lute playing in Europe, yet many makers and players still feel that the history of the Western lute really begins with the first decades of the 16th century.[1]

In the hope of casting some light upon these neglected years of lute playing I have assembled an anthology of new and neglected sources for the history of the lute before 1500,[2] together with some well-known but misinterpreted material such as the passages from Tinctoris' *De Inventione et Usu Musicae*. All of the information is practical, pertaining to such matters as the physical characteristics of the lute, its tuning, repertory, and social position.

A mid-15th-century description of the lute

In his *Liber Viginti Artium* (*c* 1460) the Jewish scholar Paulus Paulirinus of Prague describes a *cithara* which appears to be a lute:[3]

[C]ithara est instrumentum musicum communiter [sejunctum][4] ceteris propter sonorum suorum subtilitatem, habens quinque choros cordarum semper duplatas et novem ligaturas in collo, faciens sonorum varietates digitorum tamen registracione, cuius concavum pectoris clibanum habet officium, foramen vero oris; collum vero habet similitudinem canne pulmonis, super quod digiti perambulantes habent officium epigloti; percussio autem cordarum habet similitudinem penularum pulmonis a quibus vox efflatur, sed corde nervales gerunt lingue et officium quibus vox formatur. Citarista autem habet officium intellectus registrantis cantum.

The lute is a musical instrument which is generally [kept apart] from others on account of the delicacy of its sound. It has five courses of strings, always double, and nine frets on the neck making the distinctions of notes with the application of the fingers. Its hollow vessel performs the office of the [human] chest; the rose [performs the office] of the mouth; the neck [of the lute] resembles the human windpipe; the fingers running over it perform the office of the epiglottis; the striking of the strings is similar to the covering of the lungs by which the voice is blown out, but the gut strings perform the task of the tongue with which the voice is articulated. The lutenist performs the task of playing the music intelligently.

In another section of his treatise Paulus comments

Reprinted from *Early Music* 9 (1981), pp. 11–21. By permission of Oxford University Press.

that the psaltery (*psalterium*) is 'played with a quill held in the hand, like the lute' (*cum penna percutitur tenta in manu, uti cithara*).[5] From this we learn that c1460 Paulus associated the lute with plectrum playing; his account also provides the earliest literary evidence we have in the West for the pairing of lute strings.

Techniques of performance

A great deal of our knowledge about the 15th-century lute is derived from the printed treatise *De*

3 Two lutenists (one clearly singing) performing with a singer at a meal. From G. Caorsin, *De Casu Regis Zyzymy* (Ulm, 1496)

Inventione et Usu Musicae by Johannes Tinctoris, probably published at Naples (?1481-3).[6] In view of the importance of this work it is a matter of some urgency to distinguish what Tinctoris actually says from what has been attributed to him.

Firstly, Tinctoris does not say that finger plucking was a new technique,[7] nor, as far as I can discern, does he imply as much:

Et hanc [collum] sonitor manu sinistra non modo sustinet, verum etiam digitorum ipsius attactu, chordas deprimit et elevat. Altera vero, aut digitis ejus aut plectro, chordas ipsas percutit.

The player's left hand not only supports [the neck of the lute]; it also raises and lowers the strings by means of the contact of the fingers. The other hand strikes these same strings, either with the fingers or with a plectrum.

2 Lutenist (? with singer) plucking with the fingers and reading from a book of music. The music appears to have five lines with underlay and clefs. Detail from an engraving by Alart du Hameel (end of 15th century). From M. Lehrs, *Geschichte und kritischer Katalog des deutschen, niederländischen und französischen Kupferstichs im XV Jahrhundert*, 9 vols. (Vienna, 1908-34), Textband 7, pp. 219f; Tafelband 7, Tafel 204

Secondly, Tinctoris does not say that the lutenist's technique of decorating the top lines of chansons was an improvised one;[8] he says only that players encrusted top lines with *superinventiones*, or 'things found above'. The passage runs:

Siquidem nonnulli associati supremam partem cujusvis compositi cantus cum admirandis modulorum superinventionibus adeo eleganter eo personant, ut profecto nihil prestantius. Inter quos Petrus bonus Herculis Ferrarie ducis incliti lyricen (mea quidem sententia) ceteris est preferendus.
Alii (quod multo difficilius est) soli cantus non modo duarum partium, verum etiam trium et quatuor artificiosissime promunt.

Some teams play the top part of any polyphonic song you please with wondrous decorative figures composed upon it, so very elegantly that nothing is more excellent. Among whom Pietrobono lutenist to the renowned duke of Ferrara is, in my opinion, to be preferred before all others.

Others do what is much more difficult, to play a composition alone not only in two parts, but also in three and four in a most artful manner.

The tuning of the lute

Tinctoris also gives an account of lute tuning which is well known, but there are three other 15th-century

5 English instructions for tuning a lute, with other miscellaneous jottings. Cambridge, Trinity College, MS 0.2.13 (English; this section last decade of the 15th century), f.97v

4 Angel lutenist using a quill, clearly shown to be cut into a 'nib'. Detail from an engraving of the Madonna and Child with musician angels by the Master of the Death of Mary (Netherlands, 1430-40). From M. Lehrs, *Kritischer Katalog*, Textband 1, pp. 278f; Tafelband 1, Tafel 34

accounts of the subject, one of which (*a*) has been published but is generally unknown, and two more (*b* and *c*) which have been hitherto overlooked.

a. Cambridge, Trinity College, MS 0.2.13
Folios 77-99 of the manuscript compose a paper notebook compiled within the reign of Henry VII (1485-1509) which contains miscellaneous materials.[9] There are recipes of various kinds, and on f.94 there begins a series of documents in Latin and English which amounts to a small, private formulary. One on f.94 is headed 'The fourme how warauntz be made', and other documents transcribed into the manuscript include the *forma* for letters of attorney and for letters of obligation.

Folio 97v of the manuscript (illus. 5) seems to have been arranged with some care. It focuses upon literary and musical interests, and at the head of the page are four *Versus boni*. There is also a list of the eight psalm-tones in stave notation, complete with the solmization syllables appropriate to each (*re la*, etc.). A list of the seven Liberal Arts follows, and next a pair of Latin lines, beginning *lacte lava vinum*, accompanied by a neume (a punning abbreviation for *nota*). Finally there is a list of the seven sacraments.

Below the commentary on the moralizing Latin lines are four lines of Middle English headed 'To sette a lute', which have obviously been deliberately placed on this page of cultural and 'learned' concerns.

The date when these instructions were copied out cannot be determined with any degree of certainty, though they must date from the reign of Henry VII. Fortunately the documents gathered in the manuscript are dated, and therefore a reasonable *terminus post quem* can be established. The earliest date (with which we need not concern ourselves) is 1465 (f.96v), and the latest is 3 September 1493 (f.95, two folios before the lute instructions). The lines on how to set a lute were probably copied some time after 3 September 1493, but before 1509, the end of Henry VII's reign.[10] The text of the instructions reads:[11]

To sette a lute
Loke that there be .a. Trebill. Seconde trebill. Meene. Tenor/and basse . The seconde trebill to be sett a iiij[te] from the trebill/The meene a iiij[te] from the seconde trebill. The tenor a iij[de] / from the meene. And the Basse a iiij[te] from the tenor.

This is a tuning for a five-course lute with the strings referred to by English names not recorded in any other Middle English document with reference to the lute.[12] The intervals (from lowest to highest) are: fourth-third-fourth-fourth (relative pitch: *c f a d' g'*).

b. Nebrija's *Vocabulario Español-Latino*
A new source for the tuning of the 15th-century lute is Elio Antonio de Nebrija's *Vocabulario Español-Latino* published at Salamanca, possibly in 1495.[13] Nebrija defines the word *cuerda* ('string') five times, with the aid of the Greek string terminology (*nete, paranete* etc) common in medieval Latin treatises on music. These five definitions amount to a tuning for a five-course lute (illus. 6):

Cuerda de laud primera.nete.es.
Cuerda cerca de aquesta. paranete.es.
Cuerda de arriba o bordon. hypate.es.
Cuerda cerca de aquesta.parhypate.es.
Cuerda de medio.mese chorda.

Cuerda de laud primera.	nete. es.
Cuerda cerca de aquesta.	paranete. es.
Cuerda de arriba o bordon.	hypate. es.
Cuerda cerca de aquesta.	parhypate. es.
Cuerda de medio.	mese chorda

These may be translated:

First string of the lute	nete [hyperbolaion]	*a'*
String beside it	paranete [diezeugmenon]	*d'*
String above, or *bordon*	hypate [hypaton]	*B*
String next to it	parhypate [meson]	*f*
Middle string	mese	*a*

If we assemble these into their proper order we have the following arrangement (where course 1 is the highest course):

courses	1		nete	*a'*
	2		paranete	*d'*
	3		mese	*a*
	4		parhypate	*f*
	5		hypate	*B*

7 Angel lutenist with other musicians. From the translation of Bartholomaeus Anglicus' *De Proprietatibus Rerum* by J. Corbichon, revised by P. Ferget (*Proprietes des choses*, Lyons, 1491). Detail from prefatory woodcut to Book 2, on God and the angels. Reproduced by permission from Oxford, Bodleian Library, Auct. I.Q.3.35

8 Angel lutenist with plectrum. Detail from an engraving of the Madonna and Child by the Master ES (German, mid-15th-century). From M. Lehrs, *Kritischer Katalog*, Textband 2, passim; Tafelband 2, Tafel 50 (126)

9 A female lutenist. An engraving by the Master ES (German, mid-15th-century). From M. Lehrs, *Kritischer Katalog*, Textband 2, passim; Tafelband 2, Tafel 56 (137). For the lute as a woman's instrument, see also illus. 11

10 Lutenist (playing a five-course instrument) and dulcimer player. Engraving by the monogrammist b (x 8 (last quarter of the 15th century). From M. Lehrs, *Kritischer Katalog*, Textband 8, pp. 165f; Tafelband 8, Tafel 225 (544)

11 A female lutenist. An engraving by Wenzel von Olmütz (last quarter of the 15th century). From M. Lehrs, *Kritischer Katalog*, Textband 6, pp. 178f; Tafelband 6, Tafel 162 (423).

As it stands, this is unlikely, because of the gap of a diminished fifth between the fourth and fifth courses (*B-f*). I suggest that the final term should have been parhypate [hypaton] or *c*; Nebrija consistently omits the second element in each pair of Greek terms; possibly the correct order (as I am proposing it), with a double (and adjacent) occurrence of parhypate, led someone to alter the list. This would then give a tuning (relative pitch): *c f a d' a'*.

12 A lutenist accompanied by a female harpist (for this combination of instruments see also illus. 13). From a calendar published at Augsburg in 1479. Reproduced from R. Muther, *Die deutsche Bücherillustration der Gotik und Frührenaissance (1460-1530)* (Munich and Leipzig, 1884)

c. Ramos de Pareja's *Musica Practica*

We are surprisingly well informed about the tuning of the 15th-century lute, for there is yet another piece of evidence: a chapter in Ramos de Pareja's *Musica Practica* (published at Bologna in 1482, but completed some years earlier). This treatise has been in print for many years, but it appears to have gone unnoticed that the *lyra* whose tuning Ramos describes is a lute:[14]

Utuntur autem nunc quinque sic dispositis, ut grossior in tota sua extensione sonet tono sub proslambanomeno, quod dicimus Γ ut; secunda parhypate hypaton diatessaron distans ab ea, tertia hypate meson ditono altior ista; sed quarta mesen pronuntiet, quinta paraneten, diezeugmenon, sive netes synemmenon sonum emittat, diapason et diapente sonans cum prima. Nec tamen hoc de necessitate fit. Aliis enim modis diversis concorditer disponi possunt, ut prima sit proslambanomenos, secunda lichanos, tertia mese et aliae alibi, et istae similiter alibi locari possunt ad arbitrium pulsantis. Sed quia hoc nunc magis in usu est, sic potius posuimus.

Now five [strings] are used arranged so that the thickest, in all its length [i.e. unstopped] sounds a tone below proslambanomenos, which we call Γ *ut*; the second [string sounds] parhypate hypaton, set a fourth apart from the first. The third [string sounds] hypate meson two tones higher than the second. The fourth [string] makes the mese, and the fifth gives paranete diezeugmenon or nete synemmenon, making an octave and a fifth [i.e. a twelfth] with the first. However, this is not done so from necessity. Other players arrange the strings concordantly in different ways, so that the first makes prolambanomenos, the second lichanos, the third mese, and the others are set elsewhere. These [i.e. strings 4, 5] may be placed according to the wishes of the player, but because this system [the one first described] is most in use, we have given it fuller consideration.

There can be little doubt that this *lyra* is a lute. Tinctoris, as we have seen, uses the term *lyra* for the lute, Ramos' *lyra* has five courses, and the tunings he gives, easily translated from the Greek terminology into modern notation, are (relative pitch) Γ *c f a d'* (the tuning most in use) and *A d a* [?] [?] (the variant tuning of which only the first three strings are specified).

It is particularly interesting that Ramos describes the fourths around a third tuning as the most common, but not the *only* accord for the lute.

Tunings for the late 15th-century lute:

a Cambridge notebook (England, ?1490s)

b Nebrija (Spain [Salamanca], ?1495)

c Ramos de Pareja (Spanish writer published at Bologna, 1482)

d Tinctoris (native of Brabant, ?1481-3, published at ?Naples, ?c1487)

An English tutor book for the lute (1474)

During the years 1474-5 an English wool-merchant named George Cely took music lessons at Calais whilst he was in residence there as a merchant of the staple. The teacher was one Thomas Rede, a professional harpist. We know a considerable amount about Cely's studies, for a small booklet at the Public Record Office contains his own expenditure accounts for the lessons. Here Cely has noted the written materials that he bought to help him in his studies, together with the titles of songs that he learned.[15] One of the documents Cely purchased from his teacher is of particular interest to us. The note of the payment runs:[16]

Item the xiiij day off Novembyr payd to the sayd Thomas ffor a byll ffor to lerne to tevne the levte iijs vjd

which is an enormous price; Cely could have stayed in Calais for a whole week with 3s. 6d.[17]

The 'byll' must have been in English, for we have evidence that Cely's French was very rudimentary during the time that he was in Calais.[18] This payment is therefore all the more surprising since there is little evidence that instrumental tutors of any kind circulated in early Tudor England. As John Stevens has pointed out:[19]

. . . three songbooks [Ritson's MS, Henry VIII's MS, and the Fayrfax MS] contain between them almost the whole repertory of early Tudor songs—that is, of poems set to music . . . Other musical manuscripts survive, of course, from the early Tudor period . . . But they are of a different kind and do not contain vernacular songs . . . No English lute music can be dated earlier than 1540, and there are no instrumental tutors or books of that sort.

Rede was not, as far as we know, a scrivener. Cely refers to him as Thomas Rede 'harpar', and there can be little doubt that he was a professional music master (and dancing master), and possibly also a part-time minstrel. If—as seems likely—Rede copied the bills out himself, then we must view him as a combined scribe and author selling not merely his time at the desk (like any scrivener) but also selling his professional expertise. There were no printed instrumental tutors at this date as far as we know; the quality of practical teaching materials depended therefore on the professional competence of one's teacher. Pupils paid for the privilege, not merely the utility of having them, and it is easy to imagine that their prices would vary greatly according to teachers' prestige.

13 Lute and harp. Oxford, Bodleian Library, MS Douce 256 (Flemish, c 1500), f.42v

14 The lute recommended to tame the lusts of a king. From Basle University Library, MS O.II.26 (German, 1476), f.12v: Aristotle's counsels to Alexander

With this in mind, let us consider the prices charged by William Ebesham, a scrivener producing routine work for the famous Paston family in the late 1460s, or several years before Cely purchased his bills. In two letters written to John Paston II (1468 and 1469) Ebesham reviews the work he has undertaken and mentions his rates per leaf. These are 'ij^d a lef' which is mentioned twice, and 'a peny a leef' which is mentioned once and which Ebesham considers 'right wele worth'[20] ('a leef' represents two pages—i.e. the two sides of a leaf). At 'ij^d a lef', the 'byll ffor to lerne to tevne the levte' emerges as a vast document of 21 leaves (42 sides), and at Ebesham's price of a penny a leaf 'which is right wele worth', we arrive at an even more remarkable 42 leaves and 84 sides.

This evidence suggests that Cely's bill contained rather more than his description of it suggests. This hypothesis has a certain common-sense appeal; it seems rather unlikely that Rede would have sold a mere set of tuning instructions to a pupil he had been teaching to play 'xiiij davnsys and an horne pype on the levte' some weeks *earlier*, yet this is the chronology of events dictated by Cely's activities.[21]

No instrumental tutors or 'books of that sort' survive from medieval England, yet in 1474 George Cely, an Englishman probably capable of reading his native tongue only, purchased a set of instructions

15 A lutenist leading men and women in a dance in the sixth age of the world. From H. Schedel, *Liber Cronicarum* (1493), f.217r. The accompanying text includes the sentence *Cum in traiecto homines utriusque sexus super pontem coreis ac vanitatibus operam darent* ('In crossing over the bridge people of both sexes give themselves over to dances and vainglory'). Reproduced by permission from Oxford, Bodleian Library, Douce 304

for tuning the lute. The question to be asked is clear: it is true that no tutor-books survive; but could it be that tutor material circulated in a more ephemeral form than is suggested by the words 'tutor-book'? Cely's instructions were written on a 'byll' and were thus probably unbound; perhaps such unelaborate, 'loose-leaf' tutors were in wide circulation amongst literate amateur musicians and, when worn or no longer needed, were destroyed?

Ownership of lutes in 15th-century England: some evidence from wills and testaments

Cely's 'byll' of unbound sheets represents a class of document that probably made up the greater part of lay reading material in the 15th century, but which was ephemeral and therefore rarely mentioned in wills and testaments.[22]

The instruments that we find in English wills of the period do often seem to have been luxury models. The will of John Bount (1404/5), a wealthy Somerset landowner with property in Bristol, mentions a 'great harp' (*harpa magna*) and a 'gittern [? a small lute] with a woman's face [carved on the pegbox]' (*quinternam . . . cum facie damisell*).[23] Both of these instruments are mentioned along with an obviously luxury possession, 'a sword ornamented with a luxurious strap'. In the reference to the 'great harp' the use of the epithet *magna* is suggestive; perhaps a humbler instrument—such as the 'harpe smale' mentioned by Chaucer—has been passed over.[24] The mention of a 'woman's face' carved upon the gittern also reveals a telling detail. This decoration has clearly been singled out for purposes of identification, just as inventories of books sometimes mention specially decorative bindings and clasps.[25]

Sometimes, in exceptionally full inventories, or in inventories listing the possessions of relatively poor persons, these mundane instruments are mentioned, and the prices assigned to them are remarkably low. The register kept by the Chancellor of the University of Oxford contains several 15th-century inventories of private property, and a number of musical instruments appear there. 'Syre W. Lydbery' (not apparently an Oxford *alumnus*) had a 'lewt price vi^d' amongst his possessions in 1462/3,[26] while William Braggs, MA, owned a lute valued at tenpence in 1468.[27] The goods of John Hosear (not apparently a member of the University) included 'an harpe' valued at fourpence in 1463/4,[28] while Reginald Stone, Bachelor of Canon and Civil Law, left '1 harpe'

valued at two shillings among his effects at Vine Hall in 1468.[29] Simon Beryngtone owned '1 hornpipe price 1^d'.[30] The valuations given here range from fourpence to two shillings, but all the prices, save one, are below tenpence. There is little with which to compare these figures, but the evidence we do have suggests that they are extremely low. The records of Durham Priory show that a new harp could cost as much as three shillings in 1335/6,[31] while only a decade or so after the references to instruments on the Chancellor's register were written, George Cely lent his teacher Thomas Rede nine shillings 'appon an harpe'.[32] The very best harps of a leading London maker such as John Boor could cost as much as 46s. 8d. in the second decade of the 15th century.[33]

If functional instruments—like functional books—could be valued so low in the second half of the 15th century, it is hardly surprising that instruments are only rarely mentioned in wills and inventories. These references show that we must take our line of interpretation from the studies of book ownership which have been undertaken by historians. There can be little doubt that instruments were often passed over by testators and inventory makers unless they were distinguished by their decoration. Carving ('a woman's head') or luxurious appearance ('my faire lute') were probably the features that recommended instruments for inclusion, just as lavish bindings and illuminations recommended books. Thus testamentary evidence is not a definitive index of instrumental skills and interests; we cannot automatically assume that the owner of an instrument was a player, any more than we can be certain that the owner of a book was a reader.

Yet there is a positive corollary to all this. We can now see that the rarity with which instruments are listed in wills does not necessarily indicate that instruments were rarely played; on the contrary, it may be that the number of functional instruments was considerable, but that our records take no notice of the fact. As they stand, the wills and testaments reveal far more books than instruments, but it is possible that many more people owned (and used) an instrument than owned a book worth mentioning in a will. We may assume—with some justification—that not all the instruments listed in the wills were ornaments only; some of them were surely used, and we may expect that any recurrent patterns of possession genuinely reflect the instrumental interests of bourgeois amateur musicians.

The table lists all the references to instruments that have come to my notice in printed collections of English wills.[34]

Date	Name	Instruments
1404	John Bount Bristol landowner	'great harp' and gittern with carved female head
1406	John Parker cleric, doctor of medicine, York	*cithera* (?harp) in custody of a cleric, Robert Clerk
1423	Henry Bowet Archbishop of York	organ, and book of (?) organ music in his chapel
1427	Thomas Mokking cleric of London	organ
1432	Robert Wolveden treasurer of the Church of York	a *clavicimbalum* (?harp-sichord) and a lute
1438	Thomas Cooper, MA Oxford	an old *cithara* (?harp) and a broken lute
1448	Simon Beryngtone, MA Oxford	a hornpipe
1458	John Tidman chaplain, York	clavichord
1462/3	Sir W. Lydbery Oxford	a lute
1463/4	John Hosear ?	a harp
1468	William Braggs, MA Oxford	a (?) lute
1468	Reginald Stone Bachelor of canon and civil law	a harp
1488	Robert Morton gentleman	an old harp
1494	William Case escheator of Somerset	a lute

Our materials clearly show that by the final decades of the 15th century, and probably appreciably earlier, the lute was established as a five-course instrument tuned in fourths around a third. Our evidence for this tuning begins in the 1480s with Ramos de Pareja and Tinctoris. The possibility that this tuning was an Italian peculiarity is discounted by the English evidence. In view of this consistency, and the fact that this tuning was the most common according to Ramos, it probably goes back to at least the mid-century. There is thus not a shadow of doubt as to how reconstructions of 15th-century lutes should be tuned, but at the same time there is scope for experiment with variant tunings for this is sanctioned by the remarks of Ramos.

The chronology of finger plucking remains obscure. We have seen that Tinctoris mentions it, but does not describe it as new, or imply that it was an innovation. By the 1480s therefore, it was probably well established, though by no means universal. Yet the pictures consistently show plectra until late in the century, as the examples assembled here show; depictions of finger plucking before the decade 1490-1500 are not unknown, but they are rare.[35] It is time for a systematic investigation of lute iconography with a view to establishing a chronology for this technique.

The wills and inventories show us the kinds of middle-class persons who played the lute. After the angelic lutenists that abound in 15th-century pictures, and the elegant courtiers, it is sobering to find middle-class landowners, Oxford students, civil servants, and high-ranking ecclesiastics. We probably owe the lute instructions in the Cambridge notebook (illus. 5) to some kind of merchant or civil servant, or perhaps to a steward with legal responsibilities in a prosperous household. Such men doubtless performed in informal, domestic circumstances, joining forces from time to time with any other musicians or singers at hand. The case of the English wool merchant George Cely shows how the practicalities of learning the lute could be conducted; as a member of the newly literate middle class with surplus spending power Cely was able to buy a tutor-book which probably contained a great deal more than his description of it implies. By the 1470s, it would seem, there was already a lute literature.

My thanks are due to Michael Lowe, Michael Morrow, Lewis Jones and David Fallows for reading this article and making many helpful suggestions. Above all, I am grateful to Régine Page, to whom I owe almost all the information taken from wills and testaments.

[1] As long ago as 1958 Daniel Heartz characterized 1500 as a 'coupure vraiment arbitraire' in the history of the lute ('Les Premières Instructions pour le Luth', in J. Jacquot ed., *Le Luth et sa Musique*, 2nd edition (Paris, 1976), p. 87.

[2] The principal studies available at present include: P. Danner, 'Before Petrucci: the Lute in the Fifteenth Century', *JLSA* 5 (1972), pp. 4-17; I. Harwood, 'A Fifteenth Century Lute Design', *LSJ* 2 (1960), pp. 3-8; F. Hellwig, 'Lute-making in the Late Fifteenth and the Sixteenth Century', *LSJ* 16 (1974), pp. 24-38; D. Fallows, 'Fifteenth century Tablatures for Plucked Instruments: A Summary, a Revision, and a Suggestion', *LSJ* 19 (1977), pp. 7-33 (see also the other articles on the early tablatures there cited); P.

Beier, 'Right hand Position in Renaissance Lute Technique', *JLSA* 12 (1979), pp. 5-24; H. M. Brown, 'Instruments and Voices in the Performance of Fifteenth Century Chansons', in J. W. Grubbs ed., *Current Thought in Musicology* (Austin, 1976), pp. 102f (on the use of the lute). On the 15th-century lutenist Pietrobono see N. Pirrotta, 'Music and Cultural Tendencies in Fifteenth Century Italy', *JAMS* 19 (1966), pp. 127-61, L. Lockwood, 'Pietrobono and the Instrumental Tradition at Ferrara in the Fifteenth Century', *Rivista italiana di musicologia*, 10 (1975), pp. 115-33, and Fallows, op cit, pp. 27f.

[3] The text given here has been edited from a microfilm of the original manuscript, now in the library of the Jagiellonian University at Kraków (MS 257). There is no adequate edition of the material on instruments, which must be read in a confusing and inaccurate transcription by J. Reiss, 'Pauli Paulirini de Praga Tractatus de Musica (etwa 1460)', *Zeitschrift für Musikwissenschaft*, 7 (1924-5), pp. 262-4.

[4] In the manuscript the word *communiter* (line 1), which is how I read the contraction after *musicum*, is followed directly by *ceteris*. A participle seems to be required, and I have supplied *sejunctum* 'kept apart from' to complete the sense as I comprehend it. In line 8, for *efflatur*, the MS has *efflagitatur*.

[5] Reiss, op cit, p. 262.

[6] For new information about the date of the publication of this treatise I am indebted to Ronald Woodley of Christ Church, Oxford, who is completing a doctoral thesis on Tinctoris.

The text given here has been taken from K. Weinmann, *Johannes Tinctoris (1445-1511) und sein unbekannter Traktat 'De Inventione et Usu Musicae'*, corrected edition with introduction by W. Fischer (Tutzing, 1961), pp.40f. (I have removed the 15th-century pointing of the text and introduced modern punctuation of my own.) There is a text of Tinctoris' material on instruments, with English translation, in A. Baines, 'Fifteenth Century Instruments in Tinctoris's *De Inventione et Usu Musicae*', *GSJ* 3 (1950), pp. 19-26. The translations given here are mine.

[7] cf the remarks in Brown, op cit, p. 102.

[8] ibid, and Fallows, op cit, p. 28.

[9] For a description of the manuscript see M. R. James, *The Western Manuscripts in the Library of Trinity College, Cambridge*, 3 vols (Cambridge, 1900-02) 3, no. 1117. The period during which the notebook was compiled is established by a list of kings on f.12 which is in the main hand and ends with Henry VII.

[10] There is some evidence—though it is not very sound—that the text was copied before *c*1500. Folio 79 of the manuscript shows a watermark which is an anchor. Those which appear in that form (with the fold across the centre of the anchor shaft) seem to have been current up to 1490, after which there is a jump to *c*1500. A date in the early 1490s agrees remarkably well with the evidence of the dated documents in the manuscript. See V. Mošin, *Anchor Watermarks* (Amsterdam, 1973).

[11] The text has been printed by J. Handschin in 'Aus der alten Musiktheorie, V, Zur Instrumentenkunde', *Acta Musicologica*, 16-17 (1944-5), p. 2, and by S. Marcuse in *A Survey of Musical Instruments* (Newton Abbot and London, 1975), p. 417.

[12] 'Trebill', 'Meene' and 'Tenor' are well attested in Middle English as the names of vocal parts in polyphonic music. See H. H. Carter, *A Dictionary of Middle English Musical Terms* (Indiana, 1961 *R* New York, 1968), sv 'Mene', 'Tenour', and 'Treble'.

[13] Elio Antonio de Nebrija, *Vocabulario Español-Latino* (Salamanca, ?1495 *F* Madrid, 1951), sv 'cuerda'. I have restored the second element in the Greek terms.

[14] The text given here has been taken from J. Wolf ed., *Musica Practica Bartolomei Rami de Pareia* (Leipzig, 1901), pp. 16-17.

[15] For the text of the accounts, see A. Hanham, 'The Musical Studies of a Fifteenth Century Wool Merchant', *Review of English Studies*, 8 (1957), pp. 270-4. [16] ibid, p. 271.

[17] As pointed out by Hanham, op cit, p. 273. [18] ibid.

[19] J. Stevens, *Music and Poetry in the Early Tudor Court*, corrected edition (Cambridge, 1979), p. 7.

[20] For the texts of the letters see N. Davis ed., *Paston Letters and Papers of the Fifteenth Century*, 2 vols (Oxford, 1971 and 1976) 2, pp. 386-7, and 391-2.

[21] In his accounts (Hanham, op cit, p. 271), Cely records payment for the tuning instructions on 14 November 1474; he records payment for learning 'xiiij davnsys and an horne pype on the levte' on the *first* day of the same month in the same year.

[22] See M. Vale, *Piety, Charity and Literacy among the Yorkshire Gentry, 1370-1480*, Borthwick Papers, 50 (York, 1976), pp. 29f, and M. Deanesly, 'Vernacular Books in England in the Fourteenth and Fifteenth Centuries', *Modern Language Review*, 15 (1920), pp. 349-58.

[23] F. W. Weaver ed., *Somerset Medieval Wills 1383-1500*, Somerset Record Society, 16 (1901), pp. 11-14.

[24] F. N. Robinson ed., *The Works of Geoffrey Chaucer*, second edition (Oxford, 1966), p. 80, line 457.

[25] Vale, op cit, p. 30. Another Somerset will, dating from the last decade of the 15th century, contains an unequivocal reference to a fine instrument, and also seems to imply by its wording that one or more humbler instruments have been passed over (Weaver, op cit, pp. 317-18). In 1494 William Case, escheator of Somerset, made a will in the vernacular to dispose of his luxury possessions. The objects listed include 'a cheyne of goold, a basyn and lavor of siluer, myne armes printed thereon' and 'a stonding cuppe covered with gilt'. Towards the end of the document, just before disposing of his 'gowne of tawny furred with shankes', Case mentions his 'faire lute' which he leaves to a certain lady Fitz Watereyn. This is obviously a luxury instrument; the epithet 'fair' and the general context in which the reference appears leave us in little doubt. Yet the suspicion lingers that 'fair' has been included to make a distinction rather than express pride in ownership.

[26] See H. E. Salter ed., *Registrum Cancellarii Oxoniensis 1434-1469*, Oxford Historical Society, 2 vols (1932) 2, p. 101.

[27] ibid 2, p. 326; for Braggs, see A. B. Emden, *A Biographical Register of the University of Oxford to AD 1500* (Oxford, 1957), p. 247.

[28] Salter, op cit, 2, p. 129.

[29] Salter, op cit, 2, p. 327; Emden, op cit, p. 1788.

[30] Salter, op cit, 1, p. 160; Emden, op cit, p. 181.

[31] See E. K. Chambers, *The Medieval Stage*, 2 vols (Oxford, 1903) 2, p. 241.

[32] Hanham, op cit, p. 271.

[33] See F. Devon ed., *Extracts from the Issue Rolls of the Exchequer Hen III-Hen VI* (London, 1837), p. 367.

[34] This table is based upon a survey of the printed will collections listed in E. B. Graves ed., *A Bibliography of English History to 1485* (Oxford, 1975), pp. 647f. It is inevitably incomplete and makes no claim to comprehensiveness. The wills referred to here have been taken from the following sources: J. Raine ed., *Testamenta Eboracensia* 1 pp. 342-4 (John Parker), 2 p. 213 (John Tidman), 3 pp. 69-85 (Henry Bowet), and pp. 91-2 (Robert Wolveden); F. W. Weaver, *Somerset Medieval Wills*, pp. 11-14 (John Bount), and pp. 317-8 (William Case); J. R. H. Weaver and A. Beardwood, *Some Oxfordshire Wills*, Oxfordshire Record Society, 39 (1958), pp. 13-14 (Thomas Mokking); H. E. Salter, *Registrum Cancellari* (inventories) (Beryngtone, Braggs, Hosear, Stone, Lydbery and Cooper); and *Journal of the British Archaeological Association*, 33 (1877), p. 318. For a discussion of the will of Robert Morton see D. Fallows, 'Robert Morton's Songs: a Study of Styles in the Mid-Fifteenth Century' (diss., U. of California, 1979; *Dissertation Abstracts* 39 (Feb. 1979), A, pp. 4579-80; University Microfilms order no. 79-04431).

[35] It is possible that the pictures are conservative in this respect, drawing upon traditions established in model- and pattern-books that were made during the plectrum period, and never subsequently revised to keep up with developments in lute playing.

21

X

German musicians and their instruments
A 14th-century account by Konrad of Megenberg

1 'flutes . . . sometimes play together with fiddles' (see text and translation, ll.37–8). Detail from a painting of Meister Rumslaut from the Manessische Liederhandschrift (Heidelberg, Universitätsbibliothek, Cod.pal.germ.848, f.413v). German, before 1340, executed by hand G

It is impossible to say where valuable references illuminating the musical life of the Middle Ages may be found in the vast literature of the period.[1] What, for example, might we expect to learn about 14th-century music and instruments from a treatise on the education and concerns of a prince? Konrad of Megenberg's *Yconomica* provides a surprising answer.[2]

Konrad was born in 1309 and died at Regensburg in 1374. He studied at the University of Paris and rose to become a teacher there.[3] His *Yconomica*, written between 1348 and 1352, gathers material which the young sons of princes must study: *filii principum in yconomicis instruantur doctrinis*.[4] In addition to somewhat intellectual considerations drawn from Greek philosophy, from history and from the Bible, Konrad discusses many aspects of the household, including the servants, scribes, marshalls, notaries and so on who live and work within it:[5]

Capitulum quadragesimumoctavum de servis delectabilibus[6] [extract]

1 *Musicus autem est, qui sonorum armoniis aut voces canit humanas aut inanimatorum organorum clingitus clangoresque adornat, quibus animos auditorum delectat. Unde tria sunt genera eius. Vibrodus scilicet, cyrodus et aviodus. Vibrodus*
5 *est, qui arteriis et cannis naturalibus canit . . . Cyrodus autem est, qui instrumento manuali canit. Et dicitur a cyros, id est manus, et odus, cantus, quasi manualis cantor. Et cyrodorum alius cordicen, alius cannicen et tercius plagicen exstat. Cordicen est, qui in cordis cantat. Sunt autem cordicines*
10 *diversorum instrumentorum et secundum pluralitatem et paucitatem instrumentorum cordarum, sicut sunt monocorda, tricorda, tetracorda, penthacorda et policorda, et secundum varias figuraciones, sicut sunt cythare, rutte, psalteria, rubele, lute, quinterne, lyre at alie huiusmodi. Cannicen est, qui in*

Chapter 48, concerning servants who entertain

The musician is [a servant–entertainer] who either sings vocal notes with harmonies of sounds,[7] or embellishes the sounds and noises of inanimate instruments with which he delights the senses of his hearers. There are three kinds of [musician]: the singer, the instrumentalist and the imitator of birdsong. The singer is one who makes music with natural pipes and windpipes . . . The instrumentalist makes music with a manual instrument. He takes his name from *cyros*,[8] that is 'hand', and *odus*, 'song', whence 'manual singer' as it were. The first type of instrumentalist is the string player, the second the wind player, and the third the percussionist. The string player is one who makes music on strings. There are, moreover, string players of various instruments, which are distinguished both according to the number of strings (as

Reprinted from *Early Music* 10 (1982), pp. 192–200. By permission of Oxford University Press.

15 *cannis et fistulis canit, et illorum alius macrofistulus, alius*
microfistulus experitur.

Est autem macrofistulus, qui in maiori fistula canit aut sine
calamo aut sine calamo sonoro canne maiori inserto. Cuius
quatuor sunt species simplices, utpote burdunicen, musicen,
20 *tubicen et tibicen. Burdunicen est, qui in burduna aut in*
barritona quodam barrito elephantino sonorat. Musicen est,
qui in musa canit, que et bombina dicitur a sono. Bombit enim
grosso bucino sive strepitu soni et ob hoc a barritona differt.
Componitur autem musa in aliquibus instrumentis cum
25 *fistulis minoribus sicut in organis aut cum tibia sicut in*
saccitona. Tubicen est, qui in tuba masculina canit. Et dicitur
masculina a soni moderata ingrossacione ... Tibicen autem est,
qui in tibia feminea canit, que feminea dicitur a soni gracilitate
et asperitate. Unde non differunt tuba et tibia nisi per vocis
30 *grossiciem et tenuitatem, sicut vox masculi grossior est*
naturaliter ut in pluribus feminea voce. Simul eciam bene
concinunt secundum debitas proporciones in quartis, in
quintis aut octavis, sicut qualitas exigit melodie.

Microfistulus est, qui in minori fistula canit. Et voco minores
35 *fistulas, quas vulgariter flatillas nominamus, eoquod minuta*
flatillacione spiritus oris sonum reddant, sed debilem et
remissum. Unde fidulis quandoque proporcionantur in con-
cinendo. Dixi autem quatuor esse species simplices microfistuli,
quoniam ex hiis differencie complexe plures componuntur,
40 *utpote duplisonus aut bifistulus est, qui in fistula canit*
duplata; et una eademque vesica seu folliculus oris refertus
aere sonorositati sufficit utriusque. Saccisonus est, qui in
fistula saccitona canit. Et est saccitona fistula composita et
sacco coriario adunata. Componitur autem ex bombina humero
45 *fistulantis sustentata et ex tibia, cuius foramina fistulans [am-]*
plectitur digitis suis; folliculus autem bifistule parvus est, pro
quo sufficit vesica bruti animalis. Et componitur ex bombina
quadam parva et tibia sonos distinguente. Organista vero est,
qui in organis cantat. Et sunt organa pluraliter dicta propter
50 *multitudinem fistularum et crebram sonorum varietatem, ex*
quibus componuntur.

Plagicen est, qui in plagellis canit. Est autem plagella
instrumentum musicum solis plagis sine cordis et absque flatu

with monochords, trichords, tetrachords, pentachords and polychords),[9] and according to the shape of the instrument (as with harps, triangular psalteries, psalteries, rebecs, lutes, gitterns, [?]lyres and others of this kind). The wind player is the one who makes music with reeds and pipes, and of these one—the *macrofistulus*—and another—the *microfistulus*—are to be distinguished.

The *macrofistulus* is the one who makes music with a greater pipe which is either without a reed, or without a reed having been inserted into the greater, resounding pipe.[10] There are four basic types of *macrofistulus*: the one who plays the *burduna*, the player of the large reed pipe, the player of the trumpet, and the shawm player. The *burduna* player is the one who sounds a certain elephantine cry on the *burduna* or on the oliphant. The *musicen* is the one who plays the large reed pipe which is also called *bombina* ['buzzer'] from its sound. For it buzzes with a great trumpet blast or din of sound, and on this account it differs from the oliphant. The large reed pipe in some instruments is joined with minor pipes[11] as in the case of organs,[12] or with the shawm as in the bagpipe. The *tubicen* is the one who makes music with the masculine trumpet (it is called 'masculine' because of the moderate coarseness of its sound) . . . The *tibicen* is the one who makes music on the feminine shawm (called 'feminine' from the thinness and harshness of its sound). The trumpet and shawm do not differ save by the largeness and smallness of their respective sounds,[13] just as the masculine voice—as with many things—is greater by nature than the female voice. These two instruments sound well together according to due proportions in 4ths, 5ths and octaves just as the character of the melody requires.

The *microfistulus* is the one who makes music on a smaller pipe. And I call those pipes 'smaller', named 'flutes' in the vernacular,[14] because they give sound with a little blowing of the breath of the mouth, but the noise is weak and feeble. Whence they sometimes play together with fiddles. I have said that there are four basic types of *microfistulus* because more, related species are assembled from these; he is a 'double-sounder', or 'double-pipe player', who makes music with a double pipe; one and the same bladder, or little bellows, filled with the breath of the mouth, suffices for the sounding of both pipes. The bagpiper is the one who makes music on a 'bagged' pipe. This 'bagged' pipe is adapted and joined to a leather sack. The instrument comprises a large reed pipe resting on the shoulder of the player, and a shawm with holes which the player encompasses with his fingers. The bellows of the double pipe is small, for which reason the bladder of an animal suffices for it. The double pipe is made from a small reed pipe and a shawm distinguishing the notes.[15] The organist is the one who makes music on organs, and 'organs' is said thus in the plural on account of the manifold variety of sounds and the multitude of pipes from which the instrument is composed.[16]

The *plagicen* is one who makes music with percussion instruments. Such an instrument sounds only by blows, and

sonans. Unde commune est ad tympanum, cymbalum et
55 plateolas. Tympanum raucam vocem habet et bacillis ligneis
excitatur. Cymbala vero sunt tyntinabula, que martellis aut
virgulis ferreis moventur. Plateole sunt discelli, id est disci
parvi enei, qui flexibus manualibus compercuciuntur et cum
aliis instrumentis musicis pulchre sonorant. Aviodus ab
60 avibus dicitur et odus, cantus, quasi avium imitans cantus.
Talis autem cum pellicula de herba porri aut consimilis rei
diversarum avium voces dulcisonans format secundum variam
lingue sue et pellicule flexionem. Iste itaque species musici
existunt aut differencie ipsius qualescumque.

65   Gestimusus est, qui simul gestuum decencia et cantus
ornatibus homines delectat. Talis autem est, qui canit ore et
geminatis sonorat tabellis pedibus suis lepide motis eundo et
redeundo in aulica planicie dominorum. Concinunt autem ita
cantus oris, clamor tabellarum et migracio motus pedalis. Iste
70 ludus aptissime per quasdam iuvenculas exercetur.

Capitulum quadragesimumnovum ostendens, quod differencie musicales moveant ad diversas passiones anime

Oportet autem scire, quoniam diversitates melodiarum et
instrumentorum musicalium ad diversas passiones animas
excitant auditorum, utpote ad gaudium et tristiciam, iram et
benignitatem, audaciam et terrorem et sic de ceteris anime
75 affectibus diversis . . . quia instrumentorum qualitates diverse
sic melodias variant, ut animas auditorum afficiant affectibus
diversis. Nam barritona seu bombina amicorum animas
reddit audaces et conceptus suggerit animosos, sed adversantes
animas terret et hostium mentes confundit timore. Tuba vero et
80 tibia amice mentis hilaritatem excitant et hostiles animas
tristicia sternunt. Tympanum quoque raucedine sua, insultuoso
eciam sonitu fremens virtutem motivam anime ad quandam
excitare videtur agilitatem et irascibilem potenciam iam
excitatam inflammare. Quapropter hec tria concurrencia
85 organa musica in primis congressionibus bellicis aptissime
ordinantur et usitantur ad terrendum hostes videlicet et amicos
animandum.

Cithare vero alieque differencie cordigere fricaturis tytillantibus
sonantes, utpote digitorum raptibus aut pennarum fricaturis,
90 ad pietatis mansuetudinem animas inclinant humanas. Unde
pudicis gestibus et philosophicis solaciis, cum scilicet intervalla
dantur studiis, racionabiliter deputantur. Fidule autem iocositatem
persuadent animabus et tripudiis femineis sunt decenciores . . .
Modernis etenim temporibus tibie ac tube altitone fidulas
95 morigeras a conviviis communiter fugant, et altisono strepitu
certatim iuvencule saliunt ut cerve clunes illepide ac effeminaliter
agitando . . . Flatille autem fistule amorosos animos excitant
seu irritant et ad dulcorem devocionis quodammodo movent.

without strings or the introduction of wind. The type is
familiar in the drum, bell and cymbals. The drum has a
raucous voice and is struck with small wooden beaters.
Cymbala are little bells which are set vibrating with hammers
or little rods. Plateole are small discs of bronze which are
struck together with an artful turning of the hands, and they
sound beautifully with other instruments. The aviodus [is an
entertainer who is] named from avis, 'bird', and odus, 'song';
thus he is one who imitates birdsong. Such [an entertainer]
sweet-soundingly imitates the voices of various birds with
the skin of the stalk of a leek or some similar thing,
according to the varying use of his tongue and the
adjustment of the skin. These therefore are the kinds of
musician which exist, and the distinctions between them.

The gestimusus is one who entertains men with comely
movements and with ornaments of song at the same time.
There is moreover one such who sings with his mouth and
charmingly makes music with twin cymbals [?bells] on his
feet going to and fro in the clear space of the lords' hall.
The clamour of the cymbals and the motion of his feet
accord well together. This entertainment is very fittingly
performed by some young women.[17]

Chapter 49, showing how diverse kinds of music give rise to
different passions of the mind

It is also necessary to know how the diversity of melodies
and of musical instruments excites the minds of listeners to
various emotions such as joy and sadness, anger and
gentleness, boldness and terror, and thus also to other
various affections of the mind . . . the various qualities of
instruments so vary the music that they may affect the minds
of listeners with varying emotions. For the oliphant and the
large reed pipe render the minds of allies bold, and excite
brave gatherings, but they terrify hostile spirits and con-
found the minds of enemies with fear. Moreover the trumpet
and the shawm excite pleasure of the mind in one who is an
ally but depress the spirits of enemies with sadness. The
drum with its harshness and the insulting sound of its
growling excites the energy and courage of the spirit to a
certain agility and inflames an irascible, powerful vigour.
Wherefore these three concordant instruments [shawm,
trumpet and drum] are most fit to be set and often employed in the first attack of battle to terrify the enemy and
encourage allies.

Harps however, and other kinds of string instruments
sounding with light strokes (such as with the plucking of the
fingers or with the strokes of quills), incline human minds to
the mildness of piety. For which reason they are sensibly
classed amongst modest activities and philosophical pastimes
when intervals from study are given. Fiddles inspire joy in
minds, and they are therefore more appropriate to the
dances of women . . . Indeed, in modern times the shawms
and loud trumpets generally banish the sober fiddles from
the feasts, and the young girls dance eagerly to the loud
noise, like hinds, shaking their buttocks womanishly and

Quapropter organa ex ipsarum varietate ac multitudine
100 *consistencia templis, ubi divina peraguntur sollemnia, congrue*
deputantur.

Exercet autem quis musicales venustates aut sola animi
libertate, et sic laudabiles obtinent possessores, literales
quoque decencie nuncupantur; aut muneris gracia, quomodo
105 *municipes ioculatores ipsas usurpant, et sic pannausi sunt, id*
est viles et declives habentes condiciones. Sed hoc racione
possessorum accidit eis, qui propter indigencias suas exercent
eas. Omnis autem facultas lucri cupida mendica est et
ancillaris condicionis, eoquod mendicet exercicium eius. Sed
110 *mendicus artifex divites artes deformat, faciens ex domina*
famulam et de libera servam. Que de re iuvenes pauperes, qui
musicalibus insudant organis, dubias laudes exspectant.
Ambiguum etenim est ipsos pannausos fieri ioculatores.
Divites vero pro modulis decenciarum suarum adolescencias
115 *exercere poterunt, sobrie tamen, in ipsis.*

Lignum . . . abietis . . . Aeritas autem ipsius et raritas faciunt
ipsum multum sonorum, cum percutitur. Sed cum fit concavum,
non ideo sonat, quia raritas eius aerem contineri non permittit.
Qua de causa ventres instrumentorum musicalium, sicut
120 *vigelle, lire, monocordi et aliorum similium [ex] abiete facti non*
valent. Sed cooperture ventrium optime sunt ex abiete facte,
quia ille aerem in fundo vasorum musicalium concitatum per
raritates suas emittunt paulative.

rudely. Flutes arouse or exasperate amorous spirits, and to an extent move them to the sweetness of [religious] devotion. Organs therefore, on account of their variety and multitude [of flutes], are fittingly allotted a place in churches where divine services are celebrated.[18]

One cultivates the beauties of music either for freedom of the spirit alone—and thus [the beauties of music] win praiseworthy masters and may be called gentlemanly and becoming—or for the sake of reward as the municipal minstrels exploit them who are thus vulgar, having cheap and lowly status. This befalls [the beauties of music] because those who have mastered them do so because they are poor. All ability exercised for gain is beggarly, and of a maid-servant's condition, because to practise it is to play the beggar. But the begging artist perverts precious arts, making a handmaid of the mistress and a slave of the freewoman. For which reason young paupers who sweat at their instruments can expect dubious praise. It is a dubious thing for such beggars to become minstrels. The rich should exercise the young in these skills—but temperately—as a measure of their cultivation.

[Concerning the woods used by carpenters:][19] fir wood . . . its porousness and looseness of texture make it very resonant when it is struck, but when it is hollowed out it is not therefore sonorous, because its porousness does not permit the air to be contained. For which reason the bellies of string instruments such as fiddles, [?]lyres, monochords and other such are not successful if made from fir wood. But the soundboards [literally 'covers'] are best made from fir wood, because they gradually emit the air set into vibration within the instrument through their loose texture.[20]

Konrad divides the household personnel into functionaries with administrative duties, and *servi delectabiles* —servants who provide entertainment. This arrangement of material throws some light upon the musical life of the time, for he is not referring to professional minstrels, even though his players belong to households and perform for their patrons. Konrad's musicians are *servi*, and he discusses them together with carpenters, wall makers, carriers, handmaidens and so on, all of whom have chapters to themselves in this part of the *Yconomica*.[21]

We have other evidence suggesting that the court musicians of the 14th century were often closely linked with the domestic servant hierarchies of the institutions where they worked, and were distinct from the professional minstrels as conventionally conceived. Thus Constance Bullock-Davies writes in her survey of English minstrels at the great Westminster feast of 1306:

If all minstrels both at Court and in baronial hall had been professionals, the task of identifying the men and women on the [Pentecost 1306] Payroll might have been much easier. All were rewarded for 'making their minstrelsy' and, since the occasion was a festive one, there is every reason to believe that 'minstrelsy' here means entertainment of the kind usually understood when we use the word; *yet analysis of the list has revealed that numbers of the people named in it were serving in the household in other capacities and received court wages for duties far removed from singing songs, playing a musical instrument or acting in plays.* They were, among other things, heralds, messengers, sergeants-at-arms, grooms of the chamber, soldiers, sailors and watchmen. These were the amateurs whose numbers swelled the ranks of the professionals.[22] [my italics]

This distinction between professional minstrels and household musician–servants is a crucial one for Konrad. His term for the former is *ioculatores*, and he has an extremely low opinion of them. He recognizes their status as professional men, and even grants that they are civic figures (*municipes ioculatores*), but they command no respect because 'ability excercised for gain is beggarly' (*facultas lucri cupida mendica est*). Konrad even extends this harsh judgement to paupers who 'sweat at their instruments' and must develop musical skills 'because they are poor' (*propter indigencias suas*).

Here we have an important development in medieval music-making as seen through the eyes of an earnest moralist. During the 14th century, minstrels in many parts of Europe organized themselves into guilds and established their place in the administrative order of urban life.[23] Konrad is troubled by this professionalization, for he sees it as a threat to the gentlemanly excercise of music 'for freedom of the spirit alone' (*sola animi libertate*). He requires that a wise nobleman should have good music provided by his servants whose excellence lies in the fact that they are amateurs.

This presentation of the state of affairs is heavily influenced by Aristotle's view of music as presented in the *Politics*, and one of the most interesting aspects of Konrad's account of music is the way in which he is determined to see 14th-century musical life in Aristotelian terms. Aristotle shows little respect for the professional performer. He argues that Zeus did not play an instrument, and that therefore 'we are apt to regard as vulgar those who do otherwise, and we think of them as behaving in a way in which a man would not behave unless he were drunk or jesting'.[24] Konrad once refers to the professional musicians of his day as *pannausi*, borrowing Aristotle's term *banausos* for those who practise a mechanical, and therefore a common, vulgar skill.[25] He thus adopts Aristotle's position, dividing musicians into cultivated amateurs and vulgar professionals with that medieval passion for social hierarchies that often strikes the modern reader as easy élitism.

Yet Konrad is not without his Christian bias. The rise of the municipal minstrel may be a threat to gentlemanly music, but there are other signs of moral decay. The 'sober' fiddles are by no means as popular as they were at feasts; now the revellers prefer noisy trumpets and shawms, and the girls dance to the din with immodest movements (ll.94f; here and below, the line numbers refer to the Latin text).

Almost all of the musicians Konrad mentions in his account are wind players, and this emphasis needs to be accounted for in view of the apparent predominance of strings in medieval music-making. The answer may lie in one of Konrad's sources for the *Yconomica*, the commentary upon Aristotle's *Politics* by Albertus Magnus (13th century). Albertus devotes a substantial amount of space to wind instruments and Konrad may have decided to follow Albertus in this respect.[26]

2 '[shawm, trumpet and drum] are most fit to be set and often employed in the first attack of battle' (ll.85–6). An unpainted drawing from the Manessische Liederhandschrift, f.196r, executed by hand 3

Before passing on to discuss the instruments and wind music Konrad mentions, there is one final source which we must consider. Konrad's characterizations of the instruments (the 'masculine' *tuba*, the 'feminine' *tibia*, etc) are not, for the most part, his own. They come from the *Poetria nova* (*c*1200) of Geoffrey de Vinsauf. This celebrated poetry manual contains a section in which the reader is shown how to amplify and expand a description of a feast, and one of the devices Geoffrey recommends is a list of the instruments present at the celebration. Here are the relevant phrases from Geoffrey and Konrad placed side by side.[27]

Geoffrey	Konrad
tibia feminea	*Tibicen . . . in tibia feminea canit*
tuba mascula	*Tubicen . . . in tuba masculina canit*
tympana rauca	*Tympanum raucam vocem habet*
vidulaeque jocosae	*Fidule autem iocositatem persuadent animabus*

the conclusion seems inescapable that the *bombina* and *musa* were reed pipes with cylindrical bores like a bagpipe drone. This hardly accords with Konrad's statement that the *bombina* sounds 'with a great trumpet blast' (*grosso bucino*), and I am unable to explain the discrepancy.

tibia Konrad describes the bagpipe chanter as a *tibia*, and since chanters are conically bored in the main series of Western bagpipes,[31] this *tibia* is presumably a shawm (the word is sometimes glossed *scalmei* in medieval German wordlists).

tuba This word is sometimes glossed *bosun* and *tromet* in the wordlists, and there can be little doubt that Konrad uses it in its standard medieval sense of 'straight trumpet'.[32]

flatilla Konrad says that this is a vernacular (or popular) word. It is clearly a Latin version of the vernacular *floite*, *floet*, and probably covers both flutes and recorders.

String

cythara The general equivalent of this Latin word in the major vernaculars was 'harp'.[33] This is probably the meaning that Konrad assigned to it.

rutta Probably a triangular zither[34]

psalterium All of the sources I know in which this word appears next to a drawing of an instrument show pig-snout psalteries.[35]

rubela Jerome of Moravia's *rubeba* was a two-string, bowed instrument.[36] I am aware of no evidence which suggests that names on *rub-*, *reb-*, *rib-* etc stems were applied to instruments other than small fiddles.[37]

luta There seems to be no reason to doubt the meaning of this word as used by Konrad.

quinterna According to the evidence assembled by Laurence Wright, this is a piriform, round-backed, plucked instrument, formerly called *citole* by scholars.[38]

lyra Possibly the medieval lyre (which survived quite late in Germany)[39]

fidula Presumably a bowed instrument, although glosses for *figella*[40] in medieval German sources also include *lut*, *quintern* and *geyg*. This carries little weight however, for Konrad uses the words *quinterna* and *luta* elsewhere.

Percussion

tympanum A drum, but no details are given save that it is beaten with two sticks.

cymbala Small bells struck with a hammer. As in many medieval sources which mention *cymbala*, there is no indication here that a set of chime bells is meant as opposed to a few bells carried on a frame and struck for percussive rather than melodic purposes.[41]

plateole Cymbals, in the modern sense.

3 'Fiddles . . . are . . . more appropriate to the dances of women' (ll.92–3). A painting showing Herr Reinmar der Fiedler, from the Manessische Liederhandschrift, f.312r, executed by hand G.

The instruments

Wind

burduna Konrad says nothing definite about this instrument. In later Latin *burdo* has various meanings, including 'pilgrim staff', and the word was applied to the long drone-pipes of organs and the drones of bagpipes, probably because of the older meaning 'staff', or 'long rod'.[28] Konrad says that the *burduna* was played by the same musician as the *barritona* (see below).

barritona According to Konrad this instrument sounds an 'elephantine cry', and the name is clearly connected with *barritus*, 'the cry of an elephant'.[29] The instrument was perhaps therefore an oliphant.

musa The basic instrumental meaning of this word is 'pipe', and it is glossed *pfeyff* etc in numerous medieval German wordlists.[30] Konrad says that the instrument is also called *bombina* ('buzzer'), and since he states that one of the components of a bagpipe is a *bombina* resting upon the shoulder of the player (*bombina humero fistulantis sustentata*)

Summary of translations

burduna	burduna	*rutta*	triangular psaltery
barritona	oliphant	*psalterium*	psaltery
musa	large reed pipe	*rubela*	rebec
bombina	large reed pipe	*luta*	lute
tibia	shawm	*quinterna*	gittern
tuba	trumpet	*lyra*	?lyre
flatilla	flute/recorder	*fidula*	fiddle
cythara	harp	*tympanum*	drum

Cymbala and *plateole* have been left untranslated as the context demands (Konrad mentions these names and then defines them).

The loud wind music

Konrad notes that the shawm and trumpet 'sound well together . . . in 4ths, 5ths and octaves', which is perhaps a reference to some kind of polyphonic playing. He also states that this combination of instruments is used at feasts (illus.4). A 14th-century German example of what is almost certainly loud wind music has come down to us (and by coincidence it is preserved in a manuscript that incorporates a work by Konrad of Megenberg). This is the *Nachthorn* by Hermann, Monk of Salzburg, which appears in the Mondsee–Wiener Liederhandschrift (ex.1).[42] The top part is labelled *Das nachthorn und ist gut zu blasen* ('The nighthorn, and it is good to blow') while the second part is accompanied by the legend *Das ist der pumhart darzu* (illus.5). This *pumhart* may be a shawm (as later evidence suggests),[43] but it is tempting to assume that a trumpet is meant.

4 'the shawms and loud trumpets generally banish the sober fiddles from the feasts' (ll.94–5). Drawing from Nicholas de Lyra's *Postilla super libros regum et Esther* illustrating Esther 1:1–8 (Basle, Öffentliche Bibliothek der Universität, MS A.II.4, f.135v). German, 1400/01

Ex.1 Hermann, Monk of Salzburg, *Das Nachthorn* (Vienna, Österreichische Nationalbibliothek, MS 2856, ff.185v–186r)

Das nachthorn und ist gut zu blasen

Das ist der pumhart darzu

Selective index to text

Performance practice

Attitudes to musicians

I am most grateful to Régine Page, who first brought this text to my notice, and to David Fallows, who read the first draft and made many helpful suggestions. John Griffith read the translation and cleared up several troublesome points.

[1]See M. Stewart, 'Unfamiliar sources—or cooking with music', *EM* 2/3 (July 1974), pp.157–9.

[2]The modern edition of the text (so far only books 1 and 2 have appeared) is by S. Krüger, *Konrad von Megenberg Werke, 1–2, Ökonomik,* Monumenta Germaniae historica: Staatsschriften des

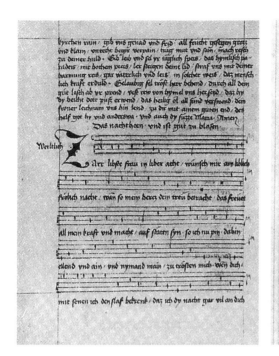 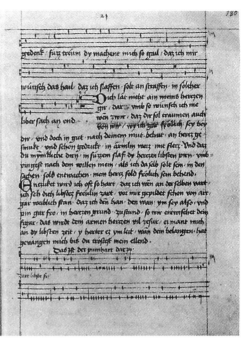

5 Hermann, Monk of Salzburg, *Das Nachthorn*: (a) beginning of top part; (b) conclusion of top part, and bottom part (Vienna, Österreichische Nationalbibliothek, MS 2856, ff.185v–186r)

späteren Mittelalters, iii/5 (Stuttgart, 1973 and 1977). The material translated here is from iii/5/1, pp.251f.

[3]For the details of Konrad's life see Krüger, vol.1, pp.xiif.

[4]Ibid, p.xxix

[5]Ibid, pp.121f

[6]The text given here is basically that of Krüger (see fn.2), and is reproduced by permission of the trustees of Monumenta Germaniae historica. I have changed the paragraph structure of Krüger's text in several places without comment, and made one editorial change of my own ([am]plectitur for plectitur in 1.45).

[7]Konrad is distinguishing a *musica humana* produced by the voice and a *musica instrumentalis* made by instruments.

[8]That is, Greek *cheiros*, of which this is the genitive form.

[9]These, of course, are not genuine names for instruments (with the exception of *monocorda*) but adjectives denoting string numbers.

[10]The distinction here would appear to be between instruments with no reeds (such as the trumpet) and instruments where the reed is not inserted directly into the pipe, but set in an assembly detachable from the pipe (e.g. a shawm).

[11]The minor pipes, as Konrad goes on to explain, are flutes and recorders.

[12]This presumably means that the long drone pipes of medieval organs were often *reed* pipes. I am not aware that this information is contained in any other medieval source.

[13]In other words they both have a predominantly cylindrical external profile terminating in a flared or tapering bell.

[14]Vernacular forms would include *floyt*, *floet* etc.

[15]Thus it is composed of a cylindrical-bore drone and a conical-bore chanter. Compare R. Weber, 'Tournebout—Pifia—Bladderpipe (*Platerspiel*)', GSJ 30 (1977), pp.64–9, pl.xvia.

[16]A convenient and neat illustration of the common medieval practice of referring to the organ as a plural conception.

[17]A remarkable description. There are similar accounts in classical sources. See P. Dronke, *The Medieval Lyric* (London, 2/1978), p.14.

[18]That is, because organs are effectively composed of 'minor pipes', or flutes which 'to an extent' move people to religious devotion.

[19]All of this section (Krüger, vol.1, pp.238–9) has been taken almost verbatim from A. Borgnet ed., *De vegetabilibus*, B[eati] Alberti Magni . . . opera omnia, 10 (Paris, 1891), p.161. Konrad also used this information in his vernacular treatise *Das Buch der Natur* (ed. F. Pfeiffer (Hildesheim, 1971), p.314), whence it was taken by Werner Bachmann in his *The Origins of Bowing* (Oxford, 1969), p.72–3.

[20]The fact that Konrad uses only two terms to describe the parts of these instruments—the *venter* ('paunch', 'belly') and the *coopertura* ('covering', 'roof')—points indisputably to the solid-carving method of construction.

[21]Krüger, vol.1, pp.245f

[22]C. Bullock-Davies, *Menestrellorum multitudo* (Cardiff, 1978), p.25

[23]The best survey of this subject (with a detailed examination of the English sources) is G. R. Rastall, 'Secular Musicians in Late Medieval England' (PhD diss., U. of Manchester, 1968), passim.

[24]Text in W.D. Ross ed., *Aristotelis Politica* (Oxford, 1957), p.259, trans. in E. Barker, *The Politics of Aristotle* (Oxford, 1946), p.341

[25]See H. G. Liddell and R. Scott, *A Greek–English Lexicon* (Oxford, rev. 1968), sv 'βάναυσος'.

[26]Albertus's commentary is printed in A. Borgnet ed., B[eati] Alberti Magni . . . opera omnia, 8 (Paris, 1891), p.789f (the relevant section).

[27]Text in E. Gallo, *The* Poetria Nova *and its Sources in Early Rhetorical Doctrine* (Paris, 1971), pp.48–9

[28]See the *Mitellateinisches Wörterbuch* (Munich, 1967–), *sv* 2*'Burdo'. For a survey of the many uses of this word in the Middle Ages see D. Hoffmann-Axthelm, 'Bourdon', *Handwörterbuch der musikalischen Terminologie* (Wiesbaden, 1972).

[29]See the *Oxford Latin Dictionary*, fasc.1 (Oxford, 1968), *sv*'bar(r)ītus'.

[30]L. Diefenbach, *Glossarium latino-germanicum mediae et infimae aetatis* (Frankfurt am Main, 1857), *sv* 'Musa'

[31]See A. Baines, *Bagpipes* (Oxford, rev. 2/1973), p.19.

[32]For a medieval illustration of a *tuba* together with this name written beside it see C. Page, 'Early 15th-century instruments in Jean de Gerson's *Tractatus de Canticis*', *EM* 6/3 (July 1978), p.341, illus.2

[33]For the German sources see Diefenbach, *Glossarium, sv* 'Cithara'.

[34]See H. Steger, *Philologia musica* (Munich, 1971), p.91f.

[35]For two examples see Page, op cit, illus.2 and 4.

[36]See C. Page, 'Jerome of Moravia on the *Rubeba* and *Viella*', *GSJ* 32 (1979), p.82.

[37]See for example the early 15th-century German gloss printed by Steger (op cit, p.110): *Rott, rubela/est parva figella.* Jean de Gerson states that the *rebecca* is smaller than the *viella* (Page, op cit, *EM* 6/3, p.347).

[38]See L. Wright, 'The Medieval Gittern and Citole: A Case of Mistaken Identity', *GSJ* 30 (1977), pp.8–42.

[39]See for example the scenes of the Apocalypse on the altarpiece of the German (Hamburg) school in the style of Master Bertram now in the Victoria and Albert Museum, London. This altarpiece probably dates from *c*1400.

[40]See Diefenbach, *Glossarium, sv* 'Figella'.

[41]See J. Smits van Waesberghe, *Cymbala*, Musicological Studies and Documents, 1 (Rome, 1951), *passim.*

[42]Facs. ed. H. Heger, *Mondsee–Wiener Liederhandschrift aus Codex Vindobonensis 2856*, Codices selecti, 19 (Graz, 1968)

[43]See S. Marcuse, *Musical Instruments–A Comprehensive Dictionary* (New York, rev. 2/1975), *sv* 'Pomhart', 'Pommer' and 'Bombard'.

The performance of songs in late medieval France

A new source

1 **King Philipus of Britain in his hall; illustration from** *Cleriadus et Meliadice* **(British Library, Royal 20 C.ii, f.1r)**

We have reached a critical stage in our understanding of the role of instruments in medieval music, both sacred and secular. Few scholars and performers in the English-speaking world now believe that instruments generally participated in liturgical music,[1] and lately some deeply entrenched views concerning the use of instruments in the secular repertories have come under scrutiny.[2] We have already reached a position where we cannot tacitly assume significant instrumental involvement in monophonic courtly songs, motets or polyphonic chansons.

Yet the study of performance practice is concerned with far more than questions of procedure—questions of what should be done; a change in performance conventions can influence the entire emotional and intellectual structure of our reaction to a particular repertory. Ultimately—and this is what raises the study of performance practice to a position of the first importance—such a change can affect the aesthetic and subjective feelings that are largely responsible for our 'sense of the past'. Consider the hints which Marix offered to performers more than 40 years ago: 'It will be best to choose instruments of contrasting sonority [for the textless tenor and contratenor parts] so as to distinguish the frequent crossing of these lines and, by contrast of timbre, to fill the emptiness of unisons'.[3]

Such counsel has inspired countless performances and has prompted some impressionistic—but compelling—analogies between the bright, uncompromising sounds of medieval instruments (as we are accustomed to imagine them) and the brilliant colours of contemporary painting, the pungent spices of medieval cookery.[4] Many seem convinced that the differentiation of timbre produced by these 'broken' instrumental groupings embodies a truth about late medieval music; 14th- and 15th-century chansons are often imagined in terms of boldly individualized lines collaborating in a polyphony which is extrovert and almost heraldic in colour, which is candid, even naïve, in its directness of address to the listener. Yet this is much more than a conception of a repertory; it is an interpretation, in miniature, of late medieval culture in France and Burgundy. We see how easily it accords with one of the most persuasive accounts of that subject ever written, Huizinga's *The Waning of the Middle Ages*: 'To the world when it was half a thousand years younger, the outlines of all things seemed more clearly marked than to us ... All experience had yet to the minds of men the directness and absoluteness of the pleasure and pain of child-life'.[5]

If this is an accurate summary of the influence of instruments—and of Huizinga—upon our thinking about this music then there are various comments by medieval theorists which must give us pause. 'Voices are more perfect than instruments', wrote Jacques de Liège during the years of Guillaume de Machaut's boyhood, 'and Art imitates Nature: there is no small

Reprinted from *Early Music* 10 (1982), pp. 441–450. By permission of Oxford University Press.

musicality in voices which instruments can never match.'[6] Instruments have been considered inferior to voices during most periods of Western music but the idea was more than a commonplace, a theoretical nicety, during the Middle Ages. The surviving musical manuscripts endorse the remarks of Jacques de Liège. Almost all the secular music which they contain can be classified as song; somewhere, and invariably in the most important place, it has words. To compose in the Middle Ages was to exploit what singers did best; to succeed was to create something that singers could control and dominate.

When we attempt to pursue these medieval priorities and establish rules to govern our performances we meet a major difficulty. This is not, as is often assumed, created by scarcity of sources; the problem is rather that the number of potentially valuable sources is legion and we do not know where we may most safely invest time and energy. Important—indeed crucial—references can turn up almost anywhere in the spectacular amount of literary and documentary material waiting to be sifted. With our present state of method and research we are at the mercy of chance finds for our understanding of performance practice, so it is inevitable that the picture we assemble from them can scarcely be regarded as more than a damaged mosaic. Here are some new fragments of the whole, gathered from a 15th-century French romance, *Cleriadus et Meliadice*, which has not been published in modern times.[7] They call much accepted thinking into question.

Cleriadus et Meliadice is a cluttered tale written to celebrate extremes of valour, sentiment and cere-monial. It caters for an insatiable appetite for adventure with many stock episodes of medieval romance: the crusade against the Saracens; the royal maiden dis-inherited by trickery, saved from murder, and forced to live in poverty until recognized by her lover; the young knight who triumphs over all his rivals, in battle and tournament, to win the heroine. Yet the author provides for a limitless interest in courts and courtesy (it is no surprise to find here and there in the work evidence of a French aristocratic and possibly royal provenance for *Cleriadus et Meliadice*)[8] and for the details of every-day life behind the ceremonial. Cleriadus, preparing to leave the port of Caradosse, having triumphed in a crusade, asks his subordinates to ensure that the army has no outstanding debts in the city; on another occasion a servant sets off to town to buy lances for

Cleriadus who has exhausted his supply in a chivalric contest, the defence of *la joyeuse maison* (ff.57r–69v, f.89v).

The author's observation of contemporary life—the detail that supports and affirms his story[9]—is grati-fyingly keen in matters musical. Throughout *Cleriadus et Meliadice* music generally follows the two main meals: first the *disner*, then the *souper*. It was often the custom in the later Middle Ages (in both France and England) for members of an aristocratic or courtly household to eat separately according to sex or rank, coming together after the meal to enjoy what came to be known as the *esbatemens* ('entertainments' or rather 'games'—implying participation by all).[10] *Cleriadus et Meliadice* incorporates a wealth of information about these *esbatemens*. In the opening pages of the romance Cleriadus and his father, the Count of Asturias, arrive at Windsor Castle while King Philipus of *Grant Bretaigne* (indiscriminately also called *Engleterre*) is at table (illus.1). Once the *disner* is finished Cleriadus enters the hall with his father's retinue; while the Count and Philipus fall into conversation he joins the company in the body of the hall:

les menestrers . . . commencerent a corner. Vng grant seigneur de la court print la belle Meliadice. Cleriadus print vne des dames et

2 Cleriadus in his chamber attended by a surgeon and three kings (f.179v)

chascun chascune se prinrent a danser. La feste dura longue piece.
Et quant il eubrent assez dansé les menestrers cesserent et se
prinrent a chanter. La oyssiez hommes et femmes bien chanter. Or
estoit Meliadice encoste Cleriadus et vng aultre cheualier de la
compaignie du conte d'Esture. Si print Meliadice a dire a Cleriadus:
'Je vous prie que nous veulliez dire vne chanchon de vostre pays;
vous auez assez oy de celles de ce pays' . . . Et lors commence
Cleriadus vne chanchon tant bien que tous ceulx de la place
l'escouterent moult volentiers. Et disoient tous que oncques mais
n'auoyent oy si bien chanter. Et mesmes le roy leissa a parler pour
l'escouter . . . (f.4v)

the minstrels began to play loud wind instruments. A great
lord of the court took the fair Meliadice. Cleriadus took one
of the ladies and all the men and women began to dance. The
entertainment lasted a long time. And when they had danced
their fill the minstrels ceased and they began to sing. There
might you have heard men and women singing well! Now
Meliadice was next to Cleriadus and another knight in the
retinue of the Count. She said to Cleriadus: 'Pray sing a song
from your country; you have heard enough songs from ours'
. . . And then Cleriadus began a song so well that all those
who were there listened to him gladly. They all said that they
had never heard anyone sing so well. Even the king himself
stopped talking to hear Cleriadus.

The *esbatemens* begin with the loud wind music of
the minstrels. When the company tires of dancing,
'they' (apparently the 'men and women' of the court)
begin to sing. Instruments are not mentioned. In these
informal, but hardly intimate circumstances, Cleriadus
is asked to sing; the company expects that young
squires aspiring to *chevalerie* will be prepared to sing
upon request. King Philipus and the Count have been
talking during the other songs—so impromptu were
the *esbatemens* on some occasions—but they both
listen to Cleriadus. The *salle* does not—at least on this
occasion—act like a modern concert hall; it is an arena
for diverse and segregated pastimes. It is no surprise to
read, in one 15th-century romance, that minstrels
'played in many places within the hall' (*juoient en
pluissieurs lieux parmy la salle*).[11]

The division of musical items into instrumental
ones performed by minstrels and songs performed by
courtly amateurs (with no reference to accompaniment)
is maintained throughout *Cleriadus et Meliadice*. Almost
invariably the minstrels play loud wind instruments,
often for dancing (illus.3):

Les menestrez commencerent a corner et chascun se print a danser
. . . (f.18r)
The minstrels began to play loud wind instruments and
everyone began to dance . . .

3 Cleriadus and Meliadice, seated, watch dancers in the hall (f.159r)

Trompettes et menestrez estoient deuant qui cornoient . . . (f.115r)
Trumpeters and minstrels went before playing loud wind
instruments . . .

trompettes sonnoyent, menestrez cornoyent, sans point cesser.
(f.122v)
trumpets sounded, minstrels played loud wind instruments,
without ceasing.

menestrez, trompettes se prinrent a corner. (f.161r)
minstrels, trumpeters began to play loud wind instruments.

les trompettes et menestrez . . . commencerent a jouer . . . Lors le
connestable commenche le basse danse . . . (f.171v)
the trumpeters and minstrels . . . began to play   Then the
connestable begins the *basse danse* . . .

Les menestrelz commencerent a corner . . . deux seigneurs
commencerent les danses . . . (f.190v)
The minstrels began to play loud wind instruments . . . two
lords began the dances . . .

There are similar references in some other 15th-
century fiction. In Antoine de la Sale's *Le Petit Jehan de
Saintré*, a remarkable work which recounts the progress
of its hero from the rank of page to higher things via
success in the lists at home and on crusade abroad,

there is a passage where minstrels play loud wind instruments and the courtiers dance, then sing:

menestrelz commencerent a corner, et les cuers joyeulz commencerent a dansser et puis a chanter . . .[12]

minstrels began to play loud wind instruments, and the joyous-hearted ones began to dance and then to sing . . .

There is a comparable reference in *Le livre des faits du bon chevalier Messire Jacques de Lalaing*, a prose narrative of the doings of an historical member of the Lalaing family in the 15th century which closely resembles a fictional romance (although a number of the more romantic exploits recounted in it are known to have taken place). Here we read that on one occasion minstrels played *trompettes* for dancing in the hall after the banquet, but then

chevaliers et dames se prirent de tous costés par la salle à danser, chanter et envoisier et faire feste . . .[13]

knights and ladies occupied every part of the hall in dancing, singing and celebrating . . .

At one point in *Cleriadus et Meliadice* there is an elaborate description of an *entremez* (an entertainment while the company is still seated at table) which shows how easily song found a place in the contexts of play and spectacle. Yet although the occasion is a festive one it is clear that only the voices of young ladies at court are heard. The professionals, the minstrels, who are playing various instruments as the *entremez* begins, are commanded to stop so that the voices may be heard. The event takes place in the courtyard of a palace where a large company is celebrating the marriage of Cleriadus and Meliadice:

Or est ainsi que auant qu'on leuast les tables apres les entremez, dont il y en eubt sans nombre, il y en vint vng vous orez quel. C'estoient .xx. jeusnes enfans de .xv. ans et .xx. pucelles de cest eage. Les filz estoient montez sur lyons priuez bien sellez de selles de joustes et bien bridez, et tous couuers tant les enfans comme les lyons de pourpre, et les .xx. pucelles estoient assizes sur licornes qui auoient moult belles selles et beaux harnas. Et estoient les pucelles vestues de pourpre de mesmez les valletons, tous leurs cheueulx gettez par derriere, et auoient chappeaulx vers sur leur teste. Et chascune pucelle menoit son valleton par vne laisse de fil d'or et de soye. En cest estat arriuerent deuant la grant table et .xl. varletz auec eulx qui portoyent grant tourse de lances. Aussi tost qu'ilz furent arriuez les pucelles descendirent et les varletz prinrent les licornes; si se tirerent les pucelles a vne part et commencerent a chanter. Et pour leur beau chant fist on cesser les instrumens adfin de les mieulx oyr, et tous ceulx et celles qui les escoutoient disoient que oncques mais n'auoient oy mieulx chanter en leur vie. Et tandis qu'ilz chantoient les valletons joustoient deuant la compagnie, et celuy qui estoit abatu se venoit rendre a le pucelle qui l'auoit amené, et celluy qui l'auoit abatu luy donnoit vne verge d'or pour sa

renchon, et puis il la donnoit a la pucelle. Et le pucelle la prenoit et luy donnoit le chapel qu'elle auoit sur sa teste, et puis le mettoit en sa main auprez d'elle et d'ung aultre. Et puis recommenchoient a jouster. Ainsi dura la jouste et la danse grant pieche. (f.170r–v)

Now it happened that before the tables were raised after the countless *entremez*, another took place and you shall hear about it. It was performed by 20 young boys, each 15 years of age, and 20 girls of the same age. The boys were mounted on tame lions well saddled with jousting saddles and well bridled; both the lions and their young riders were completely clothed in purple. The 20 girls were mounted upon unicorns which were equipped with very beautiful saddles and fair harnesses. These girls were clothed in purple like the boys; their hair was thrown back and they had green hats upon their heads. Each girl led her boy by a lead of gold and silk. In this wise they arrived before the major table accompanied by 40 valets carrying a great bundle of lances. As soon as they were there the girls dismounted and the valets took the unicorns away; then the girls went off to one side and began to sing. Because of their beautiful song the instruments were commanded to be silent so that the girls might be better heard: all those who heard them, both men and women, said that they had never heard better singing in their lives. And while they were singing the boys jousted before the company. He who was beaten came to surrender himself to the girl who had brought him in, while the victor gave him a golden rod to ransom himself, then the loser gave it to the girl. In return the girl gave him the hat that she had upon her head and he put it in his hand beside her and another [?]. Then they began the joust again. Thus the dance and the joust lasted a long while.

Few passages better illustrate the intimate relation between chivalric literature and chivalric life in the 15th century. The essence of this description is exaggeration, not fantasy. The implication that the lions and unicorns are real is not a departure from realism, but an acknowledgement that in the remote and idealized past of the story some most difficult things were accomplished in the interests of ceremonial. Compulsive chivalric themes are on display here: the fascination with youth, *jeunesse*, so candid and precocious; the undying interest in images of sexual bondage and surrender; the attraction of everything implied by play—competition, display and reward. Song is a natural adornment for such an occasion; yet even though it contributes to the spectacle there is no accompaniment. Voices suffice.

Several times in *Cleriadus et Meliadice* a distinction is maintained between 'dancing to minstrels' and 'dancing to songs'—further evidence that the author wished to keep the instrumental music of the minstrels and the vocal, amateur performances of the courtiers distinct.

This opposition is brought out at the close of the following passage (which incidentally reveals the texture of courtly manners woven around the act of dancing the *basse danse*). King Philipus of *Engleterre* has arrived at the court of the Count of Asturias to fetch his daughter, Meliadice, whom he believed dead. Cleriadus is present, and there is a great celebration:

'Je feray venir les menestres pour festier la compagnie.' Le conte luy dit que ce seroit bien fait. Adonc Cleriadus fit venir trompettes et menestres qui ja auoi[en]t festié toutte la compaignie si commencent a jouer et Cleriadus a [MS: la] querir messire Domus, le quel estoit le plus grant seigneur de toutte la compaignie . . . si la prent et la maine a Meliadice, et luy dist: 'Messire Domus, menez madame Meliadice vne basse danse.' Il s'agenoulle deuant Meliadice en s'excusant vng pou, disant que il ne sçauoit guerres danser, touttesfois Meliadice le pria qu'i[l] la [MS: qui la] menast, si fist son commandement et commencha la danse. Ceulx qui s'en sceurent entremettre prinrent dames et demoiselles tant celles de Meliadice que de celles de la contesse. Et Cleriadus print Romaine et la mena a la danse, car grant fain auoit de deuiser a elle. Et grant piece parlerent ensamble d'une chose et d'aultre. Ainsi fut la chose commencié[e] et bien entretenue tant de danser aux menestrez comme aux chansons. (f.112v)

'I will summon the minstrels to entertain the company.' The Count told Cleriadus that it would be a fine gesture. Then Cleriadus called in the trumpeters and minstrels who had already entertained the courtiers and they begin to play. Cleriadus sought Messire Domus who was the greatest lord in the whole company . . . he takes him by the hand and leads him to Meliadice saying: 'Messire Domus, lead my lady Meliadice in a *basse danse'.* He kneels before Meliadice and excuses himself somewhat, saying that he knows little of dancing; however, Meliadice entreated him that he should lead her, and so he complied with her request and began the dance. Those who knew how to perform the dance took ladies and maidens, both those of Meliadice and those of the countess. Cleriadus took Romaine and led her to the dance for he had a great desire to converse with her. For a long while they talked together of one thing and another. Thus the entertainment was begun and well conducted, both in dancing to minstrels and in dancing to songs.

We find the same distinction later in the romance when Cleriadus and Meliadice are entertained by the French king—'the greatest and noblest of all Christians' —at his court in Paris after a series of jousts from which Cleriadus has emerged triumphant:

Les danses auoient longuement duré aux menestrez, car la feste estoit moult belle . . . Quant la compaignie fut traueillée de danser aux menestrelz ilz se prinrent a danser aux chanchons . . . Le roy print Meliadice, et vne des dames de la royne, et commencha les danses aux chansons. Et la oyssiez hommes et femmes bien chanter. (f.127r–v)

The dancing to minstrels had lasted a long while, for it was a magnificent celebration . . . When the company was tired of dancing to minstrels they began to dance to songs . . . the king took Meliadice and one of the queen's ladies to begin the dancing. There might you have heard gentlemen and ladies singing well!

And again a little later during the same celebrations:

La feste aux chansons estoit ja faillie et redansoit on aux menestrez. (f.128v)

The festivity with songs was already over and the company was dancing to minstrels again.

Did amateur musicians combine vocal and instrumental music, accompanying themselves or others? *Cleriadus et Meliadice* incorporates many episodes where we might expect to find an answer to this question. It depicts a society in which instruments, like chessmen, can be called for whenever they are required to pass an hour or two.[14] Both Cleriadus and his lady are gifted harpists.[15] Contemporary illustrations sometimes show instruments stored in chambers ready for impromptu music-making. Yet 15th-century romances incorporate a number of references to segregation of voices and instruments. In *Pontus et Sidoine*, a romance dating from *c*1400 and unpublished in modern times, the hero is asked on one occasion to dance, to sing, and then to play the harp. This serves an obvious literary purpose for it emphasizes his talents by enumeration; yet each accomplishment is clearly self-sufficient:

Et apres se prindrent a chanter et a dancer. Mais a paine peurent faire dancer le sourdit, et disoit qu'il ne sçauoit dancer. Mais il fu a la dance et dança le mielx. Et apres aussi ne le pouaient faire chanter. Mais a la priere des filles du roy il chanta vne chançon le mieulx de tous. Apres ce qu'ilz eurent dancé le filz du roy et sa seur se prindrent a jouer de la herpe. Et quant ilz eurent vne piece herpé, prierent a Pontus qu'il herpast. Mais a paine le voulu faire. Et au fort herpa vng lay nouuel a merueilles bel . . .[16]

And afterwards they began to sing and dance; yet they could scarcely persuade Pontus to dance, for he protested that he had no ability for it. However, when he joined the dance he danced the best. Nor could they prevail upon him to sing afterwards, but when the daughters of the king asked him he sang a song better than any. After they had danced the son of the king and his sister began to play the harp, and when they had harped a while they asked Pontus to play but they could barely persuade him to do so. But in the end he harped a lay that was new and wonderfully beautiful . . .

There is more than a hint of such a separation of vocal and instrumental music in *Paris et Vienne* where the hero and his companion, Edardo, sing and *then* play beneath Vienne's window:

aloient de nuyt soubz la chambre de Vienne, faisant oubades de leurs chanssons, quar ilz chantoient souveraynement bien, et puys jouoyent de leur instrumens chanssons mellodyoses, comme ceulx qui de celluy mestier estoient les maistres.[17]

they were accustomed to go at night beneath Vienne's room using their songs as aubades, for they sang surpassingly well, and then they played melodious songs upon their instruments like ones who were masters of that craft.

Cleriadus et Meliadice contains some important evidence that may now be brought to bear upon this problem, for there are three occasions when music that is either possibly polyphonic (one instance) or definitely so (two instances) is performed by courtly amateurs. The first takes us to a chamber at the court of Wales where Cleriadus is recovering after wounds received in battle with a lion which had ravaged that country. He is abed, yet the setting soon loses its intimacy. Cleriadus (with four knights who keep him company) receives a visit from the King of Wales who brings a *priuee compaignie* (apparently two knights). The queen is sent for and she duly arrives together with her daughter, Cadore, and a party of waiting-women among whom there is 'a great wealth of beauties' (*grant foison de belles*). The occasion becomes a populous and convivial one and the king interprets it as ideal for a performance by Cadore, a precociously gifted singer:

Le roy demanda a Cleriadus: 'Volez vous oyr chanter ma fille?'. 'Oy, sire, s'il vous plaist.' Le roy appelle deux jeunes filz si leur commande qu'ilz chantent aueuc la fille. Adonc Cadore en commença a dire vne chanchon de si grant sentement et tant bien que Cleriadus estoit tout esmeruillié de l'oyr car elle n'auoit pas plus de sept ans . . . (f.38r)

The king asked Cleriadus: 'Would you like to hear my daughter sing?'. [Cleriadus replied:] 'Yes, please.' Then the king calls two young boys and commands them to sing with the girl. Then Cadore began to sing a song of such noble feeling, and so well, that Cleriadus was amazed to hear it for she was no more than seven years old . . .

The king calls two young boys (household pages perhaps) to sing with his daughter, but it can hardly be that one so talented needs moral support. Perhaps she performs a monophonic rondeau or some other refrain song that welcomes multi-voice performance? A particularly interesting possibility is that she performs the superius part of a polyphonic chanson while the two boys, possessing equivalent and slightly lower voices, perform the tenor and contratenor parts. There is no reference to the use of instruments.

There is some support for the 'polyphonic' interpretation of this passage in two further extracts from *Cleriadus et Meliadice*, both of them more explicit. In

each one subordinate members of the household are called upon to perform in order to accompany a courtly amateur. The first incorporates an account of Cleriadus as a composer of secular polyphony—an episode unique, as far as I am aware, in 15th-century French literature. After his battle with the lion that had ravaged the kingdom of Wales Cleriadus sets out for the court of Philipus, King of *Engleterre*. He has been separated from Meliadice for a long while and during the journey he is pleased to see one of her valets riding towards him. The valet carries a love-letter containing a rondeau written by Meliadice:

Alez vous en mon desir amoureux
Deuers celluy pour quy souuent je veille;
Luy dire tout bas en l'oreille
Qu'aultre de luy je n'ayme si m'et Dieux.

Il est tant beau et si tres gracieux;
* Alez vous en mon desir amoureux;*

Je ne quiers ne desire mieulx
Qu'a bien amer mon coeur sy appareille;
Dieu me doint oyr bonne nouuelle
Du plus leal qui soit desoubz les cieulx.
* [Alez vous en mon desir amoureux*
* Deuers celluy pour quy souuent je veille;*
* Luy dire tout bas en l'oreille*
* Qu'aultre de luy je n'ayme si m'et Dieux].* (ff.49r–v)

'I am sending you a song', writes Meliadice in her letter enclosing this rondeau, 'and I pray you to compose music for it' (*je vous prie que la veulliez mettre en chant* [f.49r]). Cleriadus arrives at a town (*ville*) and finds lodgings so that he may begin work on the setting at once:

Si tost que Cleriadus fu descendu en son logeis il demanda incontinent vne harpe . . . Quant Cleriadus fut a par luy il commença a faire les notes de la chanchon que Melyadice luy auoit enuoyée, et le fit si bien que ceulx qui l'ouoient apres chanter disoient que jamais meilleur chant n'auoyent oy. Aprez la mist sur la harpe et joua longuement. Et puis, quant il eubt tout fait, il commença a faire vnes lettres a Meliadice. (ff.50v–51r)

As soon as Cleriadus entered his lodgings he demanded a harp at once . . . When he was all alone he began to compose the music for the song that Meliadice had sent him, and he succeeded so well that those who heard it sung afterwards said that they had never heard a better song. Afterwards he put it on the harp and played for a long time. When he had done everything he began to write a letter to Meliadice.

An illustration in the British Library manuscript of the romance shows Cleriadus harping in his chamber (illus.4). No writing materials are shown (and none is mentioned in the text) even though, as we later learn,

4 Cleriadus playing the harp in his chamber (f.51v)

the setting he composes is a polyphonic one in at least two parts. What are we to understand by the fact that he 'put [the song] on the harp and played for a long time'? His work on the song seems to involve two operations: composing the music, and 'putting' the music on the harp. In his reply to Meliadice, Cleriadus emphasizes that the second stage, the only one definitely involving a harp, has already (*desia*) been accomplished, as if it were not normally completed at the time of composition:

J'ay mis vostre chanchon en chant, non pas si bien que a la chanchon apertient veu le lieu dont elle vient, et si est desia mise sur le harpe, et la vous aporteray, se dieu plait, a heure dicte. (f.51r)

I have composed music for your song, though not so well as the song deserves considering from whom it comes, and also it has already been put upon the harp, and I will bring it to you, please God, at the said time.

There seem to be two possible interpretations of these events. The first is that Cleriadus composes the superius part and then, perhaps using the harp to help himself think harmonically and contrapuntally, he composes a line (or lines) to accompany it. The second possibility—and the one that I consider more likely—is that Cleriadus composes the whole piece, superius and (at least) tenor, and then produces a harp intabulation for Meliadice who is a skilled player upon that instrument (indeed the *varlet* who brings back Cleriadus's letter finds her playing the harp in her most private chamber).[18]

Despite the involvement of a harp, the leading 15th-

century court instrument, in the above episode, Cleriadus does not use one when he is asked to perform his new composition in a hall of great splendour, purpose-built to celebrate a *pas d'armes* in which he has triumphed against all comers. King Philipus is present with many other noble ladies and gentlemen. The company is dancing:

Quant ilz eubrent longuement dansé aux menestrez ilz danserent aux chanchons. Sy commencha Cleriadus que Meliadice auoit faicte. Vng escuier de sa compaignie luy tenoit la teneur, et pensez qu'il estoit bon a oyr, car il chantoit le mieulx que on auoit jamais ouy. Et quant il eubt fait il [la] bailla par escript en la main de Melyadice. (f.70v)

When the company had danced a good while to the minstrels they began to dance to songs. So Cleriadus began to sing what Meliadice had written. A squire from his retinue held the tenor part for him and you may believe that it was good to hear, for [Cleriadus] sang better than anyone had ever heard before. When he had finished he put a written copy of the song into the hands of Meliadice.

This provides our first piece of evidence in the romance that 'dancing to songs', discussed above, could involve polyphonic music, following the pattern, by now familiar, of professional instrumental music alternating with amateur vocal music during celebration. Cleriadus is clearly singing the superius, even though the poem it carries is written from a woman's point of view, and in addition there are strong reasons for believing that the squire who 'holds' the tenor is also singing, not playing an instrument (none is mentioned). Thus, for example, Mathieu d'Escouchy, in his account of the famous Feast of the Pheasant, says that the tenor of one polyphonic song was 'held' (*tenoit la teneur*); Olivier de la Marche, working from the same official account and referring to the same piece, records that the tenor was 'sung' (*chanta la teneur*); there is ample supporting evidence for this usage.[19]

Later in the romance Cleriadus composes another song which a *varlet de chambre* carries to Meliadice reporting that Cleriadus made it 'that very morning' (f.130v). Meliadice is preparing to set out to join the French royal court in a visit to the woods and it is during the return from such an expedition, while the company is in open country (*a plain champ*) on the way to Paris, that the French king asks Cleriadus to perform a song. After elaborately rhetorical and courteous preliminaries (in which Cleriadus, faithful to the chivalric demand for modesty in practising all the arts of peace, claims that he knows nothing of singing) Cleriadus arranges a performance of the song he has recently sent to Meliadice:

Cleriadus appella vng de ses pages (lesquelz estoient tous gentilz hommes) et si appella vng de ses escuiers pour tenir teneur a luy et a l'enfant. Adonc commence Cleriadus la chanson si bien et si gentement et d'une si belle voix et nette et haulte que le roy et la royne l'ouoient tant volentiers que c'estoit merueilles. Le plus de la compaignie vinrent au tour d'eux pour les oyr. Le chanson estoit moult bonne et de bon chant, et aussi la disoit bien Cleriadus et ceulx qui luy aidoient . . . (f.133v)

Cleriadus called one of his pages (which were all of gentle status) and he also called one of his squires to hold the tenor for himself and for the child. Then Cleriadus begins the song so well and so nobly, and with such a beautiful, pure and loud voice that the king and queen heard it with marvellous willingness. The greater part of the company gathered around them to listen. The song was very good with beautiful music, and also Cleriadus and those who helped him sang it very well . . .

Once again subordinate members of the retinue are called upon to perform. A squire 'holds the tenor' as in the previous extract while Cleriadus sings. A *page* (also called *enfant*), presumably a boy of up to about 14 years of age, is also singing.[20] There is no mention of instruments and it seems clear that all the performers are singing: 'Cleriadus and those who helped him sang it very well'.

How must we assess the contribution of *Cleriadus et Meliadice* to our understanding of performance practice in 15th-century France? Can its details be trusted?

The British Library manuscript of *Cleriadus et Meliadice* was copied in an age when the relations between chivalric life and chivalric literature were so close that the modern reader 'may have difficulty in knowing whether many episodes . . . are based on facts heightened by fiction, or on fiction authenticated by facts'.[21] Aristocratic society tended to pattern its chivalric conduct on literary texts. The intimate relation of life and literature is readily apparent in the musical passages of *Cleriadus et Meliadice*. Consider the last extract quoted above. A performance of a polyphonic chanson takes place during a pause in a journey before royal personages and nobles of the highest degree; the performance involves amateurs (including a *page* drawn from the *gentilz hommes* of Cleriadus's retinue) one of whom is asked to 'hold' the tenor part; the author emphasizes that the king and the queen listen to the rendition *volentiers*. Now let us compare a well-known passage from an annalistic source, the memoirs of the Abbots of St Aubert, which relate how Philip the Good heard a polyphonic song performed at Cambrai in 1449. We are told that the performance took place during a pause before a journey and that two choirboys

(probably from the cathedral) sang together while 'one of the gentlemen held the tenor' (*un des ses Gentils Hommes tint le tenure*); Philip is said to have listened to the performance *volentiers*.[22] There are many striking points of resemblance between this account and the passage from *Cleriadus et Meliadice*: the performance during a pause in a journey; the participation by courtly amateurs, including one of the *gentils hommes* who 'holds' the tenor; the assurance that the magnates for whom the performances are undertaken listen *volentiers*. The content, style and vocabulary of the two passages are so similar that we almost seem to be dealing with a literary topos, common to fiction and annal. The truth is rather that both types of writing, romance and record, endorse one another in support of a common assumption: that it is the nature of chivalric magnates to delight in musical performances, especially those involving courtier–amateurs, or *gentils hommes*, who are pleased to 'hold' a part, when they are called upon to do so, in circumstances all the more delightful for their spontaneity. Overriding the simplest concerns—a romancer's desire to celebrate his hero, an abbot's desire to celebrate the Cambrai choristers—there is a central tenet of medieval chivalry involved: that man's capacity for virtue 'seems inseparable from his desire for beauty and his pleasure in those forms of life and love governed by an ideal of aesthetic refinement'.[23]

Like many of the finest medieval romances *Cleriadus et Meliadice* supports its themes of love and chivalry by a mode of authenticating realism—'details from everyday life that lend the narrative an air of plausibility and that allow an audience to accept, or at least suspend its disbelief in, the improbabilities of the fiction'.[24] The musical references in this romance belong, I believe, to the author's exploitation of this mode. They are not structural, they do not advance the plot; each one participates in a realism designed to allow 15th-century readers at court to recognize their own experiences, and thus almost to recognize themselves, in the idealized world of the story. This they must do, for, as with much chivalric literature of the later Middle Ages, the moral world of this narrative is in earnest and readers must be manoeuvred into a position where they may appropriate it.

I propose that in these sections of *Cleriadus et Meliadice* we have three new pieces of evidence that in later 15th-century France polyphonic chansons could be—and perhaps generally were—performed by voices only. Everywhere in this romance we meet a distinction between vocal and instrumental music. One and the same piece may be played (as Cleriadus seems to play his setting of Meliadice's rondeau) or sung, which is how Cleriadus chooses to perform his setting at court. We must imagine these pieces performed by equivalent resources, not a voice and several disparate instrumental timbres. It is possible, of course, that singers differentiated their sounds to individualize their parts, yet this still leads to what is, by the standards of an instrumentally accompanied performance, a remarkable homogeneity, as experiment shows. It is surely time to reconsider some very basic notions about the performance of late medieval chansons.

Perhaps it is also time to reassess any sense of the 15th century that we may owe to an experience of its secular music in performance. The wedding of secular music to poetry, through the voice, now appears to have been an art often segregated from the candid, ingenuous sounds of harps and lutes and from the uncompromising asperities of trumpets and shawms; chanson performances, it would seem, did not necessarily have that 'partiality for brilliant things . . . shown by the naïve pleasure taken in tinkling or clicking sounds', or those 'naïve contrasts of primary colours' that Huizinga found to be so characteristic of the 'waning' Middle Ages.[25]

Summary of information on performance practice supplied by extracts from *Cleriadus et Meliadice*

(The song performed by Cadore and two boys is assumed to be polyphonic.)

Polyphonic song

1 Performing contexts
> Performed for listeners (always)
> In a chamber (? about 20 people present)
> In the hall
> For dancing
> Out of doors (a pause during a journey)
> Performed upon request

2 Performing forces
> Three voices (a seven-year-old girl and two boys)
> Two voices (Cleriadus and a squire who sings the tenor)
> Three voices (Cleriadus, a page, and a squire who sings the tenor)
> ?Harp intabulation of a ?two-part song

3 Composition of polyphonic song
> By Cleriadus; the text, a rondeau, having been written by Meliadice
> Use of the harp by Cleriadus ?during composition
> Written copy put into circulation by Cleriadus after composition
> Composition followed by performance

Monophonic song

1 Performing contexts

> In the hall at Windsor (a company of gentlemen and ladies present)
> In the hall as part of an *entremez*
> In the hall for dancing

2 Performing forces (the singers are invariably amateurs)
> Solo voice
> Groups of courtiers
> Groups of young girls

Instruments and instrumentalists

> Minstrels invariably play loud instruments for dancing or ceremonial
> Cleriadus plays ?intabulation of his polyphonic composition upon the harp
> Minstrels are commanded to stop playing so that courtly amateur singers may be heard

[1]For a listing of some relevant bibliography see A. Hughes, *Medieval Music* (Toronto, 2/1980), items 1947ff. See also G. Reaney, 'Text Underlay in Early Fifteenth-Century Musical Manuscripts', *Essays in Musicology in Honor of Dragan Plamenac*, ed. G. Reese and R. J. Snow (Pittsburgh, 1969/R1977), pp.245–51; and J. T. Igoe, 'Performance Practice in the Polyphonic Mass of the Early Fifteenth Century' (PhD diss., U. of North Carolina at Chapel Hill, 1971).

[2]H. van der Werf, *The Chansons of the Troubadours and Trouvères* (Utrecht, 1972), p.19; L. Gushee, 'Two Central Places: Paris and the French Court in the Early Fourteenth Century', *Bericht über den Internationalen Musikwissenschaftlichen Kongress Berlin 1974*, ed. H. Kuhn and P. Nitsche (Kassel, 1980), p.143; D. Fallows, 'Specific Information on the Ensembles for Composed Polyphony 1400–1474', to appear in the proceedings of the New York conference on performance practice, October 1981 (Cambridge, in preparation) (I am most grateful to Dr Fallows for allowing me to see this paper before its publication); C. Wright, 'Voices and Instruments in the Art Music of Northern France during the 15th Century: A Conspectus', *Report of the Twelfth Congress [of the International Musicological Society] Berkeley 1977*, ed. D. Heartz and B. Wade (Kassel, 1981), pp.643–9; C. Page, 'Machaut's "pupil" Deschamps on the performance of music: Voices or instruments in the 14th-century chanson?', *EM* 5/4 (October 1977), pp.484–91

[3]J. Marix, *Les musiciens de la cour de Bourgogne au XVe siècle (1420–1467)* (Paris, 1937), p.xxi (my translation).

[4]See, for example, David Munrow's notes to his recording *The Mediaeval Sound* (Oryx EXP 46): 'The people of the Middle Ages and the Renaissance liked gorgeous colours in their clothes, sharp contrasts in their paintings, highly flavoured dishes at their table. In music they liked sounds which were bright and uncompromising.'

[5]J. Huizinga, *The Waning of the Middle Ages* (London, 1924), p.1. It would be a most worthwhile project to study the influence of Huizinga's ideas upon our conception of the sound-picture of medieval secular music. They exerted a crucial influence at an early stage; Rudolf Ficker, one of the first scholars who attempted to discuss in print the timbres and tone colours of medieval music, was indebted to Huizinga; see his study 'Polyphonic Music of the Gothic Period', *MQ* 15 (1929), pp.483–505. His concept of an 'autumn' of the Middle Ages (p.500) is directly derived from the original Dutch title of Huizinga's masterwork, and his views on the intensely coloured and brilliant quality of Machaut's music in performance seem to lead on from the notion that Machaut was a 'typical representative' of a 'moribund culture' (pp.500, 505). Signs of Huizinga's influence upon the writings of musicologists are everywhere, as for example in N. Bridgman, 'The Age of Ockeghem and Josquin', *New Oxford History of Music*, 3 (London, 1960), p.246, and H. Besseler, *Bourdon und Fauxbourdon* (Leipzig, 1950), p.207. For recent signs that *The Waning of the Middle Ages* is still casting its spell see L. L. Perkins and

H. Garey, eds., *The Mellon Chansonnier*, 2 vols. (New Haven and London, 1979), 2, p.63. For a penetrating examination of some of Huizinga's basic views see M. Vale, *War and Chivalry* (London, 1981), *passim*, esp. pp.1ff.

[6] *Jacobi Leodiensis Speculum musicae*, ed. R. Bragard, Corpus scriptorum de musica, 3 (Rome, 1955–73), i, p.54.

[7] All quotations here are taken from London, British Library, Royal 20 C.ii, a northern French or Flemish manuscript of the second half of the 15th century according to G. F. Warner and J. B. Gilson, *Catalogue of Western Manuscripts in the Old Royal and King's Collections*, 4 vols. (London, 1921), 2, p.371. For an inventory of other sources of the text, including early printed editions, see B. Woledge, *Bibliographie des romans et nouvelles en prose française antérieurs à 1500* (Geneva, 1954), and *Supplément 1954–1973* (Geneva, 1975), text no.42. For a recent survey of French prose *histoires* (and an excellent bibliographical guide) see R. Morse, 'Historical Fiction in Fifteenth-century Burgundy', *Modern Language Review*, 75 (1980), pp.48–64. I am most grateful to Dr Morse for valuable help and advice.

[8] The author speaks of the chivalry, the court and the King of France in the most flattering terms; see ff.117r, 129r, 167v.

[9] For further discussion of this point see below.

[10] Even in small households it seems to have been common for music to be reserved until after dinner. See, for example, P. Champion, ed., *Les cent nouvelles nouvelles*, 2 vols. (Paris, 1928), 1, p.132. This is perhaps the place to mention another interesting musical reference in *Les cent nouvelles nouvelles* which throws a little light on the vexed question of instrumentalists' repertory. In one story of the collection (2, p.211) a convict led to the gallows is saved by playing on his bagpipes a 'song that his companions knew very well and which began: *Tu demoures trop, Robinet, tu demoures trop'*. It is interesting that the anonymous virelai *Or sus vous dormés trop*, apparently dating from the second half of the 14th century, contains passages which seem to imitate bagpipes (an interpretation supported by the text at the relevant point: *Or tost, naquaires, cornemuses, sonnés*). The piece is edited in W. Apel, *French Secular Compositions of the Fourteenth Century*, Corpus mensurabilis musicae, 53 (n.p., 1970–72), iii, pp.42–5. Obviously there is no reason to assume that it is this very piece which is meant in the *nouvelle* (no bagpiper could play it at all); what matters is the association of a certain kind of poem with a specific instrument and its idioms. Perhaps there are more such relationships to be discovered. Further information of this kind is badly needed.

[11] *Gilles de Chin*; text published in *Publications de la Société des Bibliophiles de Mons*, 4 (1837), extract quoted from p.17

[12] *Antoine de la Sale, Le Petit Jehan de Saintré*, ed. P. Champion and F. Desonay (Paris, 1926), p.86

[13] *Oeuvres de Georges Chastellain*, 8, ed. K. de Lettenhove (Brussels, 1866), p.64. This text is full of praise for the *esbatemens* at the Burgundian court (see pp.31, 41).

[14] Thus on f.60v of the romance *harpes, fleutres, jeux d'esches et de tables et de pluiseurs aultres gracieux jeux* are called for to entertain the hero, his lady and their company of friends in a chamber. Numerous sources attest to the fact that instrumental playing and singing bore the same social weight as playing board games. In the 15th century prose version of *La fille du Comte de Pontieu*, harping, playing *tablez* and *eschiés*, and singing are described as 'the three things in which gentlemen, ladies and maidens are accustomed to take great pleasure' (*trois chosez en quoy seigneurs, damez et damoisellez seulent prendre grand deduit*); see *La fille du Comte de Pontieu*, ed. C. Brunel (Paris, 1923), p.106.

[15] Meliadice learns to play the harp 'so well that she surpassed all others' (*si bien qu'elle en estoit maistresse par dessus touttes aultres*) (f.1v); for Cleriadus as a harpist see below. It is worth emphasizing here that musical skills were not always highly regarded in 15th-century French society. It is true that they belonged in the conception of courtly accomplishment that balanced violent activity such as combat and athletics by the indoor *gieux* such as chess, but the tone of courtly life in the prose romances and *ystoires* is over-

whelmingly established by the pursuit of arms. According to a conservative author such as Antoine de la Sale 'the true lover–gentleman is not at all suited or disposed to the intellectual and holy sciences of theology, nor to decrees, laws or any other discipline of study save the very noble and illustrious science and trade of arms' (Champion and Desonay, eds., *op cit*, p.49). Since the conduct of war was so *artifficieuse et subtille* the way was open for *armes* to be regarded as a fulfilment of both the physical and ratiocinative ideals of life. Music might then be associated with the vice habitually bred at court and disastrous for the knight: sloth, or *oysiveté* (sometimes personified as a musician in 15th-century French art). It is the 'romantic' narratives such as *Cleriadus et Meliadice* where this stigma is most successfully removed from the readers' field of view. The hero of *Pontus et Sidoine* is an accomplished musician; see the text in British Library, Royal 15 E.vi, ff.209r–v, 213r (where Pontus composes a song), 217r (quoted on p.445) and 224v (where he disguises himself as a minstrel dancing to *chalumeaulx*). The hero of *Paris et Vienne* is a talented instrumentalist and singer; see R. Kaltenbacher, ed., 'Der altfranzösische Roman Paris et Vienne', *Romanische Forschungen*, 15 (1904), pp.394, 397–9, 405. The musical references in this text are discussed in H. M. Brown, 'Instruments and Voices in the Fifteenth-century Chanson', *Current Thought in Musicology*, ed. J. W. Grubbs (Austin, Texas, and London, 1976), pp.102f.

[16] British Library, Royal 15 E.vi, f.217r. For an inventory of the manuscripts of this text and of the early printed editions see Woledge, *op cit*, text no.124. [17] Kaltenbacher, *op cit*, p.397

[18] F.52v. However, the references to the use of a harp in the composition episode have a complicated literary lineage and should not, at present, be pressed too hard for information of 15th-century relevance. For analogous material see R. Lathuillère, *Guiron le Courtois* (Geneva, 1966), pp.218–9, 229, 456.

[19] G. du Fresne de Beaucourt, ed., *Chronique de Mathieu d'Escouchy*, 3 vols. (Paris, 1863–4), 2, p.147; H. Beaune and J. d'Arbaumont, eds., *Mémoires d'Olivier de la Marche*, 4 vols. (Paris, 1883–8), 2, p.359. See also G. Vale, 'La cappella musicale del Duomo di Udine dal sec. XIII al sec. XIX', *Note d'archivio per la storia musicale*, 7 (1930), p.89; the chapter approves the appointment of Domenico da Buttrio on 2 May 1395, on the condition that 'the said priest Domenico must learn to hold the tenor in singing' (*dictus presbiter dominicus debeat addiscere cantum ad tenendum tenorem*). For another example of this usage, in the French vernacular, see M.-T. Bouquet, 'La cappella musicale dei duchi di Savoia dal 1450 al 1500', *Rivista italiana di musicologia*, 3 (1968), p.257, where Antonio Giunati is mentioned 'who holds the tenor with the said choristers' (*qui tient la teneur avecque lesdits innocens*) in 1470; the terminology of 'holding the tenor' also appears in the well-known extract from the memoirs of the Abbots of St Aubert which relates how Philip the Good heard a polyphonic chanson performed by three voices in 1449. For closely related terminology in Italian see N. Wilkins, *Music in the Age of Chaucer* (Cambridge, 1979), where musical references in Giovanni da Prato's *Il paradiso degli Alberti* (c1426) are most usefully quoted and translated (pp.51–2); in one extract, a ballate by Landini (*Or su, gentili spirti*) is said to have been performed by three voices: two girls and a man *tenendo loro bordone*. I owe this reference to the kindness of Dr Fallows.

[20] I am most grateful to Dr Malcolm Vale of St John's College, Oxford, for his advice on this point.

[21] J. Leyerle, 'The Major Themes of *Chivalric Literature*', *Chivalric Literature*, ed. L. D. Benson and J. Leyerle (Michigan, 1980), p.131

[22] Quoted in J. Marix, *Histoire de la musique et des musiciens de la cour de Bourgogne sous le règne de Philippe le Bon (1420–1467)* (Strasbourg, 1939/R1974), p.67

[23] E. B. Keiser, 'The Festive Decorum of *Cleanness*', *Chivalric Literature*, ed. Benson and Leyerle, p.65

[24] L. D. Benson, 'The Tournament in the Romances of Chrétien de Troyes and *L'histoire de Guillaume le Marechal*', *ibid*, p.13

[25] Huizinga, *op cit*, pp.248, 251

The Medieval *Organistrum* and *Symphonia*
1: A Legacy from the East?

THE hurdy-gurdies known as *organistrum* and *symphonia* are perhaps the most arresting of all medieval instruments. They are certainly amongst the most enigmatic. Their parentage is obscure; their social position—embracing the court, the choir-school, the market-square and the rustic feast—is colourful but confused; the character of their music is unknown; their repertory appears to have vanished.

As always with medieval instruments, the fascination of such problems as these derives from the profound questions of cultural and technological history that they comprehend. A search for the origins of the *organistrum* and *symphonia* soon reveals an imposing theme: technical initiative in the West and its interplay with external influences transmitted via 'the great cultural symposium over which [the Arabs] presided'.[1] Is the Western debt to Islamic musical culture as significant as some Arabists have urged? How can we answer this question with respect to the *organistrum* and *symphonia*? Similarly, our grasp of these instruments' social position and function depends upon an understanding of what we might call the 'medieval soundscape' and the categories of taste imposed upon it. How did the lettered musicians of the 13th and 14th centuries regard drone-accompaniments? Had they constructed a hierarchy of string-techniques that distinguished (a) constant drones from (b) proto-polyphonic forms blurring into (c) genuine plurilinear polyphony? If so, were they prejudiced—as most modern Western listeners are—in favour of plurilinear music?[2] Can the supposed social fall of hurdy-gurdies be explained by a dependence upon drones? These are some of the questions we shall examine in the course of these studies; we begin with the vexed question of the instruments' origin.

ORIGIN AND DIFFUSION OF THE MEDIEVAL
ORGANISTRUM AND *SYMPHONIA*

In a recent book-length study of these instruments Marianne Bröcker concludes that the hurdy-gurdy is an instrument of Oriental origin

XII

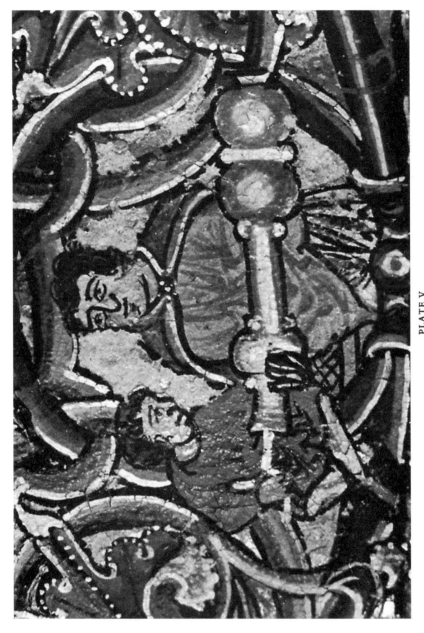

PLATE V

Douai, Bibliothèque Municipale, MS. 19 (Psalter, late-13th-century, from the Abbey of Marchiennes) f. 2 (detail).
Song-master and pupil at the organistrum or symphonia

known to the Islamic peoples in the tenth century and diffused into Europe from Moorish Spain.[3] This contention rests upon a few pieces of evidence and several inferences, none of which, in my view, will bear scrutiny.

A tenth-century work by the Ikhwān al-Ṣafā' brotherhood resident in Basra gives a list of instruments producing sustained sound including the *dawālīb* (plural of *dūlāb*), which may be translated 'waterwheels'.[4] Nothing further can be deduced concerning the nature of the *dawālīb* from this text, but scholars have linked it with the *sāz-idūlāb* mentioned in the *Cāmi 'al-alḥān* by the Persian writer ibn Ġaibī.[5] This work, it should be noted, was finished in July 1405, some five centuries after the text by the Ikhwān al-Ṣafā' brotherhood. Hitherto the relevant passage of this text has only been known in the following English paraphrase published by Farmer in 1962 (thirty years after he had examined one of the two surviving manuscripts):[6]

. . . the sāz dōlāb . . . is described as being 'in the shape of a drum'. In the interior were free (*muṭlaq*) strings which were in contact with a (rosined) wheel (*dōlāb*). On the exterior were keys which raised and lowered tangents which touched the strings and thus emitted the notes relative to the tangents. A handle outside turned the (rosined) wheel (*midrāb*) which impinged on the strings and sounded the notes touched by the tangents. The very name points to the well-known hurdy-gurdy.

This is certainly a precise description of a hurdy-gurdy; but let us consider the original text[7] (Oxford, Bodleian Library MS. Marsh 282, fol. 79ᵛ):

sāz-idūlāb. va ān bar shakl-i duhul bāshad kih bar do zuhr-i ān az khārij ghair az sathain autār bandand va ān az muṭlaqāt ast va mizrāb-i ānrā bi mahallī sākin gardānand kih imsāk-i autār kunad dar hālat-i harakat-i autār va ān ālatrā bi chīragī gardānand mānand-i charkhī kih rīsand chunānkih autār bi mizrāb rasand va asvāt-i ān autār masmū' shavand pas istikhrāj-i alḥān az ān autār kunand.

(Transl.): *sāz-idūlāb* [wheel-instrument]. It is in the form of a *duhul* [drum], on whose two backs they fasten strings from outside, but not on its two surfaces. That [the instrument] is of the independent things [?]. They place its plectrum [*mizrāb*] fixed on a place so that it touches the strings while they are moving [literally 'in the state of movement of the strings']. They make that [the instrument] go round in a clever way like a spinning wheel, so that the strings reach the plectrum and their sounds become audible. Thus they extract notes from them.

It is most illuminating to compare this translation with Farmer's paraphrase. The following points emerge: (1) although the instrument is called a 'wheel-instrument' in the Persian text, Farmer's '(rosined) wheel' is a very leading translation of *mizrāb*; (2) there is no indication

38

that the strings are in the 'interior' as Farmer would have us believe; (3) Farmer's 'keys' and 'tangents' do not exist; they appear to have been developed out of the enigmatic 'plectrum' mentioned in the original, fixed at some point on the surface of the instrument; (4) there is nothing in the original corresponding to Farmer's 'handle outside'. In short, virtually none of the features listed by Farmer which make the *sāz-idūlāb* a hurdy-gurdy positively exist! Surely we do best to leave the *sāz-idūlāb* unidentified. At least one other description of a mechanical instrument in the treatise of ibn Ġaibī left Farmer bewildered, while a large number of names for instruments in medieval Arabic sources cannot be identified.[8]

In considering the iconographical evidence, much of which derives from Spain, we must take account of recent research on the question of Arab culture in Spain and the supposed musical influence travelling northwards across the Pyrenees. Schneider, Spanke, Li Gotti and Chailley have successfully challenged the assumption of a significant musical or literary influence,[9] and it is clearly necessary to proceed with the utmost caution. We are on safe ground with the claim that Seville operated an export trade in musical instruments during the Middle Ages, but there is no *dūlāb* or anything that may (with our present knowledge) be identified with the hurdy-gurdy in the list of exported instruments drawn up by Al-Shaqandī (d.1231), or in the tally of Arabo-Spanish instruments (naming 31 items) made by Ibrāhīm al-Shalāhī (end of 13th century).[10]

Furthermore, the carvings of hurdy-gurdies from Soria (Castille) and St. Iago de Compostella (Galicia) are not the earliest known European representations as has often been maintained.[11] The Soria example dates from after c.1170, and may be appreciably later, whilst the lintel of the central door at St. Iago de Compostella was set up in 1188 and it is reasonable to place the carving of the *organistrum* at about that date.[12] The importance of these datings lies in the fact that the carving of a hurdy-gurdy at St. Georges de Boscherville near Rouen dates from c.1170,[13] and the York Psalter, with its fine illustration, from before or shortly after 1173, as suggested by the absence of Thomas à Becket in the Calendar.[14] This illustration, from the North of England, is therefore roughly contemporary with the Spanish examples and could even be slightly earlier. There is little here to weigh in favour of the view that the hurdy-gurdy originated in the Orient and was distributed from Spain northwards into France, England and Germany.[15]

Two written sources show that the hurdy-gurdy was known in northern Europe prior to the earliest indications of the instrument in the south. The manuscript Wolfenbüttel Gud. Lat. 334, written at Augsburg, contains treatises on the placement of the *organistrum* tangents. This source dates from *c.*1100—not from the 13th century as Bröcker believed—[16] and may even be earlier. The second text is the *Visio Tnugdali* (between 1149 and 1154). With the exception of the *mensura*-treatises mentioned above, the *Visio* contains the earliest instance of the word *organistrum* that I have found:[17]

... in quibus cordas et organa, tympana quoque et cytharas cum *organistris* et cymbalis canentes ...

We are now in a position to establish a chronology for the early (i.e. pre-1200) literary and pictorial materials:[18]

*c.*1100 (11th century?)	Wolfenbüttel Gud. lat. 334 (Augsburg) measurement treatise
1149–1154	*Visio Tnugdali* (Regensburg)
*c.*1160	Paris, Notre Dame
*c.*1170	Boscherville
*c.*1170 (late 12th century)	Soria
*c.*1173	York Psalter
*c.*1175–1205	*Hortus Deliciarum*
*c.*1188	St. Iago de Compostella (Cathedral)
late 12th century	St. Louis Psalter (York)
late 12th century	Riotiron
late 12th century	Moradillo de Sedano
late 12th century	Toro
late 12th century	Estella
late 12th century	St. Iago de Compostella (Bishop's palace)
12th century	Honnecourt-sur-l'Escaut

The evidence provides no grounds for assuming that the hurdy-gurdy was distributed from Spain. With the exception of the sculpture at Soria, which may be of relatively late date (and is believed to have been influenced by Western French work)[19] all the earliest evidence comes from Northern and Central Europe: Augsburg and Regensburg in Bavaria, St. Georges de Boscherville in Normandy, Notre Dame de Paris, and the north of England.

Where do matters stand? Firstly, the evidence for the existence of the hurdy-gurdy in the Orient is extremely tenuous. Secondly, the sources favour a Northern or Central European origin.

So how did the *symphonia* and *organistrum* come into being? I feel sure that the traditional view—of a Western, monastic origin—is correct. To support it, we may note that several 11th-century Latin musical treatises attach great importance to learning chant *sine magistro*. When Sigebert of Gembloux praised the achievements of the musical theorist Hucbald (d.930), he noted that the monk of St. Amand had 'so arranged the letters of the alphabet with the strings of the mono-chord that anyone, without the help of a teacher (*sine magistro*) could learn a completely unknown chant'.[20] Similarly, the assumption that chant may sometimes have to be learned without a master lies behind several remarks on the *Dialogus de Musica*, a treatise composed in the region of Milan, *c.*1000, and formerly attributed to Odo of Cluny: Once the *discipulus* in the dialogue has been taught how to manufacture a monochord, he is impatient to learn 'how I may note down a melody so that I may understand it without a teacher'.[21] In a similar vein Guido of Arezzo presents 'constant recourse to the voice of a singer or to the sound of some instrument' as two ways of becoming acquainted with an unknown melody in his *Epistola de ignoto cantu* (*c.*1030), and he relates how Pope John XIX tested the excellence of his solmisation syllables by 'learning to sing a verse without hearing it beforehand'.[22] In all these texts reference is made to the use of an instrument as a means of learning *sine magistro*. The traditional instrument for this purpose was the monochord, an oblong box with a string stretched upon it shown in numerous medieval illustrations.[23] In all probability, the hurdy-gurdy was devised as an improved monochord; the rapidly fading note of the monochord was replaced in the *schola* by the sus-tained tone of the hurdy-gurdy, a development in technology doubt-less based upon the example of the fiddle bow (distributed throughout Europe by *c.*1000).[24] The development would appear to have taken place in Germany and may have been connected with the monastic reforms of the tenth and eleventh centuries.[25] The technical expertise needed to design and build a hurdy-gurdy certainly existed within the monastic communities themselves, to judge by the case of Hermannus Contractus (d.1054), a monk of Reichenau and a musical theorist who wrote of the advantages of being able to learn music without an instructor, or *sine precentore*.[26] Hermannus is said by the chronicler Berthold (d.1088) to have been 'unequalled in making clockwork, musical instruments, and mechanical devices'. (*In horologicis et musicis instrumentis et mechanicis nulli par erat componendis.*)[27]

So far, only one medieval comment on the special value of our instruments has come to light, and this places us firmly in the world of the song-school. The anonymous author of the *Summa Musicae* (probably French, 1274–1312)[28] singles out the *symphonia quae dicitur organistrum* as particularly appropriate (together with the organ and monochord) for the *rudis cantor*. Such a man cannot mistake the notes 'which are easily perceived by fixed, labelled keys (*claves certas et signatas*) and may be performed without delay, without a friend or song master'.[29] The author is clearly thinking of a single-man instrument. However his remarks undoubtedly draw upon a tradition of usage, and we may be sure that the keys (*linguae*) of the instrument were often labelled with 'alphabets' like the face of the monochord and organ keyboard.[30] Perhaps the earliest hurdy-gurdies were designed so that a *cantor* who wished to learn a piece or correct his intonation could operate the tangents, studying them as he played, and listening to the sustained sound, whilst a colleague or song-master (see Pl. V) looked after the business of turning the wheel and, perhaps, supervised the tangent-work.[31]

I am inclined therefore to trace the development of the hurdy-gurdy to designs roughed out by men closely involved in the teaching and performance of liturgical chant. The earliest evidence points to a northern origin, and the two earliest testimonies to Bavaria. The word *organistrum* may have been coined in Germany or Flanders. As early as *c.*1130 it was used by Galbert of Bruges to denote an organ-case (*in organistro, scilicet in domicilio quodam organorum ecclesiae . . .*).[32]

One further item of evidence may be cited which supports the hypothesis of European origin. It is a well-documented fact that the movement of instruments from one culture to another is often accompanied by a transference of names. The word *symphonia* is Latin from Greek; *organistrum* looks like an invented word made up of Latin *organum* (from Greek) and suffix -(*s*)*trum*. Both words evoke the Graeco-Roman such as we find in *organum*, *monochordum* and *cymbalum*, rather than the medieval Islamic one sees so powerfully represented in *lute*, *rubebe*, and *nakers*.[33]

NOTES

1 J. Harvey, *Medieval Craftsmen*, 1975, p. 12.

2 This crucial subject requires a book to itself.

3 M. Bröcker, *Die Drehleier*, 2 vols., 1973, 1, p. 38f.

4 *Ibid.*, p. 25f.

5 *Ibid.*, p. 33. According to Farmer this work survives in two manuscripts, one in the Bodleian Library, Oxford (MS. Marsh 282), and another in the Nūr-i 'Otmānīya Library in Istanbul (see H. G. Farmer, 'Abdalqādir ibn Gaibī on Instruments of Music', in *Oriens*, 15 (1962), p. 242–248).

6 *Ibid.*, pp. 242, 246.

7 I am most grateful to Professor Ali Sharifian of Teheran University who copied the Persian text from the Bodleian manuscript and made a preliminary

translation, and to G. Morrison, Lecturer in Persian at Wolfson College, Oxford, who produced the transliteration and improved the English idiom of the translation.

8 Farmer, *op. cit.*, p. 246, and *Studies in Oriental Musical Instruments*, 2nd Series, 1939, p. 28.

9 For a convenient summary of the bibliography on this question see A. Hughes, *Medieval Music*, 2nd edition, 1980, items 1125–1139.

10 Farmer, *Studies*, 1, p. 11 and 2, p. 28.

11 As, for example, by Bröcker, Drehleier, 1, p. 43 (and *passim*), and Bachmann, W., *The Origins of Bowing*, English trans. 1969, p. 106.

12 On Soria see M. Durliat, *L'Art Roman en Espagne*, 1962, p. 29f. The façade is believed to have been influenced by the art of western France (*loc. cit.*). On St. Iago, see Georges Gaillard, 'Le Porche de la Gloire à Saint-Jacques de Compostelle et ses origines espagnoles', *Cahiers de Civilisation Médiévale*, 1 (1958), p. 465–473, and Marcel Durliat, *L'Architecture Espagnole*, 1966, p. 135.

An important point concerns the decoration on the surface of the St. Iago *organistrum* (Bröcker, Pl. 17; Bachmann Pl. 80) for Bröcker asserts that this shows signs of Arabic influence (*op. cit.*, II, p. 43). I am most grateful to Professor Marcel Durliat for the assurance that there is nothing in the decoration that does not belong to the romanesque ornamental grammar of the period (private communication).

13 On the date of Bocherville (reproduced in Bachmann, *op. cit.*, Pl. 77) see Léon Pressouyre, 'St. Bernard to St. Francis: Monastic Ideals and Iconographic programs in the Cloisters', *Gesta*, xii (1973) (The Cloister Symposium, 1972), p. 89, note 68.

14 T. S. R. Boase, *English Art 1100–1216*, 1953, p. 241–2.

15 Bröcker, *op. cit.*, 1, p. 38f.

16 *Ibid.*, 1, p. 245. On the date see Otto von Heinemann, *Die Handschriften der Herzoglichen Bibliothek zu Wolfenbüttel*, IX Band, 1913, p. 250–1. There is a facsimile of the relevant parts of the MS. in Bröcker, *Drehleier* II, Faks 1.

17 Wagner, A., ed., *Visio Tnugdali*, 1882, p. 48. On the literary affiliations of this text see J. C. Douglas Marshall, 'Three Problems in the *Vision of Tundal*', *Medium Aevum*, 44 (1975), pp. 14–22. I am most grateful to Mme A. M. Bauthier (*Lexicon du Cange*), M. Plezia (*Lexicon Mediae et Infimae Latinitatis Polonorum*), Theresia Payr (*Mittellateinisches Wörterbuch*), Olga Weijers (*Lexicon Latinitatis Nederlandicae Medii Aevi*) and Avril Powell (*Dictionary of Medieval Latin from British Sources*) for sending me their unpublished material on the words *organistrum* and *symphonia*.

18 I have omitted the carving from Civray (Bröcker, Pl. 12) as its details are of doubtful authenticity. The Notre Dame sculpture has been restored (Bachmann, *op. cit.*, Pl. 79). On the date see M. Aubert, *Notre-Dame de Paris*, 1945, *passim*.

19 Durliat, *L'Art Roman*, p. 77.

20 *PL*, 160, column 571.

21 GS. I, p. 255: 'Nunc autem qualiter cantum notare possim, ut ego illum absque magistro comprehendam . . .'.

22 GS. II, p. 44.

23 For examples see J. Smits van Waesberghe, *Musikerziehung* (Musikgeschichte in Bildern, III:3, 1969), Pls. 3, 4, 8, 14, etc.

24 Bachmann, *op. cit., passim.*

25 As suggested by J. Smits van Waesberghe in his article 'Organistrum' for the *Handwörterbuch der Musikalischen Terminologie.*

26 GS. II, pp. 149–50.

27 G. H. Pertz, ed., *Bertholdi Annales* in *Monumenta Germaniae Historica, Scriptorum* 5, 1844, p. 268.

28 This treatise is often said to be German (e.g. Bachmann, *op. cit.*, p. 79, note 45). For the evidence that points to France see *GSJ*, xxxii, pp. 84 and 86.

29 GS. III, p. 216.

30 On the monochord letters which were written on a strip of parchment placed on the soundboard see Smits van Waesberghe, *Musikerzeihung*, p. 24. For reference to the organ alphabets in original treatises see K.-J. Sachs, *Mensura Fistularum, Teil 1, Edition der Texte*, 1970, *passim.* These 'alphabets' are sometimes shown in medieval pictures and schematic representations of organs. See C. Page, 'The Earliest English Keyboard', *Early Music*, 7 (1979), Pls. 1 and 4.

31 In this connection it is interesting to note that the York psalter illustration clearly shows the tangent operator to be singing (Bachmann, *op. cit.*, plate 60).

32 For the text see H. Pirenne, ed., *Histoire du Meurtre de Charles le Bon*, 1891, p. 29.

33 See the list of names for hurdy-gurdies in S. Marcuse, *Musical Instruments, A Comprehensive Dictionary,* corrected edition, 1975, p. 253. The only name with a possible Arabic connections seems to be *gaita* (sv *Gaita zamorana*). Picken has noted that *gayda* (the Thracian bagpipe) may be connected with Arabic *ghaidā, ghaita* or *ghā'ita* (*Folk Musical Instruments of Turkey*, 1975, p. 549), but goes no further. I have always been drawn to the idea that the *gaita* group of names may be derived from Gothic *gaits* ('a goat'; compare French *chevrette* and related names), taken to the Balkans by the migrating Goths, whose speech survived in the Crimea up to the 16th century (see J. Wright, *Grammar of the Gothic Language*, second ed., by O. L. Sayce (1954), p. 380). Gothic *gaits* is from an Indo-European, not a Semitic root (cf Latin *haedus*, 'young goat').

XIII

The Medieval *Organistrum* and *Symphonia*
2: Terminology

IN the first part of this study (*GSJ* XXXV) I proposed that the hurdy-gurdies known to the Middle Ages under forms of the names *organistrum* and *symphonia* originated in the West sometime before 1100, probably in the wave of monastic creativity that followed the Benedictine Reforms of the tenth and eleventh centuries. In this second part I wish to consider the terminologies of these instruments and in particular to explore two assumptions which have long dominated our thinking:[1]

1. that *organistrum* denoted large, two-man hurdy-gurdies which were the earliest form in use and employed by clerics
2. while *symphonia* and related words denoted smaller, one-man instruments, the larger types having fallen from the cloister into the hands of travelling musicians (especially those of low degree) who reduced their size and gave them a new name.

I believe that these two assumptions are not justified by the evidence and that the true picture is a rather different one.

SYMPHONIA AND RELATED FORMS

The following table shows some major forms belonging to the '*symphonia* family' (understood at this stage to comprise a class of etymologically related words in the semantic field 'musical instrument/musical sound'):[2]

Selected Medieval Forms

Anglo-Norman	1155	*symphonies*
Old French	b.1227	*chiphonie, symphonie, cifornie*
Castilian	13th c.	*simfonia, çinfonia, çapoña, çanpoña*
Italian	14th c.	*ciunfonie, sampogna*
Middle English	c.1300	*sinfonye*
Middle Low German	15th c.	*symfenyge*
Middle High German	c.1220	*symphonien* (vb)
Latin	b.1220	*simphonia* [definitely in sense 'hurdy-gurdy']

Cognates in Modern Romance Languages

French   forms include *sampongne, zampogne, chanforgne, samphonio*
Italian   forms include *zampogna, čamporña, sampoin*
Spanish   forms include *çinfoña, çampoña, zampoña*

In addition to the forms in medieval vernacular sources (a handful of which appear above) there is a massive list of Romance cognates gathered by Wartburg and Meyer-Lübke, but roughly speaking this vast corpus of material can be classified into two major families:

    1 the *symph-* family
    2 the *samp-* family

Words of family 1 are characterised by a front vowel (*i* or *y*) in the stem syllable and a medial labial spirant -*f*/*ph*- (e.g. *symphonia, sinfonye*); forms that belong to family 2 have a back vowel in the stem (*a, o* or *u*) and a medial labial stop -*p*- (e.g. *zampogna, çampoña*). During the course of the centuries these two families have combined in some areas to produce forms such as *samphonio*.

Each family represents a distinct tradition. It is tempting to trace *samp-* words to a very early borrowing (probably popular) from Greek into pre-Classical Latin; an etymon like *sumponia* would do very well and is perhaps what we have in the Aramaic *Book of Daniel* (*sumpōnyā*). The marked prevalence of 'wind instrument' as a meaning for *samp-* words accords with this early chronology for there is sixth-century AD evidence for the circulation in the Romanised world of a derivative of Greek συμφωνία denoting a wind instrument of some kind.[3]

Now we turn to the *symph-* family and to the hurdy-gurdy. As they appear in the medieval vernaculars words of this group seem to reflect a careful pronunciation of their parent in Latin, *symphonia*, rather than a pronunciation influenced by words of the ancient *samp-* tradition. Indeed, the word first appears in any vernacular with Wace's *symphonies*, whose learned spelling is clearly designed to keep it close to its Latin parent. In view of the possibly clerical (and perhaps monastic) origin of the hurdy-gurdy this terminological evidence is striking. It certainly does not appear that *symphonia*-names are in any way 'popular' terms for hurdy-gurdies; on the contrary, they derive from a 'correct' central-medieval Latin. Nor do we have reason to believe that these *symphonia*-names are 'recent', having been inspired by some shift in the instrument's function or status.

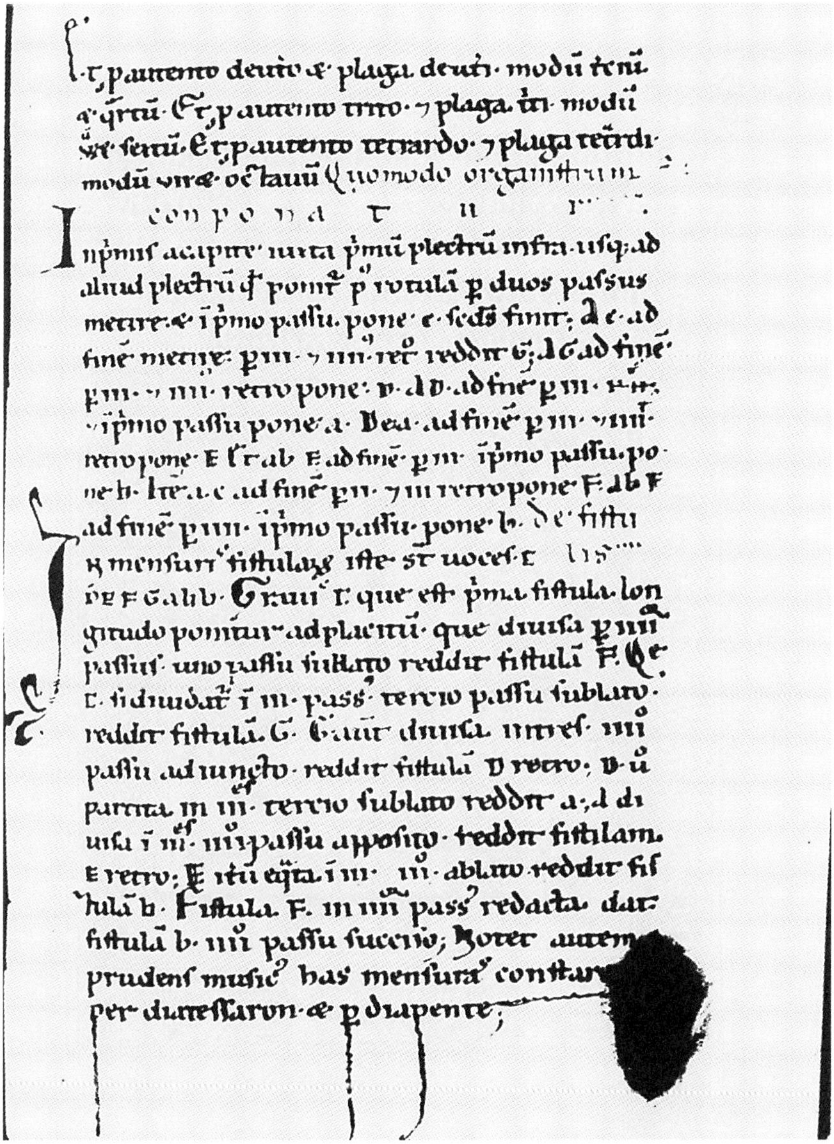

[manuscript in abbreviated medieval Latin hand — best reading follows]

et pariente deureo et plaga deureo · modū tenū
et qrtū · Et pariente tito · et plaga tri modū
sex sertū · Et pariente tertiardo · et plaga tertiardi
modū vire octauū Quomodo organistrum

I conponat

In primis accipitur iuxta primū plectrū infra usq̄ ad
aliud plectrū q̄ ponitur p rotuli p duos passus
metire · et i primo passu pone · e · sc̄ds finit · A e · ad
fine metire · p iiii · et iiii ret · reddit b; A G ad fine·
p iii · et iiii retro pone · D · a D · ad fine p iii · et iii ·
· i primo passu pone · a · D e a · ad fine p iii · viii ·
retro pone E et ab E ad fine p iii · i primo passu po
ne b · ht a e · ad fine p iii · et iii retro pone F ab F
ad fine p iiii · i primo passu · pone b · De fistu
la mensura fistularū iste sunt uoces · E · bis
De F G a b b · Graui L que est prima fistula lon
gitudo ponitur ad placitū · que diuisa p iiii
passus · uno passu sublato reddit fistula F · Qe
c sidiuidat i iii pass· tertio passu sublato·
reddit fistula G · Graui diuisa in tres · iiii
passu adiuncto · reddit fistula D retro; D u
partita in iii · tertio sublato reddit a; d di
uisa i iii · iiii passu apposito · reddit fistilam·
E retro; E itu eqta i iii · iii ablato reddit fis
tula b · Fistula F · in iiii pass· redacta dat
fistula b · iiii passu successio; Notet autem
prudens musicus has mensura constarr
per diatessaron et p diapente;

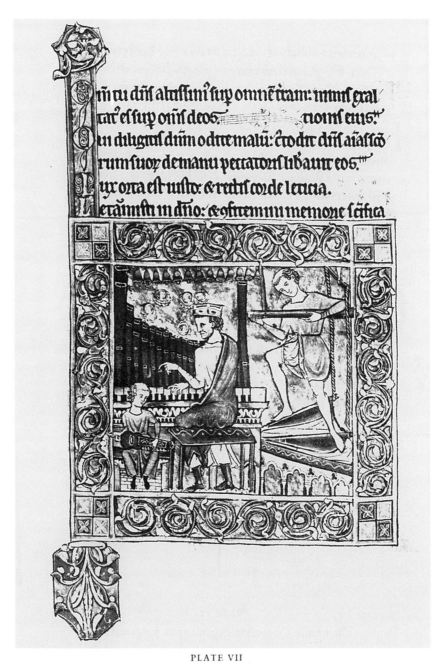

PLATE VII

Hurdy-gurdy and player; from the Rutland psalter, English, mid-13th-century, f. 97v.

Sources in which symphonia-*names are associated with hurdy-gurdies*

ENGLAND

[1] A Latin bestiary (British Library Reference Division MS. Sloane 3544, 14c).

In this manuscript a reference to dolphins, who 'crowd together and swim towards any *symphonia*' (*ad symphoniam gregatim conveniunt*, f. 43r), is linked to a painting of a figure playing a hurdy-gurdy in a boat as fish swim below (f. 42v, reproduced in Galpin, *Old English Instruments*, plate 12:1). The illustration is, in one sense, based upon a misunderstanding, since the source of the passage is Pliny, *Natural History*, 9:8 where the words *symphoniae cantu* probably refer simply to 'music' or 'harmony' rather than to an instrument.

[2] Henry of Avranches, *Versus de Sancto Thoma Archiepiscopo* (b.1220).

In this poem, which may have been written in England, Master Henry of Avranches refers to 'the *simphonia* with its winding motion' (*curvo simphonia tractu*). Presumably a hurdy-gurdy is meant.[4]

FRANCE

[3] Jean de Gerson, *Tractatus de Canticis* (c.1426).

In this source the *symphonia* is described (in a moderately technical fashion) and is clearly a hurdy-gurdy. This is the most explicit account of the *symphonia* that I have been able to find in any French source. For text and translation see my article in *Early Music*, 6 (1978), pp. 339–349.

[4] Nicholas de Lyra, Gloss on *Daniel* 3:5 (early 14th c.).

In his monumental gloss upon the bible Nicholas de Lyra specifies that the *simphonia* is an instrument played by the blind (a point noted by Gerson, by Corbechon—see below—and by numerous later writers).[5] It seems reasonable to assume that a hurdy-gurdy is meant.

[Oxford, Bodleian Library MS. Laud Misc. 152, f. 236v]
. . . accipitur simphonia pro instrumento determinato oblongo quod solent portare ceci, et digitis tangitur.
(. . . here the word *simphonia* may be understood to mean the established instrument of oblong form which the blind are accustomed to play, and it is played with the fingers.)

[5] Jean Corbechon's translation of the *De Proprietatibus Rerum* (completed 1372).

The association of the *simphonie* with blind musicians is also noted by the Augustinian friar Jean Corbechon in his translation of the *De Proprietatibus Rerum* of Bartholomaeus Anglicus. Corbechon undertook his translation at the request of Charles V and completed it in 1372. The following passage is his own addition to his original:

[British Library Additional MS. 11,612, f. 367 r–v]

. . . on appelle en france vne simphonie instrument dont les auugles jouent en chantant les chancons de geste . . .

(. . . in France we call that instrument a *simphonie* which the blind play while singing *chansons de geste* . . .)

SPAIN

[6] Sebastian de Cobarruvias, *Tesoro de la Lengva Castellana* (Madrid, 1611).

I find no Spanish vernacular reference to the *çinfonia* where it is clear that a hurdy-gurdy is meant earlier than the famous dictionary of Cobarruvias. Since it is of some interest I give it here (from a first edition: Oxford, Bodleian Library H.7.3. Art. f. 283v):

cinfonia . . . es instrumento particular de cuerdas que estan concertadas entre si en consonancias . . . Algunos pobres Franceses suelen traer vn instrumento, a modo de violoncillo, y en el vientre del cierta orden de cuerdas, que con vnas teclas que salen por defuera las arrima a vna rueda, que trayendola a la redonda con la mano derecha, tocando las teclas con la mano izquierda, la haze sonar suauamente.

(The *çinfonia* . . . is a singular instrument with strings which are tuned together in consonances . . . Some French paupers are accustomed to use an instrument in the form of a *violoncillo* and to arrange strings in the belly which, with keys that project outwardly, they place on a wheel which they turn about with the right hand, playing upon the keys with the left to make it sound sweetly.)

PORTUGAL/FRANCE

[7] Jean Cuvelier, *Chronique de Bertrand du Guesclin* (c.1380).

In his chronicle Cuvelier relates how the Englishman Matthew de Gourney was sent to the Portuguese court by du Guesclin and there entertained by the king. At one point the king calls for two of his most highly prized musicians:[6]

> '.ii. ménestrez avons qui sont en no commant;
> Il n'en y a nulz telz jusques en Oriant.
> Le rois de Bel-Marine me va souvent mandant
> Qu'envoier je li veille; mais ce est pour noiant,
> Ne m'en déliverroie pour nulle riens vivant.'
> Adont les fist mander, qu'il n'i va arrestant;
> Et cil y sont venus par itel couvenant
> Que Mahieu de Gournay dont je vous voys parlant
> Ne vit onques si noble devant roy aparant,
> Et s'avoit chascun d'eulx apres lui i. sergent

Qui une chiffonie va à son col portant.
Et li .ii. ménestrez se vont appareillant;
Devant le roy s'en vont ambdui chinfoniant.
Quant Mahieu de Gournay les va apercevant
Et les chinfonieurs a oy prisier tant,
A son cuer s'en aloit moult durement gabant.
Et li rois li a dit après le gieu laissant;
'Que vous samble? dit-il; sont il bien souffisant?'
Dit Mahieu de Gournay: 'Ne vous irai celant;
Ens ou pais de France et ou pais normant
Ne vont telz instrumens fors qu'avugles portant.
Ainsi font li avugle et li poure truant
De ci fais instrumens les bourjois entonnant:
On l'appele de la .i. instrument truant'.
Et quant li rois l'oy, s'en ot le cuer dolant;
il jura Jhésu-Crist, le père tout poissant,
Qui ne le serviront jamais en lor vivant.

? NETHERLANDS

[8] The *Summa Musice* (*c.*1300)

This anonymous Latin musical treatise, probably written in the Netherlands or in France, contains material on the *simphonia* and the *organistrum*.[7] A most important point which will emerge from the texts below is that the author uses the word *organistrum* to denote a one-man instrument.

The author's first reference to the *simphonia* occurs in a list of stringed instruments (St. Paul in Kärnten, Archiv des Benediktinerstiftes, Cod. 264/4, ff. 4v–5):

Cordalia sunt ea que per cordas metallinas, intestinales uel sericinas exerceri videntur; qualia sunt cythare, vielle et phiale, psalteria, chori, monocordium, simphonia seu organistrum, et hiis similia.

(Stringed instruments are those which are seen to operate with strings of metal, gut or silk; such are *cythare*, *vielle* and *phiale*, *psalteria*, *chori*, *monocordium*, the *simphonia* or the *organistrum*, and others like them.)

In the following passage the author alludes to the fixed keys of the *symphonia* or *organistrum* suggesting that he uses these terms to denote a hurdy-gurdy. It is also clear from this extract that he is thinking of a single-man instrument:

[ibid. ff. 12v–13]

Et si flexibilem uocem non habeat, sed dissonus fuerit, et si favorem forte, uel etiam adiutorium doctoris obiectum amiserit, curam impendat, instrumenta musica exerceat, et sepius eis vtatur qualia sunt monocordium [et] symphonia que dicitur organistrum; in organis etiam cantare laboret. In his etiam instrumentis nota a facili errare non potest, et a sono suo longius distorqueri, eo quod note per claues certas et signatas facile possunt considerari, et prompte proferri absque socio uel magistro cantore.

(And if [a singer] does not have a pliant voice—if he is a jarring singer—and if he lacks, perhaps, the good-will or the offered help of a teacher, he should take pains to busy himself with musical instruments and in particular to employ types such as the monochord and the *symphonia* which is called *organistrum*; let him also work with an organ. On these instruments it is not easy to wander from the right note, nor need a false note linger; the notes may easily be observed by means of fixed, lettered keys and may be readily produced without the aid of a friend or a song-master.)

This reference to a '*symphonia* which is called *organistrum*' is unfortunately ambiguous. Does the author treat the two terms as synonyms, or does he use *organistrum* to denote a special type of *symphonia*? The matter cannot be settled.

Conclusions: Symphonia-*names*

Yet some firm conclusions can be drawn at the end of this examination of *symphonia*-names. These names were almost certainly of learned and not popular origin, possibly going back to the earliest phase of the instrument's history. The tradition of such names was extremely widely distributed; we have encountered it in England and France (where it makes its first known appearance, in the work of the Anglo-Norman poet Wace, a Jerseyman), in Germany and the Netherlands (if that is the true home of the *Summa Musice*), in Spain, Italy and, to judge by Jean Cuvelier's *Chronique*, in Portugal.

ORGANISTRUM

We now turn to the second major medieval hurdy-gurdy name: *organistrum*. This looks like a coinage of some medieval clerk formed from the verb *organizo* 'I play an instrument/sing/in harmony' and the nominal suffix -*strum* (compare *capio/capistrum*; *moneo/monstrum*). The word was presumably coined in clerical circles; like *symphonia* it is essentially a learned name and might suggest an ecclesiastical origin for the instrument. The following survey of sources in which the word appears incorporates all the references that I have been able to find (drawing upon the resources of several medieval Latin Dictionaries not yet published as far as O).[8]

Treatises on the placement of organistrum tangents

[1] About ten of these treatises are known to exist, the earliest of which dates from *c.*1100 and is our earliest piece of secure evidence for the

existence of the hurdy-gurdy.[9] The brief treatise *Quomodo organistrum conponatur* (Pl. VI), famous for its now-rejected attribution to Odo of Cluny, yet not accurately printed hitherto, may be quoted here to show the kind of material that these treatises contain (Vienna National-bibliothek Cpv 2503, f. 42r):[10]

Quomodo organistrum conponatur

In primis a capite iuxta primum plectrum infra usque ad aliud plectrum quod ponitur post rotulam per duos passus metire et in primo passu pone *c*. Secundus finit. A *c* ad finem metire per III et IIII retro reddit *G*; a *G* ad finem per III et IIII retro pone *D*; a *D* ad finem per III et in primo passu pone *a*; de *a* ad finem per III et IIII retro pone *E*; et ab *E* ad finem per III; in primo passu pone *b*; item a *c* ad finem per II et III retro pone *F*; ab *F* ad finem per IIII; in primo passu pone *b*.

(How the organistrum is put together)

Firstly, measure from the nut which is next to the first tangent up to the other nut placed after the wheel and divide the distance into two parts; put *c* at the middle point; the half lying beyond *c* will not contain pitches. Now measure from *c* to the end and divide the distance by 3; having established this unit count back four units from the nut beyond the wheel and you will establish *G*; treat *G* as you treated *c* and you will establish *D*; measure from *D* to this nut, divide by 3 and put *a* one unit beyond *D*, measure from *a* to the nut and divide the distance by 3; having established this unit count back four such units from the nut beyond the wheel and you will establish *E*; measure from *E* to this nut, divide by 3 and put *b* one unit beyond *E*; again, measure from *c* to the nut and divide the distance by 2; having established this unit count back three such units and you will establish *F*; divide the distance from *F* to the nut by 4 and put *b* on the first step.)

This is nothing more than a means of establishing a Pythagorean diatonic scale. These organistrum treatises thus belong in the tradition of the bell, monochord and organ texts. There may indeed be some doubt as to whether bells actually existed in the form implied by *cymbala* treatises—a point argued by Hélène la Rue in *GSJ* XXXV— and I am beginning to have certain doubts about the monchord. Yet *organistra* did exist and it seems clear that these treatises were to be studied in relation to the instrument or at least a clear mental picture of it.

A striking feature of this *mensura* literature—at least as far as concerns *cymbala* and organ-pipes—is the relatively restricted distribution of the manuscripts which contain it. Smits van Waesberghe observes:[11]

During a protracted study of over 300 MSS. containing tracts on the theory of music [I have] come across no MS. of French or Italian authorship in which these measurements of *cymbala* occur. All the treatises . . . were written in Alemannic or Lorraine territory . . . A similar conclusion is suggested by the treatises on the measurements of organ-pipes, but few of which originated outside the sphere of influence of Alemannic territory.

The manuscripts containing the organistrum treatises point to a similar conclusion. In the present state of our knowledge there are grounds for regarding this organistrum literature as a phenomenon confined to Germany, Austria and Alsace.

[2] The *Visio Tnugdali* of frater Marcus (completed Regensburg, c.1143–5?).

A second source for the word *organistrum*, also of German provenance, is the *Visio Tnugdali*, a Latin account of a vision received by an Irish knight in 1149 and written by one frater Marcus for the Irish community of Benedictines at Regensburg. Marcus claims to have worked from a vernacular, presumably Old Irish. His work was probably completed about five years after 1149. In a chapter entitled *De gloria monachorum et sanctimonialium* Marcus gives the following account of a visionary landscape populated by the souls of monks and other holy persons:[12]

. . . vidit quasi castra et papiliones plurimas, purpura et bisso, auro quoque et argento et serica mira varietate confecta, in quibus cordas et organa, tympana quoque et cytharas cum organistris et cymbalis canentes ceteraque omnia musicorum genera suavissimis sonis audierat concinentes . . .

(. . . he saw what seemed to be a plain and many tents ornamented with purple and linen, with gold, silver and silk made in wondrous variety; he heard in these tents strings and *organa*, *tympana* and also *cytharas* with *organistris* and *cymbala* and all other kinds of musical instruments sounding together with the sweetest melody . . .)

Once again we notice the German connection. The earliest known manuscript containing an organistrum treatise was written at Augsburg and another was copied at Regensburg.[13] The *Visio Tnugdali* was clearly written in the heartland of the *organistrum* territory.

[3] Martin Gerbert's *Iter Alemannicum* (St. Blaise, 1765).

A new source of the word *organistrum* may be found in Martin Gerbert's *Iter Alemannicum*, an account of his antiquarian travels in Germany (also France and Italy) published in 1765. In this work Gerbert prints a Latin-German/Latin wordlist which he dates to the 12th century (an acceptable dating). One entry runs (p. 101 in Gerbert's second pagination series):

Organistrum VIII. tonis vel chordis instructum.

(Organistrum set up with eight 'strings' or notes.)

This should not be taken to imply the existence of an eight-stringed instrument for the word *chorda* is surely being used here in its technical sense of 'note'. The reference is therefore to an organistrum tuned in the normal diatonic way (lacking the upper octave in this case and presumably also either bb or $b\natural$).

Again we find the word *organistrum* in a German source.

[4] The *Hortus Deliciarum* and Gerbert's *De Cantu et Musica Sacra*.

Two further sources for the word *organistrum* take us to the Alsace/ Black Forest region and disclose a fascinating relationship between material hitherto (as far as I am aware) regarded as distinct.

The *Hortus Deliciarum*, destroyed by fire in 1870, was a massive encyclopedia of devotional texts and images produced in Alsace for Abbess Herrad of Hohenbourg between 1176 and *c.*1196.[14] The text was probably written at Hohenbourg. This work contained a page showing the Liberal Arts and various copies of the leaf survive. *Musica* is shown with three instruments, all of which are labelled with their names: *lira*, *cithara* and *organistrum*. Fig. 1 *a*, shows a copy of the drawing with the names marked;[15] Fig. 1 *b*, is a more accurate drawing of the instruments (which includes tangents for the organistrum; so much for the theory, often put forward, that this manuscript shows a tangentless hurdy-gurdy!) without the names.[16] This is presumably one of the pictures which has led many to believe that *organistrum* denoted two-man instruments; but although this example has a guitar-shaped body and is thus similar to the two-man instruments shown on sculptures at St. Iago and elsewhere, we have no way of knowing whether this artist had a team instrument in mind. Hurdy-gurdies for single-players were built in this form, and if we may judge the size of the *Hortus Deliciarum* instrument by reference to *Musica* (a dangerous process admittedly) then it would appear to be for a single player.

The same may be said of our second drawing, taken from Martin Gerbert's *De Cantu et Musica Sacra* of 1774 (Fig. 2); perhaps the artist thought of this as a single-man example.

It is a great loss that this manuscript has been destroyed. Although it is a nightmarish business trying to establish the details about the manuscripts Gerbert used, it seems clear that this one perished in the fire at his monastery, a catastrophe that took place in 1768. We are thus unable to study the originals of drawings that are of very great importance. The two *cythare* (one labelled *anglica* and the other *teutonica*) have repeatedly been drawn into the debate about the origin of the pillar-harp;[17] the drawing of the one-stringed *lyra*, showing an instrument so remarkably similar to one of that name still found in Crete, is an important document in the history of contacts in instrument-culture between East and West. The *organistrum* provides—or appears to do so—the only medieval evidence we have about the tangents of the

FIG. I (a) Musica *from the* Hortus Deliciarum (*after Engelhardt*).
(b) Musica *from the* Hortus Deliciarum (*after Bastard*).

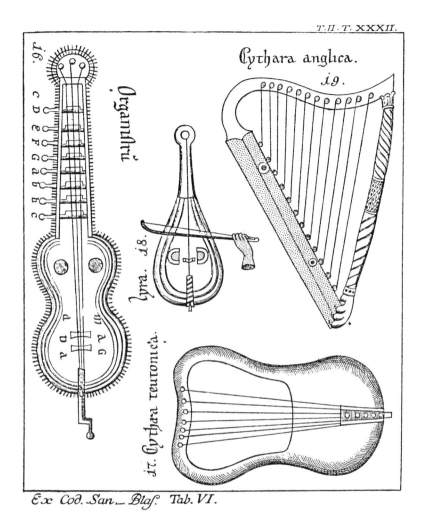

FIG. 2. *Instruments, including an organistrum, from Gerbert's* De Cantu et Musica Sacra.

instrument; here we see blades which touch all three strings at once. With a concordant tuning (such as root-fifth-octave) this mechanism would produce strict parallel organum of the type found in the *Musica Enchiriadis*—a fact which has supported many wide-ranging theories about the instrumental origin (and accompaniment) of early polyphony.[18]

It is immediately obvious that the drawing has been tampered with. To mention only a few details: the letter *E* against the third tangent is the same as the capital *E* in the legend *Ex Cod. San-Blas.* at the foot of the picture; it is clearly an 18th-century letter-form; the shading to represent convexity on the *Cythara teutonica* (and on the handle of the *organistrum*) does not look like medieval draftsmanship, nor does the highly suspect comb-effect around the organistrum which has perhaps been added to indicate that the instrument is shown in cross-section.[19]

When we compare Gerbert's drawing with the *Hortus Deliciarum* (Fig. 1, *a* and *b*) it becomes obvious that we are dealing with two very closely related sources. We have the same choice of instruments in both (save that Gerbert's drawing adds a lyre); the instruments are very similar in form (the *lyra* in each case is monochordic, and such instruments are very rare in medieval pictorial sources); furthermore all the instruments are named (another rarity), and bear the same names. The *Hortus Deliciarum* was illustrated in Alsace; Gerbert was working at the nearby monastery of St. Blaise in the Black Forest; surely it must seem that the manuscript from which he made his drawings was produced in the Alsace/Black Forest area, perhaps even in the same atelier as the *Hortus Deliciarum*? It is even possible, though I prefer the explanation just offered, that Gerbert actually encountered the *Hortus Deliciarum* on his travels (in his day it was stored at Molsheim) and that the drawings he published were taken from there. Whatever the truth of the matter we have found, once again, that the study of sources in which *organistrum* is mentioned takes us directly to German-speaking territory.

[5] A Low-German wordlist (*c.*1300).[20]

This wordlist contains the following entries arranged for the letter O:

1	organistre	simphonia
2	orgene	organum
3	orgenere	organistra
4	orgeniren	organizare

The words *orgene*, *orgenere* and *orgeniren* (2, 3 and 4) presumably refer to a pipe organ (*orgene*), the person who plays upon an organ (*orgenere*) and, finally, the act of playing an organ (*orgeniren*). It is the word *organistre* (1), glossed *simphonia*, that interests us. I believe this to be a Low-German vernacular equivalent of Latin *organistrum*. The form is what we would expect, since Low German replaces the Latin suffix -(*s*)*trum* with -(*s*)*tre* or -(*s*)*ter* (compare the forms *closter*, from *claustrum*, *plastre* from *plastrum*);[21] we would naturally expect *organistre* to come from *organistrum*, and the interpretative gloss in the manuscript -*simphonia*- suggests that this is the correct interpretation.

[6] The *Summa musice.*

The relevant passages from this text have been quoted above in the *symphonia* section. The anonymous author uses both *simphonia* and *organistrum*, and explicitly applies *organistrum* to a *single-man instrument.* In view of the evidence mentioned in section [5] above it is most interesting that Smits van Waesberghe finds evidence to locate the composition of the treatise in Liège.

[7] Heinrich von dem Türlin, *Diu Crone* (early 13th c.).

In this vast Arthurian romance of over 30,000 lines there is a form which may well be a vernacularised form of *organistrum: organiston.*[22] The termination *-on* is not a standard one in Middle High German and looks like an attempt at pseudo-Greek. Presumably it is either the Latin word *organistrum* or some vernacular equivalent of it that lies behind the spelling.

[8] The Old French translation of the *Digesta sive Pandecta Juris.*

In a supplementary volume to his *Dictionnaire de l'Ancienne Langue Française* Godefroy gives the following citation under the headword *symphoniste*:[23]

.II. synfonistre ou .II. orguenistre

Godefroy extracted these words from a manuscript now at Montpellier which I had the privilege to examine in 1979 (Bibliothèque de la Faculté de Médecine MS. H. 47, f. 261, column 4). The manuscript contains a text of the Old French version of the *Digesta sive Pandecta Juris*, a collection of legal judgements gathered under Justinian and completed in 533. Comparison with the translator's source confirm what we would expect: that both *synfonistre* and *orguenistre* are words denoting instrumentalists.[24] *Orguenistre* presumably means an organist; we would expect **orguenistrier* as a name for a player of an organistrum (compare *plastrier* 'plasterer', where the root is *plastre* from medieval Latin *plastrum* as noted above).[25]

CONCLUSIONS

At the close of our investigation we may summarise our conclusions, dovetailing them into the conclusions reached in the first part of this study:

1   The hurdy-gurdy may well have originated in the West amongst clerical communities who sought a mechanised teaching device.

2   The two major names for hurdy-gurdies in the West support this hypothesis. They are *symphonia* and *organistrum.* The first passed

into almost all the European vernaculars in a form derived from a careful Latin pronunciation. The second word, *organistrum*, also had some vernacular currency.

3   The distinction between the words *symphonia* and *organistrum* is not one of chronology: we have no reason to assume that *organistrum* was an earlier term followed later by *symphonia*-names when the instrument's form or function changed.

4   Nor is the distinction one of meaning. There is no evidence that *organistrum* denoted two-man instruments while *symphonia*-names were applied to instruments for a single player. The only firm evidence we have (the *Summa musice*) uses *organistrum* for an instrument that can be played 'without the aid of a friend or a songmaster'.

5   Nor is the distinction between *symphonia* and *organistrum* equivalent to one between learned and lay usage. There were vernacular forms of *organistrum* in areas of Low German and High German speech in the 13th and 14th centuries.

6   All the evidence suggests that the distinction between the two names was one of provenance and distribution. *Symphonia* names were distributed throughout the whole of Europe. *Organistrum* was largely confined to areas of Low and High German speech.

NOTES

1 For a relatively early (and influential) presentation of the picture, resting upon these two assumptions, see F. W. Galpin, *Old English Instruments*, 4th ed. (1965), pp. 78f: 'As with the Monochord, so with the Organistrum, for Church purposes it was greatly esteemed . . . But with the introduction of the small portative organ and the improvements made on the larger instruments the poor Organistrum left the church and cloister, and found itself, under a new name and in an attenuated form, in the hands of the wandering minstrels and the country folk. Owing to the crude chords produced by its strings it was thenceforth known as THE SYMPHONY . . .'. For some later works presenting very much the same picture see H. Panum, *Stringed Instruments of the Middle Ages* (1940) p. 307 (Panum's account of medieval hurdy-gurdies is riddled with inaccuracies and must be treated with exceptional caution); E. Winternitz, *Musical Instruments and their Symbolism in Western Art* (1967) pp. 71–2; M. Bröcker, *Die Drehleier*, 2 vols. (1973) p. 192; J. Montagu, *The World of Medieval and Renaissance Musical Instruments* (1976) pp. 29–30; S. Palmer, *The Hurdy-Gurdy* (1980) p. 37. Most recently these ideas have been enshrined in *The New Grove*, sv. *Hurdy-gurdy*.

2 The sources of the citations in this table (showing the earliest recorded forms known to me in each language) are as follows:

ANGLO-NORMAN: I. Arnold, ed., *Le Roman de Brut de Wace*, 2 vols. (1938 and 1940) lines 3702 (see MS. variants in edition) and 10551.

OLD FRENCH: E. Vilamo-Pentti, ed. [*Gautier de Coinci*] *De Sainte Leocade* (1950) line 880. A wealth of additional material from Old French sources may be had in Tobler-Lommatzsch, *Altfranzösisches Wörterbuch*, s.v *sifonie*;

CASTILIAN: the forms given in the table have been taken from the following: R. S. Willis, ed., *El libro de Alexandre* (1934) stanza 1545; this poem was composed in the 13th century; the earliest MS. (MS. O in Willis's edition) dates from the late-13th to the 14th century and reads *simfonia*. D. Julio Cajedor y Frauca, *Vocabulario Medieval Castellano* (1929), sv. *sinfonía*; R. S. Boggs, et al., *A Tentative Dictionary of Medieval Spanish* (1946), sv. *çinfonia*.

ITALIAN: the form *ciunfonie* appears in an anonymous 14th-century poem cited by Bröcker, *op. cit.*, 1, p. 204; the form *sampogna* is from Dante, *Paradiso*, 20: 24 (where it is clear that a wind instrument is meant).

MIDDLE ENGLISH: C. D'Evelyn and A. J. Mill, eds., *The South-English Legendary*, 2 vols. (1956) 2, p. 574 line 84; A selection of Middle English forms may be had from H. H. Carter, *A Dictionary of Middle English Musical Terms* (1961), sv. *Simphonye* II.

LOW GERMAN: K. Schiller and A. Lübben, *Mittelniederdeutsches Wörterbuch*, 6 vols. (1875–81), sv. *simfeni(g)e*.

MIDDLE HIGH GERMAN: P. Ganz, ed., *Gottfried von Strassburg, Tristan*, 2 vols. (1978) line 3674.

LATIN: The earliest known source, as far as I am aware, in which the word *symphonia* is used in a sense that can be demonstrated to mean a hurdy-gurdy is the *Versus de Sancto Thoma Archiepiscopo* by Master Henry of Avranches (J. C. Russell and J. P. Heironimus, *The Shorter Latin Poems of Master Henry of Avranches relating to England* (1935), p. 41). For a discussion of this poem, which dates from before 1220, see above.

MODERN ROMANCE COGNATES: These have mostly been taken from W. von Wartburg, *Französisches Etymologisches Wörterbuch*, Vol. 12 (1966), sv. *symphonia*, and W. Meyer-Lübke, *Romanisches Etymologisches Wörterbuch*, 4th ed. (1968), sv. *symphonia*.

3 For a survey of Antique and late-Antique sources in which *symphonia* appears as the name of a wind instrument see Wartburg, *op. cit.*, sv. *symphonia*.

4 For the text see Russell and Heironimus, *op. cit.*, p. 41 line 172.

5 For further information about 14th-century instruments from Nicholas de Lyra's commentary, see C. Page, 'Musical Instruments in Medieval Latin Biblical Glosses', *FoMRHI* Communication 13 (April 1976).

6 The text has been taken from E. Charrière, ed. *Chronique de Bertand du Guesclin par Cuvelier*, 2 vols. (1839) lines 10041–10067. Cuvelier was also a composer; some of his works survive (see *The New Grove* sv. *Cuvelier*).

7 The text is printed in Gerbert, *Scriptores*, 3. The extracts quoted here have been taken from a microfilm of the original. Smits van Waesberghe has proposed that the treatise was written in Paris or Liège (*Johannis Affligemensis*

De Musica (1950), p. 33); there is also a discussion of the provenance of the work in U. Michels, *Die Musiktraktate des Johannes de Muris* (1970) pp. 16–17, where it is proposed that the work is German. This hypothesis (which Michels does not, I believe, validate with complete success) fits very well with the other texts which contain the word *organistrum*.

8 For details of these see *GSJ* XXXV, p. 43 n. 17.

9 About ten treatises, that is, which actually use the word *organistrum*. The sources of these are listed by van Waesberghe in his article *Organistrum* for the *Handwörterbuch der Musikalischen Terminologie*.

10 The treatise was printed in a somewhat mangled form by Gerbert (*Scriptores*, I, p. 303) and taken from there by Bröcker (I, p. 246) and Palmer (*Hurdy-Gurdy*, p. 31); I may perhaps be forgiven for printing such a pedestrian text here in view of the inaccurate—and sometimes fantastic—things that have been said about it (e.g. by Panum, p. 293).

11 J. Smits van Waesberghe, *Cymbala* (1951) p. 33.

12 Text from A. Wagner, ed. *Visio Tnugdali* (1882) p. 48. For information about the date and provenance of this text see J. C. Douglas Marshall, 'Three Problems in the *Vision of Tundal*', *Medium Aevum* 44 (1975) pp. 14–21, and H. Spilling, *Die Visio Tnugdali* (1975). There are over 150 MSS. of the text; thus the word *organistrum* achieved a large—but in this case purely bookish—dissemination. It was also carried far afield—but again, only in learned tradition —by Vincent of Beauvais, who decided to incorporate the Tundalus material into his *Speculum Historiale*, one of the most widely copied books of his massive and influential encyclopedia. The material does not always appear in the same place, but it is often found in Book 28 chapter 101. It is also worth pointing out here that of the two examples of *organistrum* listed in R. E. Latham, *Revised Medieval Latin Word-List from British Sources* (1965), the first is taken from the *Visio Tnugdali*, while the second (dated *c.* 1325) is a reference to the Tundalus material as taken over by John of Tynemouth in his *Sanctilogium Anglie* (ed. C. Horstmann, *Nova Legenda Anglie*, 2 vols. (1901) 2, p. 310).

13 Smits van Waesberghe, *Organistrum*, details of Wolfenbüttel Cod. Gud. Lat. 334 and British Library Reference Division MS. Arundel 339 (where the instrument is named *organica lyra* in the text, but the heading is *organistrum*).

14 The information here about the *Hortus Deliciarum* has been taken from R. Green et al., eds. *Herrad von Hohenbourg: Hortus Deliciarum*, 2 vols. (1979).

15 This illustration is taken from C. M. Engelhardt, *Herrad von Landsperg* (1818) whence it was taken, somewhat elaborated, and reproduced in colour by G. Keller and A. Straub in their facsimile volume *Hortus Deliciarum* (1901), planche XI *bis*. This is the ultimate source of the 'tangentless' illustrations reproduced by many, including Panum (*op. cit.*, p. 309).

16 This illustration, which shows marks on the neck of the organistrum which I am prepared (a) to deem authentic and (b) to construe as tangents, derives from the copy made by Count Bastard. It is reproduced here from J. Walter, *Hortus Deliciarum* (1952) plate 9 (*calque en noir*).

17 See for example R. and M. Bruce-Mitford, 'The Sutton Hoo lyre,

Beowulf, and the Origins of the frame Harp', *Antiquity* 44 (1970) pp. 7–13, and H. Steger, *Philologia Musica* (1971) passim.

18 See in particular Bröcker, 1, p. 235f *et passim*.

19 Fortunately we may still compare some of the materials Gerbert used in his studies with their surviving medieval originals. For example, his copy of an elaborate diagrammatic drawing of four clerics seated to sing from the *Scientia Artis Musice* of Elias of Salomon (frontispiece to *Scriptores*, 3) is not everywhere close to its original (reproduced in J. Smits van Waesberghe, *Musikerziehung* (1969), plate 105; both Gerbert's drawing and its original are reproduced in two studies of Elias of Salomon which have appeared in *Musical Quarterly*, vols. 25 (1939) facing p. 318, and 66 (1980) p. 88). The semicircle within which the clerics sit has been bordered with elaborate foliate ornament matching 18th-century taste, while the faces of the four figures bear little relation to their originals. Small circles on the robes of two figures have been made into crescent moons; parts of text have been inverted, tacitly expanded from abbreviated forms in the original, or misread; many letter forms have been changed. By the standards of 18th-century fidelity to medieval models it is doubtless quite exceptionally accurate, yet nonetheless misleading.

20 F. B. Hettema, *Het Nederduitsche Glossarium van Bern* (1889) p. 52.

21 ibid. pp. 38 and 55.

22 G. H. Scholl, ed. *Diu Crône* (1852) lines 22094 and 22106.

23 Volume X, *Complement: Inaccoutume-Zoophyte* (1902) p. 733 column c.

24 For the original see Th. Mommsen, ed. *Digesta Iustiniani Augusti* (1870) XXI: I:38).

25 See Tobler-Lommatzsch, *Altfranözsische Wörterbuch*, sv. *orgeniste.

THE RHYMED OFFICE FOR ST THOMAS OF LANCASTER: POETRY, POLITICS AND LITURGY IN FOURTEENTH-CENTURY ENGLAND

The kings and magnates of medieval England knew how to exploit - and how to suppress - the influences of topical songs, and many medieval English chronicles contain scraps of verse that quicken as we read the violent narratives that enfold them. Yet hardly any topical poetry - either within the chronicles or elsewhere - is preserved with the music that may often have added its own quality of wit to satire and of zest to eulogy.[1] Some of the surviving verse must have been sung; Langtoft relates that one of the English topical rhymes embedded in his *Chronicle* was *chaunté* by the Scots; two poems on the death of Piers Gaveston in a fifteenth century manuscript at Cambridge are contrafacta of hymns by Fortunatus whose melodies they are presumably intended to share.[2] Yet this is a small body of material with which to explore the kind of questions we wish to ask: how were the associations of pre-existent melodies harnessed to new political causes? How complex was the meaning that such songs could generate? What kinds of subject matter attracted this form of creation? What techniques can we use to recover tunes for poems preserved without music? We need more material to investigate these issues and fortunately more is now at hand: an office for "St" Thomas of Lancaster (d 1322) in British Library MS Royal 12 C. xii.[3] The poems of this office are preserved without music (see plate 1) but the melodies can be recovered in all save two cases; the search reveals how a poet (or poets, the distinction matters little here) exploited the liturgy for a purpose in which propaganda and hagiography were inextricably mixed, turning old melodies saturated with liturgical meaning to the service of a controversial new cult.

One of the most dramatic events in the devotional life of medieval England took place on 22 March, 1322, when Thomas earl of Lancaster was led from his own hall at Pontefract and beheaded for his part in the armed baronial opposition to Edward 11:[4]

> Þo sette þai oppon his heued in scorn an olde chapelet, al-to rent and torn, þat was nouȝt worþ an halpeny; and after þai sette him oppon a lene white palfray, ful vnsemeliche and ek al bare, wiþ an olde bridel; and wiþ an horrible noyse þai drow him out of þe castel toward his deþ, and caste on him meny balles of snowe . . anone a ribaude went to him, and smote of his heuede . . . Allas þat euer soche a gentil blode shulde ben don to deþ with-outen cause and resoun!

The execution was possibly illegal; it was definitely a mis-take.[5] Edward consented that Thomas should be buried by the monks of St John's priory at Pontefract and almost immediately a cult developed centering upon the tomb near the main altar.[6] This devotion certainly had a political element - prayer and pilgrimage masked protest - yet the emblematising drive of medieval devotion to the saints must soon have turned the Thomas of 1322 into an image, eroding the pragmatism of the cult.[7] Many pilgrims may have recognised that Thomas's claim to sainthood lay as much in his kin as in his conduct; it was royal blood that was spilled at Pontefract: *Vas regale trucidatur*, says Thomas' Office, *regni pro remedio*, and royalty enjoyed a privileged relationship with the king of Heaven.[8] On Earth, nobility of blood allied to greatness of station and honour were a "grand spur to love amongst the laity" as the author of the *Vita Beati Thome Comitis Lancastrie* affirms.[9] The pilgrims flocked to Pontefract and news of the cult was carried to Edward at the York parliament of 1322; his investigators found "the whole country" testifying to the miracles according to one pro-Lancastrian continuator of the *Brut* Chronicle.[10] Edward commanded the priory doors to be closed but the cult broke out at St Paul's in London where there was a plaque which Lancaster had put up to commemorate Edward's affirmation of the Ordinances.[11] Miraculous cures were effected in the building and on 28 June, 1323, Edward wrote to bishop Stephen of London about this "certain plaque . . . on which there are likenesses, images or diverse pictures including, amongst others, a figure of Thomas, formerly earl of Lancaster", emphasising that the miracles were a "diabolic deception" and the cult *absque auctoritate ecclesie Romane*.[12] He had the plaque removed but we do not need the testimony of the *Cronique de London* to surmise that this did little to weaken Lancaster's hold over the people's minds.[13] It seems that many other commemorative objects existed in private hands - plaques showing scenes from his life, bowls engraved with his image - that Edward could not suppress and the moment he fell there ceased to be anything subversive about them. The official status of Thomas's cult changed at once. A matter of days after Edward's deposition Henry of Lancaster wrote to the Archbishop of York, William Melton, seeking the establishment of a commission to investigate Thomas's miracles; Melton duly wrote to the Holy See testifying to the importance he attached to the question.[14]

Thomas's cult inspired poetry as well as piety; no doubt poets with Lancastrian sympathies were quick to see the potential of events at Pontefract and London. The remains of what must have been a large quantity of Latin verse in Thomas's honour are scattered here and there, some of it unpublished like the following stanzas - a fragment, perhaps, from a liturgical Office:[15]

> Thomas de Lancastria comes commendatus,
> Miles ex malicia morti iudicatus,
> I[u]stus pro iusticia fuit decollatus,
> F[u]it mors mesticia cuncti comitatus.

> Ab etate tenera devotus degebat,
> Pietatis viscera pauperi pandebat,
> Miserorum misera pondera pollebat,
> Vir verax, vera, varia virtute verebat.

The most extensive series of poems in Lancaster's praise appears in a manuscript dating from the first half of the fourteenth century: British Library MS Royal 12 C. xii. The legends which accompany three of the poems - *Antiphona*, *Prosa* and *Sequentia* - suggest that we are dealing with texts intended for liturgical use. There are no melodies but the poems encode a secret: the incipits refer the singer to chants he already knows.

The poem *Pange lingua gloriosi comitis martirium* (Appendix 5) provides a clear example. The incipit points us to Fortunatus's famous hymn *Pange lingua gloriosi proelium certaminis* for Easter; we think at once - as we are surely intended to do - of Lancaster's execution in the liturgical time of Quadragesima, *ante Passionem*.[16] Fortunatus's hymn celebrates Christ's battle with his adversary, the Devil, and thus the liturgical associations of the melody nourish the hagiographer's effort. He makes much of his model poem, copying not only the syllable-count and verse-form but also internal pieces of text which he either borrows or echoes:[17]

FORTUNATUS

Pange lingua gloriosi / comitis . . .	*Pange lingua gloriosi* proelium
De parentis utriusque . . .	*De parentis* protoplasti
Dux fidelis suum gregem . . .	*Crux fidelis* inter omnes

These relationships are clearly not accidental. The metrical and formal identity, graced by verbal affinity then carried to a sub-verbal level of perception - and persuasion - by the melody, establishes an implicit comparison between Thomas and Christ (at one point the author is almost explicit: Lancaster becomes a "victor on the third day in line 11).[18] The aim of the poem is to glorify and emblematise Thomas in a way that is endorsed by historical reference; he becomes an image of the "pious earl" and the "royal flower of knights" amongst the characters and scenes of his earthly drama. The framework is almost chronological, each stanza embodying a critical moment in a static grasp that resists narrative. The real world is close at hand; the name of Lancaster's betrayer, pointed by the musical logic, lingers between stanzas:

> . . . .
> dum dolose defraudatur
> per sudam Hoylandie.   (Appendix 5, stanza 5)

The search for more "liturgical meaning" in Lancaster's Office is rewarded. *Copiose caritatis* (Appendix 7) proves to be a contra-factum of an antiphon for St Nicholas, while *Sospitati dat egrotos* (Appendix 3) is based upon a prosa for the same saint interpolated into the ninth respond at Matins.[19] This poem attempts a systematic exploitation of its model:[20]

137

Nicholas	*Sospitati dedit egros* olei *perfusio*
Thomas	*Sospitati dat egrotos* precum Thome *fusio*
Nicholas	Nicholaus naufrag*antum affuit presidio*
Thomas	Comes pius mox lang*uentum adest in presidio*

There are several reasons why our poet should have wanted to link Thomas with St Nicholas. The celebration of miraculous healing *ex eius tumba* forms an important element in the liturgy for Nicholas and few personal names were more appropriate to Thomas than that of this saint; John Myrk interprets it as "praysyng of þe pepull" and there are related etymologies in the *Legenda Aurea*, including *victor populi*.[21]

So far we have seen our poet at work with well-known materials but the solution to two further puzzles - the music of *Summum regem honoremus* (Appendix 4) and *O iam Christi pietas* (Appendix 6) reveals him at work with more recondite sources that throw much light on Lancaster's office and the circumstances in which it was composed. The answer suggested itself to me when I noticed the following stanza in a sequence contained in University College Oxford MS 78a, a missal according to the use of Hereford:[22]

> O miranda sanctitas
> per quam [Christi] pietas
> sic mundo profecit;
> nam mutus et cecitas,
> gutta, claudus, surditas
> et gibbus defecit.

Lancaster's poem begins:

> O iam Christi pietas
> atque Thome caritas
> palam elucessit.
> Heu! nunc languet equitas
> viget et impietas,
> veritas vilessit.

The schemes of metre and rhyme are the same (this is a close relative of the Middle English tail-rhyme stanza) and the rhymes are identical. There is the shared clause *Christi pietas* (where *Christi* can be confidently restored to the imperfect text of the first poem on the authority of a reading in an early-sixteenth century printed Hereford Breviary).[23] If this stanza was the model for our poem then its subject matter is exactly what is required for it relates the miracles of St Thomas of Hereford.

Important details now fall into place. It is established that the scribe who copied our Office was the main scribe of the celebrated miscellany, British Library MS Harley 2253; he appears to have been active in Ludlow.[24] A little searching with this provenance in mind reveals that the poem for Lancaster entitled *Summum regem honoremus* (Appendix 4) is a contrafactum of *Summi regis in honore*, a sequence which exists (with varying content but with the same incipit and form) in three versions: one for St Thomas of Hereford, one for St

XIV

138

Ethelbert of Hereford and one for the Virgin (to whom, together
with St Ethelbert, Hereford cathedral is jointly dedicated).[25] When
clerics familiar with the use of Hereford sang Lancaster's piece a
wealth of liturgical meaning would be released and channelled into
the new cult; Thomas would be implicitly compared with St Ethelbert,
a martyr of royal blood said to have been murdered by a king - the
parallels would assuredly not be seen as accidental; he would also
be assimilated to his namesake, Thomas of Hereford, canonised in 1320
or only two years before Lancaster's execution. Thomas of Hereford
had been Simon de Montfort's chancellor - a fact hardly likely to be
forgotten at a time when Lancaster was apt to be compared with
Simon.[26] Yet there may be a closer link between the two men. The
anonymous author of the *Vita Beati Thome Comitis Lancastrie* relates
that it was Thomas of Hereford who baptised Lancaster; he even
claims that the bishop made a prophetic speech during the ceremony
about Lancaster's destiny, capitalising upon the traditional symbolic
relationship between baptiser and baptised by claiming Lancaster as
his *filius spiritualis*.[27] We cannot assess the truth of these
stories as no other source deals with Lancaster's youth;[28] perhaps
it was fabricated by a pro-Lancastrian author who, like the compiler
of our office, wished to establish and then to exploit a link
between Lancaster and the renowned bishop of Hereford only recently
canonised.

Where might this have happened? The evidence points strongly
to the diocese of Hereford. The three sequences beginning *Summi
regis in honore* do not appear, as far as I am aware, outside of
books conforming to the use of Hereford. Certainly our copy of
Lancaster's office, which exploits these sequences, seems to come
from the Herefordshire-Shropshire area. It was doubtless copied by
someone who recognised the peculiarly localised liturgical meaning
it was trying to exploit. There were numerous clerics in the
dioceses of Hereford and Worcester pursued after 1322 for their pro-
baronial sympathies;[29] our poet could well have been such a man,
perhaps one wishing to make an impression on Adam of Orleton, bishop
of Hereford until 1327, whose household was not without a pro-
baonial element and who, arraigned in 1324 for not following the
king north in the campaign which led to Lancaster's death, conceived
an *inexorabile odium contra regem et eius amicos* according to the
chronicler le Baker.[30]

How were these pieces used? We do not know for certain that
they were ever performed liturgically - or, indeed, that they were
ever performed at all. It was quite in order for poets to write
Offices for "saints" before they were officially canonised but it
does not follow that it was always permissible to sing them.[31] Yet
we do possess a fifteenth century polyphonic setting of a text in
honour of Thomas and it must seem unlikely that such a piece would
have been composed without the prospect of a performance.[32] As far
as the years after Edward's deposition are concerned liturgical
performance remains a possibility for our office. But it is also
possible that they were intended for use as political songs. We
remember that two Latin poems on the death of Gaveston survive (one
praises Thomas in its first line) which are contrafacta of hymns by
Fortunatus including *Pange lingua gloriosi proelium certaminis*;

these topical poems were certainly not intended for liturgical use. The idea of hymn-melodies torn from their liturgical setting and set adrift in a world of domestic and public performance need not surprise us; John Stevens pointed out long ago that some plainsong hymns had currency as popular songs in later-medieval England.[33]

We have some evidence that Lancaster's downfall caused a stir amongst singers. In 1323 Edward II made a progress to the north that brought him to Pickering in August. Whilst there he took seisin of Thomas's confiscated manors. He then proceeded to Whorlton castle where two women, perhaps minstrels, named Alianore le Rede and Alice de Whorlton sang songs of Simon de Montfort for which they were subsequently paid three shillings.[34] It seems almost inconceivable that Edward, finding himself in the north only a year after Boroughbridge, would relax with stories of this great rebel to whom Lancaster was often compared. It seems more likely that the songs, clearly circulating in the area, were such that Edward would wish to hear to sense the temper of the region. Perhaps some popular feeling and lore about Thomas was finding expression? There was certainly more such feeling in the halls and refectories of Herefordshire clerics where our songs may have been delivered.[35]

NOTES

[1] Two familiar instances of the influence of song are: Roger of Hoveden's story of the (French) *cantores et joculatores* hired to sing the praises of Richard I (*Chronica Rogeri de Hoveden*, Rolls Series 51, III, p.143), and the story of Lucas de Barre, blinded by Henry I for his songs, told by Orderic Vitalis (*The Ecclesiastical History of Orderic Vitalis*, ed. M. Chibnall, 6 vols. (Oxford, 1972-80) VI, pp.352-5). As far as I am aware no political poetry appears with music in any medieval English chronicle source, although it is interesting to find one Latin topical song, *Vulneratur karitas*, laid out for music (which was never supplied) in British Library MS Harley 746, ff.103v-4, a miscellany of legal and documentary materials. A later reader (?s.xiv) has scribbled the opening words of the poem and some musical notes on f.107.

[2] *The Chronicle of Pierre de Langtoft* (RS 47) II, p.234; the songs on the death of Gaveston, *Vexilla regni prodeunt* and *Pange lingua necem Petri* are preserved in Cambridge, Trinity College MS O. 9. 38, f.64r/v. They have been printed (without music) by T. Wright, *The Political Songs of England*, Camden Society 6 (London, 1839) pp.258-61. I have edited the poems with their music for a forthcoming edition to be published by Antico Editions.

[3] The text of this office is printed in Wright, *Political Songs*, pp.268-72. For a description of this manuscript and an inventory of its contents see G. Warner and J.B. Gilson, *Catalogue of Western Manuscripts in the Old Royal and King's Collections in the British Museum*, 5 vols. (London, 1921) II, pp.26-9. The office is also printed in W. Sparrow Simpson, *Documents illustrating the History of St Paul's Cathedral*, Camden Society n.s. 26 (1880) pp.12-14. I have resisted Sparrow Simpson's emendation of the MS *sudam Hoylandie* (in *Pange lingua gloriosi comitis martirium*, Appendix 5) to *Judam Hoylandie* which I do not find entirely convincing, even though I have no explanation to offer for the mysterious *sudam*.

[4] *The Brut*, ed. F.W.D. Brie, EETS OS 131 and 136 (1906 and 1908) I, p.223. For an account of the circumstances leading up to this event see J.R. Maddicott, *Thomas of Lancaster, 1307-1322: A Study in the Reign of Edward II* (Oxford, 1970). As the dates in his title reveal, Maddicott is not concerned with the development of Thomas's cult in his book (although it is briefly discussed on pp.329-30); most of the studies of the subject date from the nineteenth century. They include Lord Houghton, "Observations on the History of Thomas, Earl of Lancaster", *Journal of the British Archaeological Association*, 20 (1864) pp.16-18; Richard Holmes, *Pontefract* (Pontefract, 1878) pp.152f; Alex D.H. Leadman, "The Battle of Boroughbridge", *Yorkshire Archaeological and Topographical Journal* 7 (1881-2) pp.330-60. See also H. Tait, "Pilgrim-signs and Thomas, Earl of Lancaster", *The British Museum Quarterly* 19 (1954) pp.39-46.

[5] The judgement against Thomas was annulled in the first parliament of Edward III (*Rotuli Parliamentorum*, II, pp.3-5, where Henry of Lancaster claims that his brother *noun resonablement estoit jugge a la morte par un proces erroyne contre lui adonques fait*). See M.H. Keen, "Treason Trials under the Law of Arms", *Transactions of the Royal Historical Society*, 5th Series, 12 (1962) p.102.

[6] Various chronicles mention the location of the tomb (e.g. *Flores Historiarum*, RS 95, III, p.206) but it had not been traced when C.V. Bellamy's excavation report was published ("Pontefract Priory Excavations 1957-61", *Thoresby Society* 49 (1962-4)). Janet Walker informs me, on the basis of her examination of the late C.V. Bellamy's as yet unpublished notes, and following consultation with the members of the excavation group, that there is no evidence to connect any of the burials excavated

141

in the priory church with the tomb of Thomas of Lancaster.

7   The cult lasted well into the fifteenth century - and indeed until the Reformation - when its political impetus must have been spent. There is, for example, a rubricated obit for *Sancti thome martiris comitis Lancastrie* in the calendar of a fifteenth century Missal from St John's, Pontefract, now Cambridge, King's College MS 31 (the entry covers two lines for 22 and 23 March). There was a guild of St Thomas in Pontefract at this time dedicated to preserving and improving commemorative sites and monuments. Miracles continued well into the century. Blood flowed from Thomas's tomb in 1466 (as it had done in 1359) according to an *Abbreviata Chronica* (ed. J.J. Smith in *Cambridge Antiquarian Society Publications* 1 (1840-6) p.10); this event is said to have caused *maxima fama* in England and allusion is made to other miracles of *beatus Thomas* (*loc.cit.*). Relics were still kept in the fifteenth century. See Alexandra F. Johnston and Margaret Rogerson, *Records of Early English Drama: York*, 2 vols. (Toronto, 1979) II, pp.637 and 858-9.

8   This is the most complex issue surrounding Lancaster's cult and one that must be studied by a qualified historian. It does not bear directly upon the issues raised here.

9   *Anecdota ex codicibus hagiographicis Johannis Gielemans* (Brussels, 1895) p.94. This *Vita* is preserved in a manuscript now Vienna Nationalbibliothek Ser.nov.12708; there it is divided into nine sections and it is just possible that this ninefold division is connected with the readings of Matins.

10   V.H. Galbraith, "Extracts from the Historia Aurea and a French 'Brut', (1317-47)", *English Historical Review* 43 (1928) p.216. Very few of Lancaster's miracles are documented. Some are listed in the *Vita* (pp.98f) and several in the *Brut*. A passage in the *Flores Historiarum*, III, p.214, promises a separate treatment of Lancaster's miracles in another work. I have found no evidence that this was ever undertaken.

11   *Croniques de London*, ed. G.J. Aungier, Camden Society 28 (1844) p.46. This same chronicle reports that the plaque was later replaced.

12   *Foedera*, II, part 1, p.525. According to the *Cronique de London* Edward had the *tabula* and the accompanying wax images removed on the feast of the translation of St Thomas of Canterbury, Lancaster's celebrated namesake with whom he was sometimes compared (as in the first poem of our office, Appendix 1). The *Flores Historiarum*, III, pp.213f, confirms that the plaque contained an image of Thomas in armour. For a painting of a *vir armatus*, probably Thomas, see Bodleian Library MS Douce 231, f.1.

13   *Cronique de London*, p.46.

14   Both Letters are printed in *Historical Papers and Letters from the Northern Registers*, ed. J. Raine (RS 61) pp.339-42. The modern MS reference and foliation is: York, Borthwick Institute Reg.9A, ff.205v-6. Lancaster was never actually canonised, despite the assertion to the contrary in Walsingham, *Historia Anglicana* (RS 28) II, p.195.

15   MS e Mus. 139, f.85r. I have omitted: a hypermetric *cuius* in line 4; a redundant compendium (?*pra*) before *pondera* in line 7. Line 8 as it stands has one syllable too many; perhaps it should read *Homo verax, varia virtute verebat*. *Homo* might easily have been changed to *vir* by a scribe over-zealous for alliteration and word-play.
    For other "liturgical" material in honour of Lancaster see the note by T. Taylor and J.T. Micklethwaite in *Archaeological Journal* 36 (1879)

pp.103-4, which incorporates material from a fourteenth-century English
Book of Hours now Baltimore, Walters Art Gallery MS W.105, f.13v (compare
Cambridge, Clare College MS 6, f.144). For *Ave Thoma, gemma milicie* and
Miles Christi gloriose from Cologne, Historisches Archiv der Stadt Cod.
W.28, ff.84v and 146r, see *Analecta Hymnica*, 13, p.7, and 28, p.321. For
a fifteenth century English polyphonic setting of the latter see *Fifteenth
Century Liturgical Music*, ed. Andrew Hughes, Early English Church Music 8
(London, 1964) pp.10-11.

16   *Adae Murimuth Continuatio Chronicarum* (RS 93) p.36 and p.280.

17   Fortunatus's poem is quoted from MGH *Auctorum Antiquissimorum* IV, part 1
(Berlin, 1881) pp.27-8.

18   *Agonista fit invictus/statim die tercia.* An association between Thomas
and Christ seems to linger in a passage of the *Flores Historiarum*, III,
p.206, where Lancaster, led to execution, *non contendit neque clamavit*
(*cf.* Matthew xii 19).

19   The texts of the ninth respond and its verse could scarcely be more
appropriate: R *Ex eius tumba marmorea sacrum resudat oleum quo liniti
sanantur ceci , surdis auditus redditur et debilis quisque sospes
regreditur.* V *Cateruatim ruunt populi cernere cupientes que per eum
fiunt mirabilia.* Our author clearly capitalises not only upon the
liturgical meaning of the prosa but also of its context.

20   Here is the full text, transcribed from the Hereford Antiphoner (Hereford
Cathedral Library MS P. 9. vii, f.229v; for the choice of source see below):
Sospitati dedit egros olei perfusio / Nicholaus naufragantum affuit
presidio / Releuauit a defunctis defunctum in biuio / Baptizatur auri uiso
iudeus inditio / Uas in mari mersum patri redditur cum filio / O quam probat
sanctum Dei farris augmentacio / Ergo laudes Nicholao concinat hec concio /
Nam qui corde poscit illum propulsato uicio / Sospes regreditur.

21   *Mirk's Festial*, ed. T. Erbe, EETS ES 96 (1905) p.11, and *Jacobi a Voragine
Legenda Aurea*, ed. Th. Graesse (Leipzig, 1850) p.22.

22   F.188r. This is part of the sequence *Magne lucem caritatis* for St Thomas
of Hereford (text in *Analecta Hymnica*, 40, p.302); unfortunately there
seems to be no copy of this sequence in existence with music. For details
of this manuscript see S.J.P. van Dijk, "Handlist of the Latin Liturgical
Manuscripts in the Bodleian Library Oxford", 1 (1957) p.150 (typescript
handlist), where the MS is said to be from St Dubricius', Whitchurch
(Monmouthshire).

23   See the text in *Analecta Hymnica*, *loc.cit.*

24   Carter Revard, "Three more Holographs in the Hand of the Scribe of MS
Harley 2253 in Shrewsbury", *Notes and Queries*, n.s. 28 (1981) pp.199-200.
The scribe is known to have been active in the period 1314-49.

25   The texts for Ethelbert and Thomas of Hereford are in *The Hereford Breviary*,
ed. W.H. Frere and L.E.G. Brown, 3 vols., Henry Bradshaw Society (London,
1903, 1910 and 1915) II, pp.174 and 351. The version for the Virgin is in
Analecta Hymnica 40, p.82. The music for Ethelbert's sequence is preserved
in the Hereford Gradual (British Library MS Harley 3965, f.113r/v) and this
appears to be the only complete surviving melody for any of these three
poems. It has been used to restore music to Lancaster's sequence (Appendix
4). The version for the Virgin also appears in the manuscript but with
blank staves; possibly it was intended for the same melody as Ethelbert's

version but the absence of music at the close of the preceding sequence suggests rather some hiatus in the copying (ff.127v-8). It is certain, however, that the version for Thomas was associated - at least in some centres - with a different tune. I am grateful to Andrew Wathey for drawing my attention to a bifolium of an antiphonal in Gloucester Diocesan Records Office (numbered 14 in N.R. Ker, *Medieval Manuscripts in British Libraries*, 2, Abbotsford-Keele (Oxford, 1977) p.971); f.1-1v contains the last section of Thomas of Hereford's sequence with music different from that associated with Ethelbert in the Hereford Gradual.

26   *Chronica Monasterii de Melsa* (RS 43) II, p.131.

27   *Vita*, pp.93 and 98.

28   As pointed out by Maddicott, *Thomas of Lancaster*, p.3.

29   R.M. Haines, *The Church and Politics in Fourteenth Century England: The Career of Adam Orleton c1275-1345* (Cambridge, 1978) p.140.

30   *Chronicon Galfridi le Baker*, ed. E.M. Thompson (Oxford, 1889) p.16.

31   A particularly interesting case is provided by the Office for John Dalderby, bishop of Lincoln, who was never canonised. This Office (Lincoln-shire County Records Office Dj/20/2) has been systematically compiled and is elaborate (there is full provision for three Nocturns at Matins each with three psalms and three Great Responsories); there is rubrication. Yet the hand is a cursive one and the leaves were clearly never intended to be bound into a liturgical book. They represent a kind of liturgical document often mentioned in inventories - the unbound quire or bundle of leaves - but very rarely encountered. Lancaster's Office in Royal 12 C. xii may well have been taken from some more systematic, yet transient and informal source.

32   Edited in Hughes, *op.cit.*, pp.10-11.

33   John Stevens, *Music and Poetry in the Early Tudor Court*, Corrected edition (Cambridge, 1979) p.50.

34   J.W. Walker, "Robin Hood Identified", *The Yorkshire Archaeological Journal* 36 (1944-7) p.30.

35   I am most grateful to Dr Peter Newton, FSA, of the Centre for Medieval Studies at the University of York, to Mr Andrew Wathey, of Merton College, Oxford, and to Mr Edward Wilson, of Worcester College, Oxford, for their help in the preparation of this article.

APPENDIX

THE OFFICE OF THOMAS OF LANCASTER

BRITISH LIBRARY, MS ROYAL 12 C.XII

TEXT   The manuscript spellings have been retained, save that the
scribe's consonantal *u* is everywhere reproduced as *v*. Punctuation
and capitalisation are mostly mine.

MUSIC   Ligatures are indicated by slurs.

1   Antiphona   GAUDE THOMA, DUCUM DECUS   (Music Unidentified)

       Gaude Thoma, ducum decus, lucerna Lancastrie
       Qui per necem imitaris Thomam Cantuarie
       Cuius capud conculcatur pacem ob ecclesie
       Atque tuum detruncatur causa pacis Anglie;
       Esto nobis pius tutor in omni discrimine.

2   Oratio

       Deus, qui pro pace et tranquillitate regnicolarum Anglie beatum
       Thomam martirem tuum atque comitem gladio persecutoris occumbere
       voluisti, concede propicius, ut omnes qui eius memoriam devote
       venerantur in terris premia condigna cum ipso consequi mereantur
       in celis, per Dominum nostrum.

3 Prosa SOSPITATI DAT EGROTOS Music: Hereford Cathedral MS P.9.VII f.229ᵛ

Sos--pi--ta--ti dat e-gro-tos pre-cum Tho--me fu--si--o;

Co--mes pi--us mox lan-guen-tum a-dest in pre--si--di--o;

Re--le--van--tur ab in-fir-mis in-fir-mi suf-fra-gi--o;

Sanc-ti Tho-me quod mon-stra-tur sig-no-rum in-di--ci--o

Vas re--ga--le tru--ci--da--tur reg-ni pro re--me--di--o.

O quam pro--bat sanc-tum du-cem mor-bo-rum cu - ra - ti - o!

Er-go lau--des Tho--me sanc-to ca-na-mus cum gau--di--o,

Nam de-vo-te   pos-cens il--lum sta-tim pro--cul--du--bi--o

Sos-------pes   re----gre----di----------------tur.

4 Sequencia SUMMUM REGEM HONOREMUS Music: British Library, Harley MS 3965
f.113^{r-1}

Sum--mum re--gem ho--no--re--mus dul--cis pro me-------mo--ri--a

Mar--ti--ris, quem col--lau----de--mus sum--ma re--ve--ren------ci--a.

Tho------mas co----mes ap--pel--la--tur ste--ma--te e--gre--gi--o;

Si-----ne cau----sa con--demp--na--tur, na--tus tho--ro re--gi--o.

Qui cum ple--bem to--tam cer--nit la--bi sub nau--fra--gi--o,

Non pro iu--re mo--ri sper--nit le--ta--li com--mer--ci--o.

O flos mi--li--tum re--ga--lis, tu--am hanc fa--mi--li--am

Sem--per con--ser--ves a ma--lis, per--du--cens ad glo--ri--am. AMEN

5 [Hymnus] PANGE LINGUA   Music: Hereford Cathedral, MS P.9.VII f.94^v

Pan--ge lin----gua glo--ri--o----si co----mi--tis mar--ti--ri--um,

San--gui--nis--que pre--ci--o---si Tho---me flo--ris mi--li--tum,

Ger--mi--nis--que ge--ne--ro--si lau--dis, lu--cis co-----mi--tum.

XIV

De parentis utriusque
regali prosapia
prodit Thomas, cuius pater
proles erat regia,
matrem atque sublimavit
reginam Navarria.

Dux fidelis suum gregem
dum dispersum conspicit,
emulumque suum regem
sibi motum meminit,
mox carnalem iuxta legem
in mirum contremuit.

Benedicti Benedictus
capitur vigilia;
agonista fit invictus
statim die tercia;
dire neci est addictus,
ob quod luget Anglia.

Proht dolor! azephalatur
plebis pro iuvamine,
suorumque desolatur
militum stipamine,
dum dolose defraudatur
per sudam Hoylandie.

Ad sepulcrum cuius fiunt
frequenter miracula;
ceci, claudi, surdi, muti,
membra[1] paralitica,
prece sua consequuntur
optata presidia.

Trinitati laus et honor,
virtus et potencia
patri, proli, flaminique
sacro sit per secula,
que nos salvat a peccatis
Thome per suffragia. Amen

---

[1] MS: menbra

6   O IAM CHRISTI PIETAS   (Music untraced, but almost certainly
      taken from a section of the sequence MAGNE LUCEM CARITATIS
      for St Thomas of Hereford)

      O iam Christi pietas
      atque Thome caritas
        palam elucessit.
      Heu! nunc languet equitas
      viget et impietas,
        veritas vilessit.
      Nempe Thome bonitas
      eius atque sanctitas
        indies acressit,
      Ad cuius tumbam sospitas
      egris datur, ut veritas
        cunctis nunc claressit.

7 [Antiphona] COPIOSE CARITATIS Music: Hereford Cathedral, MS P.9.VII f.230

Co----pi--o--------se ca--ri--ta--tis Tho--ma pu-----gil stre--nu--e,

Qui   pro   le---ge li--ber---ta------tis de--cer----tas--ti An--gli--e,

in--ter--pel--la pro   pec--ca--tis nos--tris   pat--rem glo--ri--e,

Ut as--cri----bat cum be---a--tis   nos ce--les-----tis cu--ri--e. AMEN

Gaude thoma ducum decus lucerna lancastrie q̄ p̄ comune utilitatis thomam comitem cui caput amputans pacem observacio anima dedicas, causa pacis anglie ora pro nobis pie cure in ora disciplinae, orā.

Deus qui pro pace et tranquillitate regnicola anglie beatum thomam martyrem tuum atque comitem gladio persecutoris decumbere voluisti concede quesumus ut omnes qui ei memoriam devote venerantur in terris premia condigna cum ipso consequi mereantur in celis per dominum.

Oportebat deus egrotos panes thome suscipere. Concessit mox languentem adest in presidio. Felonam ab iniuriam infirmis sufficiam. Est thome quod in constans signorum indicio vas regale tendat regni pro remedio. Qui p̄ prolata sermum dicere moerebis constitio. Ergo laudes thome tibi animam congaudendo. Peram devote posses illibistatim pande bona suffices reddas.

Regnantem. Omnium regem in honorem dulcis p̄ memoriam maior vir quem collendens summa reverencia. Thomas comes appellatur stemmate egregio. Sine causa condempnatum nato thoro regio. Qui cum plebem totam cerniret labi et manciparo utrum pro ipse mori igni letali commercio. Sed hos militum regalis tuam hanc famulum. Serum conserues a malis per ducens ad gloriam amen.

Plange lingua gloriosi comitis martyrium sanguinis p̄ profi thome plora militum dimin̄ q̄ credat placuere suas comitam de pecus utriusque regali progenia prodit thomas cui pater pro les erit regia militem atq sublimatur regimen nantauria.

Eripe prodis suum aucugem domino Dominum constret comiti q̄ sum regem q̄ motu memmit auce aternale mis lego in uno comite et Benedicta virtus capit uirgilia agonista sic inuidi pietas de dom. Que uia est addicens ob quod luget anglia.

Prohibe dolor acephalat plebis p̄ uniuerse prior p̄ desolat nostri stepmane on dolose desistat psici hoplandie. Ad sequi spuatur cui sunt regmonum miuiti eco claudis sundi uiuo.

Deus proles querens quod uara fides reperta legumis mortis psana uinis auia peplat

Lumley

IN THE DIRECTION OF
THE BEGINNING

As they charted Everyman's progress on the march to Doomsday medieval scholars saw that the arts had evolved by an accumulation of inventions and discoveries. The Italian scholar Polydore Vergil gathered this learning into a book on 'the inventors of things' published in 1499, but he was defeated by a musical instrument called *clavicymbalum* — one of the earliest names for the harpsichord:[1]

> Many musical instruments have been devised in very recent times whose inventors have now passed into oblivion. Among these, the following are worthy of admiration and all praise on account of the sweetness of their music . . . *monochordia,* and *clavicymbala* . . . the inventors of these lie hidden in the darkest night, to the great detriment of their renown.

Our age prefers comprehensive, impersonalised causes to the vivid parade of individuals that served for a past in the Middle Ages, yet it still seems that the harpsichord is not entirely out of place in the *De Inventoribus Rerum*. Some musical instruments are tools, their linea-

---

[1]Quoted from *Polydori Vergilii Urbinatis de Inventoribus Rerum Libri Tres* (Venice 1499) 1[viii] — 1[ix]. For the speculations of Anselmi (1434) concerning the inventor of the *monocordum* (apparently a clavichord) see G. Massera, ed., *Georgii Anselmi Parmensis De Musica* (Florence, 1961), p. 126. It is worth recording that one medieval document in which a person is attributed with the invention of the clavicimbalum has come down to us. In 1397 one Johannes Ludovicus wrote a letter at Padua to his son Petrus de Thomasiis. The letter is full of gossip about mutual friends and colleagues, and at one point Johannes mentions a 'Magister Armannus doctor artium, qui fuit socius tui magistri Iohannis, juvenis bone conversationis et bonorum morum, ingeniosus multum et inventor unius instrumenti, quod nominat clavicembalum . . .' (Master Hermann doctor of arts, who was a friend of your Master John, a young man of good behaviour and character, very ingenious and inventor of an instrument which is called clavicembalum . . .) The text is printed in Arnaldo Segarizzi, 'La Corrispondenza familiare d'un medico . . .' in Atti della I.R. Accademia . . . degli Agiati in Rovereto, 3d series, xiii (1907), 224-5.

ments worn smooth by the accumulated experience of generations into a form that is a profile of the task to be done, and it rarely makes sense to speak of their 'origin'. Their history may prove to be a synopsis of the great cultural symposium of Eurasia extending far beyond our knowledge, and crowded with movement:

> It is the nature of instruments to migrate, with or without their masters, through an organic process, or by force. They accommodate themselves on foreign soil like living matter, add new parts or lose others, or change the manner of playing, the tuning, their volume or shape.[2]

But some instruments spring from a humus of accumulated skills and creative mastery over raw materials when a technician discerns a problem and devises an apparatus to circumvent it. Such a man is indeed an *auctor,* as Polydore says. But what is the precise nature of his role? Are we to take an evolutionary view and assume that a technological innovation such as the harpsichord is precipitated by an accumulating need which spurs designers to take a creative step?[3] Is it rather that the inventor identifies potential for growth, and creates conditions in which it may be fostered?

The harpsichord appears to have fulfilled all the conditions necessary for a successful invention. The rapid spread of the instrument in 15th-century Europe suggests that it solved a problem shared by an international community of musicians receptive to innovation.[4] The

[2]E. Gerson-Kiwi, 'Migrations and Mutations of Oriental Folk Instruments', *Journal of the International Folk Music Council,* iv (1952), p.17. Attempts to determine the 'origin' of instruments are rarely more than searches for the points where they disappear from view. Thus Werner Bachmann's study *The Origins of Bowing* (London, 1969; translated from the original German by Norma Deane) is about the *earliest evidence* for the bow, and is conducted upon the assumption that the date and provenance of that evidence must furnish a clue to the *origin* of the bow. This does not follow, as Laurence Picken has pointed out (*Folk Musical Instruments of Turkey* [London, 1975], p.323). We may base theories upon the content of our evidence, but scarcely upon its pattern of survival.

[3]The problem is discussed in another connection, but in medieval contexts, by Elizabeth L. Eisenstein, in her richly discursive book *The Printing Press as an Agent of Change* (2 vols., Cambridge University Press, 1979), i, p.32*f,* and *passim.*

[4]The spread of the instrument is most fully documented by pictorial sources. See Edmund A. Bowles, 'A Checklist of Fifteenth-century Representatives of Stringed Keyboard Instruments', in Edwin M. Ripin ed., *Keyboard Instruments: Studies in*

creative step may have been taken by a pottering notary who cared nothing for music; it is equally possible that a professional instrument maker with a keen eye for musical trends was responsible. But *why* was the instrument so successful?

Our story might begin with the chekker, first named in the account books of King John the Good (1360), and frequently mentioned thereafter in written sources. Yet despite the abundance of material we know very little about this instrument, save that *the* chekker probably never existed; names for stringed keyboard instruments were associated with shapes rather than with their actions in the Middle Ages, and chekkers in different places at different times may have had all sorts of mechanisms under their lids.[5]

The chekker materials illustrate a central problem in any discussion of the origin of the harpsichord; they lead us everywhere but in the direction of musical life. Certainly some of the documentary references to the chekker (and other keyboard instruments) reveal telling details about players and their patrons, but most of the verse and prose sources benefit only the student of *ordo* in medieval literary

---

Keyboard Organology 1500-1800 (second edition, New York, 1977), 11-17, and plates 1-31a. This checklist (which also includes clavichords and other forms) may be supplemented by Christopher Page and Lewis Jones, 'Four More 15th-century Representations of Stringed Keyboard Instruments', *Galpin Society Journal* xxxi (1978), 151-155, and plates xi-xii, and by Page, 'The Myth of the Chekker', *Early Music*, vii (1979), 489, plate 8. A further example (a clavichord in the intarsia of the choir of Modena Cathedral) has been brought to my attention by Mary Remnant.

[5]Page, 'The Myth of the Chekker', *passim*. Edwin M. Ripin assembled many references to this instrument in his article 'Towards an Identification of the Chekker', *Galpin Society Journal*, xxviii (1975), 11-25. A reference to the chekker overlooked in Ripin's article and in mine, now brought to my attention by David Fallows, illustrates the point that *the* chekker is a myth. In 1485 one Jean Cholay, *organiste et chantre de la saincte chapelle de Chamberi,* was sent from Geneva to Chambéry to fetch *les petites orgues dit exchaquiers,* 'the little organs called chekkers' (Marie-Thérèse Bouquet, 'La Cappella Musicale dei Duchi di Savoia dal 1450 al 1500', *Rivista Italiana di Musicologia,* iii (1968), 243 and 275). Yet the chekker known to Jean de Gerson in the early fifteenth century was undoubtedly a stringed keyboard instrument (Ripin, *op cit,* plates 3 and 4; Page, *op cit,* plate 6); we therefore have evidence for the existence of two families of chekkers. See further Tess Knighton, 'Another chekker reference', *Early Music,* viii, (1980), 375, discussing a fifteenth-century Aragonese document which mentions an instrument called 'organ or chekker' *(orgue o scaquer).*

XV

composition. The pictorial sources are also deeply involved with formalised procedures; each has a place in a lineage of replicas fostered by workshop pattern books and *repertoria*. A new scion may be more of an emblem of notions about space, imagery and decoration than a fresh response to musical life.

As an alternative approach we might focus upon medieval machine-technology, following the lead of Edmund Bowles who argues that "the contemporary tradition of scientific instrument building associated with astronomical devices and automata" established a technological basis for the development of stringed keyboard instruments.[6] Yet such reasoning remains static until we can *demonstrate* a causal connection between the two technologies. To give a convincing account of automata building does not necessarily make its techniques seem pregnant with possibilities for the harpsichord and clavichord. Nor does it explain why the harpsichord existed in the days of Arnaut of Zwolle (d. 1466), a keen student of scientific and musical instruments, but not in the lifetime of Hermannus Contractus (d. 1054), a musical theorist "unequalled in making clockwork, musical instruments and mechanical devices" according to the chronicler Berthold.[7]

Sooner or later we find ourselves retreating from the mass of literary and documentary material to questions about music and musical life in the later Middle Ages. Are there reasons for the emergence of the harpsichord at this time that we can identify? If so, how intimately are they related to the development of music before 1400? It has often been said that the harpsichord is a mechanised psaltery;[8] this is true, and it is equivalent to saying that the harpsichord is a keyed box of quill-plucked open strings, which is scarcely to get beyond describing the instrument; how much do we really know about the music and techniques of the fourteenth century psaltery? Why should anyone have wanted to mechanise it — and why then? I

[6]Edmund A. Bowles, 'On the Origin of the Keyboard Mechanism in the Late Middle Ages', *Technology and Culture*, vii (1966), 152-62.
[7]The chronicle of Berthold (d. 1088) is printed in G. H. Pertz, ed., *Monumenta Germaniae Historica*, Scriptorum V (Hanover, 1844). The reference to Hermannus (p.268) runs: *In horologicis et musicis instrumentis et mechanicis nulli par erat componendis.*
[8]As for example by Raymond Russell, *The Harpsichord and Clavichord* (2nd edition, revised by Howard Schott, London, 1973), p.13: "The earliest forms of the harpsichord were the result of attempts to mechanise the psaltery . . .".

propose that the invention of the harpsichord was precipitated by a drive in the string playing of all Medieval art music towards plurilinear texture, deeply involved with the evolution of a written musical tradition and associated concepts.

STRING PLAYING IN THE MIDDLE AGES

At one extreme of the string-playing spectrum we may distinguish monolinear procedures in which the solo-musician never sounds notes simultaneously, and at the other, plurilinear music in which one player controls the simultaneous outflow of two or more individualised lines.[9] In between there are a host of illiterate techniques characterised by the simultaneous sounding of notes, including fixed, moveable, constant and interrupted drones, and parallel intervals. Such playing may be termed *polyphonic,* and I shall henceforward use the term in this special sense. It consists of auxiliary noises clustering around a central element — the 'thing' which is played:

monolinear	polyphonic	plurilinear

The history of string playing in medieval art music is one of movement along this spectrum from polyphonic to plurilinear playing. The roots of this development perhaps lie in the ninth century, when the stimulus of secular vocal and instrumental polyphony drove textured singing into liturgical celebration, formerly dominated by monolinear chant.[10] Treatises such as the *Enchiriadis de Mu-*

[9]Compare Ernst Emsheimer, 'Some Remarks on European Folk Polyphony', *Journal of the International Folk Music Council,* xvi (1964), 43-46; Bachmann, *Origins, passim,* but especially 100*f,* and 149-151; *idem,* 'Die Verbreitung des Quintierens im euorpäischen Volksgesang des späten Mittelalters', in Walther Vetter, ed., *Festschrift Max Schneider zum 80. Geburtstage* (Leipzig, 1955), 25-29; and Anthony Baines, 'Ancient and Folk Backgrounds', in *idem,* ed., *Musical Instruments through the Ages* (2nd revised edition, London, 1969), 221-2.

[10]Compare Marius Schneider, *Geschichte der Mehrstimmigkeit* (2 vols., Berlin, 1934-5), *passim,* and on the question of instrumental influence on early organum, M. Vogel, 'Zum Ursprung der Mehrstimmigkeit', *Kirchenmusikalisches Jahrbuch,* xlix (1965), 57-64. An important aspect of this question concerns the possible use of instruments to accompany early organum, carrying instrumental playing into the world of literate musical practice. See Andreas Holschneider, *Die Organa von Winchester* (Hildesheim, 1968), 131-144, and *idem,* 'Instrumental Titles to the Sequentiae of the Winchester Tropers', in F. W. Sternfeld *et al.,* ed., *Essays on Opera and English Music in honour of Sir Jack Westrup* (Oxford, 1975), 8-18.

sica[11] show that a propaganda campaign was launched to legitimise the new techniques by placing them in the learned — and primarily Boethian — tradition of speculation about consonance and dissonance. The writers who initiated this campaign created a revolution in Western musical consciousness. Once the written musical tradition had been generated, an irreversible conceptual step was taken. Henceforward, practice and development came to rest upon articulated principles maintained by the exercise of literacy.

These principles were founded not upon metre or melody, but upon notions of consonance and dissonance which eventually influenced instrumental playing. We can see the process at work with startling clarity in Jerome of Moravia's *Tractatus de Musica,* a compendium of music theory composed in Paris late in the thirteenth century. This work closes with a chapter on the tuning of two bowed instruments, the *rubeba* and the *viella,* which is a crucial document bearing directly upon our story.[12] Jerome's tunings for the latter instrument are ideal for droning, and they therefore show that the age of textured fiddle playing was not yet over. However, Jerome also mentions an advanced technique that betrays the irruption of literacy-based thinking about consonance and dissonance into this area of instrumental practice.[13]

> One thing must be finally noted, namely that which is most difficult, serious and excellent in this art: to know how to accord with the *borduni* in the first harmonies any note from which any melody is woven. This is certainly easily known from the second [Guidonian] hand, which is only used by advanced players . . .

[11]The only edition is in Martin Gerbert, *Scriptores Ecclesiastici de Musica Sacra Potissimum* (3 vols., St. Blasien, 1784; reprinted Milan, 1931) i, 152a-173b; there is a useful translation of the work in Leonie Rosenstiel, *Music Handbook (Musica Enchiriadis),* (Colorado Springs, 1976). The contexts of the treatise are discussed in Willi Apel, 'The Earliest Polyphonic Composition and its Theoretical Background', *Revue Belge de Musicologie,* x (1956), 129-37.

[12]The text is edited with facsimile, translation and commentary in Page, 'Jerome of Moravia on the *Rubeba* and *Viella',* *Galpin Society Journal* xxxii (1979), 77-98.

[13]Ibid, 93.

IN THE DIRECTION OF THE BEGINNING

The annotator of Jerome's treatise, Pierre de Limoges (d. 1306), offers the following explanation of the technique:[14]

> Because the D *bordunus* [a string running off the fingerboard] must not be touched with the thumb or the bow, unless the other strings touched by the bow produce notes with which the *bordunus* makes any of the aforesaid consonances, namely fifth, octave and fourth etc. . . .

Jerome and Pierre tell us far less than we wish to know about this technique, but we can see what was happening nevertheless. The tangle of textured sound associated with the drone-based tunings of the *viella* was being combed through by applying the *ratio* of written music theory until discrete chords, susceptible of description in the contemporary language of consonance and dissonance, were revealed.[15]

A development from polyphony to plurilinear playing (or to chordal techniques based upon the texture of written polyphony) overtook many of the art-chordophones of Europe during the Middle Ages. It happened to the lute in the fifteenth century, when players pushed the 'auxiliary noise' techniques clearly implied by sixteenth century sources[16] in the direction of plurilinear playing. Eventually the pressure became so great that the old technique burst, and the plectrum gave way to the fingers. It happened to the harp during the fourteenth century (and possibly earlier). We have striking twelfth and thirteenth century evidence for the currency of textured harp-playing,[17] and plurilinear harping can be traced to the

[14]Ibid. For the identification of the annotator, see 78-9.

[15]Bachmann, *Origins,* 102f gives an account of the technique which is not, in my view, correct. The matter must await a separate study.

[16]As for example in the drone tuning prescribed by Hans Newsidler for *Der Judentanz* in his collection *Ein newgeordnetkunstlich Lautenbuch* (Nuremberg, 1536). See Michael Morrow, 'Ayre on the F♯ string', *Lute Society Journal,* ii (1960), 9-12.

[17]Particularly in the descriptions of the performance of Breton lays. For the central documents see Constance Bullock-Davies, 'The Form of the Breton Lay', *Medium Aevum,* xlii (1973), 18-31.

age of Machaut, when the models, as far as we can tell, were vocal ones.[18] We are describing the dawn of intabulation.

Why was the psaltery mechanised? A significant part of the answer to this question surely lies in the movement from polyphony to plurilinear playing which I have offered as a model of literate string playing in medieval Europe. That the psaltery had become a rationalised polyphonic — or at the very least chordal — instrument by the Renaissance is implied by the testimony of men such as Merlin and Cellier, Mersenne and Kircher, all of whom take an interest in the instrument and mention the performance of chordal or polyphonic music upon it.[19] Mersenne's evidence goes further, for in his diagram of a psaltery with its lowest string a fourth below the next we may perhaps find an echo of medieval technique. Pictorial sources frequently show players with a finger or two spread over the lowest course of their instruments, perhaps sounding a drone while the other hand performs the melody.[20] Mersenne's reference to coursing in fifths 'to augment the harmony' may also be a relic of medieval practice.[21]

By the early fifteenth century it seems that some psaltery players were intabulating the parts of polyphonic chansons. In his poem *Pratique du Psalterium Mystique* the French theologian Jean de Gerson

[18]See below, p.8. It is worth pointing out that the composer Richard de Loqueville was a harpist, and so too, perhaps, was the composer Baude Cordier (see Craig Wright, *Music at the Court of Burgundy 1364-1419: a Documentary History* (Institute of Medieval Music, Musicological Studies, xxviii, 1979), 132. Both of these musicians were active c.1400. There can be little doubt that players such as these executed plurlinear music.

[19]François Merlin and Jacques Cellier, *Recherche de plusieurs singularités* (Paris, Bibliothèque Nationale, MS français 9152, folio 171[R]); Mersenne's material on the psaltery (*Harmonie Universelle: Tracté des Instrumens*, Livre Troisiesme, Proposition XXVI) is translated in R. E. Chapman, *Harmonie Universelle: The Books on Instruments* (The Hague, 1957), 224-6. In the Latin version (*Harmonicorum Libri*, 1636, 71f), Mersenne adds little. For Athanasius Kircher's material see *Musurgia Universalis* (Rome, 1650), 495. On p.496 Kircher gives a fragment of music for the psaltery in tablature, but it is of a very rudimentary character.

[20]There are several examples in the famous *Cantigas* miniatures (Madrid, Biblioteca de el Escorial, MS j-b-2, ?Seville, c.1280-3), folios 89, 96v and 260. Drawings of two of these appear in Hortense Panum, *The Stringed Instruments of the Middle Ages* (London, 1940), figures 121 and 123. Compare also figures 119 and 133.

[21]Chapman, op cit, 224. The point is made by Bachmann, *Die Verbreitung*, 26.

(d. 1429) describes how a solitary heart *(ung cuer seulet)* is visited by Comfort, who says:[22]

Sces tu que veult Dieu que ie face?	Do you know what God wishes me to do?
A toy m'envoye de sa grace.	In his grace he sends me to you.
Quoi, dist le cuer qui s'esiouy	"What?", says the heart, rejoicing
Quant la voix de confort ouy,	when it hears the voice of Comfort,
Sa face lieve et son oreille.	looking up and paying attention.
Confort tantost si s'apareille	Comfort at once prepares himself
A monstrer ung psalterium	to show a psaltery,
Aultrement dit canticordum.	otherwise called *canticordum.*
Prens le, dit il, et bien le note	"Take it", he says, "and play well
A teneur et contreteneur	with tenor and contratenor
. . .	. . .

The *psalterium* of course, is both psaltery and book of psalms; Comfort is advising the solitary heart to turn to the classic medieval book for private devotion. Yet the musical level of the allegory stands intact, and Gerson seems to be referring to the performance of tenor and contratenor parts.

The *Pratique du Psalterium Mystique* was probably written c. 1424-6, and we have evidence from exactly this period which suggests that two (or more) parts of polyphonic chansons were intabulated for the harp, an instrument then very close to the psaltery in character. A tapestry, possibly from the 1420's, now in the *Musée des Arts Decoratifs* at Paris, shows a female harpist reading from a music rotulus upon which is written *De ce que fol pense.*[23] The music is stylised into a ran-

---

[22]Mgr Glorieux, ed., *Jean Gerson: Oeuvres complètes* (Tournai, 1960-73), 7, 421.
[23]Reproduced in Nigel Wilkins, *Music in the Age of Chaucer* (Cambridge, 1979), 30. For a discussion of this picture (with a reproduction) see Howard M. Brown, 'Instruments and Voices in the Fifteenth-Century Chanson', in J. W. Grubbs, ed., *Current Thought in Musicology* (University of Texas Press, 1976), 100, and plate 6.

dom array of marks, but the text indicates that the piece in question may be the chanson with this incipit by Pierre de Molins. The player of a diatonic harp or psaltery would have no difficulty in rendering the superius and tenor (example a) or the tenor and contratenor (example b) of this piece:

Pierre de Molins *De ce que foul pensé* [Ballade] After Willi Apel, ed, *French Secular Compositions of the Fourteenth Century,* Corpus Mensurabilis Musicae, 53, (American Institute of Musicology, 1970), 1, p.159 (triplum omitted).

De ce que fol pense is markedly diatonic in character, yet other chansons of the period introduce chromatic inflections in a way that would have demanded an adjustment of psaltery technique, and there is evidence that such adjustments were made. The music library of the University of California, Berkeley, houses a fourteenth century manuscript containing a treatise on instruments, which, as I have argued elsewhere, is probably by the composer Jean Vaillant (d. 1361).[24] Here were find a diagram of a psaltery with five quadru-

[24]See Page, 'Fourteenth-century Instruments and Tunings: a treatise by Jean Vaillant? (Berkeley, MS 744)', *Galpin Society Journal,* xxxiii (1980), 17f. The name IOHHAN VAIANT is produced by a head-letter and internal acrostic located in the introduction to the Latin text. Such *internal* acrostics are found elsewhere in late-medieval poetry. For an example from a French poem by Charles D'Orleans, see Ethel Seaton, *Studies in Villon, Vaillant and Charles D'Orleans* (Oxford, 1957), p.v. (The Vaillant of this study is not our author.)

ple courses, each course comprising two pairs a tone or a semitone apart (aabb ccdd eeff ggaa ♮♮cc). Between the courses there are sharps and flats which appear at the end of lines drawn half way across the soundboard.[25] The sequence of pitches they create, together with the course pitches, is as follows:

$$a \; b \; [\; \sharp \;] \; c \; d \; [\; \flat \;] \; e \; f \; [\; \sharp \;] \; g \; a \; [\; \flat \;] \; \natural \; c \; [\; \sharp \;]$$

These sharps and flats perhaps indicate variants in the tuning; if we regard the basic series as a C major octave with two notes below, then we can see how they would be useful. The b♮ (in both octaves) provides a sharpened leading note, and the e♭ the minor third. F♯ is the most common chromatic inflection in the music of the fourteenth century. By tuning each string in a pair to different notes, the player of such a psaltery could push his instrument to almost complete chromaticism.

The notion that players of these instruments intabulated tenor and contratenor parts may seem hard to reconcile with the small size of many psalteries as revealed in some (but by no means all) pictorial sources. Since these two parts do not form an adequate solo texture we might be tempted to assume that psaltery players accompanied singers who performed cantus lines, but who were forced to an anomalously high pitch by the range of the instrument. Such reasoning must rest upon assumptions about late-medieval pitch that may or may not be justified, but psaltery players do seem to have aimed at a lower pitch than we might assume on the basis of much iconographical evidence. Psalteries appear to have been strung with wire, at least from the thirteenth century onwards. In his treatise *De Proprietatibus Rerum* (completed, or a revised version edited, c. 1250), the English scholar Bartholomaeus records that the strings for the *psalterium* are best made of copper and silver *(de aurichalco et etiam de argento)*[26], while Jean de Gerson mentions strings for the *psalterium* of

---

[25]The diagram is reproduced in Page, *op cit*, plate V.

[26]For the text, see Hermann Müller, 'Der Musiktraktat in dem Werke des Bartholomaeus Anglicus De Proprietatibus Rerum', *Riemann-Festschrift*, (Leipzig, 1909), 241-55.

silver or bronze *(argenteas vel ex electro)*[27] in his *Tractatus de Canticis* (1424-26). Returning to the matter in his *Collectorium Super Magnificat* (1427-8) he refers to gold and copper *(auro vel auricalco)*[28]. That these *psalteria* are what we are calling psalteries is confirmed not only by the numerous European sources of the period in which *psalteria* are both named and drawn, but also, in the case of Gerson, by internal evidence.[29] It is significant in this connection that the earliest information about the string materials of keyboard instruments shows that metal was used — a tradition of stringing that was doubtless taken over directly from earlier psalteries; no other instruments (save the Irish harp) can be associated with metal stringing before the late fifteenth century.[30]

Whatever the reasons for the use of metal strings on psalteries, precious metals or alloys containing them would have produced strings achieving a lower pitch at a given length and tension than could be achieved with gut or metals of a lower density, such as iron. It is also noteworthy that Gerson recommends a light touch upon the psaltery *(leviusque tangendas)*[31]; perhaps the strings were customarily kept at low tension to permit deeper pitches?

Our evidence suggests that during the fourteenth century some psaltery players carried the technique of their instrument in the direction of plurilinear playing, responding to a drive in Western string technique deeply involved with the development of a written musical

---

[27]Glorieux, op cit, 9, 532. For a corrected text with translation and commentary see Page, 'Early Fifteenth-century instruments in Jean de Gerson's *Tractatus de Canticis*', *Early Music*, vi (1978), 339-349 [Editor's Note: It is possible that in the context electrum refers to an alloy of gold and silver.]

[28]Glorieux, op cit, 8, 521.

[29]For a list of some of the labelled drawings, (with two examples) see Page, "Early Fifteenth-Century Instruments', 340 and plates 2 and 4. For reproductions of two more see Laurence Wright, 'The Medieval Gittern and Citole: A case of Mistaken identity', *Galpin Society Journal*, xxx (1977), Plates 1 and 2. In all of these sources the *psalterium* is shown as a 'pig-snout' psaltery. For Gerson's internal evidence, see Page, op cit, 347.

[30]The earliest evidence for the string-materials of keyboard instruments appears to be that given by Paulus Paulirinus of Prague in his *Liber Viginti Artium* (c.1460), now in the Library of the Jagiellonian University at Cracow (MS 257). See Standley Howell, "Paulus Paulirinus of Prague on Musical Instruments", *Journal of the American Musical Instrument Society*, v-vi (1979-80), 9-36.

[31]Glorieux, op cit, 9, 532; Page, "Early Fifteenth-century Instruments', 346-7.

tradition and habits of mind nurtured by it. With a quill in each hand, players intabulated the tenor and contratenor parts of chansons and, no doubt, the superius and tenor parts. Variant tunings were introduced to permit more chromatic inflections, for the Renaissance ideal of fidelity to the texture of vocal originals was already fostered.

The harpsichord was surely invented to drive the technique of the quill-plucked string even further in these three directions: greater polyphonic potential, increased downward compass, and fuller chromaticism.[32] There are good reasons why a cross-fertilization between the psaltery and the organ should have occurred in the fourteenth century. The English Robertsbridge Codex shows that an advanced art of keyboard intabulation, based upon full chromaticism, existed at this time,[33] but there can have been little opportunity for *domestic* performance of such repertory. Organists could not use a portative for this music; they were restricted to positive organs lodged in places where they were needed for liturgical celebration. What was required was a portable instrument to which organists could transfer their keyboard technique. If this instrument could dispense with bellows (which required a second person) so much the better. Psalteries of an ideal type were already in existence (plate 1).

This brings us up to the earliest known stringed keyboard instrument, the chekker, first mentioned in the accounts of John the Good for 1360, then a prisoner in England. The location may be significant for there is evidence that a special variety of chekker existed, called the 'English chekker'.[34] We do have some idea of how professional stringed-instrument making evolved in England as a specialised craft,[35] and a very early maker, John de Toppclyf (1366) is one of several artificers whose trade makes a precocious appearance in York after the Black Death. (Other craftsmen include those prac-

---

[32]There is no evidence that any of the *very earliest* stringed keyboard instruments were fully chromatic as far as I am aware.

[33]The music is printed in Willi Apel, ed., *Keyboard Music of the Fourteenth and Fifteenth Centuries* (American Institute of Musicology, *Corpus of Early Keyboard Music*, i, 1963), 1-9.

[34]Ripin, op cit, Appendix 2, presents the evidence.

[35]See Page, 'String-Instrument Making in Medieval England and Some Oxford Harpmakers 1380-1466', *Galpin Society Journal*, xxi (1978), 44-67.

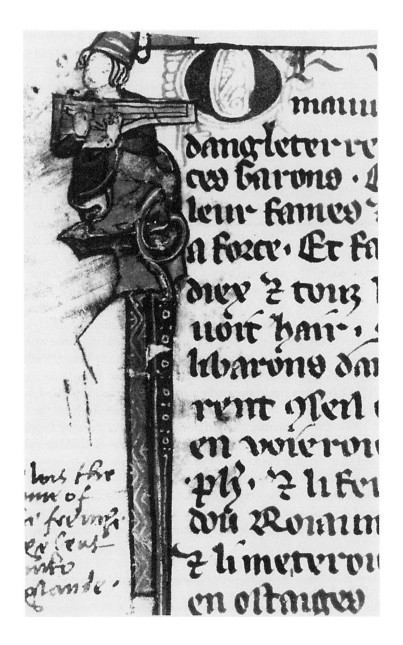

Plate 1. Oxford, Bodleian Library, MS Rawlinson B. 170 (French, beginning of 14c), folio 5ᵛ. Fragments of a chronicle from c1214-60, and fragments from the *Grandes Chroniques de France* from Philip Augustus to 1212.

tising the artistic trades of clock and color making).[36] The earliest known London maker was active in the final decades of the four-teenth century, and a long line of makers begins at Oxford in 1360.[37] Perhaps the remarkable impetus given to professional stringed-instrument making in fourteenth-century England fostered experi-ment with keyboard instruments, including a proto-harpsichord?

ACKNOWLEDGEMENTS

My thanks are due to David Fallows, Jeremy Montagu, John Caldwell, Lewis Jones and Andrew Wathey who read the first ver-sion of this paper and made many helpful suggestions.

[36]Ibid, p.59.

[37]The earliest London maker known to me (antedating those listed in the above study) is recorded in 1390-1 (Staffordshire Record Office, D 641/1/2/4, m.4, Ac-count of Nicholas Bradshawe, receiver general of Thomas, Earl of Stafford). I am most grateful to Miss Elizabeth Gue of Somerville College, Oxford, for this refer-ence. For the Oxford makers, see, in addition to the above, *Galpin Society Journal*, xxi, (1979), 135.

Music and Chivalric Fiction in France, 1150–1300

When the meal drew to a close the lady who had served the wine produced a harp and began to play it so sweetly that it was a wondrous thing to hear. So Sir Gawayn listened to her very willingly for a while until he began to feel the cold, for his tunic was not at all well dried. And when the cold got to him he rose up and went to the great fire which was in the middle of the Hall and took a stool and sat down before the fire, turning his shoulder and his back [to the flames] and warmed himself until he slept, as one who had been afflicted the whole day with the rain and the wind.[1]

I TAKE this artless description of harping in a Great Hall to be a depiction of life in the castles of thirteenth-century France and as lifelike as the wicked draught which tortures Sir Gawayn. Like many similar passages in Old French fiction, it seems to transport us directly into a realm of domestic and amateur music-making which, at this date, can barely be glimpsed upon the horizon of other sources such as manuscript paintings and archives.[2]

A lady plays a harp and her music is 'a wondrous thing to hear'. This balance of objective detail and subjective assessment accounts for the special interest of many references to music in Old French fiction; there are no other sources from the twelfth and thirteenth centuries which

---

1 H.O. Sommer, ed., *The Vulgate Version of the Arthurian Romances*, 8 vols. (Washington, 1909–16), 7, Supplement, *Le Livre d'Artus* (Washington, 1913), pp. 173–4. I retain Sommer's orthography:

   Qvant uint en la fin du mengier si traist la damoisele cele qui auoit serui du uin une harpe et comenca a harper tant do[l]cement que ce estoit merueilles a oir et a escouter . si lescouta messires Gauuain une piece molt uolentiers tant que il comenca a refroidier que sa robe nestoit mie bien essuiee . et quant il senti la froidure si se leua et uint au feu que granz estoit en mi la sale et prent il meismes un quarrel et sa[s]iet desus deuant le feu et li torne lespaule et le dos et se chaufe tant quil si endort come cil qui toz estoit debatuz tot le ior entier de pluie et de uent. Compare the episode in E. Stengel, ed., *Li Romans de Durmart le Galois* (Tübingen, 1873), lines 3217ff.

2 On thirteenth-century French pictorial sources see G. Foster, *The iconology of musical instruments and musical performance in thirteenth-century French manuscript illuminations* (diss. City University of New York, 1977). Foster concludes, quite rightly in my view, that pictorial material of this date has considerable limitations as a source of information about musical life and performance practice. As for archival sources, relevant documents are not plentiful from the thirteenth-century (and are extremely scarse for the twelfth). Furthermore there are very few documentary sources from any period of the Middle Ages which shed light upon the musical activities of courtly amateurs. Most financial records, for example, bear upon secular music only insofar as they record various kinds of transactions involving the services of minstrels. For some thirteenth-century examples, see A. Henry, ed., *Les Ouvres d'Ardenet le Roi*, 1 (Bruges, 1951), *passim*, but especially p. 65ff.

Reprinted from *Proceedings of the Royal Music Association* 111 (1984–85), pp. 1–27.
By permission of Oxford University Press.

engage so often and so candidly with the aesthetic pleasure given by music. Nor, perhaps, is there anywhere else to go for a sense of that most elusive quality of life in the past: atmosphere. The lady who plays the harp has previously served wine and now she offers after-dinner music to the guests in the Hall. These narrative details define the ambience of the musical scene: the entertainment is being offered in a casual but courteous spirit. Like the wine, it is a garnish to the meal which the guests are free to accept or to decline according to their pleasure.

The real focus of the passage is not the lady but Sir Gawayn. Even so, every movement which this famous knight makes defines the atmosphere of the musical event a little further:

> So Sir Gawayn listened to her very willingly . . . and when the cold got to him he rose up and went to the great fire which was in the middle of the hall . . . turning his shoulder and his back [to the flames] and warmed himself until he slept.

This is a glimpse of the reality beneath the metal plates of chivalry. Without his armour, and exhausted after a long journey, one of the greatest knights of Christendom is as vulnerable as a tortoise without a shell. Gawayn rises to warm his tired body by the fire but there is no suggestion that this inattentiveness to a lady's harping will damage his reputation as one of Camelot's most amorous knights. This is presumably because the performance (if that is the right word) takes place in a Great Hall, a place whose characteristic ambience can be recovered from a wealth of literary references to its appearance and function. A Great Hall was usually a wide, open space where a large fire sent smoke into the rafters; it was the usual setting for festive minstrel-music[3] and a thoroughfare which echoed to the clatter of trestle-tables being set up for meals. The 'feel' of life in the Great Hall was therefore quite unlike that of inner rooms and chambers – places where more scrupulous behaviour might have been expected of Sir Gawayn. Thus it seems that the lady harpist in our extract is one who, by virtue of her sex and tender age, may be asked to leave her chamber and play in this public and minstrellish space.[4]

'The past is another country', wrote L.P. Hartley; 'they do things differently there'. The passage we have just examined suggests that

---

3 For examples see the texts gathered in E. Faral, *Les jongleurs en France au moyen age*, 2nd edition (Paris, 1971), Appendix 3, items 60, 63, 68, 113, *et passim*, and E. Bowles, 'Musical Instruments at the Medieval Banquet', *Revue Belge de Musicologie*, 12 (1958), pp. 41–51.

4 There are many indications in medieval literature that musical accomplishments were regarded as particularly appropriate to young girls (much as they were in nineteenth-century England). The evidence of didactic literature addressed to women is particularly revealing here. See A. Hentsch, *De la littérature didactique du moyen age s'addressant spécialement aux femmes* (Cahors, 1903), pp. 89 and 107, and J. Ulrich, ed., *Robert von Blois sämmtliche Werke*. 3 vols., (Berlin, 1889–95), 3, p. 70, lines 453–68.

chivalric fiction may sometimes enhance our awareness of how musical things were done in the medieval past. Yet it is *fiction*; surely medieval storytellers were free to wield the power of Merlin's sorcery and to distort life as they pleased? How may the more reliable references to music in their tales be distinguished from their less reliable ones?

One thing can be conceded at once: it is impossible to prove anything about musical life in the Middle Ages on the basis of chivalric fiction alone. Our description of a lady's harping in a Great Hall is believable in the simple sense that it does not strain our credibility, but we would surely be on firmer ground with an archival record of some kind or perhaps a passing reference in a sober historical chronicle? I am sure that we would, but I am also convinced that nothing like the harping-scene of the *Livre d'Artus* is to be found in the known archives and chronicles of the twelfth and thirteenth centuries. This observation can be widened into a claim that (as far as musical life is concerned) the testimony of chivalric fiction is mostly unsupported with regard to exactly the details likely to interest us most.

Yet what gradually happens during a reading of these tales is that passages emerge whose veracity there seems no good reason to doubt:[5]

> Quant il orent mangié a grant plente tant comme il leur plot, li rois escoute et ot en une chambre qui estoit encoste de lui touz les diuers estrumenz dont il eüst onques oî parler en sa vie; si sonoient tout ensamble li vn avec les autres si tres doucement qu'il n'avoit onques oîe melodie que tant li fust douce ne plesanz a oîr.

> When they had eaten their fill as much as they wished, the king [Arthur] listened to and heard in an adjacent chamber all the various instruments that he had ever heard speak of in his life; they played all together, each one with the others, so very sweetly that he had never encountered music which seems to him so sweet or pleasant to hear.

This passage has obviously been gilded with hyperbole to give it a heraldic brilliance. Arthur listens to 'all the various instruments that he had ever heard speak of in his entire life' and he 'had never encountered music so sweet or pleasant to hear'. Yet hyperbole is not a particularly

---

5 J. Frappier, ed., *La Mort le Roi Artu* (Geneva and Paris, 1936), pp. 16 7. This is an exceptional reference; it seems that musicians have been gathered together to provide concerted instrumental music, for listening, in a chamber specially set aside for the purpose. I do not know of any directly comparable reference in Old French fiction. It may be that the anonymous author of *La Mort le Roi Artu* is recording some thirteenth-century antecedent of a practice recorded in association with King Charles V of France by both Froissart and Christine de Pisan. Froissart describes an occasion when after-dinner music is provided for Gaston Phébus and Charles by players of *bas* instruments in the *chambre de parement* of the castle of Toulouse; Christine de Pisan recounts a very similar event at Paris in 1377 (once again the music is played by *bas* instruments, this time in the *chambre de parlement*). See Kervyn de Lettenhove, ed., *Oeuvres de Froissart*, 25 vols. (Brussels, 1870–7), 14, p. 75, and S. Solente, ed., *Le livre des fais et bonnes meurs du sage Roy Charles V*, 2 vols. (Paris, 1936 and 1940), 2, pp. 108–109.

4

sophisticated literary strategy. Old French narrators often apply it like
paint and it is easy to strip away. In this passage a simple grain of sober
and almost domestic description lies beneath the gilt. In the events
leading up to this musical scene Arthur arrives at Morgan's castle and is
received in the Great Hall (the usual place for a ceremonial reception).
Next, he is led into a private chamber to take his meal (again, an accepted
custom in the thirteenth and fourteenth centuries).[6] These details evoke a
narrator attentive to patterns of use within a castle complex and suggest
that the 'concert' arranged for Arthur in a nearby chamber is another
example of his scrupulosity. It is also striking that the music is not
performed *before* Arthur but is played in an adjacent room – a detail which
the author is perhaps unlikely to have invented. It is tempting to regard
this passage as a record of contemporary practice.[7]

6   For a superb account of this custom, this time in the most sophisticated of all Middle
    English Arthurian romances, see J.R.R. Tolkien and E.V. Gordon, eds., *Sir Gawayn and the
    Green Knight*, second edition, ed. N. Davis (Oxford, 1967), line 853ff.
7   The question of whether medieval romances do, or do not, incorporate verisimilar
    references to social customs and practices reduces to a matter of faith: when reading
    these texts one either chooses to believe in the realism of details which seem credible
    and consonant with external evidence, or one does not choose to believe in them. It
    would be possible to present very sophisticated arguments in favour of atheism in this
    regard, for modern developments in literary theory have opened the study of literature to
    profound philosophical issues that turn upon how words mean, whether they mean what
    we take them to mean when we use them, and whether they mean anything; immersion
    in such questions will not fill us with confidence that medieval literature can reveal
    much about contemporary reality. Yet neither will it reassure us that we know, or can
    reasonably say, anything about the external world of objects and actions. On moral and
    humanitarian grounds I dissent from the sceptical view that imaginative literature in
    general, and medieval romance in particular, cannot reveal objective truths about the
    past; such scepticism ultimately deposes the notion of objective truth and leaves no
    basis for rational enquiry.
       A more traditional ground for atheism would be to argue, in the best positivist
    tradition, that medieval romances, being 'literature', must be sharply distinguished from
    the objective records of fact (especially archives) which are the proper materials of the
    historian. This argument can be met in two ways.
       Firstly, any historian who wishes to adopt this rigorously positivist line will need to
    base his historical credo almost entirely upon archival sources, yet 'literary' works
    (especially chronicles and saints' Lives) have long been exploited by historians. Indeed,
    a distinction between 'factual' writing and 'fictional' writing is hard to maintain in the
    contexts of the thirteenth century when the biography of a historical figure such as
    William Marshall could be written in verse and dressed out with many of the
    conventions of chivalric romance, and when a prose chronicle, such as Villehardouin's
    La Conquete de Constantinople, is strewn with verbal tags and hyperboles drawn from
    vernacular epics such as *The Song of Roland*.
       Secondly, it is simplistic to draw a firm distinction between *history* and *story*. The
    modern historian does not write in a scientifically objective language which is devoid of
    rhetorical colouring and transparent to its object, for such writing is not possible to
    achieve. This is not to deny that historians may make objective statements about the
    external world; it is merely to urge that a firm distinction between the language of
    historical fact and the language of literary fiction is not possible and there is therefore no

So far I have suggested that chivalric fiction embodies details of musical life which may be reasonably assumed to be realistic. That is a simple claim, of course, and in the contexts of both literary studies and musicology it is nothing new.[8] Now I wish to go further and to maintain that these tales can supply us with complexes of detail and judgment which help to frame a history of music in medieval France.

Let us glance first at the things which such a history will *not* contain. It will not have much to say about polyphony; organum, motet and conductus rarely appear in the world of Gawayn or Galahad.[9] Nor will it reveal much about specific troubadours and trouvères and the reception of their works.[10] On the other hand a history of music based on chivalric fiction would be directly concerned with performance practice in the most comprehensive sense (who performed for whom, where, to what effect, and so on); it would also be closely involved with the activities of courtly amateurs (whose doings can barely be documented from any other kind of source) and with the life and work of minstrels. On a deeper level chivalric fiction helps to interpret the ideals of the aristocratic class from which many troubadours and trouvères sprang (and to which most courtly monody, of whatever origin, ostensibly refers for its moral and aesthetic values). Indeed these narratives may be our only guide to the place where

cause for the historian to disdain imaginative literature *per se* on the grounds that it may sully the nature of his discourse. See, for example, H. White, *Metahistory: The Historical Imagination in Nineteenth Century Europe* (1974) and S. Bann, *The Clothing of Clio : A Study of the Representation of History in Nineteenth Century Britain and France* (Cambridge, 1984).

8 Old French fiction has been mined for its information about medieval music since at least the late sixteenth century. See, for example, C. Fauchet. *Recueil de l'Origine de la langue et poesie francoise, ryme et romans* (Paris, 1581), pp. 72–3. Modern works which exploit medieval literature in this way are too numerous to mention.

9 Of the tiny handful of references to polyphony in Old French literature the most striking is to be found in Wace's *Brut* of 1155, in a passage describing the festivities at Arthur's coronation. See I. Arnold, ed., *Le Roman de Brut de Wace*. 2 vols., Société des Anciens Textes Français (Paris, 1938 and 1940), 2, lines 10421–4. However, Wace is following his source closely at this point, Geoffrey of Monmouth's *Historia Regum Britannie*, completed at Oxford c. 1136. See A. Griscom and R.E. Jones., eds., *The Historia Regum Britanniae of Geoffrey of Monmouth* (London etc.), 1929), p. 456. For other passages which probably refer to polyphony see L. Wright, '*Chanter a gresillon(s)* and *chanter es gresillons*', *Medium Aevum*, 35 (1966), pp. 231–5, and Y. Rokseth, *Polyphonies du XIIIe Siècle*, 4 vols., (Paris, 1935, 1936 and 1939), 4, pp. 65–7, 84, 219–220. There is a terminological problem with some of the texts cited by Rokseth, however. It is far from certain, for example, whether Old French *motet* customarily refers to a polyphonic genre when used in the non-specialist contexts of vernacular poetry and prose.

10 The most famous references to trouvères (complete with citations of songs) in Old French fiction are in Jean Renart's romance of *Guillaume de Dole* (ed F. Lecoy, Classiques Français du Moyen Age (Paris, 1962), lines 844ff, 1451ff, 3620ff, 4120ff and 5228ff). See also P.B. Fay and J.L. Grigsby, eds., *Joufroi de Poitiers* (Geneva, 1972), lines 3601–3692 (the troubadour Marcabrun), and J.E. Matzke and M. Delbouille, eds., *Le Roman du Castelain de Couci et de la Dame de Fayel par Jakemes*, Société des Anciens Textes Français (Paris, 1936), *passim*.

6

music lay in the minds of secular magnates – men who knew more of the stable, the fencing-yard and the tournament field than they knew of masses, motets and modal rhythms. It is this last, deeper level of reference that I wish to pursue in the first half of this paper by focusing upon chivalric ideology and the rise of the troubadours and trouvères.

1 EPIC AND ROMANCE

To open the earliest and most famous of the French epics, *The Song of Roland* (c. 1080), is to be transported into a world where companies of knights do combat for a communal and aggressively Christian purpose: Charlemagne's crusade against the Saracens in Spain. Roland has his being in the army of Charlemagne; he does nothing alone, and there is little sense in the poem that his (or anybody's) life is a journey of private conflict and conscience.

When we leave Roland at Roncesvals and turn to Arthur at Camelot the world has changed. The epic community of knights, bound together by a common struggle, has vanished; the age of Abelard, and of the new luxurious castles with their individually heated chambers, required a new kind of knight. In contrast to Roland who rides with the army of Charlemagne, the romance knight travels alone in search of some testing adventure or some material advancement in the world. Leaving the court, he journeys along forest paths and tracks where he is tried by mortal and faery enemies. In this scheme of things the court is a secure place where the knight's values are shared and endorsed; it is the point from which he departs to be tested and to which he usually returns when the test has brought him either success or failure.[11] The walls of the court are therefore built against the challenge of the outside world; they enclose a luxurious hostelry whose significance is sustained by a realistic and hyperbolical portrayal of its luxuries, including music. This is why there is much more musical activity in romance than in epic and why the romancers are generally committed to presentations of musical life which may be idealized or gilded with hyperbole but which are generally plausible and charged with the significance of music in courtly civilization.

A glance at the world of Arthur, Gawayn or Galahad is enough to show that chivalric fiction mirrors the key place of music in the social and intellectual revolution which accompanied the second feudal age (roughly

---

11 The Middle English *Sir Gawayn and the Green Knight* (see note 6) is a Romance plot of classic design. Sir Gawayn must leave Arthur's court and journey through wild country to have his valour and constancy tested in the wilderness at the Green Chapel; he then returns to Camelot where the community of knights is strengthened by his success in the test. In the text this scheme is playfully varied (the real test is over by the time Gawayn reaches the Green Chapel; what he receives there is only his 'result'); yet the outlines of the archetypal Romance plot are clear and lucid throughout the tale.

1050–1300). From our distance it seems that the greatest achievement of these centuries in the West was to widen the range of human experience judged to be consequential. In Romance it is not merely the heroes' deportment in council or combat that matters, although that was virtually all that mattered in the world of Roland; the Romance knight lives in a place where adventures are often solitary and where a measure of freedom from sudden summons to war has enlarged the scope of intimate and private life; he reflects the new stability and security of Western Christendom which found itself largely free of external enemies by the end of the eleventh century. A Gawayn or a Galahad must know how to talk with ladies in a chamber or at a castle window-seat; he must converse elegantly and play the harp if asked.

Within secular aristocratic society the fountainhead of these changes lay with an idea without parallel in the history of warriorhood: that the male's ardour for honour and his ardour for erotic experience are conjunct and almost indistinguishable impulses.[12] Music, always the food of love, was intimately involved with this new sexuality.

The earliest verse-romance of the Middle Ages reveals the link between self-awareness, music and love in a most revealing way. The south-German *Ruodlieb* of c. 1050 recounts the career of a young noble warrior (*miles*) who is forced to leave his homeland. At one point in the narrative Ruodlieb stays at a castle where a young girl lives with her mother; he is entertained with music there but he is far from satisfied with the playing of the castle harpers:[13]

> Meanwhile Ruodlieb and his nephew go with the mistress to where the harpers are playing. When Ruodlieb heard how badly he played the melody (though that harpist was the best pupil of the art among them) he said to the mistress: 'If there had been another harp here. . .'. 'There is', she said, 'a harp here and there is no better; my lord played upon it whilst he lived. Through its music my thoughts languished in love. No one has touched it since he died'.
>
> . . . [two lines of text missing here] . . .
>
> Plucking now with two fingers of the left hand, and now with the right, he renders very

---

12   This is the most distinctive contribution of medieval chivalry to the ethic of warriorhood and the bibliography devoted to it, both by historians of literature and historians of chivalry, is enormous. For a guide through the maze of theories which have been offered to explain it see R. Boase, *The Origin and Meaning of Courtly Love* (Manchester, 1977). Among the works which have been devoted to the subject since the appearance of Boase's book one of the most impressive is R.H. Bloch, *Medieval French Literature and Law* (University of California Press, 1977).

13   For the original see E.H. Zeydel, ed., *Ruodlieb* (Chapel Hill, 1959), p. 110. The translation is mine, though I have drawn extensively on the facing-page version offered by Zeydel. On the *Ruodlieb* as the first surviving example of a medieval verse-romance see P. Dronke, 'Ruodlieb : The Emergence of Romance', in *Poetic Individuality in the Middle Ages : New Departures in Poetry 1000–1150* (Oxford, 1970), pp. 24–6 and 33–65.

8

sweet melodies as he touches the strings, producing many variations with great distinctness. He who was entirely unversed in moving his feet in a dance or in beating time with his hands learned both of those things quickly. The harpists, who formerly had boldly struck the strings in minstrel fashion, listened silently and did not dare play.

Once Ruodlieb has played three melodies the mistress of the castle asks him to play so that her daughter may dance with Ruodlieb's nephew:[14]

He carries this out, performing refrains now pausing one note away from the final, now pausing upon the final, in an admirable and decorous way.

A noble string-player who performs so well that he eclipses professionals, with everything which that implies about the strength of the hero's commitment to polite, social skills: this is a new figure in medieval literature. It is not only Ruodlieb's warriorhood which is consequential in this poem but also the courtliness of his behaviour; epic heroes do not often deal in the delicacy of sentiment which prompts Ruodlieb to ask for a harp with a scrupulously unassuming subjunctive: 'If there had been another harp here . . .' (*Ibi si plus harpa fuisset*);[15] the poet knows that his hero can put the professionals to shame, but he also believes (and here he anticipates Castiglione by five centuries) that the courtier should maintain a nonchalent modesty at all times.

Rudlieb plays for a small company in which there are ladies. There is nothing amorous in his own conduct but a close association between string-playing and passion runs through this musical episode. The *harpa* which Ruodlieb plays is no minstrel's instrument; it was once the private possession of a castellan and it is powerfully associated with the sexual longing of his widow. Her thoughts 'languished in love' every time her lord played upon it and the instrument continues to cast its spell; once

---

14 Zeydel, op. cit., p. 110: *Quem per sistema siue diastema dando responsa/Dum mirabiliter operaretur ue decenter.* It is particularly striking that the author seems to be describing the performance of something closely akin to the later-medieval *estampie*: (1) Ruodlieb's music is danced to, (2) it has a reprise or refrain of some kind (*responsa*) and (3) it appears to have open and closed endings. With respect to this last detail, which is perhaps the most interesting of all, my translation of the words *sistema siue diastema* ('now pausing on a note away from the final, now pausing upon the final . . .') is based upon the definitions of these terms given in the *De Musica* of John 'of Afflighem': 'diastema . . . occurs when the chant makes a suitable pause, not on the final, but elsewhere . . . systema . . . [occurs] whenever a suitable pause in the melody comes on the final . . .'. I borrow the translation from W. Babb and C.V. Palisca, *Hucbald, Guido and John on Music* (Yale University Press, 1978), p. 117; for the original, see J. Smits van Waesberghe, ed., *Johannis Affligemensis De Musica cum Tonario*, American Institute of Musicology, Corpus Scriptorum de Musica, 1 (Rome 1950), p. 80. If, as seems likely, John wrote in southern Germany around 1100, then he is well placed to be our intepreter of musical terminology in the south-German *Ruodlieb* which may have been composed during his lifetime.

15 I owe this point to Dronke, '*Ruodlieb*', p. 54.

Ruodlieb's nephew and the lady's daughter have danced to the hero's playing they are 'strongly aglow' for one another.[16]

2   NARCISSISM

By following through the conceptions of male talent to be found in chivalric fiction it is possible to establish a social context for the art of the troubadours and trouvères. Two central themes emerge: narcissism and eloquence.

We have already glimpsed the revolution in warrior-ethics whereby the warrior's ardour for honour merged with his erotic ardour. As I interpret it, the cause of this revolution was the emergence in the aristocratic societies of the eleventh and twelfth centuries of male sexual narcissism. An epic knight may have a magnificent physique, but he is always seen through the eyes of his admiring male peers in the banqueting hall, in the council chamber or on the battlefield. Women barely figure in these places and therefore the epic hero's magnificence is without any sexual nuance. Here, for example, is Ganelon before the war-council of Charlemagne in *The Song of Roland*:[17]

> De sun col getet ses grandes pels de martre
> E est remes en sun blialt de palie;
> Vairs out [les oilx] e mult fier lu visage.
> Gent out le cors e les costez out larges
> Tant par fut bels tuit si per l'en esguardent.
>
> He has thrown back his great marten-fur from his neck and is left standing in his under-tunic of silk; his eyes are flashing and his face is haughty. His body is fair and his sides are broad. He was so fine that all his peers watch him.

'He was so fine that all his peers watch him'; this is a man seen by men. What a difference, then, if we move forward a century to encounter one of the earliest French romances, the *Roman de Horn* of c. 1170. Here is a man whose beauty is seen through the eyes of a woman who desires him to distraction:[18]

> [Rigmel] pense de Horn, ki ele tient trop fier,
> . . . .
> 'Cheveus ad lungs e blois, que nul n'en est sun per;
> Oilz veirs, gros, duz, rianz, pur dames esgarder;
> Nies e buche bien faite pur duz beisiers prester . . .'

16   Zeydel, op. cit., pp. 110–3.
17   F. Whitehead, ed., *La Chanson de Roland* (Basil Blackwell, 1970), lines 281–5.
18   M.K. Pope, ec., *The Romance of Horn by Thomas*, 2 vols., Anglo-Norman Text Society (Oxford 1955 and 1964), 1, lines 1250, 1255–7. Compare lines 1050ff where Horn's beauty is described as radiant and angelic. On the presentation of the hero in this poem see J.D. Burnley, 'The *Roman de Horn* and its ethos', *French Studies*, 32 (1978), pp.385–97.

10

Lady Rigmel thinks of Horn, whom she thinks too proud,
. . . .
'He has long blonde hair so that none can equal him; he has blue eyes, large, sweet and laughing to look upon ladies; he has a fine nose and mouth to give kisses . . .'

We have become so accustomed to regard 'courtly love' as a male idealization of female beauty that it may come as a surprise to find, here in the first generation of French romance, an idealization of male beauty as seen by a woman. Yet it is this new awareness of male sexuality and narcissism which underlies the courtly cult of love.

And, of course, the courtly cult of music. For the musicologist the most striking aspect of Horn is not his physical beauty but the way in which his sexual attractiveness centres upon his musical accomplishments. Horn is a skilled harpist.

The author of the *Roman de Horn* builds an extended episode around his hero's musical abilities. In a royal chamber, 'strewn with flowers, yellow, indigo and vermillion', Horn gathers with some other young courtiers for entertainments. He is travelling incognito. At one point a harp is called for and Lenburc, the Irish princess, begins to play. Having performed several pieces, she remarks that she has heard a magnificent *lai* but that she only knows half of it. Eventually the harp passes to Horn; needless to say he knows the song and to the astonishment of all the company he begins to sing and play it with surpassing mastery:[19]

Lors prent la harpe a sei,	qu'il la veut atemprer.
Deus! ki dunc l'esgardast	cum la sout manïer,
Cum ces cordes tuchout,	cum les feseit trembler,
Asquantes feiz chanter	asquantes organer,
De l'armonie del ciel	li poüst remembrer!
Sur tuz homes k'i sunt	fet cist a merveiller.
Quant ses notes ot fait	si la prent a munter
E tut par autres tuns	les cordes fait soner:
Mut se merveillent tuit	qu'il la sout si bailler.
Et quant il out (is)si fait,	si cummence a noter
Le lai dont or ains dis,	de Baltof, haut e cler,
Si cum sunt cil bretun	d'itiel fait costumier.
Apres en l'esturment	fet les cordes suner,
Tut issi cum en voiz	l'aveit dit tut premier . . .
Tut le lai lur ad fait,	n'i vout rien retailler.

Then he took the harp to tune it. God! whoever saw how well he handled it, touching the strings and making them vibrate, sometimes causing them to sing a melody and at other times join in harmonies, he would have been reminded of the heavenly harmony. This man, of all those that are there, causes most wonder. When he had played his notes he made the harp go up so that the strings gave out completely different notes. All those present marvelled that he could play thus. And when he had done all this he began to play the aforesaid lai of Baltof, in a loud and clear voice, just as the Bretons are versed in

19 Pope, op. cit., lines 2830–44.

such performances. Afterwards he made the strings of the instrument play exactly the same melody as he had just sung; he performed the whole lai for he wished to omit nothing.

The problem of what the author means by a *lai* need not concern us here;[20] what matters is that it is clearly a song (Horn both sings and plays during the performance) inspired by love (Horn's love for Rigmel) and composed by a nobleman. The whole episode seems to assume a milieu where there is an intense interest in new songs and their composers. When the Irish princess Lenburc announces that she has heard a marvellous *lai* the response from the young courtiers gathered in the chamber is immediate: 'God! If I might only hear it', exclaims one; 'who composed it, fair sister?'[21]

The *Roman de Horn* was composed around 1170. It is surely no coincidence that this is almost exactly the period of the first trouvères? The story of Horn – and there are others like it – seems to mediate a contemporary interest in the composition of love-songs by well-born composers – we immediately think of trouvères such as Conon de Béthune and the Chastelain de Couci. These tales show how closely their lyric art must have been involved with the male narcissism which lies at the root of chivalry and 'courtly love'. They are an unexplored deposit of the art of the trouvères.

3   ELOQUENCE

We have glanced at the theme of narcissism; in the twelfth century, or so I have suggested, the revolutionary notion of the warrior as one whose ardour for honour was embroiled with his sexual allure brought musical skills, and particularly love-song, within the scope of warrior accomplishment. This brings us to our second theme: eloquence. How did the new cult of song-making and courtesy grow out of the old martial ethos of epic?

Part of the answer may lie in the cult of eloquence. Here we must retrace our steps to *The Song of Roland* and the threshold of the twelfth century. If we turn back to the years around 1080 and to the most famous of the French epics we find that Roland is *proz*, headstrong and brave, whilst his friend Oliver is *sage*, wise and circumspect. Now it is almost exactly at this time – the end of the eleventh century – that the adjective *prudens*, 'wise', becomes by far the most popular epithet to join to the word *miles* in Latin narrative texts.[22] In other words the ideal knight of c. 1100 was closer to Oliver the *sage* than to Roland the *proz*.

How did the knight develop and display his *sagesse*? Above all, I suspect,

20   I deal with this question at length in *Voices and Instruments in the Middle Ages* (forthcoming).
21   Pope, op. cit., lines 2788–9.
22   This contrast is discussed in Alexander Murray's richly discursive book *Reason and Society in the Middle Ages* (Oxford, 1978), pp. 125–7.

12

in the soundness and the eloquence of the counsel which he gave his feudal lord. In *The Song of Roland* the pagan king Marsilie calls upon his dukes and counts for counsel:[23]

> Cunseilez mei . . . mi savie hume

and the poet dwells upon the *sagesse* of the pagan warrior Blancandrins: 'He was one of the wisest pagans; he was a knight well-endowed with the qualities of a vassal; he was a man of valour to serve his lord'.[24]

In some measure, I suggest, the lyric art of the troubadours and trouvères began as a transference of the chivalric eloquence which a knight was expected to display before his male peers into the realm of leisure passed in mixed company. In some chivalric narratives both kinds of eloquence are associated. In the epic of *Folque de Candie*, for example, Thibaut is said to be *amez de dames et sages de plaidier*: 'loved by ladies and wise in pleading a case'.[25] And why is Thibaut loved by the ladies? Because, as the author explains elsewhere, of his *beles paroles*, his attractive eloquence.[26]

The fictional figure of Thibaut is given some historical dress in Conon de Béthune, the knightly trouvère who was active in the late twelfth and early thirteenth centuries. In 1203 we find him conducting delicate negotiations at Constantinople on behalf of the Crusaders; he was chosen, it seems, because he was *sage . . . et bein emparlez*; 'wise . . . and most eloquent'.[27]

4 A NEW SONG ARRIVES AT COURT

It is time to manoeuvre a little closer to the milieux where the songs in the troubadour and trouvère chansonniers flourished. As we turn the pages of those manuscripts we are left with a puzzling sense of being close to the world in which the songs thrived and yet far away from it. They leave us wondering about the circumstances in which courtly interest in lyric art was fostered and maintained. Did minstrels and trouvères take these songs from court to court? Did the arrival of a new song create a stir of anticipation and lead to a flurry of questions about its composer? If so, has all this activity left any imprint outside of the chansonniers? I believe it has left a marked impression upon chivalric romance.

A striking example is provided by the prose romance of *Guiron le courtois*, composed in the first half of the thirteenth century. An extensive episode

---

23 Whitehead, *La Chanson de Roland*, line 20.
24 Ibid., lines 24–6.
25 O. Schultz–Gora, ed., *Folque de Candie*, 3 vols. (Dresden etc. 1909, 1915 and 1936), 2, p. 2 line 9899.
26 Ibid., line 12512.
27 J.E. White Jr. ed., *La Conqueste de Constantinople* (New York, 1968), p. 90. Cf. p. 69.

in this romance relates how Meliadus, the father of Tristan, composes the first *lai* that was ever made (again, the precise meaning of this term does not matter here) in honour of the queen of Scotland whom he loves. Meliadus reveals his plight to one of his knights, a friend since childhood and the most gifted harpist in the world after himself. The knight immediately offers to learn the *lai* and then to travel to Arthur's plenary court and perform it to the queen of Scotland as a confession of love. Meliadus agrees to this plan and the knight learns the *lai*.[28]

Here, surely, is a literary mediation of the jongleurs who sometimes learned and transmitted the songs composed by troudadours and trouvères?[29]

~ The story then relates how the knight travels to the court of King Arthur. Once there he begins to stir up excitement over the arrival of a new song at court. First, he tells the queen of Scotland that Meliadus has composed a song in her honour; 'tomorrow I will harp it myself before you', he assures her, 'in the full court'.[30] Next, he seeks out Sir Gawayn, a connoisseur of *noveax chant*:[31]

---

28 London, British Library, MS Add. 12228, ff.218–219. *Guiron le courtois* has not been published in modern times and the early printed editions are not adequate for the present purposes. The surviving manuscripts of the work are fully catalogued in R. Lathuillère, *Guiron le Courtois* (Geneva, 1966). MS Add. 12228 is of special interest in that the musical scenes of the romance are lavishly illustrated with coloured miniatures. For an example see *The New Grove* sv. 'Performing practice'.

29 The best-known examples of such minstrels are those mentioned in the (mainly thirteenth-century) *Vidas* or 'Lives' of the troubadours. See J. Boutière and A.H. Schutz, eds., *Biographies de Troubadours*, 2nd edition (Paris, 1973), including pp. 39 (Guiraut de Borneill), 68 (Bertran de Born). For a striking northern example see J.E. Matzke and M. Delbouille, eds., *Le Roman de Castelain de Couci et de la Dame de Fayel par Jakemes*, Société des Anciens Textes Français (Paris, 1936), lines 356–420.

There is a similar episode to this one from *Guiron le Courtois* in the hitherto unpublished section of the *Roman de Perceforest*, probably composed between 1330 and 1350. Lionnel, a knight, composes the words of a *lai* which he wishes all *vrays amans* should know. A minstrel-harpist approaches Lionnel and offers to compose music for it so that it may be sung 'in many assemblies and in many a noble celebration'. Lionnel agrees, requesting that the music should match the *pitoiable* mood of the poetry. This the minstrel does: '*Sire*' [says the minstrel] '*vous prometz que se vous le me voulez aprendre, au plaisir du dieu souverain, je le feray ancores jouer en mainte assemblee et en mainte noble feste*'.
'*Par ma foy, mon amy*', dist Lionnel, '*je te diray voulentiers les motz mais il n'a point de chant, et se tu en vouloies faire ung pitoiable comme est le dit, je t'en scauroie bon gre*'.
'*Certes, sire*', dist le menestrel, '*je le feray voulentiers*'. Adont le preu Lionnel lui dist les moz du lay tant de fois qu'il le sceut par coeur. Ce fait, le menestrel tira sa harpe hors du fourreau et fist dessus ung chant . . . pitaux. . . . British Library, MS Royal 19 E. iii, f. 139v.

30 *Demain le harperai ge devant vos meesmes en pleine cort.* British Library, MS Add. 12228, f. 220v.

31 '*Missire Yvayn, vos qui tant vos alez delytant en noveax chant, ge vos promet que vos porriez demain oir un chant novel tout le meillor et le plus dolz et le mielz acordant que vos onques oissiez jor de vostre vie*'.
'*Ha! por Deu*', fait missire Yvayn, '*quant il est si bons, or me dites qui le fist, se Dex vos doint bone aventure*'.
'*Certes*', fet il, '*le meillor chevalier del monde le fist, ce est li rois Melyadus de Loenoys . . . demain le porriez vos oir apres hore de manger*'. *Ibid.*, ff. 220v–221.

14

> 'Sir Gawayn, you who delight in newly-composed songs, I promise you that you may
> hear one tomorrow, the best and the sweetest that you have ever heard in your life.'
> 'By God', cried Gawayn, 'since it is so good, tell me who composed it'.
> 'Certainly', said the knight, 'the best knight in the world composed it, that is to say
> Meliadus of Leonnois . . . you may hear it tomorrow'.

Sir Gawayn is so excited by the arrival of a new song at court that he goes
directly to a lady gifted with a fine voice and takes her aside to give her the
news:[32]

> He said to her, smiling: 'Tomorrow a new poem and a new melody will come to court, the
> best and the finest that has ever been brought here . . . the best knight in the world
> composed it. If you could hear it first and teach it to me I would be your knight, so God
> help me!'
> 'Tell me', said she, 'who has brought it to court? Is he a knight or a minstrel or a harper?'
> 'Indeed', he replied, 'it is a knight of Leonnois, a knight of King Meliadus who sings
> extremely well'.

We are deep in the realm of Arthurian fiction here and yet the world of the
contemporary trouvères could scarcely be closer. These passages provide a
literary image of 'grass-roots' activity in the world that nourished the art of
courtly monody in France. They show us the great appetite for *noveax chant*
(the phrase recalls countless trouvère poems); the aristocratic trouvère;
the emissary who learns the song and carries it to a court and stirs up
excitement over its arrival; the eagerness to know who composed the new
piece; the impatience to acquire the song for one's own repertory ('if you
could hear it first and teach it to me I would be your knight, so God help
me!'); the careful distinction between words and music ('tomorrow a new
poem and a new melody will come to court') implying a connoisseurship of
each; the interest in the social condition of the singer who brings the song
('Is he a knight or a minstrel'?); the keen sense that the performance of the
song is a forthcoming attraction that will be performed at an appointed
time before 'the full court'. We are looking through the chansonniers here
to the chambers, corridors and galleries of thirteenth-century France
where the art of the aristocratic trouvères was cultivated and enjoyed.

*   *   *

So far I have been treating Old French fiction as if it were an enormous
stained-glass window with panels of clear glass revealing the world

---

32 . . . *li dit tout en riant: 'Demain vendra a cort un dit novel et un son novel tout le meillor et le plus*
mielz dit que onques fust aportez a cort . . . le plus meillor chevalier del monde le fist. Se tu puissiez ore
faire que tu la preissez premierement et puis la me feisses savoir, ge seroie ton chevalier, se Dex me doint
bone aventure'.
'Or me dites', fet ele, 'qui est cil qui la porte a cort, est il chevaliers ou jugleor ou harpeor?'
'Certes', fait il, 'il est chevaliers et est de Leonoys, et est chevaliers del roi Melyadus et chante molt bien,
se sai ge bien veraiement car je l'ay oi'. Ibid., f. 221.

beyond. Now it is time to step back and consider the pattern which all the panels form. I wish to suggest that many passages from chivalric fiction are closely akin to one-another, both on the level of narrative content and of verbal technique. In other words there are certain genres of musical reference in Old French fiction and each individual passage may be seen as a mobilization of the conventions of the genre.[33] By identifying these genres we are able to deal with this narrative material in a systematic way and to answer precise questions about individual passages: are there other passages like this one? how does this one differ from its fellows? and so on. The search for these motifs leads into as dense a forest as ever beset Sir Gawayn, strewn with more than a million lines of verse and prose. I can only hope to reach a high vantage-point and to discern where the tracks lie.

The main path seems to divide references which offer a generalized view of a multifarious activity from references which offer a more particularized view of a specific activity. An example of the generalized view might be a list of musical entertainments offered at a feast, and examples of the more particularized view would include descriptions of solo minstrels performing. These two types of 'view' – the generalizing and the particularizing – are not watertight categories; indeed, they are not really categories at all but only expressions of the two most fundamental patterns in the material.

We are in the depths of the forest already and it is time to go hunting for examples. The Appendix presents a typology of some principal genres of musical reference in epic and romance setting them out in relation to what I call the 'Reviewing Register' (a generalized view of a multifarious activity) and the 'Focusing Register' (a more particularized view of a specific activity). The list opens with a genre which offers the most common and stable manifestation of the generalized view, THE FEAST. Here is a characteristic and influential example, from Chrestien's romance of *Erec*, probably composed in the 1170s:[34]

> Quant la corz fu tote asanblee,
> . . .
> An la sale grant joie ot;
> chascuns servi de ce qu'il sot;
> cil saut, cil tunbe, cil anchante
> li uns sifle, li autres chante,
> cil flaüte, cil chalemele,
> cil gigue, li autres vïele . . .

---

33 I am steering close here to some of the work on formulaic and oral-formulaic composition in medieval literature. See particularly D.H. Fry, 'Old English Formulaic Themes and Type-Scenes', *Neophilologus*, 52 (1968), pp. 48–54.
34 M. Roques, ed., *Erec et Enide* (Paris, 1952–3), lines 1983, 1987–1992.

16

> When the court was assembled ... there was great celebration in the hall; each [minstrel] offered what he knew how to do; he leaps, he tumbles, he conjures, one whistles, the other sings, he flutes, he plays the reed-pipes, he plays the *gigue*, another fiddles ...

There is implicit hyperbole here, for although Chrestien does not exaggerate at the level of the individual phrase the cumulative effect of the passage is to evoke a feast so abundant and so luxurious that it almost defies description in discursive terms. Therefore Chrestien declines to describe it and contents himself with listing its parts. His use of asyndeton ('he leaps, he tumbles, he conjures') evokes a narrator who is so delighted with what he sees on every side that a more circumstantial description is beyond his powers, and this sense of multifarious grandeur is heightened by parataxis; when Chrestien records that 'he leaps, he tumbles, he conjures', without indicating the sense relations between the three phrases, we cannot tell whether the actions of leaping, tumbling and conjuring happen together and at the same time, or happen apart and at different times; our minds resolve the problem in favour of a vague sense that everything is happening in a single, magnificent moment, which is exactly what Chrestien wants. He also reinforces our sense of vague splendour by declining to name anyone; the entertainers are evoked by distributive pronouns ('he does X ... he does Y' and so on) in another deliberate evasion of detail.

Chrestien's aim seems to be to reinforce the association between lavish entertainment, including music, and the excellence of courtly civilization – an association which is so fundamental to the place of music in romance that the language of FEAST passages (and there are very many of them)[35] tends to settle into a series of signals and formulas. The relation between the narrative voice and what is being described, for example, usually resolves into a direct relation between spectator and spectacle; formulas such as 'there you might have heard ...' sustain the fictional implication that the narrator is only reporting what he experienced and that his account of the feast is therefore an authentic one. In the same way the lists of musical entertainments usually adhere to a consistent plan: they generally follow a meal and are therefore often signalled by some such formula as 'when the meal was over ...', or 'when the table cloths were lifted away ...' (see Appendix, 1:3).

The majority of musical references in Old French fiction follow some broadly similar pattern to the lines from *Erec* which we have just examined: they provide a general picture of some splendid or admirable event; they evade giving precise details in an attempt to evoke a magnificence which defies discursive description; their language is in some measure formulaic and cannot be tacitly assumed to record a fresh perception of contemporary reality.

35. For examples see Faral, op. cit., Appendix 3, numbers 60, 63, 92, etc.

In contrast to such passages there are others of a different order which can be more quickly described in that they focus upon some particularized action. Some examples are provided by section 4 of the Appendix, SINGING ON HORSEBACK. This is a common genre of reference in both epics and romances, and the example quoted at the head of section 4 is a representative one:[36]

> Thus Boefs mounts his swift palfrey . . . all a-singing he begins to ride.

These two lines focus upon a single, closely-defined sequence of actions. There is no time for the pervasive hyperbole of Feast passages and the veil of anonymity, so impenetrable in passages of the Feast type, is lifted; the protagonist is named in the first line (as in five other references in this set; see Appendix, 4:9). There is little sign of stereotyped diction or syntax.

Those lines about Boefs de Haumtone – 'Thus Boefs mounts his swift palfrey . . . all a-singing he begins to ride' – are not particularly interesting (save in that they suggest, as do many other passages, that a great deal of musical life was lived on horseback during the twelfth and thirteenth centuries). Yet by laying the reference to Boefs alongside similar passages we are able to isolate the ones which *are* interesting. This is what I have attempted to do in the Appendix under the number 4:9. As we compare the extracts assembled there it becomes clear that one of them takes a decisive step beyond the conventional boundaries of its genre: the lines from the epic of *Les Quatre Fils Aymon:*[37]

> Aallars and Guichars begin a *son*, the words were from Gascony and the music from the Limousin, and Richars provides a fine *bordon* beneath. One can hear them from a long way off. There is no *rote*, *viele* or *psalterion* that would have pleased you as much as these three barons.

We are prepared for the idea of a band of men singing together as they ride: we encounter it in *Les Narbonnais* and in *Claris et Laris*. We are also prepared for the music they sing to be called a *son*. But the author breaks the mould of the genre when he reveals that the words of the song are from Gascony, that the music is from the Limousin (the lands around Limoges), and that one of the three men accompanies the other two by singing a *bordon* underneath their melody. If the epic of *Les Quatre Fils Aymon* dates from the late twelfth-century, as is commonly believed, then this would seem to be the earliest known reference to concerted singing involving the term *bordon* (here in verbal form).[38] Presumably the author is describing some kind of unwritten polyphonic practice?

---

36 A. Stimmung. ed., *Der Anglonormannische Boeve de Haumtone*, (Halle, 1899), lines 863 and 865.

37 F. Castets, ed., *La Chanson des Quatre Fils Aymon* (Montpellier, 1909), lines 6599–6604.

38 For a comprehensive collection of literary references in which the term *bordon* (in various forms and spellings) appears, see B. Trowell, 'Faburden – New Sources, New Evidence; a Preliminary Survey', in E. Olleson, ed., *Modern Musical Scholarship* (Stocksfield etc, 1980), pp. 28–78.

18

A second example of a reference which reaches beyond the confines of its genre carries us forward to written repertory. Section 6 of the Appendix embraces performances by solo minstrels. Often there is some passing reference to what is performed in these contexts,[39] but a passage from the thirteenth-century romance of *Claris et Laris* is exceptional for the way it describe's the minstrel's performance routine. At one point in this romance knights and ladies listen to a minstrel in the open air:[40]

> La escoutoient bonement
> .I. conteor, qui lor contoit
> Une chançon et si notoit
> Ses refrez en une viele,
> Qui assez iert et bonne et bele.

There they listened attentively to a minstrel, who sang them a song and performed the refrains on his fiddle which was both good and beautiful.

This *chançon* with its refrains may be a rondeau (or some similar form), and this deduction seems to be reinforced by certain features in the poet's description of the scene. The minstrel performs *En mi . . . d'une praierie* which is near *la rive de mer*, and both of these phrases are key registral terms in the thirteenth-century repertory of rondeaux and simple refrain songs. Compare the following incipits of lyrics quoted in Jean Renart's *Guillaume de Dole*:[41]

> C'est la jus *en la praele*
> C'est la gieus *en mi les prez*
> Sor la *rive de mer*
> Mignotement alez
> Tout la gieus, *sor rive mer*

This is not to claim that the author has scattered clues to the nature of the minstrel's song here and there in his account of its performance, only that his imaginative apprehension of this musical scene is impregnated with poetic formulae which suggest that the *chançon* is a monophonic rondeau or virelai such as *C'est la gieus en mi les préz*, whose music has survived (Ex. 1).[42] These few lines may be our only guide to the way in which such songs were performed with instruments during the thirteenth century. I take it that the fiddler is singing the song and doubling the refrains upon his fiddle (perhaps sustaining a drone all the way through; some such technique is

---

39 For some examples of references belonging to this genre see Faral, op. cit., Appendix 3, numbers 59a, 109, 172c etc.
40 J. Alton, ed., *Li Romans de Claris et Laris* (Tübingen, 1884), lines 9940–3.
41 F. Lecoy, op. cit., lines 1846ff; 5440ff; 2523ff;
42 F. Gennrich, *Rondeaux, Virelais und Balladen*, 2 vols., Gesellschaft für Romanische Literatur, 43 (Dresden, 1921 and Göttingen, 1927), 1, p. 10.

Ex. 1: C'est la gieus en mi les préz

C'est la gieus en mi les préz, J'ai a - mors a ma vo - len - té! da - mes i ont baus le - véz. Ga - ri m'ont mi oel. J'ai a - mors a ma vo - len - té, te - les com ge voel.

implied by Jerome of Moravia's account of the tuning of the fiddle in his *Tractatus de Musica*.[43]

As they are inventoried in the Appendix, each of these genres of musical reference comprises a set of universal conditions: 'if X then Y, but not Z': if a courtly amateur plays an instrument in public then, if male, he will often be travelling incognito or about some subterfuge, and so on. In other words the presentation of musical life in chivalric fiction is subject to a complex set of rules. How are we to read these patterns, and what is their deep structure? I would like to close with three themes which seem to me to run deeply through the whole corpus of material assembled in the Appendix.

A monophonic universe. In recent years musicologists have repeatedly stressed that monophonic music was the staple fare in both secular and sacred contexts throughout the Middle Ages.[44] Chivalric fiction bears this out, for in more than a million lines of narrative material the existence of polyphony is scarcely even acknowledged.[45]

Chivalric integrity. In many ways the position of any *chevalier* who was not a great lord was akin to that of the *jongleur*: both relied upon the generosity of their masters and were in competition for their surplus spending power.[46] The *chevaliers* were thus inclined to insist upon their social superiority and to avoid any taint of minstrelism in their own behaviour. Chivalric fiction seems to embody an anxiety within the knightly class that the musical

43 C. Page, 'Jerome of Moravia on the *rubeba* and *viella*', *Galpin Society Journal*, 32 (1979), pp. 77–98.

44 See D. Fallows, 'Specific Information on the Ensembles for Composed Polyphony' in S. Boorman, ed., *Studies in the Performance of Late-Medieval Music* (Cambridge, 1983), p. 109.

34 See note 9.

46 This point emerges with some clarity in certain Old Provençal narratives where liberal patrons are mentioned who are generous to both *cavayers* and *joglars*. See, for example, *Jaufre* (?c. 1170) in R. Lavaud and R. Nelli, eds., *Les Troubadours*, 2 vols. (Bruges, 1960–66), 1, p. 44, lines 79–84.

20

accomplishments proper to a courteous knight should not appear to diminish the gap between *chevalier* and *jongleur*. Thus there is often some kind of distance placed between the knight and the display of his musical powers. In the *Roman de Horn*, for example, the hero is travelling incognito and under an assumed name when he sings and plays the harp at court. In *Guiron le Courtois* we are not allowed to see King Meliadus performing his own *lai* to the harp; this is done by a knight on his behalf. In this same romance Gawayn is presented as a fine singer, but we do not see him perform; he only sings as he rides, expressing his fine state of physical and mental health in an un-selfconscious way. Women, on the other hand, frequently perform 'on stage' in *Guiron le Courtois*.[47]

Modesty, or rather something akin to Castiglione's cult of nonchalance, emerges as a crucial element in the knight's bearing when he shows his musical skills. In contrast to the minstrel who needed to vaunt his abilities, the knight required to be asked to perform. Horn does not play until he is asked, while the knight in *Guiron le Courtois* who performs Meliadus' *lai* makes a great show of modesty and will not consent to play until he is almost overwhelmed with requests to do so:[48]

> [The lady Orgayne] said to the knight: 'I have been told that you know how to sing and to play the harp; I beseech you, seeing these ladies present, that you show a little of the skill that you have acquired.'
> The knight, who wished that there should be more requests than that of the lady alone, replied that he no longer had any skill in singing. Then all the ladies entreated him, and when he saw that they asked him so earnestly, and that even the knights who were there did the same, he replied: 'then pass me the harp . . .'

Anti-intellectualism. On the whole, chivalric fiction looks askance upon the Liberal Arts, so important in contemporary clerical tradition. When they are mentioned they may be surrounded by an unmasculine, unchristian and even unnatural aura, being studied by women, by Saracen children, or by visitors from the seductive and dangerous world of faery. Such is the reflection which clerical learning and the Islamic contribution to Western science finds in the mirror of chivalric narrative.

As for reading and writing as accomplishments of the *chevalier*, they are hardly ever mentioned. There is a striking passage in *Maugis d'Aigremont*, an epic of the first half of the thirteenth century, where the hero is taught to *lire e chanter*, the pair of verbs habitually associated with the distinctive skills of the cleric.[49] I have no doubt that this poet wishes to present his

47 British Library, MS Add. 12228, ff.221v–222.
48 *[Orgayne] li dist: 'Sire chevalier, l'en m'a fait entendant que vos savez chanter et harper; ge vos pri que vos voiant cestes dames en faiciez partie de ce que vos en savez'.*
  Li chevalier, qui voloit qu'il en eust autre priere que de la damoisele solement, respont qu'il navoit ore talent de chanter, et toutes les dames le prient adonc, et quant il voit qu'eles le prioient si ententivement, et li chevaliers meesmes qui illuec estoient le prient autresint, respont: 'Or me faites baillier cele harpe . . .'. Ibid., f. 222r.
49 P. Vernay, ed., *Maugis d'Aigremont* (Berne, 1980, lines 4361ff.

hero as a literate musician, for he even reinforces the idea with some technical terminology derived from music theory: Maugis can sing *par ordre de game*, 'according to the form of the gamut'.[50] Such terminology is almost unknown to chivalric fiction and it is no surprise to find that Maugis is taught these exotic skills by an inhabitant of the faery realm.

I end with a relatively modern writer, Gerard Manley Hopkins:

> Oh the mind, mind has mountains, cliffs of fall
> Frightful, sheer, no-man-fathomed.

The chivalric narratives of medieval France may sometimes reveal how music was performed: where, when, by whom and to what effect. As such they have some value as a record of performance-practice in the broadest sense of the term. But they are also a door into a vanished country of the mind, frightful in some ways and no-man-fathomed in many: the mind of the secular aristocrat whose thinking was not closely touched by the seven Liberal Arts of clerical tradition and still less by the Renaissance humanism that is our heritage. His was a mentality in which music was embroiled with a generous and extravagant ethic which, after salvation, was the greatest preoccupation of every twelfth and thirteenth-century magnate: the ethic of chivalry.

---

50 Ibid., line 637.
   I am grateful to Professor J.H. Marshall, Professor J. Stevens, Dr David Fallows, Laurence Wright, Régine Page and Ann Lewis for their comments upon the first draft of this paper.

APPENDIX

SELECTIVE TYPOLOGY OF MUSICAL REFERENCES IN FRENCH NARRATIVE FICTION TO 1300

The following typology describes some of the most important genres of musical reference in Old French fiction. It is based upon the following texts:

ROMANCES

Amadas et Ydoine
Athis et Prophilias
Attila
Beaudous
Le bel inconnu
Blancandrin et l'orgueilleuse d'Amour
La Chastelaine de Vergi
Le chevalier au lion (Yvain)
Le chevalier de la Charrete
Li chevaliers as deus espees
Claris et Laris
Cligés
La Confrere d'amours
Le conte du Graal (Perceval)
Le court d'amours
Durmart le Gallois
Eledus et Serene
Eracle
Erec et Enide
Escanor
L'estoire del Saint Graal
L'estoire de Merlin
Fergus
Floire et Blancheflor
Floriant et Florete
Galeran de Bretagne
Gautier d'Aupais
Guillaume de Dole
Gille de Chyn
Gligois

Guillaume d'Angleterre
Guillaume de Palerne
Guiron le Courtois
Hunbaut
Ille et Galeron
Ipomedon
Jehan et Blonde
Joufroi de Poitiers
Kanor
Le lai d'Aristote
Le livre d'Artus
Le livre de Lancelot del Lac
La manekine
Meraugis de Portlesguez
Les mervelles de Rigomer
La mort le roy Artu
Narcisus
Partonopeu de Blois
Peliarmenus
Philomena
Piramus et Tisbé
Prose Tristan (read in Vienna 2542)
Protheslaus
Robert le Diable
Le roman d'Auberon
Le roman de Laurin
Le roman de Silence
Le roman de Thèbes
Le roman de Troie
Le roman de la Violette

EPICS

Aiol
Aliscans
Ami et Amile
Anseîs de Carthage
Anseÿs de Metz
Auberi le Bourgoin
Aye d'Avignon
Aymeri de Narbonne
Boeve de Haumtone
La bataille Loquifer

Garin le Loheren
Gaufrey
Gaydon
Gerbert de Mez
Girart de Roussillon
Girart de Vienne
Godefroid de Bouillon
Gormont et Isembart
Gui de Bourgogne
Hervis de Metz

Brun de la Montagne
La chanson d'Aspremont
La chanson de Godin
La chanson de Guillaume
La chanson des quatre fils Aymon
Le charroi de Nimes
La chevalerie d'Ogier de Danemarche
La chevalerie Vivien
Couronnement de Louis (verse redations)
Doon de Maience
Doon de Nanteuil
Doon de la Roche
Les enfances Guillaume
Les enfances Renier
Les enfances Vivien
L'entree d'Espagne
Fierebras
Floovant
Florence de Rome
Folque de Candie

Hugues Capet
Huon de Bordeaux
Jehan de Lanson
Jourdain de Blaye
Maugis d'Aigremont
Moniage Guillaume (verse redactions)
La mort Garin le Loherain
Les Narbonnais
Otinel
La prise de Cordres et de Sebille
Macaire
Prise d'Orange (verse redactions)
Raoul de Cambrai
Le siége de Barbastre
Tristan de Nanteuil
Voyage de Charlemagne
Yon

THE 'REVIEWING' REGISTER

1 THE FEAST

1.1 Essentially a listing of the musical (and other) entertainments offered at some courtly function,

1.2 usually a feast, and therefore in the hall,

1.3 and in this context often clearly signalled by some formulaic reference to the termination of the meal, often with *Quant* . . . or *Apres* . . .

> Quant les tables furent levees . . .
> Quant les tables ostees furent . . .
> Quant cho vint apres mangier . . .
> Apres disner i eut . . .
> Apres mengier . . .

1.4 The occasion of the feast is often a royal marriage (under the influence of *Brut* lines 10543ff and *Erec et Enide*, lines 1983ff)

1.5 The doings of professional entertainers, especially instrumentalists and singers, loom very large in these lists of entertainments at feasts. Many such lists are mainly strings of instrument-names (a rhetorical procedure acknowledged in Geoffrey de Vinsauf's *Ars Poetica* (c. 1200)).

1.6 However, many lists also include references to the doings of courtiers, primarily dancing (see 2.1–13), tale-telling, and (for the men) the playing of chivalric sports (such as fencing and jumping). In this case there may be moments of focus on specific activities.

1.7 There is a single, stable literary purpose for almost all such material: it emphasizes the luxury and abundance of the scene whilst reinforcing the image of the court as a stable point of departure and point of return for all 'romance experience'.

1.8 In accordance with this fixity of purpose there is a fixity of technique. Syntax is highly stereotyped and built of paratactic formulae, including the following, where (in the first four examples) a cultivated vagueness of sense – suggesting a feast so magnificent

24

that it all but defies description in discursive terms – is intensified by anaphora and asyndeton:

li uns	VERB	li autres	VERB
cil	VERB	cil	VERB
li alquant	VERB	li plusor	VERB

la ot . . . . .   (la ot . . . . .)

la oïssiez . . .
la peüssies oïr . . .

1.9   The total effect of the entertainment and its music is often expressed by the formula

        grant joi/noise (de)mener

1.10   The formulae listed in 1:8 may introduce references ranging from a couplet to a dozen lines. There are other formulae allowing narrators to signal the presence of music in a single line, including:

      (et) VERB et VERB (et) VERB cil jongler

Cantent et notent, vïelent chil jongler	*Hervis de Metz* 569
Cantent et harpent, vïelent cil jongler	*Hervis de Metz* 7929
e cantent et vïelent et rotent cil gugler	*Voyage de Charlemagne* 413
e cantent et vïelent et rotent cil geugler	*Voyage de Charlemagne* 837

2 THE CAROLE

     Après disner i eut vïeles,
     Muses et harpes et freteles,
     Qui font si douces melodies,
     Plus douces ne furent oïes.
     Après coururent as caroles
     Ou eut canté maintes paroles.

Jehan et Blonde 4761–4766

2.1   A dance performed by courtly amateurs and often mentioned in FEAST passages (1.1–10), often as an entertainment taken up when the company tires of the music offered by minstrels, or when the celebrations are carried beyond the hall and into the open air.

2.2   *Carole* references therefore often follow the material inventoried in 1.1–10 (as in the example from *Jehan et Blonde* quoted above).

2.3   The dance is often performed outdoors

2.4   to songs which the courtiers sing for themselves

2.5   and which may be accompanied by the instrumental music of minstrels.

2.6   Sometimes, but not frequently, the *caroles* seem to be purely instrumental and provided by minstrels (few texts can be securely interpreted to have this meaning).

2.7   The *caroles* are performed by a mixed company of men and women

2.8   or by women alone

2.9   and are especially associated with young girls (in numerous references the young girls are said to dance *caroles* while the young men indulge in chivalric sports such as fencing).

2.10   As implied by 2.3, the ethos of the *carole* is predominantly 'pastoral', and it is associated with the freshness and candour of youth. Whence *caroles* are particularly associated with the younger (and perhaps probationary) members of courtly society and are often danced by *puceles, puceletes jouvenceles, meschines, escuiers, bachelers* and *vallets*.

2.11   *Carole* (verb *caroler*) is the most common word for dancing, although *danser, treschier* and *baler* are also used.

2.12   In the tradition of lyric-insertion established by Jean Renart's *Guillaume de Dole* some thirteenth-century romances give the texts (and occasionally the music) of these *caroles*, a degree of explicitness that carries such references away from the Reviewing Register towards the Focusing Register.

2.13   Occasionally the *carole* seems to take the form of a joyous train of courtiers, both male and female, moving across open country. Here the genre blends with the SINGING PARTY genre (3.1–6).

3 THE SINGING PARTY

A genre embracing several classes of reference where courtiers entertain themselves, often as part of a feast when the meal is over and some (or all) of the courtiers have either tired of the minstrels or have chosen this form of entertainment from the first.

3.1   In a group, indoors (in hall or chamber), or outdoors, courtiers sing

3.2   and dance *caroles* (never in the chamber)

3.3   and perhaps tell stories or read romances (the key verb being *conter*).

3.4   The entertainment may be mixed with references to chivalric sports

3.5   and may take place indoors or (perhaps more often) outdoors.

3.6   Large *caroles* danced outdoors to the singing of courtiers often blend with the motif of the journey or formal progress enlivened by instrumental music.

THE 'FOCUSING' REGISTER

4 SINGING ON HORSEBACK

> Boefs si en mounte le palefrei corser . . .
> Tretot en chantaunt comence a chivacher

Boeve de Haumtone 863–5

4.1   Outside the *carole* (2.1–13) and the singing party (3.1–6) the courtly amateur rarely sings except when riding (for the singing of *lais* to the *harpe* see 5.1–10). The hero or some other important character (generally male) sings having just mounted his horse, or

4.2   sings during the course of a journey on horseback.

4.3   His song is commonly described as a *son*.

4.4   He may be holding a hunting bird.

4.5   Sometimes he is alone

4.6   and sometimes with others who sing with him (in which case the genre may blend with the SINGING PARTY 3.1–6).

4.7   By singing, the hero expresses his fine state of mental and physical health (in epics before the late 12th century)

4.8   and also his courtliness and amorousness of bearing (in romance, and in many of the later epics).

26

4.9   There may also be a powerful suggestion (at least in epic) that the singing protagonist is enjoying his last moments of light-heartedness before some disaster, and even that his singing is an expression of a false sense of security.

> Quant Gui l'entent, si ist de son donjon,
> En sa compengne son senechal Milon,
> Ostes et Dreues, que sont si compangnon.
> Es mulez montent, qui furent au perron,
> A l'ostel vindrent trestuit chantant un son,
> Et li frere se drecent.
>
> *Les Narbonnais* 1000–5

> Ferraus repaire et vait nontant .I. son,
> Et Amaufrois disoit .I. lay breton.
>
> *Gaydon* 7778–9

> Jolyvement chauntaunt comence a chevacher.
>
> *Boeve de Haumtone* 1144

> Parmi .I. bois s'en vont [no baron] chantant
> Et molt grant joie demenant.
>
> *Claris et Laris* 15319–20

> Gilles et tout si compeignon
> Vienent cantant une canchon.
>
> *Gille de Chyn* 533–4

> . . . vient [.i. chevalier] .i. esprevier paisant
> Et .i. noviel sonet cantant.
>
> *Mervelles de Rigomer* 15199–200

> Aallars et Guichars commenceront .i. son,
> Gasconois fu li dis et limosins li ton,
> Et Richars lor bordone belement par desos;
> D'une grande huchie entendre les puet on.
> Ainc rote ne viele ne nul psalterion
> Ne vos pleüst si bien comme li troi baron.
>
> *Les Quatre Fils Aymon* 6699–6604.

5 THE LAI/HARP COMPLEX

5.1   A courtly amateur
5.2   who is generally a protagonist or an important character in the narrative, is a gifted harpist
5.4   and harps pieces, in public, called *lais*,
5.5   and can usually compose them,
5.6   and often sings them to his/her own accompaniment.
5.7   There is a slot for some technical description of the performance, usually a tuning procedure.
5.8   The tale in which the courtly harper appears will normally have a 'Celtic' setting (Brittany, Cornwall, Wales; Arthurian Britain is a particular favourite)
5.9   and the harpist will often be in disguise when he performs (or be travelling incognito). This does not usually apply if the character is female.
5.10   If not a major protagonist of the tale the harpist will often be the messenger and ally of a protagonist, carrying his *lai* as a message or commemoration on the protagonist's behalf to one in a foreign realm for whom the *lai* has some special meaning.

6 THE SOLO PERFORMANCE

6.1   A solo musican, often a minstrel, performs. If a courtly amateur, then he/she is usually

6.2   a courtly amateur disguised as a minstrel for some purpose
6.3   or a character wrongly brought up as a minstrel following some tragedy, subterfuge or treachery following his birth,
6.4   or a character within the lai/harp complex (see 5.1–10).
6.5   If the solo performer is an instrumentalist, or a singer/instrumentalist, then the instrument will generally be a *vïele* unless the reference falls within 5.1–10.
6.6   If the solo musician is a vocal performer without an instrument then he is usually a narrator of saints' lives or epic tales.
6.7   The genre provides a slot for some passing reference to what the musician plays (which may or may not be filled), and narrators seem to have been free to fill the slot as they wished.
6.8   A special sub-genre of references to courtly, amateur instrumentalists centres upon the private musician/retainer of Charlemagne in epic tradition (*Chanson de Guillaume* and *Aye d'Avignon*).

7 COURTLY ACCOMPLISHMENT

Many epic and romance heroes are praised for their accomplishments which are often itemized in detail.

7.1   In both Epic and Romance chivalric skills and sports (jousting, fencing, leaping etc) predominate in the lists of male accomplishments, and the main arts of peace are chess and draughts.
7.2   It is exceptionally rare for a male to be praised for an ability to sing or to read. References to a hero having mastered the 'vii ars' are also very rare, though rather more frequent in connection with women.
7.3   Outside of 5.1–10 (and of texts relating to Aristotle's education of Alexander) it is almost unknown for a male to be praised for instrumental skills; exceptions are *Florimont*, which is related to the Alexander material, the *Roman de Horn* and *Eracle* where, in both cases, the ability to play the harp is presented as a skill cultivated by the nobility of the past.
7.5   In accounts of female education and accomplishment both singing and playing are sometimes mentioned, and perhaps the seven Liberal Arts.

The performance of Ars Antiqua motets

This article is dedicated to the memory of Professor Frank Harrison, a scholar whose delight in the sound of medieval music was an inspiration to all who knew him.

1 A young cleric (perhaps a student at the University of Paris) offers money to a girl who, to judge by the frame-drum (? or tambourine) in her hand, is off to dance in a carole. From a 13th-century Bible moralisée produced in Paris (London, British Library MS Harley 1526, f.31r).

Sequitur bene psallite ei . . . id est non vane leticie lascivie sicut illi qui cantant mundo in motetis, cantilenis et choreis . . .[1]

Praise the Lord well . . . not with vainglorious and wanton pleasure like those who sing for the world in motets, lyrics and dance-songs.

The author of these words, the early 14th-century and renowned theologian Pierre de Palude, suggests an association between the motet and the sprightly dances (or *caroles*) that were performed in streets and churchyards by young men and women. He clearly despises the 'wanton pleasure' that motets provide, and the implication is that they share the joyful and primaveral colours always worn by secular music in the Middle Ages.

The treatise *De Musica* by de Palude's contemporary, Johannes de Grocheio, presents an altogether different picture.[2] When Pierre speaks of the motet he opens a window that lets in the sound of dance music; Johannes de Grocheio, in contrast, closes a door that shuts the motet into all the solid and professional chambers of Parisian life. Such music should not be performed for the laity, he declares, because it only baffles them; let these pieces be sung for the *litterati*— in other words for the theologians, the Masters of Arts,

Reprinted from *Early Music* 16 (1988), pp. 147–164. By permission of Oxford University Press.

the prosperous lawyers and the successful physicians who thrived on the banks of the Seine.[3]

The paradox of the 13th-century motet is that it is both playful and learned at the same time. Though Pierre de Palude and Johannes de Grocheio disagree, it is clear that each represents part of the truth; surveying the repertory as a whole, each fulfils a helpful role as guide. Pierre was right to speak of motets and dance songs in the same breath, for some Ars Antiqua motets incorporate scraps of dance songs (see ex.1). These quotations give many motets a light and informal air, confirming the impression that the genre's social background lies, in part, with the amorous interplay between Parisian students and the local girls with their ring-dances. Even in 'learned' pieces the freshness of dance music is rarely far away (see ex.2).

Ex.1 A dance-song, or rondet de carole, whose words are preserved in the early 13th-century romance of Guillaume de Dole by Jean Renart, and whose music can be reconstructed from a 'quotation' in a two-part motet. From F. Gennrich, Rondeaux, Virelais und Balladen (Dresden, 1921), i, p.10

Ex.2 Triplum, bars 1–8, of Ut celesti possimus/Cum sit natus hodie/Hec dies as it appears in the Bamberg MS. From Anderson, CMM, lxviii, no.21

On the other hand, Johannes de Grocheio was well-advised to emphasize the learned appeal of a genre in which two, sometimes three, songs are performed at the same time, their texts and melodies colliding together in a way that seems to obliterate the very lightness and charm that has been admired (ex.3). And while the upper parts possess a melodiousness that may have an instant appeal for the modern listener, the tenor parts do their best to sound like a three-inch tape-loop. With unyielding determination they repeat their rhythmic (and often melodic) material, thus effacing the very qualities which most modern performers and listeners regard as the essence of medieval chant: an expressive melodiousness and a freedom from any mensural organization.

Above all, it is in the texture of these pieces that the force of Johannes de Grochcio's words about the learned character of the motet may be sensed. The harmony is intellectual—or at least highly controlled—in a way that may seem to be at odds with the gracious and appealing melodies from which the vertical sonorities are made. With a strictness of method that rivals the scholastic philosophy of the 13th century, virtually every perfection in a motet (represented by a dotted crotchet in ex.3) opens with a perfect consonance. This was usually an open 5th or octave, but it could also include the $\frac{8}{4}$ chord (the first sonority of bar 5 in ex.3) which even medieval theorists regarded as less *jocundus* than the $\frac{8}{5}$. The harmonic structure of an Ars Antiqua motet is therefore subject to a rigorous counting process, and for 13th-century musicians this was part of the mystique of measured music; in their eyes *mensurabilis* was to *musica* as *sapiens* is now to *homo*, implying a new departure in evolution with reason emerging triumphant after untold ages in which men had been governed by instinct alone.

Poised between the serious and the playful—between 'earnest and game', to borrow a phrase from Chaucer—the 13th-century motet offers much to modern performers and listeners, and by collating several hints in contemporary treatises with the results of practical experiment it becomes possible to reconstruct, at least in part, the manner of their performance. Needless to say, this cannot be a wholly objective enquiry, and what follows is based upon my own experience with professional British singers, most of whom received their training in the choir of some cathedral or collegiate establishment in England.

What kinds of voices were used for motets in the 13th century? I believe that the existence of something like the counter-tenor voice must be granted at the outset. In his *Scientia artis musice* of 1274, the French theorist

Ex.3 Encontre le tans/Quant fuellent/In ordorem, **from Thomas**, Robin and Marion motets, ii

Elias of Salomon describes a form of improvized organum in which four associates double a chant at the 5th, octave and 12th,[4] and when a plainsong with a range of seven or eight notes is performed in this way the lowest and highest sounding notes in the organum will lie some two octaves and a 5th apart. This is a very generous compass (sufficing for most of Dufay's music, for example) and it may be concluded that some 13th-century churches could muster singers with a compass of 20 notes between them. If Elias intends that one or more of the singers should be boys, he does not say so;[5] nor does he say whether the chant should be transposed downwards from its customary range to make the parallelism possible. The most plausible interpretation of his directions would seem to be that the lowest part in this organum was sung in something approximating to a bass voice while the upper part was sung by some kind of high tenor who could move into falsetto.

However, the mere existence of such voices does not prove that they were used in composed polyphonic music where the total compass used before 1300 never attains 20 notes and is often restricted to ten or even less. Elias is describing a technique which the Parisian *discantores* who performed motets would have regarded as rudimentary; it is possible that different standards of performance were involved in the two repertoires.[6] It may be added that the sound of Elias's organum would have been so thick—especially in a resonant acoustic—and so full of interlocking harmonics, that the singer on the top of the texture would not necessarily have been required to possess a voice good enough to be exposed in motets.

A survey of the compass used in motets, taken together with the evidence of certain literary sources, makes it possible to assemble a rather more definite

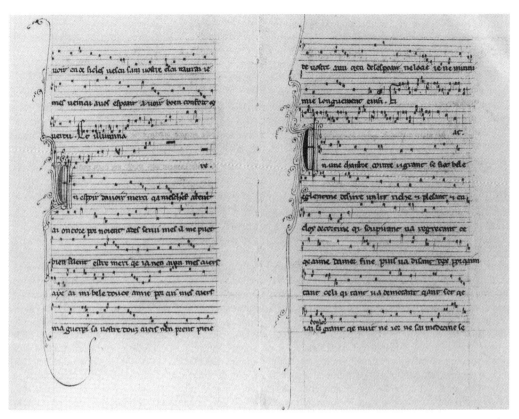

2 This and illus.3 and 4 show pieces from the earliest layer of Ars Antiqua vernacular motets, as found in the tenth fascicle of W2. They have been chosen to show how systematically the first motet composers raided the contemporary monophonic tradition for poetic styles. On this opening are the two part motets En espoir d'avoir merci/Fiat and En une chanbre cointe et grant/Et gaudebit The first is a brisk and informal version of the high-style love language of the trouvères, ubiquitous in the motet repertory. The second attempts the manner of a chanson de toile (literally 'a song to sing while spinning cloth', a minor but fascinating genre in the monophonic song repertory). W2, f.232v. and 233r.

picture of the voice types used in this repertory. For example, many of the motets in the Bamberg manuscript (probably dating from c.1285) exploit a range of around eleven notes from top to bottom,[7] while some individual voice parts also employ this compass.[8] It would therefore seem that 13th-century motets were conceived to exploit the resources of two, three or four equal voices; one singer, in other words, could normally perform any part in a motet—tenor, duplum, triplum or quadruplum—without undue difficulty. The result would have been a well-blended sound with each part distinguished by its text rather than by its colour.

This conclusion needs some modification, perhaps, for practical experience suggests that it will often be wise to place the tenor part with a singer who is at his best about a 3rd lower than his colleagues. If this means that the tenor line always falls to the same person so much the better, for there is no greater asset to performers of this music than a singer who has accepted the initially thankless task of confining himself to tenors so that he can master their idioms and styles.

If motets were performed by identical (or by nearly identical) voices then a cherished assumption about medieval music may be called into question. It is often claimed that Gothic polyphony is essentially linear in character and that modern performers must therefore make each melodic line stand out, perhaps with the aid of contrasting instrumental timbres: a fiddle for the tenor, a harp for the duplum, and so on.[9] We shall

153

return to the question of instrumental participation; for the moment let us concede the linear character of the motet, a genre where each line above the tenor has a well-wrought melody and its own text. That said, however, the evidence of voice ranges suggests that blend, and not contrast, is the guiding colour principle of the Ars Antiqua motet. This is quintessentially music for singers, designed to exploit the sounds of Latin and Old French as put into song by voices of very similar type singing in very much the same kind of way. Experience suggests that the contrasts between the voices of any motet become both more subtle and, strange though it may seem, more apparent when the piece is essentially monochromatic. I would therefore tentatively propose that Ars Antiqua motets, whether sacred or secular, preserved much of the sound world originally associated with the liturgical *clausulae* from which they were ultimately derived.

The question of performing pitch is a delicate one since it is generally accepted that there was no absolute pitch standard in the Middle Ages (none, that is, with more than a strictly local influence, since the members of individual religious communities may have followed a note provided by a bell or by an organ, if they possessed one). The musical sources suggest a certain amount of movement in performing pitch, for while 'transposition' cannot exist without reference to a standard pitch, it may be significant that some motets survive in variant versions a 5th apart (although the question remains open as to whether there may be some purely notational reason for these shifts).[10]

Even allowing for this movement, however, it may be possible to define the pitch range most commonly employed for motets in the 13th century (at least when they were sung by men). Long ago Yvonne Rokseth drew attention to the number of literary sources from the 13th century in which singers are praised for the *haut* or *alta* quality of their voices, and concluded that the favoured pitch of 13th-century polyphony was 'as high as possible'.[11] Does this mean that motets should be performed by women or falsettists at the top of their range? Almost certainly not. Let us look again at Old French *haut* and its Latin parent *alta*. It is now well-known (although it was perhaps not altogether clear to Rokseth) that these two terms meant both 'high-pitched' and 'loud' during the Gothic period.[12] This high/loud ambiguity is convincingly demonstrated by a hitherto unnoticed text of *c*1340, a sermon by Armand de Belvezér containing a brief discussion of a figure of speech current among singers:

consuevit dici quando aliquis frater habens vocem sic altam sic pulchram quod eo cantante non est in ecclesia angulus quem non faciat resonare.[13]

when a brother has a voice so *alta* and so beautiful it is customary to say that when he sings there is not a corner of the church which he cannot make resound.

Here it seems that an *alta* voice is a loud one that sets every corner of a church echoing with sound, and yet in another passage from the same source the word *alta* clearly means 'high-pitched':

Est autem sciendum quod aliquis dicitur habere vocem altam qui pre aliis cantat altius .v. punctis . . .[14]

It should be noted that any man is said to have an *alta* voice who sings five notes higher than his fellows . . .

There is nothing surprising about the convergence of the two meanings 'high-pitched' and 'loud' upon a single word, for if a singer wanders high then he will be loud unless, in deference to contemporary taste or to musical context, he 'covers' the sound in order to become less conspicuous or to soften the contrast between the lower and the higher regions of his voice. Nor is there anything surprising about the praise which medieval writers lavish upon loud and high voices, for modern experience shows that audiences admire them still; hence the present popularity of sopranos and tenors as opposed to contraltos, baritones and basses. In the Middle Ages, as now, singers who could soar above the common run, and who could even rise above their professional colleagues, won lavish praise.

In the 13th century the standard for judging whether a man had an *alta* voice was probably set by choral plainchant, the music likely to have established a sense of what most male singers could achieve in terms of range, and therefore to have defined what was 'high'. The entire plainchant repertory lies, for the greater part, within the compass of about a 9th; for most men who can sing reasonably well (but who have not received a special training designed to increase their range upwards) its optimum position may be tentatively placed in the region of *C–d'*. As we have seen, Armand de Belvezér records that *alta* singers could sing a 5th above the common run, suggesting that the 'high' male singers of the 13th century were high tenors with a total compass of about *C–a'* but mostly working in the upper octave of this range. These 13 notes are sufficient for most of the Ars Antiqua motets that have been preserved.

Both the theorists and the musical sources confirm

that a ritardando was often employed in the penultimate measure of a motet. The theorists usually referred to this device as *organicus punctus*,[15] a term that likens it to the musical effect of two-part organum where, at least in the earlier 13th century, an upper voice executed an elaborate but (it may now be supposed) rhythmically free melody over the sustained and unmeasured notes of the tenor.[16] The musical

Ex.4 Conclusion of Pucelete bele/Je langui/Domino, from the Montpellier codex, f.193v. The penultimate note of the triplum, marked with a fermata in the transcription, is written as a longa in the manuscript and clearly indicates a ritardando. The penultimate bars of the motetus part are also 'stretched'. In performance the semiquavers in parallel 4ths at the start of the penultimate bar should obviously lock together, and therefore the time should be strict at this point. As so often in this repertory, it is best to begin the ritardando late, on the second beat of the penultimate perfection or possibly even further forward (as signalled for the top part by the original notation).

sources also reveal the ritardandi that performers used in the penultimate bars of motets, for there are many instances where the rules of mensural notation break down as the scribes introduced long note values where they do not belong. These can neither be performed nor transcribed strictly; they are clearly designed to indicate a ritardando (see ex.4).[17]

The theorists also mention the device of an internal ritardando, however, and these pauses can be of considerable help in shaping a piece. They are described in the later layer (?1270s) of the anonymous treatise known since Coussemaker as the *Discantus positio vulgaris*; the author discusses the ways in which the modal patterns of motetus parts accord with the modal patterns of tenors thus:

Et primo de primo modo. Cujus quidem tenor aliquando concordat cum motheto in notis, sicut hic: Virgo decus castitatis [ex.5], et tunc semper nota longa de motheto notae longae correspondet de tenore et brevis brevi et e converso. Pausa vero utriusque valet unam brevem, nisi simul pauset uterque cum tripla, et tunc pausae cantus ecclesiastici tenentur ad placitum.[18]

Firstly, concerning mode 1. The tenor can concord somewhat with the motetus in notes, as in *Virgo decus castitatis*, and then a long note in the motetus will correspond to a long note of the tenor, and a breve to a breve, and vice versa. The pause of each [the motetus and the tenor] is worth one breve unless both of them pause with the triplum, and then let plainchant pauses be held for as long as may be pleasing.

The writer is referring to pieces with passages in which both the tenor and the motetus lock together in mode 1 rhythms, producing extended passages of note-against-note writing (see ex.5). He then says, quite correctly,

Ex.5 Res nova mirabilis/Virgo decus castitatis/Alleluya, from Anderson, op cit, no.95 (triplum omitted)

that when such parts rest the pause will be worth one breve (a quaver after the customary reduction of note values in the earlier motet repertory by a factor of 16): $\quad \downarrow \quad \flat \mid \downarrow \quad \flat \mid \downarrow \quad \flat \mid \downarrow \quad \gamma$

However, he goes on to say that when there is a third part,[19] then the places where all three parts—tenor, motetus and triplum—phrase together are to be marked not by a measured pause of a breve, but by an unmeasured pause *ad placitum* such as would be employed in plainchant (*cantus ecclesiasticus*).

How were these internal pauses executed? The anonymous *Compendium musicae mensurabilis artis antiquae* (c1300) offers the advice that when the three parts of a motet phrase together, the penultimate notes before the general pause should be unmeasured:

quando [inveniuntur] tres cantus insimul concordantes, facientes insimul suas pausas, tunc debent in tenore et in moteto et in triplo fieri duo tractus ad significandum quod penultime note inmensurabiles fieri debent . . .[20]

when three parts [are found] concording with one another and making their pauses together, then two strokes should be made in the tenor, motetus and triplum to signify that the penultimate notes are to be sung in an unmeasured way . . .

155

The writer even gives an extract from a double motet showing how this notational device should be employed. Unfortunately it is incomplete, as is the only independent source of the piece, which lacks the tenor part.[21] By collating the two sources, however, it is possible to arrive at a plausible reconstruction of what was intended (ex.6).

Ex.6 Quomodo fiet/O stupor/**tenor, reconstructed from** Compendium musicae mensurabilis artis antiquae (c1300) **and D-Mbs lat.5539, ff.76v–78r.**

In practice, this device of an internal pause will often make good musical sense. A constant overlap of musical and poetic phrases is the essence of motet style, so when all the parts phrase together something is clearly called for in performance. These concerted pauses form an admirable check against the tendency of the brisker motets to rollick and become relentless.

Ex.3 shows how composers sometimes took these internal pauses for granted and disposed the musical material around them in a strategic fashion. In bar 7, for example, the general pause coincides with the end of an unusual sequential figure in the duplum. The triplum also changes character at this point; after the crowded movement of the first six bars it thins to a series of longs, which by bar 10 have developed into the smooth trochaic figures that form the bulk of the triplum material throughout the piece. The general pause in bar 37 has comparable significance; in bar 34 the composer signals that something is approaching by changing the rhythmic mode in the upper voices from mode 1 to mode 3; after the general pause in bar 37 the triplum immediately returns to mode 1 while the

duplum retains mode 3 until bar 48, creating a new counterplay of rhythms. It is almost always worthwhile to register these changes of mode in performance; they will stand a good deal of emphasis. Modes 2 and 3, when they make *brief* appearances like these, and especially when they are momentarily set against mode 1, may sometimes be emphasized by detaching the quavers in a forceful way, though this would be impractical for pieces cast entirely in these two modes.

Perhaps the most perplexing performance problem of all concerns what is to be done with the wordless tenor parts. Here the answer must vary according to the texture of the motet. In general, the individual tenor notes in an Ars Antiqua motet behave like momentary pedal points. In a passage like the one shown in ex.7, the first sonority of each perfection is invariably a perfect consonance with the tenor forming the root. Next, the upper parts move towards the consonance that will open the next perfection, but the tenor remains stranded at the point where it began. This feeling of a perfect consonance which sounds and then dissolves during the course of the bar is highly characteristic of the Ars Antiqua motet; it accounts for the momentary pedal-like effect of almost every perfection in our example. In pieces where the tenor moves in this way it will usually be wise to choose a sustained sound for the tenor part. In most cases the ideal solution will be to vocalize the tenor, perhaps using as a cue any syllable (or syllables) of plainchant text that may accompany it.[22] This style

Ex.7 Par une matinee/Mellis stilla/Domino, **bars 1–10, from Thomas, Robin and Marion motets, i**

of performance has hardly ever been adopted by early music ensembles so far, but it should never be forgotten that the motet emerged from a tradition of liturgical and therefore of exclusively vocal polyphony;[23] the one thing that is certain about these motet tenors is that 13th-century musicians would have considered them idiomatic for singing.

Mark Everist has recently drawn attention to an intriguing piece of evidence that bears upon this problem.[24] In the manuscript *GB-Lbm* Cotton Vespasian A.XVIII the motet *Amor veint tout/Au tens d'esté/Et gaudebit* appears with the chant text *Et gaudebit* stretched under the tenor part. There is nothing striking about that, of course, for motet tenors were often written down in this way. Here, however, it seems that the scribe had some definite plan in mind, for the tenor melody appears twice, with the syllable *gau-* placed exactly at the point where the repetition begins, while *-bit* is placed at the end (see ex.8). None of these details corresponds to the original Gregorian underlay, so it may be that the scribe intended the performer to change his syllable at a point that would emphasize the structure of the piece, introducing a change of vowel colour at the crucial moment. Might this have been a common practice? Experiment shows that if vocalization is used to supply the lack of a chant cue then the crucial factor in success or failure is usually the vowel that has been chosen. The vowel *o* (as in southern English 'pot') can become somewhat ominous in a resonant acoustic, seeming very dark and very large, while *i* (as in southern English 'feet') can produce a much brighter and (paradoxical though this may seem) less intrusive colour; being a high front vowel it lends itself very well to precise, meticulous articulation. It is ideal for ex.3.

A major performance problem is created by the brevity (sometimes extreme) of these motets. The obvious solution is to perform three-part pieces once through as a duplum/tenor duet and then again with the triplum. This is not entirely satisfactory, however, for in some cases it cannot be done without turning the performance into two distinct renditions, each with its own tempo and movement, because there are many duplum parts in the motet repertory which must be sung with more pace when they are to be exposed than when they participate in a three-voice texture.[25] Furthermore there are many two-part motets (which cannot be treated in this 'layered' fashion) that are irredeemably short, and in performance it is probably best to accept that these pieces were as brief as they

Ex.8 The tenor of Amor veint tout/Au tens d'esté/Et gaudebit as it appears in GB-Lbm Cotton Vespasian A. XVIII, f.164v–165r, from Everist, op cit.

look on the page. Another worry is that the passage often cited as evidence of such 'layered' performance, from the *Speculum Musicae* of Jacques de Liège, proves to be referring to something quite different—the practice of performing a motet voice entirely alone, as a free-standing song.[26] Perhaps this provides the best guide. A plausible solution may be that the duplum and triplum were sometimes performed as solo songs without the tenor, each with its own pace and character, and that the performers then joined forces to create the motet, each adjusting the pace of his line as seemed necessary.

What were the customary performing forces? The evidence that can be brought to bear upon this question is unfortunately very slim indeed. It seems to be universally agreed that most medieval polyphony was intended for soloists, although specific information

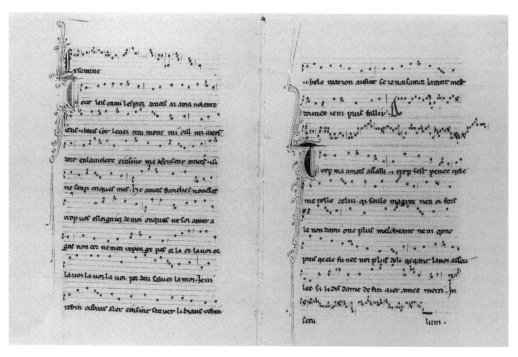

3 **The two-part motets** Tout leis enmi les prez/Do [minus] **and** Trop m'a amors asalli/In seculum. **The first begins with a quotation (both verbal and musical) from the dance-song, or** rondet de carole, **shown in the text as ex.1.** W₂, f.247v and 248.

about the Ars Antiqua motet is lacking.[27] Instrumental participation (in addition, that is, to instrumental performance of the textless tenor parts) is a possibility, but there is no firm evidence for this practice and no obvious reason why it should be recommended.[28]

The more subjective areas of performance practice where modern singers have only their own musical instincts to guide them may now be considered. To a large extent, I believe, the things that may profitably be asked of singers performing Ars Antiqua motets are much the same as those required in any accurate ensemble singing.

Something is often to be gained by pitching these motets in a way that lifts the singers on the upper parts away from the comfortable range where they can coast or croon. When the music is lifted above this range the relatively higher pitch brings many things under closer control because the vocal cords are vibrating more quickly and because the singers, recognizing that danger is only about a tone away, begin to work hard in a fashion that is always beneficial to this music (and perhaps to any music; modern critics generally seem to

admire performers who introduce an element of risk into their performances). Few motets last more than two minutes, even at the most lugubrious speeds, and they therefore ask both singers and listeners to make a concentrated effort. If they are sung in a forthright manner (that is to say with a good supply of wind and a great deal of busy vowel and consonant formation towards the front of the mouth) then it becomes possible to approach the crispness of diction, fullness of tone and scrupulous intonation that these pieces surely demand. It seems probable that the 'high' and 'loud' singers of the 13th century were praised for their ability to perform in this way.

In music as densely texted as this, and so dependent for its success upon a burst of energy, the manner of articulation is of cardinal importance. The motet emerged as a form when words were added to pre-existing sections of melismatic polyphony,[29] and it succeeds very well in performance when the two elements in this history—melisma and text—are allowed to co-exist. This can be achieved by singing the lines in a legato fashion and by allowing the words to look after the articulation. Many singers will instinctively attempt to 'enliven' chains of mode 1 rhythms, for example, by imposing a kind of automatic articulation, 'coming away' during the course of the longer notes and almost turning

into

which soon tires the ear. It will usually make good musical sense to maintain full tone and volume through the course of every long note value in a 13th-century motet; if the words are clearly pronounced then they will establish an appropriate manner of articulation.

A correct historical pronunciation of every text is therefore a great asset in the performance of this music.[30] Old French possessed many consonants that have softened a little down the centuries, or that have faded away altogether, and these crisp sounds help to project the principal features of medieval motet style in performance. Most notable amongst these are a texture in which two (or three) assertive and clearly articulated songs seem to compete for mastery, and a crowded sound picture in which the piece appears to be on the point of bursting the taut intellectual constraints that bind it together.

The importance of historical pronunciation to the shaping of phrases is considerable. In a line like the following, for example,

En   a - mours

the listener should hear not only the final *s* of *amours* but also the rolled *r* immediately before it; both sounds must be rapidly produced at almost the last possible moment. In this way the word *amours* points the end of the melodic phrase in a most decisive manner. When lines ending in consonants follow one another in rapid succession (as when lines rhyme on -*er* verbs), the effect on melodic phrasing can be very marked indeed.

Two further points can contribute substantially to a successful performance of these pieces. The first relates to the shape of each note. When singing Ars Antiqua motets (and, perhaps, any medieval music) it is important that each note should start firmly with as much—or nearly as much—tone as it is ever to possess. A firm beginning counts for a great deal, and notes which are blown up like a balloon during their duration seem out of place in this repertory.

The second point concerns tuning. It is plain that singers of the 13th-century attached great importance

to accuracy in this respect. The music treatises of the period devote considerable space to the mathematical basis of intervals, confirming the impression that medieval singers regarded polyphony as an advanced method of producing musical beauty by means of meticulous measurement. It is necessary only to glance at Ars Antiqua motets, with their abundance of perfect intervals, to realize that high standards must have been aimed for. Unless the intervals of octave, 4th and 5th are placed with precision (and with far more than is required to place 3rds and 6ths, whether major or minor) a 13th-century motet will tend to sound feeble and needlessly dissonant. The supreme goal is therefore accuracy, together with the strong, straight tone without vibrato that allows the ear to savour the purity of the perfect intervals and to detect the distinctive buzz that they possess when true.

What of the imperfect intervals, the 3rds and 6ths? Here it is almost always profitable (at least in French pieces—English music of this period is altogether different) to steer towards the Pythagorean tuning whose principles are expounded time and again in medieval treatises on music. The technical details of this tuning can be found in many places;[31] the immediate practical consequences for the modern performer are straightforward and easily summarized. All perfect intervals are pure. All notes with a semitone step above them need to be raised (in other words E, A and B natural should, in most circumstances, be noticeably high). Major 3rds and 6ths should be appreciably wider than in equal temperament, giving a sense of strain to cadences where a major 6th widens to an octave or a major 3rd moves outwards to a 5th. Finally, all tone steps may be allowed to expand a little; it is never required in the Ars Antiqua motet that a tone step be narrowed.

This brings us to what is perhaps one of the most delicate questions about the performance of these pieces: the question of tempo. Some 14th-century theorists distinguish between 'fast', 'medium' and 'slow' manners of execution,[32] but this is of no more practical help to the modern singer of medieval music than the doctrine of 'high', 'middle' and 'low' styles in rhetoric is a help to readers of Chaucer's poetry. Indeed the comments of the theorists, most of whom are discussing 14th-century notational practices when they broach this subject, reduce to little more than a codification of what would be expected, namely that the fewer note values a piece contains, the faster it goes. Crudely speaking, this means that a piece made

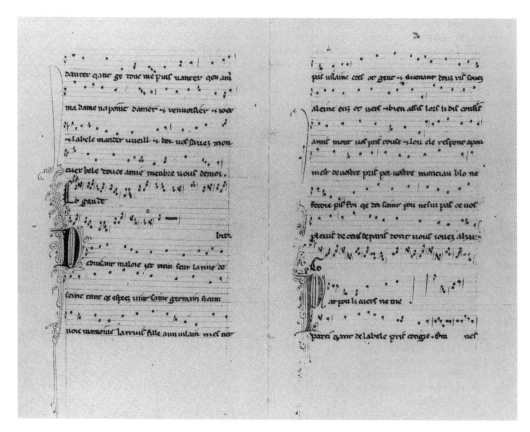

4 The two-part motet Deduisant m'aloie/Go. This is an ingenious adaptation of the genre of the pastourelle (where a man, often a knight, meets a shepherdess or comes upon rustics as they sing or indulge in other country pleasures). Here the encounter takes place outside the walls of Paris in the suburb of St. Germain (prez . . . saint germain in the second line of the motet). W₂, f.251v and 252.

up exclusively (in modern transcription) of crotchets and quavers can go appreciably faster than one where the quavers are frequently (or even occasionally) broken into pairs of semiquavers.

Where the theorists fail, modern performers must use their own musical judgement. The principal objective is to overcome the consequences of the triple time which dominates Ars Antiqua polyphony. To some extent, perhaps, this is not an historical problem, for it may be imagined that 13th-century performers were not troubled by the relentless ternaries of the motet; when did they ever sing as many motets in sequence as today's musicians are required to do in one concert? Whatever the answer may be, the art of handling rhythm in 13th-century motets is a subtle one that must be acquired. I do not believe that the

problem is one of speed. No doubt many modern singers are liable to sing these pieces too fast— especially when they have learned their parts well and have become confident—and it will be wise to correct this tendency as soon as it makes itself apparent. Nonetheless, the speed of music has no necessary connection with its iterative qualities in performance; a fast piece in triple time need not be more emphatically 'in three' than a slow waltz where each beat is felt individually.

I prefer to suggest that the triple-time problem in 13th-century polyphony is essentially one of stability. The prime danger in this music is that modern singers, confronted by a motet transcribed with the customary bar lines, will start to compress the second beat of the bar and then lunge—very slightly, but nonetheless fatally—towards the beginning of the next bar. It becomes especially serious with the use of the very common rhythmic figure

which seems ideally designed to cause trouble. Many singers will tend to 'come away' from the crotchet a little (probably around the start of the second beat); they will then come back and hammer the notes of the triplet figure in the hope of making them distinct. In doing so they will rush on to the next crotchet. If this occurs, the advice should always be to begin the long note with as much tone and conviction as it is ever to possess, to keep this tone and conviction absolutely steady throughout the note, and then to toss the triplets away as lightly as possible—to treat them as ornaments, in other words, which they are, rather than as tune, which they are not. The secret of success is rhythmic accuracy of a scrupulous kind. It must also be remembered that in this, as in all medieval music, perfect consonances accent themselves; there is no need to accent the start of a bar.

Two further considerations prove useful in shaping a performance. The first relates to the balance of the voices. As suggested above, medieval motet style exploits the excitement that can be created when the listener feels that the two or three upper parts are strenuously competing for attention. The triplum is generally rather more active than the duplum in the Ars Antiqua repertory (see ex.9), but this does not mean that in a double motet, for example, the busier part should be the more assertive one in performance. In ex.9 the singer of the duplum will do well to sing as if the triplum were not there; in practical terms this means giving long notes (minims in this example) full tone and commitment throughout their written value, without 'coming away'.

A second consideration relates to harmonic colouring. The composers of Ars Antiqua motets were remarkably strict in their adherence to the theorists' rule that every perfection should begin with a perfect consonance. Accordingly, it will often make musical sense to emphasize the places where this rule is broken. Ex.10 shows an extract from a double motet where the appearance of a *refrain* (a pre-existing piece of text and/or music)[33] in the triplum, coinciding with one complete statement of the tenor, is introduced by an uncharacteristic 6–5 movement at the beginning of bar 17 (uncharacteristic, that is, for the start of a

Ex.9 **Conclusion of** Par une matinee/Mellis stilla/Domino, **from** Thomas, Robin and Marion motets, i

Ex.10 **Extract from** Je m'en vois/Tels a mout/Omnes, **from Anderson,** op cit, **no.90**

perfection). There are also two stark (but in performance surprisingly gracious) dissonances at the opening of the second perfection in bar 19 and of the first perfection in bar 20.

Whatever tempo is chosen, the basic pulse should be absolutely strict. Medieval singers regarded polyphony as an art of accurate measurement and the terms which they associated with musical excellence include *recta* (correct), *integralis* (whole), and (perhaps most frequently of all) *regularis* (disciplined).[34] One theorist of the mid-14th century, for example, records that the tenor parts of motets are best performed 'in a whole and secure fashion'.[35]

Ornamentation was probably a major factor governing the choice of tempo. 'Let anyone who wishes to indulge in practical music beware that he does not exult too much in his voice', warns Johannes de Muris,[36] though there can be no doubt that his words often went unheeded by singers determined to show off their skill. References to liturgical singing in the writings of outraged churchmen suggest that polyphony was performed with Romanesque exuberance and Gothic flamboyance in the 12th and 13th centuries; even when allowances have been made for the exaggerated language of these moralists, the impression remains that polyphony, whether sacred or secular, was declaimed by singers determined to enjoy the experience and to make an impression. According to the late 13th-century writer Elias of Salomon, the task of keeping control over their exuberance fell to the *rector*,[37] who was required to correct any colleague who ornamented his part excessively by whispering a reproach into his ear. Elias is discussing improvized polyphony, but even motets, which look so busy with their chafing texts, were sometimes ornamented. An anonymous (possibly English) theorist of the 14th century makes this clear:

Sciendum secundum curiam romanam et francigenos et omnes musicales cantores quod tenor, qui discantum tenet, integre et solide pronunciari debet in mensura, ne supra discantantes dissonantiam incurrant; et hoc ratio exigit nam super instabile fundamentum stabile edificium construi non potest, sic nec instabilem tenorem vix sine dissonantia discantus pronunciari potest. In motetis quippe et rundallis ac etiam in aliis cantilenis tenor prout figuratur pronunciari debet, tamen non est contradicendum tenorem pronuncianti, et pulcras ascenciones et descenciones facienti, quando sentit se discantu non impedire, sed pocius comendandum.[38]

It should be known that according to the singers of the Roman curia, according to the French and according to all musical singers, the tenor, which holds the polyphony together, must be performed in a whole and secure fashion in strict measure, lest those who are singing the upper parts fall into discord. And this principle imposes itself in many things, for just as a stable building cannot be constructed upon a shaky foundation, neither can polyphony be sung over a shaky tenor without discord. Certainly, in motets, rondelli and also in other kinds of music the tenor must be sung just as it is written; however there should be no reproach for the singer of the tenor who makes beautiful

ascents and descents when he senses that he is not becoming entangled in the polyphony; he should rather be congratulated.

Here it seems that the performer of the tenor may be allowed to make 'beautiful ascents and descents' if he can do it well enough not to become entangled in the upper parts and produce cacophony. If this was acceptable in the performance of a tenor, the *fundamentum totius cantus*, it is likely that singers of duplum, triplum and quadruplum voices would also have been free to decorate their lines. The melodic variants found in the motet repertory, readily available for study in several collected editions, may give some clue to the character of this ornamentation (see ex.11).

Ex.11 Au cuer ai un mal/Ja ne m'en departirai/Jolietement, **duplum. Upper stave from Bamberg MS (Anderson, op cit, no.53, lower stave from GB-Ob Douce 139, f.179v (as ed. M. Everist, Five Anglo-Norman Motets (1986), p.10). To facilitate comparison I have halved the note-values of Anderson's edition.**

The Ars Antiqua motet seems to come into its own when it has one singer on each part—a singer with a strong, straight tone who is able to go directly to the centre of the note and who, in return for complete freedom from instrumental doubling, can tune intervals in a tactical way, now wide, now narrow, according to the demands of the texture. The beauty of this music—and perhaps of all medieval music—surely lies in the opportunity it gives us to savour clear and fresh sounds being combined with perfect accuracy, and without any thickening from vibrato or any other source that might overscore the lines that make up this delightful geometry.

I am most grateful to David Fallows, Daniel Leech-Wilkinson, Mark Everist, Jeremy Summerly and Shane Fletcher for their comments upon an earlier draft of this article.

Christopher Page is senior research fellow in music at Sidney Sussex College, Cambridge, and director of the ensemble Gothic Voices.

[1]*F-T* MS 144, vol.1, f.305*r*. Pierre de Palude, *In psalmos*.
The bulk of the 13th-century motet repertory is available in the following editions: H. Tischler, *The earliest motets: a complete comparative edition*, 3 vols, (Yale Univ. Press, 1982); *idem*, *The Montpellier codex*, 4 vols, (Madison, 1978 and 1985); G. Anderson, *Compositions of the Bamberg manuscript*, Corpus mensurabilis musicae [CMM], lxxv (1977); *idem*, *The motets of the manuscript La Clayette*, CMM, lxviii (1975); *idem*, *The Las Huelgas manuscript*, CMM, lxxix (1982). The motets of the Montpellier codex, the major 13th-century collection, are also available in Y. Rokseth, *Polyphonies du XIIIᵉ siècle*, 4 vols, (Paris, 1935–48). A recent performing edition that may be highly recommended to male singers (for all the pieces either lie in—or have been transposed to fit—the range of tenors and baritones) is W. Thomas, *Robin and Marion motets*, 2 vols, Antico edn, AE 22 and 25 (1985 and 1987). A third volume is in preparation.
On the performance of motets, see E. H. Roesner's introductions to two reprints of L. Schrade, *Polyphonic Music of the Fourteenth Century: Le Roman de Fauvel* (Monaco, 1956/R1984), v–vii; and *The Works of Philippe de Vitry* (Monaco, 1956/R1984), v–vi; H. Tischler, *The style and evolution of the earliest motets (to c1270)*, Musicological Studies and Documents, xl (Henryville, 1985), i, p.207ff; *idem*, *op cit*, *The Montpellier codex*, i, pp.xxxii–xxxiii; Rokseth, *op cit*, *Polyphonies*, iv, p.41f; Thomas, *op cit*, *Robin and Marion motets* (introductory sections to both volumes); P. Jeffery, 'A Four-Part *In Seculum* Hocket and a Mensural Sequence in an Unknown Fragment', *JAMS*, xxxvii (1984), pp.1–48; and C. Page, 'The performance of medieval polyphony', in H. M. Brown and S. Sadie, eds, *Handbook of Performance Practice* (in the press).

[2]Text in E. Rohloff, ed., *Die Quellenhandschriften zum Musiktraktat des Johannes de Grocheio* (Leipzig, 1972); for comments on the motet, see p.144. Eng. trans. (to be employed with considerable caution) by A. Seay, *Johannes de Grocheo [sic] Concerning Music* (Colorado Springs, 2/1973), esp. p.26

[3]For this identification of those whom Johannes de Grocheio means by the litterati (to which he adds 'illis, qui subtilitates artium sunt quaerentes' (those who are investigating the finer points of the arts)) see, for example, the sermon which the 13th-century Dominican, Humbert of Romans, writing in Paris, addressed *Ad omnes litteratos* in *Sermones Beati Umberti Burgundi* (Venice, 1603), 2 vols, sermon lvi: 'ut patet in Medicis, et Advocatis, et Magistris in liberalibus artibus, et in similibus'.

[4]See M. Gerbert, *Scriptores* (St Blasien, 1784/R1963), iii, p.57ff, and also J. Dyer, 'A thirteenth-century choirmaster: the *Scientia Artis Musicae* of Elias Salomon', *MQ*, lxvi (1980), pp.83–111.

[5]It is possible that the upper level of such organum was sometimes performed by boys in the 13th century; in the absence of any explicit testimony, however, it is probably safest to assume that the singers envisaged by Elias were adult males.

[6]Compare, for example, the practice of 'fifthing', a technique for singing in parallel 5ths with contrary motion at the beginnings and ends of phrases; this was regarded as a preparatory stage in the training of a true *discantor*. See S. Fuller, 'Discant and the theory of fifthing', *Acta Musicologica*, l (1978), pp.241–75.

[7]For examples with a total compass of eleven notes, see Anderson, *op cit*, CMM, lxxv, nos 3, 8, 9, 11, 18, 22, 23, 28, 36, etc. Ranges of a 10th (nos 4, 7, 12, 13, etc) and a 12th (nos 2, 10, 16, 17, 24, 26, 27, etc) are also fairly common. The compass of a 14th in no.48 is unusual. The average total compass of the motets in the Bamberg anthology is 11.5 notes. For a discussion of the ranges in the Montpellier motets, see Tischler, *op cit*, *Montpellier codex*, i, p.xxxiii.

[8]For some eleven-note voice-parts, see Bamberg nos 16 (both triplum and duplum), 18 (triplum, where the total compass of the piece is an 11th), 22 (duplum, again where the whole piece spans but an 11th), 30 (duplum), 38 (duplum), 47 (duplum), etc.

[9]See, for example, Tischler, *op cit*, *Montpellier codex*, i, p.xxxii, where reference is made to the 'distinct rhythm, phrasing, text, and timbre of the several lines of music' in motets. See also G. Reaney, 'Voices and Instruments in the Music of Guillaume de Machaut', *Revue Belge de Musicologie*, x (1956), pp.3–17 and pp.93–104. I have already questioned this view in 'The performance of songs in late medieval France: a new source', *EM*, x/4 (Oct. 1982), pp.441–50. Cf D. Leech-Wilkinson, 'Machaut's *Rose, lis* and the problems of early music analysis', *Music Analysis*, iii/1 (1984), pp.25–6, fn.13.

[10]The notational explanation may perhaps be that scribes wished to avoid certain accidentals wherever possible. A piece requiring F♯ in the triplum, for example, and possessing no other accidental, would become free of all such markings if written out 'in C'.

[11]Rokseth, *op cit*, *Polyphonies*, iv, pp.46–8

[12]The point is well made in E. Bowles, 'Haut and Bas: the Grouping of Musical Instruments in the Middle Ages', *Musica Disciplina*, viii (1954), pp.115–40.

[13]*F. Armandi de Bellovisu . . . Sermones plane divini assumptis ex solo Psalterio Davidico Thematis*, (Lyons, 1525), f.75*v*

[14]*Ibid*, f.156. The passage continues: 'sed altiorem si .x. altissimam autem si .xv. hoc enim nunquam visum fuit'. Thus a singer was said to have a 'higher' voice if he could sing ten notes above the common run, and 'highest' if he could sing fifteen, 'but this is unheard of'. Whether this represents genuine usage, or merely Armandus's determination to pursue the issue of 'high' voices through the comparative and superlative stages of the adjective *alta*, is difficult to determine. As far as 'highest' voices are concerned, Armandus is clearly propelled by passion for neatness at this point since he acknowledges, in effect, that the term can never be used, for such voices are 'unheard of'.

[15]Anonymous 1 in C.-E.-H. de Coussemaker, *Scriptorum de musica*, iii, p.362. The device of the final ritardando was probably carried over from plainchant; for the technique of drawing out a chant 'slightly near the end', see C. Palisca, *Hucbald, Guido and John on Music* (New Haven, 1979), p.139

[16]This is still a matter of controversy; for recent literature see Page, *op cit*, 'The performance of medieval polyphony'.

[17]Needless to say, these ritardandi must be carefully controlled, and should hardly ever begin earlier than the second beat of the penultimate bar.

[18]S. M. Cserba, ed., *Hieronymus de Moravia O. P. Tractatus de Musica*, (Regensburg, 1935), p.193

[19]His term is *tripla* ('cum tripla'), where *triplo* would have been the expected form. It is possible that the author, having seen the neuter plural *tripla* in other writings, construed the form as a feminine nominative singular. I am otherwise unable to explain *cum tripla*, but have no doubt that a third part is meant.

[20]F. A. Gallo, ed., *Compendium musicae mensurabilis artis antiquae*, Corpus Scriptorum de Musica [CSM], xv (1971), p.71. As Gallo points out, (p.65), the 'content of the work refers to the moment of transition from the Franconian teaching to the notation of the fourteenth century'.

[21]*D-Mbs* 5539. See G. Reaney, *Manuscripts of Polyphonic Music (cl320–1400)* (München-Duisburg, 1969), p.78

[22]This question is discussed in Jeffery, *op cit*.

[23]The unconvincing arguments that have been advanced in favour of instrumental participation in the Notre Dame clausula repertory have been finally exploded by E. Roesner, 'The performance of Parisian organum', *EM*, vii/2 (Apr.1979), pp.174–189.

[24]M. Everist, ed., *Five Anglo-Norman Motets* (Antico Edition, 1986), AE 24

[25]An example is provided by the motet *Quant vient/Ne sai que/Amoris [Johannes]*, in both the Bamberg and Montpellier manuscripts. The most recent edition is in Thomas, *op cit*, *Robin and Marion motets*, i, pp.13–15. The duplum and tenor survive as a two-part work in some sources (the *Roman de Fauvel*, for example, where the duplum bears the text *Veritas arpie*), and the duplum, which has only two note values, seems to demand a brisk tempo if it is to be exposed in a layered performance of perhaps dotted minim = 100. The duplum, a much more active line, requires a tempo in the region of

dotted minim = 48. In order to make the motet work in performance as a three-part composition it is necessary to take the tempo from the triplum, and for the duplum singer to perform his line in a way that will feel very slow to him.

[26]Rokseth, *op cit*, *Polyphonies*, iv, p.221. See also R. Bragard, ed., *Jacobi Leodiensis Speculum Musicae*, CSM, iii/7, (1955–73) p.9.

[27]For a more detailed account of instrumental practice in Ars Antiqua music, see Page, *op cit*, 'The performance of medieval polyphony'. It has been suggested (for example, by Tischler, *op cit*, *The Montpellier Codex*, i, p.xxxiv), that the instruments sometimes named in motets are a guide to the instrumentation of these pieces. The striking feature of Tischler's comprehensive listing of references in the Montpellier corpus is that the most popular instruments of 13th-century culture, the harp and fiddle, are missing. The case of the motet *In seculum viellatoris* remains as puzzling as ever. .

[28]The often-cited passage from the *Roman de la Rose* in which Pygmalion plays the portative organ and sings *Motet ou treble ou teneüre*, probably refers to the performance of motet voices as isolated monophonic songs. For the text, see E. Langlois, ed., *Le Roman de la Rose* (Paris, 1914–24), line 21041. On the portative organ, see Page, *op cit*, 'The performance of medieval polyphony'. See also L. Gushee, 'Two Central Places: Paris and the French Court in the Early Fourteenth Century', in H. Kühn and P. Nitsche, eds, *Bericht über den Internationalen Musikwissenschaftlichen Kongress Berlin 1974* (Kassel etc, 1980), p.143.

[29]The earliest motets and their source clausulae can now be examined in bulk in the complete and comparative edition by Tischler, *op cit*, *The earliest motets*.

[30]The standard guide is J. Alton and B. Jeffery, *Bele Buche e Bele Parleure: a guide to the pronunciation of medieval and renaissance French*

for singers and others (London, 1976). The usefulness of this volume is immeasurably increased by the accompanying cassette.

[31]For a clear exposition of the Pythagorean system and its mathematics see J. Backhus, *The Acoustical Foundations of Music*, (London, 1970), p.116f. See also Page, *op cit*, 'The performance of medieval polyphony'. The subject of tuning in medieval music has principally been investigated in terms of keyboard temperaments, with a marked emphasis upon the 15th century; see, for example, M. Lindley, 'Fifteenth-century evidence for meantone temperament', *PRMA*, cii, (1975–6), pp.37–51, and *idem*, 'Pythagorean Intonation and the Rise of the Triad', *RMA Research Chronicle*, xvi (1980), pp.4–61.

[32]Roesner, *op cit*, pp.vi–vii.

[33]The standard guide to the *refrain* material is still N. Van den Boogaard, *Rondeaux et refrains du XIIe siècle au début du XIVe* (Paris, 1969).

[34]See, for example, the *Ars discantus secundum Johannem de Muris* in Coussemaker, *op cit*, *Scriptores*, iii, p.110.

[35]*Ibid*, p.362

[36]*Ibid*, p.60

[37]Dyer, *op cit*

[38]As the manuscript *GB-Lbm* Cotton Tiberius B.IX was severely damaged in the fire of 1731, I have followed the early 18th-century copy (*GB-Lbm* Add. MS 4909, f.54r), checking this, where possible, against the original (f.213v). There seems no reason to believe that the 18th-century transcript is unreliable. Indeed it is more reliable than the text which Coussemaker printed in his *Scriptores*, iii. The same material also appears in the *Quatuor principalia musica* (*op cit*, iv, p.295).

A Treatise on Musicians from ?c.1400: The *Tractatulus de differentiis et gradibus cantorum* by Arnulf de St Ghislain

THE historian John Keegan was one of the first to ask the simple yet searching question: what actually happens in combat? It is well known that English footsoldiers received a charge by French knights at the battle of Agincourt in 1415, but what took place when men and horses collided? Keegan gives his answers in *The Face of Battle*,[1] and it may be time for musicologists to modulate the sonorous questions that he poses there for their own purposes. What actually happened, for example, when a motet by Johannes Ciconia was performed in northern Italy *c*.1400? When friends and associates gathered together to hear such music, what was the nature of their various musical aptitudes and interests? Did women participate in the performances? What was the role of instrumentalists? Some of these questions, no doubt, will never find an answer; there are no medieval chronicles devoted to musical gatherings as there are chronicles – and many other writings – devoted to battles like Agincourt. None the less, literary and iconographical sources are among those which may still have something to reveal about 'the face of performance' (to coin a phrase after Keegan's own), and the purpose of this article is to examine the contents of one that has been unjustly neglected: the *Tractatulus de differentiis et gradibus cantorum* by Arnulf de St Ghislain. This brief treatise classifies the kinds of musicians who performed or admired polyphonic music and is therefore quite exceptional among the works loosely classified as medieval music theory.

Little is known for certain about the author.[2] He presumably came from St Ghislain, a town in Hainaut which had grown from a small

I am most grateful to Dr David Fallows, who first drew the treatise by Arnulf de St Ghislain to my attention and who read an earlier version of this article, to Roy Gibson and to Dr Daniel Leech-Wilkinson. I owe a special debt of gratitude to Prof. Bonnie J. Blackburn and to Leofranc Holford-Strevens for many helpful comments and corrections.

[1] John Keegan, *The Face of Battle* (London, 1976).

[2] There are almost no bibliographical or biographical sources pertaining to Arnulf de St Ghislain. Those that do exist (such as the *Biographie nationale de Belgique*, i (Brussels, 1866), s.v. 'Arnulphe de Saint-Ghislain') are manifestly based on Gerbert's text alone. Among the most reliable of the materials deriving from Gerbert's text is the discussion, with translation, of one section of the *Tractatulus* in Hugo Riemann, *Geschichte der Musiktheorie*, trans. Raymond H. Haggh (Lincoln, Nebraska, 1962), 184. The entry 'Arnulph of St Gilles' in *The New Grove Dictionary of Music and Musicians* (London, 1980) leaves something to be desired, as does the entry 'Arnulf von S. Gillen' in *Die Musik in Geschichte und Gegenwart* (Kassel, 1939–51; hereafter *MGG*). See below, note 5.

Reprinted from *Journal of the Royal Music Association* 115 (1992), pp. 1–21. By permission of Oxford University Press.

village in the tenth century to become a place of some consequence in the fourteenth.[3] Ciconia, Binchois and Dufay (to name only some major composers) were born within a few days' ride of Arnulf's native town. It is possible that Arnulf was a monk at the Benedictine abbey of St Ghislain, but this has not been confirmed and his name was so common that the discovery of a monk bearing such a name in any abbey records would not be decisive.[4] Nor would anything be definitively established by the discovery of an Arnulphus de Sancto Gilleno in the registers of some other ecclesiastical institution or university – always assuming that the title 'magister' which is given to Arnulf in the unique manuscript of his treatise indicates that he held a university degree. That manuscript, now to be found in the Archiv des Benediktinerstiftes in St Paul im Lavanttal, appears to have been copied in the early fifteenth century and the *Tractatulus* must therefore date from before that time.[5] A possible pun on the Latin word *prolatio*[6] and the importance which Arnulf attaches to the expert musicians' skill with *musica ficta* (of which more below) are consistent with the suggestion that it was composed during the fourteenth century.

A newly edited text of the *Tractatulus de differentiis et gradibus cantorum* is given in the Appendix to this article, together with an annotated English translation. For the purposes of the following discussion it will be helpful to paraphrase the major points of the treatise.

---

[3] See Daniel van Overstraeten, 'Du hameau à la ville: Saint-Ghislain du Xe au XIVe siècle', *Autour de la ville en Hainaut: Mélanges d'archéologie et d'histoire offerts à Jean Dughoille et à René Sansen* (Ath, 1986), 175–83.

[4] The case is complicated by the tendency for the names Arnulf and Arnoul (the former being etymologically distinct from the latter) to be confounded in the fourteenth and fifteenth centuries. See, for example, *Table chronologique des chartes et diplômes imprimés concernant l'histoire de la Belgique*, ed. Alphonse Wauters, i (Brussels, 1866), 523. For the extraordinary frequency of the name Arnoul in the Low Countries during the fourteenth and fifteenth centuries (with variants Arnols, Arnut, Arnu, Arnulf and others) see *Chronique et geste de Jean des Preis dit d'Outremeuse*, ed. Stanislas Bormans, introductory volume (Brussels, 1887), 38–41.

[5] There has been much confusion about the manuscript which contains Arnulf's treatise. It is certain that Gerbert used (and knew) only one manuscript of the *Tractatulus* and that the manuscript in question is the one employed here, St Paul im Lavanttal, Archiv des Benediktinerstiftes, MS 264/4. For Gerbert's account of the manuscript see *Scriptores ecclesiastici de musica*, ed. Martin Gerbert, 3 vols. (St Blasien, 1784), iii, 189–90. The identification is beyond doubt, not only because of the congruence between Gerbert's text (allowing for errors of transcription) and the manuscript text, but also because a substantial amount of Gerbert's third volume is derived from the St Paul manuscript and printed by him in the order in which the items occur there. It has repeatedly been claimed in the modern literature that this manuscript has been lost (see, for example, the article 'Arnulf von S. Gillen' in *MGG* and the article 'Eustacius Leodiensis' in *The New Grove Dictionary*), so it is pleasing to be able to report that it is still housed in the Archiv des Benediktinerstiftes where it has surely been since the late eighteenth century. Gerbert (*Scriptores*, iii, 189) says that the manuscript had been sent to him from Paris, and this led L. Royer to suggest that Bibliothèque nationale MS lat. 7370, already long mislaid in 1913, might be the book in question ('Catalogue des écrits des théoriciens de la musique conservés dans le fonds latin des manuscrits de la Bibliothèque Nationale', *L'année musicale*, 3 (1913), 206–46 (p. 222)). This was only a guess (whose quality cannot now be judged) but it apparently led Hüschen to declare in his *MGG* entry on Arnulf that there are two manuscripts of Arnulf's treatise, the St Paul manuscript and MS lat. 7370. This is a simple error of simple origin. There is only one known source of Arnulf's treatise. For further, brief information on the date and provenance of the manuscript, with bibliography, see Christopher Page, *The Summa musice: A Thirteenth-Century Manual for Singers* (Cambridge, 1991), 1.

[6] *Intercedente prolationis gracia melioris* ('with the intercession of the pleasantness of a more pleasing performance'). It is clearly very uncertain whether a pun is intended.

SUMMARY OF THE *TRACTATULUS DE DIFFERENTIIS ET GRADIBUS CANTORUM*

There are four principal kinds of musician (*cantor*):

I. The first degree comprises those who are ignorant of the *ars* of music and not even acquainted with plainchant. They 'sing their parts in the reverse of the way in which they should' and presume to correct trained musicians in the throng (*turba*) where they pollute whatever is more correctly performed.

II. The second degree comprises those lay persons who may be entirely lacking in musical *ars* but who are none the less drawn by 'a zeal for sweetness'. They cultivate the company of trained musicians (*musici*) so that 'natural industriousness and practice (*usus*) can make good their deficiency in *ars*'. Among them are certain clerics who compose difficult compositions for instruments such as the human voice would scarcely presume to execute. Others 'recollect' (*recordantur*) the pieces that have been composed in this way.

III. The third degree comprises those who may suffer from a defective voice but who 'keep the glorious treasures of the *ars* and *disciplina* of music in the sanctuaries of their breasts, acquired . . . by the efficacy of study'. Their *scientia* compensates for their natural inability and they teach their pupils to perform what they cannot perform themselves. The theory of musical teaching flows from their breasts. They do not make themselves into sophists but profess 'real music'.

IV. The fourth degree in order, but the first in honour, comprises those whom natural instinct, aided by a sweet voice, turns into true nightingales. By the acquisition of *ars* they sing according to rule with *modus, mensura, numerus* and *color*. They are adept at making *musica ficta* adjustments. The blessed felicity of both Nature and art adorns these musicians.

Among them are female musicians. They divide semitones into indivisible microtones and with their sound, more angelic than human, they steal away the hearts of those who listen to them, like the Sirens. That women should sing so well is due to the subministrations of *ars*, improving upon Nature.

With the aid of this treatise the diligent reader may discover in what class of musician he should consider himself to be.

This paraphrase gives the substance of Arnulf's opinions but it conveys neither the virulence of his style nor the scriptural resonances of his diction. The bad and presumptuous singers of category I, for example, are described with a sustained, bestial imagery that is all the more pervasive because it is never configured into a direct comparison. These inept but arrogant musicians 'gnaw' musical consonances and 'devour' them; they sing *brutali clangore*; they tread the pearls of music beneath their feet and so become the swine of *Matthew* vii. 6: 'Give not that which is holy to the dogs, neither cast ye your pearls before swine, lest they trample them under their feet and turn again and rend you.' As this last instance suggests, and as the commentary to the translation given below attempts to illustrate, Arnulf's language establishes the kind of scriptural reminiscence that was profoundly (almost subliminally) persuasive to clerics who passed their lives ruminating upon the Vulgate Bible. For example, when Arnulf speaks of the musicians he admires most – the expert singers of polyphony placed in category IV – his language assumes an almost sacramental quality as he compares the fruits of their expertise to the good harvest which the Israelites are enjoined to bear to the Promised Land in *Leviticus* xxiii. 10: 'When ye be come into the land which I give unto you . . . then shall ye bring a sheaf of the first fruits of your harvest.' In contrast, Arnulf presents the ignorant musicians of category I as almost diabolic, for they stifle this good harvest with the weeds of their ignorance, imitating the enemy in *Matthew*'s second parable of the sower: 'His enemy came and sowed tares among the wheat, and went his way.'

A single metaphor controls the imagery of the treatise, for throughout the *Tractatulus* Music is personified as the ruler of a realm. The inept but arrogant musicians of category I are exiles and must dwell beyond her borders; the diligent but ungifted musicians of II, in contrast, are permitted to be members of her household (*familia*), while the learned 'theorists' of III sit as judges in her tribunal (*pro tribunali* . . .), ruling in her affairs and giving the highest honours to the musicians of IV, the skilled singers of polyphony.

Unusual as it is, the *Tractatulus de differentiis et gradibus cantorum* has something in common with the writings of other theorists; ignorant and presumptuous singers are chastised in several treatises on measured music, for example, just as they are in many manuals of plainchant reaching back to *c*.1000 and beyond.[7] Taken as a whole, however, the *Tractatulus* is not like any other kind of Latin writing that we usually associate with the medieval music theorists, and Arnulf's stated aim – which is to enable each reader with musical interests to define his own position within a hierarchy based upon musical ability, innate and acquired – does not closely resemble anything in the acknowledged purpose of writers such as Jacques de Liège. Where should we look for its models and the origins of its concerns?

The desire to classify musicians according to some criterion of excellence is as old as the *De institutione musica* of Boethius (to look no further). It is well known that a chapter in the first book of that treatise defines the supreme musician, the *musicus*, as a gentleman connoisseur who has studied the rational principles of music and who is therefore qualified to pass judgment upon performances without ever lowering himself to the servile position of the singers and instrumentalists who actually make music.[8] This patrician view of excellence in the art reflects the master–slave relationship of late antiquity with sharp clarity and could not survive unchanged in the monastic culture of the early Middle Ages. A monk had the 'work of God', the liturgy, to perform every day, and it was his duty (at least in theory) to go into the fields with hoe and scythe. He might share the antique senators' longing for rural quiet and studious repose, but he could not so complacently inherit his pagan forebears' disdain for labour in general and for practical music-making in particular.

---

[7] See, for example, the remarks of Jacques de Liège in *Jacobi Leodiensis Speculum musice*, ed. Roger Bragard, 7 vols., Corpus scriptorum de musica, 3 (American Institute of Musicology, 1955–72), vii, 22–4. For an example in a plainchant treatise see Page, *The Summa musice*, 144.

[8] *Anicii Manlii Torquati Severini Boetii . . . De institutione musica libri quinque*, ed. Gottfried Friedlein (Leipzig, 1867; repr. 1966), i, 34. Translation in Calvin M. Bower, *Fundamentals of Music: Anicius Manlius Severinus Boethius* (New Haven and London, 1989), 50–1.

Throughout most of the Middle Ages, therefore, the teaching of Boethius with regard to the *musicus* was modified by writers who were not consciously reinterpreting the great Roman theorist but reading him in the only terms that made sense to their minds.[9] Whereas Boethius had sought to draw a firm distinction between lowly performers on one hand and lofty critics on the other, it was more urgent for medieval writers to distinguish ignorant singers of plainchant, mere *cantores*, from those who had studied such matters as the gamut and modal theory, to say nothing of musical notation. The latter, the informed practitioners, were the new *musici*, and the supremacy of such singers, defined by Arnulf de St Ghislain (with a characteristic turn towards aesthetic considerations) as persons of superb natural gifts, raised yet further in esteem by their informed expertise, is the major theme of the *Tractatulus*.

The gradual penetration of written record into both the theory and the practice of plainchant created the context for most medieval discussions of musical ability. Such discussions are rarely systematic; Arnulf's *Tractatulus* is exceptional from this point of view. When medieval writers broach the subject of musical skills it is almost invariably in terms of a contrast between what might be called 'informed' and 'uninformed' practice: 'informed' implying some kind of literate support (whether in the form of musical notation or of concepts derived from literacy-based musical theory), and 'uninformed' implying no literate support of any kind for the musical techniques employed. The distinction between informed and uninformed practices arose for discussion amongst the theorists because the relationship between memory and written record, like the relationship between improvisation and composition, became more – not less – complex during the thirteenth and fourteenth centuries.

A passage from the threshold of that period may serve to illustrate the point. The authors of the *Summa musice*, a treatise on plainchant and polyphony from *c*.1200, define a *musicus* as a singer who can learn a new chant from musical notation without hearing anyone sing it first. We instantly recognize this concept of notation as a system of storage from which a melody can be retrieved without reference to any ancillary memory of it; we may also be inclined to regard this concept of notation in the *Summa musice* as a stage in the progress towards major dependency upon writing, and the consequent unburdening of memory, that has been so important in the culture of Europe since the Renaissance. However, the authors of the *Summa musice* do not in the least regard musical notation as a substitute for memory; they recommend that a singer should learn chant by heart so that he can sing without books – vulnerable objects that are often unavailable, or not yet finished, when they are required.[10] The relationship between memory and writing is here still fluid and, by the standards of the twentieth century, unpredictable.

[9] For an account of these developments see Christopher Page, 'Musicus and cantor', *The Everyman Companion to Medieval and Renaissance Music*, ed. David Fallows and Tess Knighton (forthcoming); for a wealth of documents see the entry by Erich Reimer, 'Musicus-cantor', in the *Handwörterbuch der musikalischen Terminologie*.

[10] See Page, *The Summa musice*, 67 (the definition of the *musicus*) and 128: 'they who cannot sing a chant without books are speedily brought to grief in that they seem to become dumb and know nothing of chant when the books are elsewhere or are not ready'.

6

With the continuing evolution of polyphonic techniques in the twelfth and thirteenth centuries the relationship between informed and uninformed musical practices became increasingly complex. Some of the polyphonic techniques in use, such as the elaboration of a melodic line over a slower-moving chant, were clearly improvisatory in origin, and yet they were so close to the techniques which achieved written form, developed into musical 'compositions', that the theorists were compelled to distinguish between polyphony performed *ex arte* (invoking principles derived from music theory, perhaps using musical notation) and polyphony performed *ex usu* (that is to say entirely by ear and memory). The importance of such thinking in establishing a context for Arnulf's treatise can be measured by a passage in Johannes de Grocheio's *De musica* of *c*.1300. In this treatise we find Johannes using terms and concepts that resemble those of Arnulf, including *industria naturalis* and *usus*, and it is significant that they appear in his discussion of two-part organum, a musical art where the boundaries between informed and uninformed practice were flexible:[11]

> Quidam autem per experientiam attendentes ad consonantias tam perfectas quam imperfectas cantum ex duobus compositum invenerunt, quem *quintum* et *discantum* seu *duplum organum* appellaverunt. Et de hoc plures regulas invenerunt, ut apparet eorum tractatus aspicienti. Si tamen aliquis praedictas consonantias sufficienter cognoverit, ex modicis regulis poterit talem cantum et eius partes et eius compositionem cognoscere. Sunt enim aliqui, qui ex industria naturali et per usum talem cantum cognoscunt et componere sciunt.

> Some persons, moreover, studying both the perfect and the imperfect consonances in practice, devised a kind of music in two parts, which they called *quintus, discantus* or *organum duplum*. They have invented many rules concerning this, as will be apparent to anyone who looks into one of their treatises. However, if anyone will have studied the aforesaid consonances in a sufficient manner he will be able to have an understanding of such music, its constituent parts and its composition in only a few rules. For there are some who are familiar with such music, and who know how to compose it, entirely by natural industriousness and by practice.

Arnulf's angry reference to those musicians of category I who, *organizantes*, produce barbarous results, may well refer to singers who thought it an easy matter to improvise over a chant but who were ignorant of plainchant (as Arnulf reveals) and also unfamiliar with the classification of intervals; it is easy to imagine how such musicians might have violated the rules of consonance when they sang by failing to see when a cadence was possible or by failing to end a section on a perfect consonance. By the time of Arnulf, it would seem, the limits of even such extemporized techniques were closely defined by the rules of *ars*; *usus* alone could take one only so far.[12]

---

[11] Text from Ernst Rohloff, *Die Quellenhandschriften zum Musiktraktat des Johannes de Grocheio* (Leipzig, 1972), 138. Compare the remarks of Jacques de Liège in *Jacobi Leodiensis Speculum musice*, ed. Bragard, vii, 23.

[12] I am grateful to Dr Daniel Leech-Wilkinson for his comments upon Arnulf's use of the term *organizantes*.

As Table 1 reveals, Arnulf de St Ghislain is directly concerned with the concepts of *usus* and *ars*, for he explains the ways in which the various natural aptitudes and incapacities which people display are blended with folly, diligence and intelligence to produce different kinds and degrees of musicians. The new intricacies of mensural notation, the increasing *subtilitas* of the works which composers produced, and the density of the ancillary Latin literature of 'theory' had clearly produced a musical culture in which many kinds of ambition and achievement were displayed within the relatively public forum that Arnulf calls the 'throng', *turba* (of which more below). His discussion reveals that there were musicians who lacked *ars* and could not be redeemed (I), while others were deficient in *ars* but diligently attempted to compensate by *usus* (II). There were others who possessed a fine knowledge of *ars* but no ability whatever to benefit by *usus* (III), while the supreme musicians united *ars* and *usus* (IV).

TABLE 1

THE HIERARCHY OF MUSICAL ABILITIES IN THE *TRACTATULUS DE DIFFERENTIIS ET GRADIBUS CANTORUM*

IV	ARS	naturalis instinctus et mellice vocis organo
		ARS cantorie
		Nature et ARTIS felicitas
		potentia, actus, habitus
III	ARS	artis scientia supplet impotentia naturalis
II	USUS	dispositio Nature et industria naturalis
		USUS supplet quod ARTIS deficit
		zelo dulcedinis
I		nulla naturalis dispositio

Despite the almost scholastic appearance of this terminology, Arnulf's treatise hints at the social as well as the intellectual complexity of the Ars nova. The ignorant performer who believes himself able to correct the expert; the gifted performer who regards the musical scholar with a mixture of respect and condescension; the amateur with a modest talent anxious to learn what he can – all of these are evoked in the *Tractatulus*.

So far we have dealt exclusively with vocal music, but Arnulf also provides evidence that the relationship between informed and uninformed musical practice – between *ars* and *usus* – was particularly complex in the sphere of instrumental music.[13] A century or more before Arnulf, the anonymous author of the Pseudo-Ovidian Latin poem *De vetula* distinguishes between 'whatever written music provides *or hands have learned from*

---

[13] For a discussion of medieval instrumental traditions and their relation to literate musical techniques see Christopher Page, *Voices and Instruments of the Middle Ages* (London, 1987), *passim*.

hearing's instruction' (my italics).[14] In the first decades of the fourteenth century, Engelbert of Admont declares that instrumentalists work entirely *ex usu*,[15] that is to say by manual dexterity and aural tradition. As late as the fifteenth century, theorists such as Johannes Gallicus (d. 1473) and Conrad of Zabern (d. 1478–81) still speak of instrumentalists who make and compose music without any knowledge of literacy-based theory.[16]

It may be significant in this context that the only reference to instrumental playing in Arnulf's treatise appears in the account of those who are 'entirely lacking in musical art'. Arnulf reports that some clerical instrumentalists (he does not appear to be thinking of minstrels) compose pieces for instruments that are distinctively instrumental in the sense that they contain difficulties such as the human voice would scarcely presume to negotiate. We think of the more elaborate monophonic *istampitte* of the fourteenth century, perhaps, or even of some compositions in the Faenza codex where there is a good deal of figuration to intimidate a fourteenth-century singer but not, perhaps, an organist or string-player.[17] Furthermore, it seems that the composers of these instrumental works do not use notation, for Arnulf mentions other clerics who 'recollect' the pieces which are composed in this way, and this presumably refers to the transmission of these instrumental compositions by memory rather than by written record. Arnulf is apparently describing a musical culture in which singers are the finest performers of composed polyphony, while instrumentalists work at a significantly lower level of attainment, performing compositions which have distinctively instrumental characteristics and which are produced (and transmitted) without recourse to musical notation.

Before leaving the question of sources and context for the *Tractatulus* we may note that there may be another, more specific, source for what Arnulf has attempted, and one that becomes apparent when his treatise is compared with literary sources which are not generally used by historians of music: handbooks compiled for the use of confessors. Towards the end of his treatise, Arnulf decrees that musicians who are both ignorant and arrogant should be 'excommunicated from all communion with musicians' (*excommunicatosque pronunciat ab omni communione cantorum*). This metaphor is precise: Arnulf is speaking of bad singers as if they were excommunicants, denied communion. This is not exceptional language for a fourteenth-century theorist to employ; there is something similar in the *Speculum musice* of Jacques de Liège.[18] None

---

[14] *Pseudo-Ovidius De vetula*, ed. Paul Klopsch (Leiden and Cologne, 1967), 196: 'quicquid vel musica scribit / vel didicere manus auditu indice tacto / pulsu vel tractu vel flatu . . .'.

[15] *De musica, Scriptores*, ed. Gerbert, ii, 289. The whole of this section of Engelbert's treatise merits comparison with Arnulf's *Tractatulus*.

[16] For the remarks of Johannes Gallicus see the *Ritus canendi vetustissimus et novus, Scriptorum de musica medii aevi nova series*, ed. Edmond de Coussemaker, 4 vols. (Paris, 1864–76; repr. 1963), iv, 303–4; also edited in *Johannes Gallicus 'Ritus canendi'*, ed. Albert Seay, 2 vols. (Colorado Springs, 1981), i, 10. For the comments of Conrad of Zabern see *Die Musiktraktate Conrads von Zabern*, ed. Karl Werner Gümpel (Wiesbaden, 1956), 186.

[17] As early as the 1280s the theorists remark upon the ability of instruments to exceed the human voice in agility. See, for example, the comments of Anonymous IV in *Der Musiktraktat des Anonymus 4*, ed. Fritz Reckow, 2 vols. (Wiesbaden, 1967), i, 39 and 45.

[18] *Jacobi Leodiensis Speculum musice*, ed. Bragard, vii, 94–5.

the less, it is tempting to suppose that Arnulf's use of this metaphor can be traced to the manuals of confession,[19] for it was the purpose of these books to classify trades, helping the confessor to decide whether the supplicants who came to him were fit to proceed to communion. By the early thirteenth century we already find that such manuals discuss different kinds of musician – that is to say different kinds of minstrel – and there are many clear rulings in these handbooks which refuse minstrels the right to be admitted *ad ecclesiasticam communionem*.[20] Arnulf's *Tractatulus*, with its decree that bad singers should be exiled *ab omni communione cantorum*, can be interpreted as a most unexpected exploitation of what was originally a penitential motif: the classification of musicians according to their virtues and failings, and thus according to their right to receive the sacrament of bread and wine.

Arnulf explains the purpose of his treatise in disarmingly simple terms: he has written so that 'the diligent reader may at last discover . . . in what category or degree of musician he should consider himself to be'. In a medieval context we inevitably discern a moral impulse in this motive, and a severe one. Some musicians, it would seem, did not know their place. It may be significant therefore that the word Arnulf uses to denote a musical gathering is *turba* ('a crowd', 'a throng', even 'a rabble'), rather than the more serene *societas* ('a company', 'a gathering') used in a similar context by Jacques de Liège.[21] Apparently, Arnulf wishes to imply a somewhat animated performing context which has a predominantly high tone (being a *scolata . . . turba*), in which there is free discussion (the less skilled musicians being keen to converse with the experts)[22] and in which gifted singers are increasingly troubled by those who have almost no ability but who none the less push themselves forward to take control.[23] The mixture of abilities in the *turba*, indeed, is one of Arnulf's themes. As he reveals, and as we may have long suspected, the social contexts for secular polyphonic performance in the Middle Ages bore little resemblance to the modern concert with its insistence upon the distinction between performer and listener. Arnulf does articulate the concept of 'a listener' (*auditor*), but he can scarcely avoid doing so since a performance in the *turba* did not involve everyone present; none the less, he implies no firm distinction between those who perform and those who do not, for all the musicians whom he describes (with the exception of the 'theorists' who have no practical talent) are anxious to make music, apparently within the same *turba*, according to their abilities. Similarly, he

---

[19] For some of the thirteenth-century manuals of confession which discuss musicians see Christopher Page, *The Owl and the Nightingale: Musical Life and Ideas in France, 1100–1300* (London, 1990), *passim*, but especially pp. 19–29.

[20] The phrase is from the *Penitential* (*c.*1216) of Thomas Chobham; see *Thomae de Chobham Summa Confessorum*, ed. F. Broomfield (Paris and Louvain, 1968), 291.

[21] *Jacobi Leodiensis Speculum musice*, ed. Bragard, vii, 95.

[22] *Ut in plerisque cum cantoribus gratius garriendo concordent* ('so that in most things [musicians lacking in musical art but keen to learn] may be of one mind with accomplished musicians by conversing with them in a more pleasant fashion'). See note j to the translation, however; it is possible that Arnulf is referring to the wish of these untrained musicians to sing with the experts rather than to converse with them.

[23] Arnulf's use of the verb *plebesco* ('to become notorious') sanctions the assertion that this kind of behaviour was on the increase.

gives no hint of anything which we can recognize as professionalism; if money was involved at any stage in drawing the musical *turba* together (perhaps to hire minstrels or to ensure the attendance of some gifted choirman) Arnulf says nothing of it. It is noteworthy in this connection that modern scholars are inclined to associate medieval secular polyphony with small groups of connoisseurs and literati,[24] but Arnulf's words suggest something more diversified, active and mobile. We should perhaps also conceive of something more populous than a 'small group'; Jacques de Liège, we recall, speaks of the *magna . . . societas* where he listened to motets,[25] and Arnulf's term *turba* has an offspring in Middle French *tourbe*, defined by one of his contemporaries as a gathering of 26 people.[26] (The definition seems strangely precise, but it is worth having.)

Who were the people who joined the kind of *scolata turba* to which Arnulf refers? Many of them, we may assume, were men in clerical orders, since Arnulf seems to regard an ignorance of plainchant as a mark of the very worst and most presumptuous musicians. The company was not entirely clerical, however, for Arnulf is careful to specify that musicians of category II, those who are 'entirely lacking in musical art [but who are] none the less drawn by a zeal for sweetness', are principally laymen. These remarks indicate a combined lay and clerical presence in the *turba* (as do the comments of Jacques de Liège). A final point in this connection is that Arnulf's description of female singers, though fraught with difficulties to be discussed shortly, none the less suggests that a *scolata turba* was not necessarily an entirely masculine affair – with all the limitations which that would place upon its tone and social character – but may have broadened to accommodate women with a taste for polyphonic music and some performing ability. We think of Guillaume de Machaut's lady in the *Voir dit*, Perronne, clearly a devotee of Machaut's polyphonic songs and, to judge by Machaut's own letters to her, a competent performer and perhaps more.[27]

Continuing with the general implications of the *Tractatulus*, we find that the text has some bearing upon the aesthetics of late medieval music. In recent years, musicologists have increasingly chosen to emphasize what might be termed the 'Pythagorean' complexion of medieval thought about music and poetry. The fondness for scrupulous measurement, and the severely intellectual concept of beauty which is implicit in the writings of so many theorists, make it seem that medieval musicians approached polyphony 'with an enthralled but objective curiosity as a contemporary

---

[24] See, for example, *Motets of French Provenance*, ed. Frank Ll. Harrison, Polyphonic Music of the Fourteenth Century, 5 (Monaco, 1968), xi: 'This type of piece . . . would generally have had as listeners an intimate company of cognoscenti.' This remark is based upon the famous comment about the milieu of the motet in Paris *c*.1300 by Johannes de Grocheio, but Grocheio is not always observing contemporary conditions; he is often describing how, in his judgment, things ought to be. See Page, *The Owl and the Nightingale*, 148.

[25] *Jacobi Leodiensis Speculum musice*, ed. Bragard, vii, 95.

[26] The definition is from the *Somme rural* (1395) of Jean Boutillier, Bailli de Tournai: *pour le nombre de .xxvi. se fait tourbe et multitude*. Cited in Frédéric Godefroy, *Dictionnaire de l'ancienne langue française*, 10 vols. (Paris, 1880–1902; repr. New York, 1961), vii, col. 748.

[27] For details see Sarah Jane Williams, 'The Lady, the Lyrics and the Letters', *Early Music*, 5 (1977), 462–8. I am most grateful to Dr Daniel Leech-Wilkinson for allowing me to consult his forthcoming study of the *Voir dit* and its letters.

astronomer might contemplate the workings of his astrolabe'.[28] However, Arnulf's treatise suggests that a more sensual appreciation of musical beauty may sometimes have prevailed, at least among performers. Arnulf admires musical learning, and he knows the true weight of the words *scientia* and *disciplina* which he applies to it, but his impatience with those who pursue the more speculative aspects of music theory reveals an aesthetic bias. He is only prepared to respect musical scholars who abandon sophistries and give their attention to *realis musica*: to 'real music'.[29] The tone of those words, and their brusque good sense, are instantly familiar to a modern musician.

It is Arnulf's glorification of performance, however, that most vividly reveals his aesthetic bias: that is to say his preference for sensation over contemplation. In his judgment the glory of the supreme musician is the practical aptitude which is freely given by Nature, not the theoretical learning which is arduously acquired by study. This natural gift, as Arnulf understands it, comprises inherent musicality (*naturalis instinctus*) and a beautiful voice. The finest kind of musician is therefore a performer, not a theorist, and without denying the importance of the theorists as judges of music and musicians[30] the *Tractatulus* sets the musically gifted and learned performer above the merely learned theorist.[31] Indeed, it is implied in the *Tractatulus* (and this is surely one measure of Arnulf's identification with performing musicians above all others) that those who become learned in music do so because Nature has not chosen to grant them any practical talent. One becomes a scholar, in other words, when one cannot become a performer. Once again the modern musician may feel at home.

Turning now to the kinds of music which were performed in the *turba*, the *tractatulus* is of special interest because 'real music' for Arnulf de St Ghislain is undoubtedly composed polyphony. He despises the musicians who are not yet acquainted with plainchant, a remark which may be judged in relation to the standard doctrine of the theorists that a good knowledge of plainchant is the essential foundation of *musica mensurabilis*.[32] Expert musicians, in contrast, are those who perform in *modus, mensura, numerus et color* (all of these words possess a technical sense in fourteenth-century discussions of mensural music and its notation), and these supreme musicians possess an outstanding talent which

[28] Christopher Page, 'Polyphony before 1400', *Performance Practice*, ed. Howard Mayer Brown and Stanley Sadie, 2 vols. (London, 1989), i, 79.
    [29] Compare the comments of Jacques de Liège in *Jacobi Leodiensis Speculum musice*, ed. Bragard, vii, 25: 'Et quid valet subtilitas ubi perit utilitas?' ('And what is the good of subtlety if one loses usefulness thereby?').
    [30] Arnulf is careful to emphasize that 'the ear and eye of a trained man . . . declare a practical musician worthy of praise'.
    [31] Compare Nino Pirrotta, *'Ricercare* and Variations on *O rosa bella'*, *Music and Culture in Italy from the Middle Ages to the Baroque* (Cambridge, Mass., and London, 1984), 145: 'In a letter [apparently written in January 1429] addressed to Leonardo Giustinian, Ambrogio Traversari blandly but resolutely inverts, in order to praise his friend, one of the fundamental assumptions of scholastic musical culture, that the *musicus'* knowledge was superior to the *cantor's* practical skills.' I owe this reference to Dr David Fallows.
    [32] Compare the comment of Jacques de Liège in *Jacobi Leodiensis Speculum musice*, ed. Bragard, vi, 202: 'Qui igitur ignorat planum [cantum] frustra tendit ad mensuratum' ('He who is ignorant of plainchant will proceed without profit to measured [music]').

Arnulf greatly admires: the ability to take a notated composition and apply *musica ficta* adjustments to it with such fluency that music which was 'dissonant at first hearing sweetens by means of their pleasant performance and is brought back to the pleasantness of consonance'. Behind these words we can glimpse trained singers running through a composition and deftly registering each unsuccessful vertical sonority 'at first hearing' and simultaneously remembering the adjustment that will be needed the second time to bring the moment back 'to the pleasantness of consonance'. Although it is impossible to be specific (for we do not know where the *Tractatulus* was written) we may presumably imagine that secular chansons and motets were among the pieces performed in the *turba*.

It is this concentration upon polyphony that gives Arnulf's treatment of voices and instruments a special interest. Since the later 1970s, several studies have emphasized the importance of *a cappella* scorings in the performance of sacred and secular polyphony during the fourteenth and fifteenth centuries,[33] and Arnulf's treatise may support some of the more radical recent thinking about the role of instruments in medieval polyphony for the most favoured musicians in Arnulf's account are singers; hardly anything is said about instrumentalists. Would this have been the case if Arnulf were really looking back over more than half a century of French (and perhaps Italian) polyphonic song habitually performed by voices and instruments? His supreme performers are obviously singers, but he classifies instrumentalists among those who may be 'entirely lacking in musical art'.

In presenting his inventory of performers, Arnulf gives an account of the figure in medieval musical life whom we have come to call the 'theorist' (III). Beneath his insistent claim that these individuals lack any practical gifts we glimpse a kind of person, and this gives some life to what is otherwise a rather inert term. Arnulf's account suggests that the constant elaboration of mensural theory in the fourteenth century produced a class of studious individuals, some of whom had no practical talent but who were none the less attracted by polyphonic music and perhaps attracted still more by the intellectual rigour of its theory. There may never have been a time in the history of music so kind and receptive to such enthusiasts as the fourteenth century; it must often have happened, when new music was tried, that the notation of the copies gave trouble to the singers, either because of inaccuracies in the manuscripts or because a singer had not mastered a rule. It was then that the advice of

---

[33] See Howard Mayer Brown, record review in *Early Music*, 15 (1987), 278; David Fallows, 'Specific Information on the Ensembles for Composed Polyphony, 1400–1475', *Studies in the Performance of Late Mediaeval Music*, ed. Stanley Boorman (Cambridge, 1983), 109–59; Lawrence Earp, 'Texting in 15th-Century French Chansons: A Look Ahead from the Fourteenth Century', *Early Music*, 19 (1991), 194–210; Christopher Page, 'Machaut's "Pupil" Deschamps on the Performance of Music', *Early Music*, 5 (1977), 484–91; idem, 'The Performance of Songs in Late Medieval France', *Early Music*, 10 (1982), 441–50; idem, 'The English *A cappella* Heresy', *The Everyman Companion to Medieval and Renaissance Music* (forthcoming); Dennis Slavin, 'In Support of "Heresy": Manuscript Evidence for the *A cappella* Performance of Early 15th-Century Songs', *Early Music*, 19 (1991), 178–90; Craig Wright, 'Voices and Instruments in the Art Music of Northern France during the 15th Century: A Conspectus', *Report of the Twelfth Congress [of the International Musicological Society] Berkeley 1977*, ed. Daniel Heartz and Bonnie Wade (Kassel, 1981), 643–9.

those who had studied notation in detail became vital. Such men – who may well have included physicians, lawyers and even merchants – would count among the *doctores* and *approbati magistri* whose opinions the theorists of the fourteenth century cite so freely, and whom it would be naive to identify solely with 'theorists' in the reduced sense of the word which is common in modern discussions of medieval music (i.e. 'writers on music, especially those whose works survive').[34] Arnulf may be describing such a situation when he remarks that these learned men 'teach their pupils to perform the notes in concord which they cannot perform themselves by instructing them according to rule'. It is noteworthy that Arnulf thinks of such scholars as teachers rather than writers; the question of authorship is not uppermost in his conception of the theorist as it has become in ours, and his use of the term *doctrina verbalis*, 'verbal teaching', to denote what these scholars impart, is perhaps deliberately poised between speech and writing. His description supports the proposal that it may be better to call the theorists 'teacher-reporters'.[35]

The account of female singers in the *Tractatulus* is perhaps the most intriguing and certainly the most complex section of the treatise. The problem is not one of terminology, nor even one of meaning in the narrow lexical sense; it is a matter of tone. There was such a powerful misogynistic resonance in much of the language and imagery which medieval writers possessed to speak of women that only an author exceptionally vigilant to accidental ironic nuance and determined to speak well of women could hope to use it in an unreservedly positive way. The case of Arnulf's *Tractatulus* is very uncertain. He begins with the remark that the female sex, the 'other part', is 'so much the more precious the more it is rare', an aphorism which has an ambiguity that is too nicely poised to be accidental. It is followed by an extended comparison between female singers and the Sirens, the mythical creatures who bewitched the ears of those who heard them and drew them to destruction. At first sight, this may appear to succeed as an enthusiastic description of female charm, as heightened by music, with overtones of courtly lyric and romance ('they steal away their hearts . . . in secret theft'). Moreover, upon second reading, the apparent compliment to female singers may seem all the more gracious and ingenious for having been accomplished with literary materials (the Siren comparison) which had been employed for centuries in a thoroughly misogynistic context. Once again, however, it seems that Arnulf has chosen language with an ironic tinge. And what are we to make of the way these women singers 'divide semitones into indivisible microtones'? Is Arnulf praising their tuning – in particular their strategic widening or narrowing of intervals for musical effect? There seems no reason to assume that this would have been a particularly female accomplishment and the matter is therefore very uncertain. On balance, I incline to the view that Arnulf does indeed intend to praise female singers of polyphony for their exquisite artistry, but he has surely done so with a

---

[34] For an example of such a reference to the authority of (unspecified) *approbati magistri* see the treatise of Anonymous I (*De musica antiqua et nova*) in Coussemaker, *Scriptorum*, iii, 349.

[35] Ernest Sanders, 'Consonance and Rhythm in the Organum of the 12th and 13th Centuries', *Journal of the American Musicological Society*, 33 (1980), 264–86 (p. 271, note 25).

touch of irony that, as a male author, with a zest for language, he found irresistible.

The *Tractatulus de differentiis et gradibus cantorum* sheds light on various matters that other, better-known writings of the Middle Ages rarely or never elucidate: the various kinds of musician which a contemporary could discern; the use of voices and instruments in polyphony; the absolute dominance of singers and (perhaps) the importance of female performers; the composition and dissemination of instrumental pieces; the markedly aesthetic view of music which is easily neglected by the modern scholar concentrating upon the writings of other theorists, be they theoreticians of music or of poetry. It is such an unusual document that it hardly comes within the realm of medieval music theory as conventionally established; it stands alone.

APPENDIX

EDITION AND TRANSLATION OF THE *TRACTATULUS DE DIFFEREN-TIIS ET GRADIBUS CANTORUM* BY ARNULF DE ST GHISLAIN

ST PAUL IM LAVANTTAL, ARCHIV DES BENEDIKTINERSTIFTES, MS 264/4, ff. 66ᵛ–68

[f. 66ᵛ] Tractatulus de differentiis et gradibus cantorum a magistro Arnulpho de Sancto Gilleno editus

Existimo quod nunc temporis quatuor principales sunt differentie cantorum. Prima plebescit in illis, ut convenit, qui artem musice prorsus
5 ignari, nullo etiam naturalis dispositionis suffragante beneficio, per fatue sue presumptionis ausum temerarium, planam nundum gnari musicam, musicales actamen consonantias avido morsu rodere et verius devorare precentando satagunt, et in sue corrixationis latratu dum clamore rudiunt altius asino et brutali clangore terribilius intubant, cachephaton evomunt,
10 organizantesque per antifrasin faciunt in musica irregulariter barbarismum atque execrabili sue presumptionis falso cecati putamine se ipsos in se iactitant cantores posse postponere seu preire precipuos, ipsosque in turba quasi corrigere vel dirigere se impudenter offerunt ut apud homines musici videantur qui nec tantum de musica sapiunt ut ducantur,
15 semper cum consonantibus nichilominus dissonantes et soloestico fedantes vicio in scolata musicorum turba quidquid profertur regularius adeo cantoribus intollerabiles et nocivi, quemadmodum puram segetem zizania suffocat succrescens, quibus nec imponi potest silencium, quod non minus censetur viciosum in ipsis; verum contumaciter perinde clamitat avidius
20 quos suis pedibus conculcare non pudet: auro preciosiores armonicas Musice margaritas. Hii sunt profecto quos musicalis edicit auctoritas irrevocabiliter a suorum metis finium exulare quinimo in quos ipse favor Musice conspuit indignantis.

Secunda vero differentia patet in illis laycalibus qui, licet sint totius artis
25 musicalis expertes, zelo tamen ducti dulcedinis delicatas aures suas ad quevis musicalia prebent, attentius adamantes et associantes musicos et, veluti panthera boni odoris quevis insequntur animalia et apis ob dulcorem mellis argumentat, [f. 67] in studium propositos studiosius prosecuntur, florum et spicarum musicalium messis manipulos colligentes quos possunt,
30 ut in plerisque cum cantoribus gratius garriendo concordent et frequentius usitando in multis musicalibus quodammodo habilitentur et reddantur experti ut quod artis in eis deficit usus suppleat et industria naturalis. Ex istis nonnullos videmus clericos qui in organicis instrumentis difficilimos musicales modulos quos exprimere vix presumeret vox humana adin
35 veniunt atque tradunt per miraculosum quoddam innate in eis inventive Musice prodigium, reliquos autem qui que sic gesta sunt et tradita paulo minus laudabiliter recordantur, et interdum inventoris laudem convenit gracialis industria recordantis. Hii re vera de foro Musice sunt et quibus nimirum ipsa favere creditur nosque in filios adoptare a dumo sua et
40 speciali familia ab promissa familia sua clementia non exclusos.

Tertia est et aperte comprobatur in illis qui in suorum sacrariis pectorum gloriosos possident artis et discipline musicalis thesauros virtute studii laudabiliter acquisitos, qui licet defectum patiantur in organo ad alta digne proferenda que sapiunt, verumptamen vivax artis scientia sup
45 plet in ipsis impotentiam naturalem ut quod per se promere notaliter

consonando nequeunt per discipulos fieri procurant, propositos regulariter
edocendo ipsisque musicales communicando divitias et margaritas, Musice
digne dignis revelando secreta. De eorum namque pectoribus nedum
fluunt theorica musicalis doctrine fluenta; verumptamen practizantes in
50 illa facto pandunt et opere unde auris sapientis et oculus practicum
musicum indicant laude dignum, nam quod habet in habitu exhibet audiendum et speculandum in facto. Tales non sophisticantur in musica sed
realem musicam profitentur, et quamvis in cantando fastidiant auditores
hunc defectum in ipsis redimit eorum facundia dum per doctrinam ver-
55 balem artis regulas eloquntur.

Quarta ordine, dignitate prior, attenditur clarere glorianter in illis
[f. 67ᵛ] quos naturalis instinctus, suffragante mellice vocis organo,
figuraliter reddit philomenicos, meliores tamen multo Nature munere
philomenis et laude non inferiores alaudis, in quibus nobilis acquisitio artis
60 cantorie organum naturale dirigit regulariter in modo, mensura, numero
et colore, miro modulamine in consonantiis vicissitudines variando, et
varietate pluriformi modorum novelle recreationis adducit materiam in
animo auditoris, qui etiam, intercedente prolationis gracia melioris, in-
culta queque et m[i]nus decenter exhibita musicalia, ad incudem sui gut-
65 turis reportata, quasi remonetando gratiorem reducit in formam. Quis
enim non mirare poterit quo proferendi magisterio proportio musicalis
artis, primaria traditione dissona, eorum super artificiali docescat et ad
consonantie gratiam reducatur? Hos profecto utraque Nature scilicet et
artis beata felicitas decorat superpellatos, eosdemque ipsa Arismetice filia,
70 cooperante Natura beatiori, coronatos dyademate lacteque sue dulcedinis
enutritos ad cumulum perfectionis eduxit. Porro isti sunt quos tercia cantorum prescripta differentia, auctoritatem iudiciarie potestatis exercens in
musica, et pro tribunali sedens pretorii musicalis in solio tamquam predic-
tos, potentia, actu et habitu que cantorem venustum perficiunt iuste in
75 cantoribus prepolentes iudicat, cum non inveniantur in aliquo defectivi. E
quibus pars altera, favorosi videlicet sexus feminei, que quanto rarior
tanto preciosior, dum in dulcinomi gutturis epigloto tonos librate dividit in
semitonia, et semitonia in athomos indivisibiles garrit, ineffabili lascivit
melodiomate quod magis putares angelicum quam humanum. Hinc
80 mulieres – dee ymo verius syrene terrestres – incantatas aures incarminant
audientium quorum corda, pleraque tali ebrietate sopora, invisibili furto
subripiunt subreptaque et voluntari facta sue servituti subiugant ter-
restremque perducunt naufra-[f. 68]gantes sui, heu! gratia carceris, in
Caribdim in qua nullum redemptionis genus vel precium locum tenet.
85 Unde licet Natura dignitate atque prioritate precedat, in eo saltem
Musicam Natura honorare videtur quod in tali opere mirabiliter quodammodo prevenerit ars Naturum, nam quod Natura per se non velle facere
dissimulat artis subministrata servicio perfecit. Quid Natura derogat aut
deperit si artis adiuncta ingenio decoretur? Nonnullos namque interdum
90 videmus forme inferioris gratiores in acquisita virtute ubi in formosis
naturaliter sua pulcritudo, silescit, cum in eis morum decor et virtus deficit
acquisita.

Igitur cantores primos – si cantores dici debeant cum non sint ipsi musici
– omni gradu comparationis indignos, anathematis percussos sententia,
95 Musica dampnat veluti temerarios incursiores, lese sue maiestatis in
crimine excommunicatosque pronunciat ab omni communione cantorum.
Illi vero qui iuxta secundam differentiam sunt cantores, quia dispositiones
Nature in eis ponit industria unde innatam per usus exercitium proferunt

musicam, tamquam boni in gradu [positivo] cantorum digni habentur
100 statui positione. Hii autem quos tertia describit differentia, quia arte et
scientia positivos precellunt, tamquam meliores in comparativo gradu
iuste statuendi concedentur. Verum illos quos quarta differentia pre-
conizat, quoniam perfectos utpote quibus Natura, artis subministrante
misterio, nil denegat, tamquam musicos optimos ad supperlativum
105 gradum in cantoribus iustior sublimat existimatio.

Salva opinionis sententia sanioris, demum in huius opusculi serie sedulus
speculetur inspector in qua differentia vel in quo gradu inter cantores se
regere debeat, ut quisque in gradu suo qui musicam sapiet cantare sepius
delectetur semper hiis quibus debetur maioritas deferendo, ululansque
110 ferinum discat ydiota suum continere tumultum.

Explicit tractatus magistri Arnulphi.

TEXTUAL NOTES
14   tantum] cantum
37   inventoris] inventoriis
40   ab promissa familia sua clementia] ab promissam familiam suam
     clementiam
47   communicando] ?comitando
71   cumulum] tumulum

TRANSLATION

A brief treatise concerning the different kinds and degrees of musicians, compiled by master Arnulf de St Ghislain
I consider that there are four principal kinds of musician at the present time.
The first is becoming notorious – as is fitting – in those who are utterly ignorant
of the art of music, who do not profit from the benefit of any natural aptitude,
who are not yet acquainted with plainchant, but who none the less try to gnaw –
indeed to devour – musical consonances with a hungry bite[a] as they lead the singing[b] through the impetuous rashness of their ridiculous presumption. When they
bray with the din of their brawling bark louder than an ass, and when they
trumpet more terribly than the clamour of a wild animal, they spew out harsh-
sounding things. Singing their parts in the reverse of the way in which they
should,[c] they produce barbarism in music contrary to rule; falsely blinded by a

---

[a] 'To gnaw – indeed to devour – musical consonances with a hungry bite' renders *musicales actamen consonantias avido morsu rodere et verius devorare*. *Rodere* ('to gnaw') is a pungent verb in
medieval Latin, often associated with violent and gnawing envy; see, for example, Hans Walther,
Die lateinische Sprichworter (Göttingen, 1982–6), 12753 (*Invidia . . . rodit*), 12801 (*Invidus odit se,
rodens alios perit ipse*) and 22314 (*Pravus homo rodit*). The verb *devorare* is more violent still and
has animalistic associations, deeply coloured by its many appearances in scripture. Compare *Genesis*
xxxvii. 33 and xliv. 28 (*bestia devoravit*), *Exodus* x. 12 and *Deuteronomy* xxviii. 38 (where *devoro*
denotes the action of locusts). It also conveys the destructive rapacity of fire (*Numbers* xvi. 39;
Deuteronomy, v. 25 and ix. 3).
[b] 'As they lead the singing' is a somewhat literal translation of Arnulf's *precentando*, but his insistence upon the way in which these inept musicians of the first category leap up to take control of
any performance that they attend suggests that a translation adhering to the literal sense of *precento*
('to sing before, in front') may be advisable.
[c] 'Singing their parts in the reverse of the way in which they should' renders *organizantesque per
antifrasin*. The participle *organizantes* presumably implies some kind of polyphonic practice,
although it might be rendered more loosely as 'putting their music together' or something of that
kind. Antiphrasis is the use of a word in a sense that is the opposite of its proper sense or which conflicts with it (such use of rhetorical and grammatical terminology to create a vocabulary for describing musical phenomena associated with no technical vocabulary of their own is very common in
medieval music theory and continues in this passage with the terms *cachephaton* and *barbarismum*).

despicable delusion that arises from their presumption, they boast in their hearts that they can disregard excellent singers and surpass them, and they impudently offer themselves in the throng to give correction or leadership to these same [excellent singers] so that they who do not even know enough about music to be led, and who are always producing dissonance amongst those who are concordant, may give the appearance of being trained musicians. With their ineptitude they constantly pollute whatever is more correctly performed in the learned throng of musicians; they do this to the point where they become intolerable and noxious to trained musicians, as when the weed springs up and stifles pure corn.[d] They cannot be silenced, and this is to be judged as no less than a vice in them. Truly [such a musician] correspondingly, stubbornly and all the more avidly lays claim[e] to the things which he is not afraid to trample under his feet: the harmonious pearls of music which are more precious than gold.[f] They are indeed those whom Music's authority proclaims to be irrevocably exiled from the borders of her territory, and upon whom the favour of indignant Music spits.

The second category [of musician] is manifest in those lay persons who, even though they are entirely lacking in musical art, are none the less drawn by a zeal for sweetness and so lend their pleasure-loving ears to any music, attentively cherishing trained musicians and associating with them. Just as all animals follow the sweet-smelling panther,[g] and the bee buzzes towards the sweetness of the honey,[h] so these musicians studiously follow the aforementioned trained musicians in their study, gathering what handfuls of the harvest of musical flowers and of corn-ears[i] they can so that in most things they may be of one mind with accomplished musicians by conversing[j] with them in a more pleasant

If it does indeed refer to polyphony, then *organizantesque per antifrasin* may have a technically precise meaning; that meaning can be guessed at (the performance of a polyphonic part at the wrong octave – an abuse described by some theorists?) but not established.

[d] *Quemadmodum puram segetem zizania suffocat succrescens.* In a passage characterized by virulent language this is the most virulent of all. The reference is to the second parable of the sower in *Matthew* xiii. 24–32 where the weed is spread on the field by the *inimicus* and the weeds are eventually burned in fires which foreshadow the fate of those who stifle the good crop.

[e] *Perinde clamitat avidius*; given the context and diction of this passage, which relates how unschooled musicians try to take charge of the 'throng' (*turba*) it is tempting to hear in this use of *clamitat* an echo of *Proverbs* i. 21: *in capite turbarum clamitat.*

[f] *Quos suis pedibus conculcare non pudet: auro preciosiores armonicas Musice margaritas.* Matthew vii. 6: *Nolite . . . mittatis margaritas vestras ante porcos ne forte conculcent eas pedibus suis.* The image of the pearl trodden beneath the feet of swine, which sustains the bestial imagery of this section, is not in the least stale in medieval scriptural commentary (see, for example, the *Glossa ordinaria, Patrologia latina*, ed. Jacques Paul Migne, 221 vols. (Paris, 1844–64), cxiv, col. 108). In the commentary tradition it is not merely the beauty, purity and value of the pearl which contribute to the image but also the way it lies hidden (*in absconditio latet*) and must be prised from the shell (*apertis conchis eruitur*). By alluding to Matthew's passage Arnulf emphasizes not only the great value of advanced musical learning but also the great difficulty of acquiring it.

[g] The panther was believed to possess a sweetness of breath which enraptured and drew all other animals. Compare Baudouin de Condé: *Tout ensement con la pantere / Cui les bestes sivent et tracent / . . . Por la douce alaine qu'il porte* (Adolf Tobler and Erhard Lommatzsch, *Altfranzösisches Wörterbuch* (Berlin, 1925–), s.v. *pantere*).

[h] 'The bee buzzes' renders *apis . . . argumentat.* The sense of the verb may seem, at first sight, somewhat strained in this context, but *argutus* ('clear-sounding, murmuring, melodious') is used of insects in classical Latin.

[i] *Florum et spicarum musicalium messis manipulos colligentes quos possunt.* Here the diction owes much to *Leviticus* xxiii. 10, no doubt a deliberate echo since in that passage God speaks to the Hebrews who are soon to enter the Promised Land and who are enjoined to gather *manipulos spicarum* when they come there; by implication, musicians of this category thirst after the company of those who are both naturally gifted and thoroughly trained in the art as the Hebrews thirsted after Israel.

[j] 'Conversing' translates *garriendo*, from *garrio*, 'to chatter, prate or talk'. However, at line 78 the closely related form *garritat* clearly means 'to sing', and we are perhaps to understand that

fashion and may somewhat improve their ability and become experienced by
more frequent practice in many musical matters; thus natural industriousness
and practice can make good their deficiency in art. Among these we may see
some clerics who compose and perform[k] most difficult musical compositions for
musical instruments, such as the human voice would scarcely presume to execute, with the aid of a certain wonderful token of inventive Music in them, and
[we see] others also who recollect[l] the pieces which have been composed and performed in this way, which is only a little less praiseworthy; sometimes the
gracious industry of the one who remembers [the composition] matches the
laudable enterprise of the composer. Truly, these musicians are from the court
of Music, and those whom she is thought certainly to favour we should also adopt
as sons from her household and personal retinue, not excluded – by her clemency
– from the promised retinue.

There is a third kind of musician, clearly discerned in those who keep the
glorious treasures of the art and discipline of music in the sanctuaries of their
breasts, acquired in a praiseworthy fashion by the efficacy of study. Even if they
suffer from a defective voice so that they cannot properly perform what they
know aloud, none the less the vigorous knowledge of art compensates in them for
their natural inability. Thus they teach their pupils to perform what they cannot
perform themselves by instructing them according to rule and by sharing
musical riches and pearls with them, revealing the secrets of music in a fitting
fashion to those fit to receive them. What is more, the theory of musical teaching
flows in streams from their breasts, and yet by being practising theorists they extend their activities with deeds and undertaking, for it is the ear and eye of a
trained man that declare a practical musician worthy of praise, because a listening and a careful consideration reveal what the performer has in him in practical
terms.[m] Such [musicians] do not make themselves into musical sophists but profess real music, and however much they displease listeners when they sing, that
failing is redeemed by the fertility of their minds when they explain the rules of
the art in words.

The fourth [kind of musician] in order, but the first in honour, is considered
to shine gloriously in those whom natural instinct, aided by a sweet voice, turns
into very nightingales as it were (although better than nightingales in their
natural gift) who yield nothing in praiseworthiness to the lark. The acquisition
of the noble art of singing guides such a singer's voice according to rule in
modus, measure, number and *color*, in varying changes of harmony with a
wonderful melodiousness, and it gives the listener a fresh means of recreation in
a manifold variety of ways; with the intercession of the pleasantness of a more
pleasing performance [the art of singing] gives a more delightful form to
anything inelegant and imperfectly performed when it is brought to the anvil of

---

musicians of this second category study so that they may sing with trained musicians and not simply
converse with them.

[k] 'Perform' renders *tradunt*, from *trado*, whose meanings include 'to hand over, to deliver, to
transmit, to teach', but at line 67 *primaria traditione dissona* clearly means 'dissonant at first hear-
ing/performance', whence the translation 'perform' here. It is possible, however, that Arnulf is referring to the diffusion of these instrumental compositions, in which case a translation such as 'hand
down' or 'disseminate' would be advisable.

[l] 'Recollect' translates *recordantur*, from the deponent verb *recordor* ('to recollect, call to mind').
The *Revised Medieval Latin Word List*, ed. R. E. Latham (London, 1965), s.v. *recordor*, gives two
instances of this verb in the sense 'to record' (citations from 1198 and the fifteenth century). This
passage may therefore refer to the production of notated copies of instrumental compositions, but it
may be doubted whether Arnulf wishes us to understand that musicians of this category were familiar
with musical notation.

[m] 'For it is the ear and eye . . . practical terms'. This passage renders a somewhat obscure section
in the Latin (lines 50–2).

the throat – minting it anew, as it were. Who will not marvel to see with what expertise in performance some musical relationship, dissonant at first hearing, sweetens[n] by means of their skilful performance and is brought back to the pleasantness of consonance? Truly, the blessed felicity of both Nature and art adorns these enrobed musicians; [Music], the very daughter of Arithmetic, aided by Nature who is yet more blessed, leads these same musicians forward crowned with a diadem and nourished with the milk of her sweetness, to the height of perfection. Indeed, these are the musicians whom the third kind of musician described above, exercising the authority of judicial power in music and sitting on the throne of the musical court of law, rightly judges to be the most excellent among musicians in respect of the faculty, action and turn of mind which make a pleasing musician,[o] since they are found to be lacking in nothing. Among these there is a second group – that is to say of the favoured female sex – which is so much the more precious the more it is rare; when it freely divides tones into semitones with a sweet-sounding throat, and divides semitones into indivisible microtones, it enjoys itself with an indescribable melody that you would rather deem angelic than human. So it is that these women – goddesses, or indeed rather earthly Sirens – enchant the bewitched ears of their listeners and they steal away their hearts, which are for the most part lulled by this kind of intoxication, in secret theft, and having snatched them and made them subject to their will, they then enslave them and lead them, shipwrecked by the beauty, alas! of their prison, into an earthly Charybdis in which no kind of redemption or ransom is of any avail. Thus, although it is fitting that Nature take pride of place with honour and with precedence, Nature evidently honours Music in this matter because in music-making such as this art precedes Nature in a certain marvellous way because what Nature pretends to have no wish to do Music accomplishes by the subministrations of art. What does Nature dispraise or diminish if it is adorned with the skill of art? We may sometimes see people who are of less pleasing appearance but who are none the less more attractive in their acquired virtue, while the beauty of those who are naturally beautiful is mute because they lack comeliness of conduct and acquired virtue.

In conclusion, musicians of the first kind – if they may be so called, since they have no training – are unworthy of any degree of comparison and are smitten with a sentence of anathema, condemned by Music as audacious invaders, and she decrees that they be excommunicated for the crime of *lèse-majesté* from all communion with musicians. Those who are musicians of the second category are thought worthy to be classified in the [positive] degree, being good persons whose natural inclinations are strengthened by application, whence they perform innate music by diligent practice. Those who fall within the third category are rightly granted a station in the comparative degree; being better, they exceed those in the positive degree in both art and learning. Those, indeed, who are described in the fourth distinction are yet more justly held in lofty esteem; being the best musicians in the superlative degree, they are perfect musicians to whom Nature, with the subministrations of the mystery of art, denies nothing.

Without prejudice to the judgment of wiser opinion, the diligent reader may at last discover in the course of this brief work in what category or degree of

---

[n] 'Sweetens' renders *docescat*, which would appear to be a form of *dulcescat* heavily influenced by the orthography (and perhaps the pronunciation) of Middle French *douce*.

[o] 'Faculty, action and turn of mind' renders *potentia, actu et habitu*, which is terminology of a scholastic and ambitious kind. For Aquinas, for example, these terms form a closely related group in which, crudely speaking, *potentia* ('faculty') denotes the power to accomplish something, *actus* ('action') denotes action, while *habitus* ('turn of mind') is a disposition to act well or badly (*A Lexicon of St Thomas Aquinas*, ed. Roy J. Deferrari, Sister M. Inviolata Barry and Ignatius McGuinness (Baltimore, Maryland, 1948), s.v. *actus*, *habitus* and *potentia*).

musician he should consider himself to be, so that everyone who would know how to make music in his degree may delight in it more often, always deferring to those to whom obedience is owed, and the bellowing fool may learn to control his bestial noise.

Here ends the treatise of master Arnulf de St Ghislain.

The following is a list of false readings in the text of Arnulf's *Tractatulus* published in *Scriptores*, ed. Gerbert, iii; it does not include discrepancies in orthography between Gerbert's text and the manuscript.

Scriptores, iii	MS
316a	
generibus	gradibus
ubivis	verius
regulariter	irregulariter
tuba	turba
scholastico	soloestico
primam	puram
316b	
ut	et
flores	florum
317a	
concinit	convenit
reipsa	ipsa
eosque	nosque
et	ut
communicando	comitando
numeris	margaritas
317b	
vocis	nature
adcquisitor	acquisitio
quod	quo
coram	eorum
vera	beata
eosdem	eosdemque
destitui	defectivi
dulcisoni	dulcinomi
318a	
. . .	athomos
lascivitque	lascivit
decet	dee
incarminantes	incarminant
naufragium	naufragantes
adiuta	adiuncta
318b	
integerrimae	in crimine
propositorum	positione
ministerio	misterio
feminine	ferinum

XIX

Le troisième accord pour vièle de Jérôme de Moravie

Jongleurs et « anciens Pères de France »

Le troisième accord pour la vièle décrit par Jérôme de Moravie (Tractatus de Musica, chapitre 28) a fait l'objet d'interprétations contradictoires. Le texte du manuscrit ne présente toutefois aucune ambiguïté. Cet accord pourrait avoir été destiné à l'interprétation des chansons de geste. L'intérêt porté par Jérôme de Moravie à ce répertoire s'explique par un sentiment de fierté de la France ; ce répertoire contribuait par ailleurs au combat de l'Eglise - et notamment de l'ordre des Frères prêcheurs - contre le paganisme et l'hérésie ; il véhicule enfin une certaine propagande cléricale.

On a cru longtemps qu'un passage très important dans le *Tractatus* de Jérôme de Moravie renferme une sérieuse erreur. Je me réfère au chapitre 28. C'est là que Jérôme décrit les accords utilisés sur deux instruments à archet : la *rubela* et la *viella*. Depuis 1828 au moins, date de la première publication de ce chapitre (en traduction française)[1], bien des musicologues ont présumé que l'un des accords que Jérôme nous donne pour la vièle est inexact. Je ne suis pas de cet avis. J'aimerais suggérer que l'accord a été parfaitement compris par Jérôme et a été fidèlement transcrit dans le manuscrit. Cet accord, souvent supposé faux, soulève des questions importantes au sujet des traditions musicales orales au temps de Jérôme.

La vièle était le principal instrument pour la musique profane et Jérôme décrit trois accords différents pour celui-ci. Il fait aussi l'inventaire des notes que chaque corde peut produire, et décrit (très brièvement d'ailleurs) une technique avancée. C'est le troisième accord qui présente un problème, et je crois qu'il serait préférable pour nous de l'aborder à partir des deux premiers accords.

La figure ci-contre montre les trois accords. Ils sont disposés sur des dessins schématiques avec les cordes placées en chœurs comme, d'après moi, ils étaient situés sur les instruments de Jérôme[2]. Dans le premier accord, la corde marquée D se trouve sur le côté de la touche. J'ai aussi transcrit les accords en notation moderne, bien que cette notation n'implique rien quant au diapason des instruments de Jérôme, sujet sur lequel nous ne savons rien de précis.

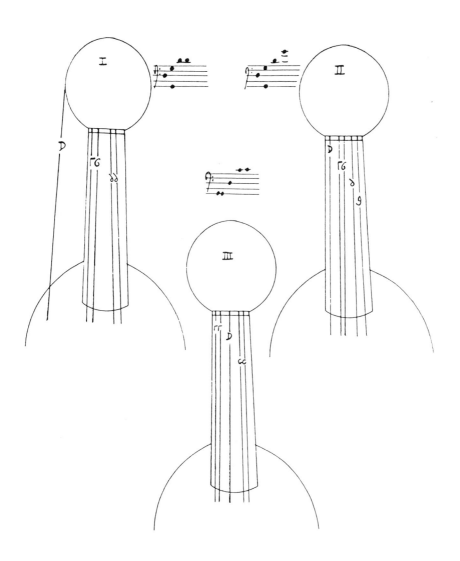

Les trois accords pour vièle décrits par Jérôme de Moravie.

Le troisième accord pour vièle

Ces deux premiers accords produisent une *accordatura*. Ces accords permettent à l'artiste de faire des coups d'archet sur les cordes de chaque côté de la corde qui produit la mélodie, et de telles techniques ont été reproduites avec succès par des joueurs modernes. Ce genre de technique musicale permet facilement à la vièle de devenir un instrument idéal pour s'accompagner : un développement nécessaire à une époque où la plupart des musiciens jouaient tout seul.

Le troisième accord réserve une surprise. Il y a un espace d'une septième entre la corde du milieu et les deux cordes supérieures. Un agrandissement de cet accord tel qu'il se trouve dans le manuscrit montre qu'on n'y trouve aucune lettre ambiguë ou mal formée. Cependant malgré cela, de nombreux musicologues ont réécrit le troisième accord, ou bien l'ont dénaturé, ou encore complètement ignoré [3].

Un changement décisif survint quand, en 1964, fut publiée l'édition originale allemande du livre de Werner Bachmann, *Die Anfänge des Streichinstrumentspiels,* un des ouvrages les plus stimulants sur la musique médiévale. L'œuvre de Bachmann illustre l'importance cardinale de l'ethnomusicologie pour notre sujet. Ayant étudié les accords utilisés sur les instruments folkloriques en Europe, Bachmann tira la conclusion que le troisième accord n'a rien de surprenant. « Il est possible, écrit-il, que ce type d'accord ait été créé pour des instruments sur lesquels seulement une corde, d'habitude la plus haute, produisait la mélodie… la corde *c* était parfaitement adéquate pour le vaste répertoire de mélodies archaïques à quatre ou cinq notes, et son redoublement renforçait la trame mélodique pendant que les autres produisaient un bourdon complexe. » [4]

Je suis convaincu que cette interprétation est la bonne. Je ne suggère pas que c'était le *seule* manière d'exploiter le troisième accord, mais je crois vraiment que c'était l'une des principales. D'après cette interprétation, l'accord produisait ce que l'on voit dans l'exemple 1.

Exemple 1

Le troisième accord pour vièle

Bien que l'interprétation de Bachmann soit convaincante, elle comporte un élément d'imprécision. Il parle du répertoire « des mélodies archaïques à quatre ou cinq notes » sans vraiment dire ce qu'il entend par là. Quel était ce répertoire ? Cela m'étonnerait que Bachmann ait eu une idée précise à ce sujet, au delà de la notion qu'il doit y avoir un genre de musique médiévale primitive, folklorique, et qui n'a jamais été écrite. J'aimerais suggérer, maintenant, qu'il doit être possible de deviner la nature des mélodies archaïques et très limitées que l'on jouait avec le troisième accord.

En rassemblant des références ayant trait à la musique dans les œuvres vernaculaires et latines de la France médiévale, j'ai été impressionné par le lien étroit qui semble avoir existé entre la vièle et les épopées françaises, ou chansons de geste. Les chansons de geste sont des poèmes narratifs, souvent très longs, qui racontent les exploits des héros carolingiens tels que Roland et Olivier, ou des barons guerriers. La plus ancienne et la plus connue est, bien sûr, *La Chanson de Roland,* qui date environ de 1080. Ces poèmes présentent souvent l'image paradoxale d'une France qui est perçue comme le centre de la Chrétienté en lutte contre les infidèles, mais aussi qui est déchirée par des conflits tragiques entre les chevaliers refusant de sacrifier quoi que ce soit de leur indépendance et de leur orgueil.

La Chanson de Roland, comme toutes les chansons de geste, est composée en laisses, ce qui veut dire des groupes de vers, la longueur des groupes étant variable. Chaque vers finit par une assonance, ou, dans les épopées les plus récentes, par une rime. Voici le commencement de *La chanson de Roland*[5] :

I

Carles li rei, nostre emperere magnes,
Set anz tuz pleins ad estét en Espaigne,
Tresqu'en la mer cunquist la terc altaigne.
N'i ad castel ki devant lui remaigne,
Mur ne citét n'i est remés à fraindre,
Fors Sarraguce, ki est en une muntaigne ;
Li reis Marsilie la tient ki Deu nen aimet,
Mahumet sert e Apollin recleimet ;
Ne s poet guarder que mals ne l'i ateignet. Aoi.

Le troisième accord pour vièle

II

Li reis Marsilie esteit en Sarraguce,
Alez en est en un verger suz l'umbre,
Sur un perrun de marbre bloi se culched,
Envirun lui plus de vint milie humes.
Il en apelet e ses dux e ses cuntes :
« Oëz, seignurs, quel pecchét nus encumbret :
Li empereres Carles de France dulce
En cest païs nos est venuz cunfundre.
Jo nen ai ost qui bataille li dunne,
Ne n'ai tel gent ki la sue deru[m]pet :
Cunseilez mei cume mi savie hume,
Si me guarisez e de mort e de hunte. »
N'i ad paien ki un sul mot respundet,
Fors Blancandrins de Castel de[l] Valfunde.

Ces deux laisses sont de longueurs inégales ; alors comment les jongleurs chantaient-ils ces chansons de geste ? On sait que le seul témoignage médiéval que nous possédons se trouve dans le *De musica* de Jean de Grouchy, un contemporain parisien de Jérôme. Il nous dit (dans un passage qui ne manque pas de difficulté textuelle) que la même musique doit être répétée pour chaque ligne de la laisse [6].

La solution musicale dont parle Jean de Grouchy est peut-être la seule possible. Il est impossible de chanter une chanson de geste de la même manière que les stances d'une chanson de trouvère, par exemple, car dans ce genre les stances sont toutes de la même forme, et s'ajustent ainsi à la même mélodie. Avec la solution de Jean de Grouchy, il était possible de chanter n'importe quelle laisse épique, qu'elle fut composée de cinq ou de deux cents lignes. Chaque ligne avait le même air. Décrire cela comme une « solution » au « problème » de chanter les chansons de geste est quelque peu fallacieux, bien sûr, car il est vraisemblable que cette manière de chanter ait été aussi vieille que l'épopée française elle-même : c'est-à-dire qu'elle remonte au XIe, voire au Xe siècles [7].

Nous sommes, peut-être, maintenant sur la trace de notre répertoire, archaïque et disparu, des mélodies répétitives pour le troisième accord de Jérôme de Moravie. Notre Appendice cite neuf témoignages littéraires qui ont rapport à l'exécution des chansons de geste. Il est difficile de juger de la

Le troisième accord pour vièle

valeur de tels témoignages en termes précis. Ce qui est clair, cependant, c'est que cette liste couvre plusieurs genres littéraires différents : une épopée, un roman de chevalerie, un sermon, un commentaire scolastique, un poème moralisateur et un poème satirique. Cette transgression des frontières entre genres et langues, latin et vernaculaire, suggère que notre argument n'a pas été trop biaisé par un groupe particulier de conventions littéraires.

Il est impossible de discuter ici de tous ces textes. Je crois cependant que trois d'entre eux présentent un intérêt particulier et valent bien une brève mention.

Le texte numéro VII est tiré d'un sermon du XIIIe siècle. Le prêcheur dit que les joueurs de vièle sont habitués à raconter les exploits de Charlemagne et de Roland. Il est donc doublement important, continue-t-il, que les prêcheurs, « les joueurs de vièle de Dieu », racontent les exploits des saints. J'imagine que cette comparaison entre les joueurs de vièle et les prêcheurs était utile parce que ces joueurs chantaient vraiment les louanges de Charlemagne et de Roland et étaient bien connus pour cela.

Pour en venir du latin au vernaculaire, le texte numéro VI est remarquable pour une raison différente. Le *Dit des taboureurs* est un poème dans lequel les joueurs de vièle expriment leur colère envers les ménestrels amateurs, la plupart des paysans, qui fabriquaient des tambours et des instruments à vent et s'en allaient jouer dans les villes, volant ainsi le pain de la bouche des musiciens de vièle. Dans la stance citée, le poète, au nom des vièleurs, identifie le répertoire qui, selon lui, justifie le respect qu'on leur doit. Ce ne sont pas les motets, non plus les *conducti* ou même les chansons des trouvères. En fait, le genre que ces vièleurs sont si fiers de jouer est absent de nos sources musicales. Il s'agit d'un répertoire entièrement narratif tiré des chansons de geste, dont les héros cités sont Auberi le Bourgoing, Girart de Vienne, Tierri l'Ardennois, Guillaume au court nez et Aymeri de Narbonne. Tous ces personnages nous sont très bien connus.

Enfin, le texte numéro IV, tiré du *Roman de la Violette* de Gerbert de Montreuil, montre que les exécutants des chansons de geste chantaient et jouaient quelquefois en même temps. Dans le passage cité, le héros du roman, Gérard de Nevers, s'est déguisé en ménestrel ; lorsqu'on lui demande d'exécuter son morceau il bondit et commence à « chanter et vieler ensemble ». Il chante une laisse qui fait partie de l'épopée appelée *Aliscans*. Seuls les trois premiers vers de cette citation épique figurent dans l'Appendice.

Un troubadour et sa vièle : Perdigon, chansonnier provençal (XIIIᵉ siècle).
(Paris, B.N., ms. fr. 124473, fol. 36)

Le troisième accord pour vièle

L'instrument utilisé pour accompagner la chanson de geste est la *viella* dans les textes latins, et la vièle dans les œuvres vernaculaires. Je n'ai trouvé aucun témoignage de l'utilisation d'autres instruments. Cela concorde avec le témoignage du *Dit des taboureurs* où les vièleurs prétendent que l'épopée leur appartient et en font la source de leur prestige.

Nous pouvons maintenant rassembler les fils de notre histoire. Je soutiens la suggestion de Bachmann qui dit que le troisième accord pour vièle de Jérôme est destiné à fournir cinq notes de mélodie et un bourdon, et qu'il n'était donc guère approprié aux genres de la musique médiévale que nous connaissons à travers nos sources musicales. Cependant, cet accord aurait pu être idéal pour jouer la musique, très répétitive, des chansons de geste auxquelles la vièle est étroitement associée dans les textes littéraires.

Le seul fragment qui peut être associé avec certitude à la chanson de geste est préservé dans *Le Jeu de Robin et Marion,* par un contemporain de Jérôme, Adam de la Halle [8]. Cette mélodie *(exemple 2)* convient parfaitement au troisième accord pour vièle décrit par Jérôme ; s'agit-il d'une coïncidence ? Un chanteur utilisant cette mélodie et jouant le même air sur la vièle, comme Gérard de Nevers semble le faire dans *Le Roman de la Violette,* produirait une mélodie ainsi qu'un accompagnement dense pour renforcer sa voix. Il est à déplorer qu'il n'existe pas d'autre mélodie pour chanson de geste !

Pourquoi Jérôme aurait-il inclus un accord pour le répertoire des chansons de geste dans son traité ?

Exemple 2

Le troisième accord pour vièle

D'abord, il y a la fierté de la France, la *Gallica superbia,* qui était si connue au Moyen Age. Si l'on considère la variété des héros qui sont associés à la vièle sur notre liste de textes, on découvre qu'ils appartiennent tous à ce que les poètes du XIIIᵉ siècle appellent « La matière de France ». Charlemagne, Roland, Guillaume au court nez, Aymeri de Narbonne : ils étaient les barons dont les vies de combat formaient le passé de la France. Jean de Grouchy avait ressenti cela lorsqu'il appelait les héros comme Charlemagne les *antiqui patres,* les « pères anciens » de France [9]. Nous commençons à comprendre pourquoi les musiciens du *Dit des Taboureurs* sont si fiers de chanter et de jouer les chansons de geste.

Après la fierté, l'hérésie. Le sujet de nombreux poèmes épiques se rattache directement à la lutte contre l'Islam, *La chanson de Roland* étant l'exemple le plus connu. Dans beaucoup de chansons de geste, la terre de France est le centre d'une magnifique entreprise martiale au cœur de laquelle tous les membres de la classe chevaleresque s'engagent dans les actions, à la fois défensives et offensives, contre les forces de l'Islam. En tant que frère dominicain, Jérôme faisait partie d'un ordre religieux engagé qui occupait une position vitale dans le combat de l'Eglise contre le paganisme et l'hérésie sous toutes ses formes.

Troisièmement, et sans doute plus complexe que les autres raisons, il y a un genre de propagande cléricale dans beaucoup de chansons de geste. Dans le monde des épopées il est question de pouvoir, c'est certain, mais il n'y a pas vraiment d'appareil gouvernemental proprement dit : pas de notaires, d'administrateurs ou d'avocats. Il y a des prêtres et des évêques, mais il n'y a pas de sacerdoce systématique. Ce qui apparaît dans les épopées, c'est la violence d'une aristocratie martiale qui ne peut restreindre son orgueil destructif et son agressivité. Pour ceux qui écoutaient les chansons de geste au temps de Jérôme, le message subliminal était puissant : voici ce qu'était la France avant la bureaucratie cléricale et le ministère des ordres religieux. Si cela semble un peu fantasque, souvenons-nous que c'est exactement en ces termes « politiques » que Jean de Grouchy interprète la valeur sociale des chansons de geste dans le contexte parisien. Il remarque, avec raison, que les vies des héros épiques comme Charlemagne, se passaient en batailles et dures épreuves : *proelia et adversitates* ; il ajoute ensuite que les chansons de geste contribuent à la sécurité de Paris. Et comment ? Il dit que c'est parce que les travailleurs et les gens de la classe moyenne qui les écoutaient en viennent à réaliser que leur condition présente est relativement facile et

Le troisième accord pour vièle

agréable. Il leur fallait donc travailler avec un esprit calme. « Ainsi, dit Jean de Grouchy, la ville [de Paris] entière est protégée ».

Un sermon du XIIIe siècle décrit comment les ménestrels de Paris prenaient position sur le Petit Pont, près de Notre-Dame, pour raconter les exploits de Roland et Olivier. Les gens attroupés, touchés par ces histoires tristes et violentes, en versaient des larmes [10]. Jean de Grouchy et Jérôme, passant par le Petit Pont pour se rendre au quartier latin, étaient souvent, sans doute, témoins de ces scènes. Les artisans et les marchands ambulants écoutaient ces chansons de geste ; lorsqu'ils levaient les yeux vers la façade de Notre-Dame, ils ne pouvaient s'empêcher de penser que la puissance du roi associée à celle du clergé les avait sortis d'un passé héroïque mais tumultueux, pour leur offrir un présent où il y avait un espoir de paix et de salut. Il n'est pas étonnant, donc, que Jérôme ait voulu retenir par écrit — et de manière exacte — un accord dont les musiciens se servaient lorsqu'ils exécutaient des chansons de geste.

1 - F.-L. Perne, « Notice sur un manuscrit du XIIIe siècle », *Revue Musicale,* 2 (1828), 457-67 et 481-90.

2 - C. Page, *Voices and Instruments of the Middle Ages* (Londres, 1987), p. 126-32, et pour le texte du chapitre 28, id., « Jerome of Moravia on the *rubeba* and *viella* », *Galpin Society Journal,* 32 (1979), p. 77-8.

3 - Voir les versions de Perne et de Gérold (*La musique au Moyen Age* [Paris, 1932]), p. 382, entre autres.

4 - Ma traduction, d'après la version anglaise de N. Deane, *The Origins of Bowing* (Oxford, 1969), p. 104.

5 - Texte de F. Whitehead, *La chanson de Roland* (Oxford, 1970).

6 - E. Rohloff, *Die Quellenhandschriften zum Musiktraktat des Johannes de Grocheio* (Leipzig, 1972), p. 132.

7 - Voir J. Stevens, *Words and Music in the Middle Ages* (Cambridge, 1986), p. 199-267.

8 - J. Chailley, « Du *Tu autem* de Horn à la musique des chansons de geste », *Mélanges René Louis* (Saint-Père-Sous-Vezelay, 1982), tome I, p. 21-32.

9 - Rohloff, *Die Quellenhandschriften, op. cit.,* p. 130.

10 - B. Hauréau, *Notices et extraits de quelques manuscrits latins de la Bibliothèque nationale* (Paris, 1890-3), tome III, p. 317.

Le troisième accord pour vièle

APPENDICE

I

XIIe S., ANONYMOUS, *LE MONIAGE GUILLAUME* (SECONDE RÉDACTION)

Hui mais orès canchon de fiere geste,
Chil jougleour en cantent en vïele.

II

c1175-1200, JEAN BODEL, *LA CHANSON DES SAISNES*

Cil bastart jougleour qui vont par ces viliaus
A ces longues vïeles à depeciés forriaus
Chantent de Guiteclin…

III

1195-6, EGIDIUS OF PARIS, *KAROLINUS*

De Karolo, clari preclara prole Pipini,
Cuius apud populos venerabile nomen in omni
Ore satis claret, et decantata per orbem
Gesta solent melicis aures sopire viellis.

IV

?1227-9, GERBERT DE MONTREUIL, *LE ROMAN DE VIOLETTE*

« Faire m'estuet, quant l'ai empris,
Chou dont je ne sui mie apris. »
Chanter et vïeler ensamble
Lors commencha, si com moi samble,
Con chil qui molt estoit senés,
Un ver de Guillaume au court nes,
A clere vois et o douch son :

(Suit un extrait de la chanson de geste d'*Aliscans*, vers 3036 f)

Crans fu la cours en la sale a Loon ;
Mult ot as tables oisiaus et venison.
Ki ke mangast le car ne le poisson, etc.

Le troisième accord pour vièle

V

?c1262-3, Albertus Magnus

comoedi… sunt, qui facta heroum canunt in viellis

VI

XIIIᴱ s., Anonyme, *Dit des Taboureurs*

Mès qui bien set chanter du Borgoing Auberi,
De Girart de Viane, de l'Ardenois Tierri,
De Guillaume au cort nez, de son père Aimeri,
Doivent par tout le monde bien estre seignori.

VII

XIIIᴱ s., Anonyme (? Nicholas de Biard), *Sermon*

Laudate Dominum in sanctis ejus. Viellatores gesta proborum militum utpote Karoli, Rolandi, solent libenter narrare ; quanto magis
predicatores, qui sunt viellatores Dei, gesta sanctorum que sunt lau-
dabiliora in infinitum debent narrare.

VIII

XIIIᴱ s., Anonyme, *Poeme moral*

Et teus est ki ne viut a la karole aler,
Mais bien voet tote jour oir d'Aiol parler ;
Ne cuide nul mal faire s'il ot bien vieler.
Mais jou cuic qu'il ne puent sans pecie escoter.

Car cou c'aie a l'ame, cou k'atent a Jesu,
Se bien set li jouglere les dois movoir menu,
S'i me dist que Rollans abati Fiernagu
E k'Aious fu gabes por l'anciien escu ?

IX

XIIIᴱ s., Anonyme, *Doon de Nanteuil*

Il est einsint coustume en la vostre contrée,
Quant uns chanterres vient entre gent henorée
Et il a endroit soi sa vielle atremprée
Ja tant n'avra mantel ne cote desramée
Que sa premiere laisse ne soit bien escoutée…

SOURCES : (I) W. Cloetta, *Les deux rédactions en vers du Moniage Guillaume*, 2 vols, SAFT (Paris, 1906 and 1911), I, p. 139. (II) F. Menzel and E. Stengel, *Jean Bodel's Saxenlied*, 2 vols (Marburg, 1906 and 1909), vers 27-9. (III) M. L. Colker, « The 'Karolinus' of 'Egidius Pariensis' », *Traditio*, 29 (1973), p. 199-325, vers 9-12. (IV) D. L. Buffum, *Le Roman de la Violette*, SAFT (Paris, 1928), vers 1400. (V) A. Borgnet, *Beati Alberti Magni Opera Omnia*, 8, p. 748. (VI) A. Jubinal, *Jongleurs et trouvères* (Paris, 1835), p. 164-9. (VII) J. J. Techener, *Description raisonnée d'une collection choisie d'Anciens Manuscrits, de Documents Historiques et de Chartes, Réunis par les soins de J. J. Techener*, I (Paris, 1862), p. 273. (VIII) E. Herzog, « Ein Fragment des *Poème moral* », *Zeitschrift für Romanische Philologie*, 32 (1908), p. 60. (IX) P. Meyer, « La chanson de Doon de Nanteuil : fragments inédits », *Romania*, 13 (1884), p. 12.

Johannes de Grocheio on secular music: a corrected text and a new translation

It has long been recognized that Johannes de Grocheio's *De musica*[1] is an outstanding source of information about Parisian musical practice *c.* 1300. However, the critical text of the treatise published by Rohloff in 1972 can be improved by returning to the manuscripts,[2] and the pioneering English translation, by Albert Seay, can now be corrected in some important particulars.[3] The purpose of this article is therefore to present a corrected text and a new (annotated) translation of Johannes de Grocheio's remarks about secular music, both monophonic and polyphonic, generally regarded as the most important part of his treatise.[4]

To judge by Grocheio's comments on measured notation, he was writing *c.* 1300; he mentions Franco (whose *Ars cantus mensurabilis* was probably compiled *c.* 1280, according to current opinion), and he refers to the division of the tempus 'into two, into three, and in the same way on up to six'.[5] The text deals with Parisian musical practices, and Grocheio's thoroughness in this regard leaves no doubt that he had sampled the musical life of the capital; his passing references to Aristotelian concepts such as *forma et materia*, and to commentaries upon the *De anima* (among other books), suggest that he had studied in Paris, presumably by attending a

---

[1] I adopt this title since it is the one that Grocheio employs himself; see E. Rohloff, ed., *Die Quellenhandschriften zum Musiktraktat des Johannes de Grocheio* (Leipzig, 1972), p. 171.

[2] Some of Rohloff's interpretations and readings are challenged and discussed in P. A. M. DeWitt, *A New Perspective on Johannes de Grocheio's Ars Musicae*, Ph.D dissertation, University of Michigan (1973). After some years of independent work on French music in the thirteenth century I have returned to this dissertation and found many points of agreement. For further material of interest and importance, see T. J. McGee, 'Medieval Dances: Matching the Repertory with Grocheio's Descriptions', *The Journal of Musicology*, 7 (1989), 498–517, and D. Stockmann, '*Musica Vulgaris* bei Johannes de Grocheio', *Beiträge zur Musikwissenschaft*, 25 (1983), 3–56.

[3] A. Seay, trans., *Johannes de Grocheo [sic]: Concerning Music*, 2nd edn (Colorado Springs: Colorado College Music Press, 1974).

[4] This article incorporates and develops the results of research presented in C. Page, *Voices and Instruments of the Middle Ages: Instrumental Practice and Songs in France, 1100–1300* (London, 1987), *passim*, but especially pp. 196–201; *idem*, *The Owl and the Nightingale: Musical Life and Ideas in France 1100–1300* (London, 1989), *passim*; and *idem*, *Discarding Images: Reflections on Music and Culture in Medieval France* (Oxford, 1993), Chapter 3, *passim*.

[5] For the text see Rohloff, *Die Quellenhandschriften*, p. 138.

Plainsong and Medieval Music 2, 1, pp. 17–41 © 1993 Cambridge University Press

course of lectures.[6] There is no proof that he proceeded to take a degree, however (for this was not an automatic step), and it may be wise to keep an open mind about the note in the Darmstadt manuscript of the text where he is given the title 'magister' and named as a resident teacher at Paris ('regens Parisius');[7] the scribe may have been guessing on the basis of what he had read in the treatise. (It is note-worthy that the word 'Parisius' is added in a later hand.) If modern scholars are agreed that the treatise was written in Paris then it is partly because Paris exerts an extraordinary magnetism in most areas of Ars Antiqua studies; one might well argue that it is a quintessentially *provincial* activity to classify and describe the musical forms and fashions of a capital. Viewed in this light, the *De musica* might have been written in any part of France.

Johannes de Grocheio was almost certainly a Norman by birth. It is conceivable that he took his name from the coastal hamlet of Gruchy some 12 km west of Cherbourg, but a much more tempting hypothesis is that he belonged to the distin-guished Norman family of de Grouchy. The de Grouchys are first recorded in the eleventh century (as 'de Groci') and were to become a distinguished minor family in the military history of France.[8] They possessed several fiefs between Rouen and Gournay-en-Bray. The family name derives from the region of Gruchy, near Blainville, about 16 km to the south-west of the de Grouchy lordship of Montérolier (see the Map). In view of the Norman fiefdoms of the de Grouchys it is striking that Normandy is the only provincial region of France that Grocheio mentions in his treatise (see the section below on the *ductia*). It may also be significant that Grocheio, by his own account, explored some important aspects of his treatise in a discourse with a certain Clement, who has recently been identified as a monk of the Benedictine Abbey of Lessay in Normandy.[9] It is possible that Grocheio had some link with this important monastic house, a community of more than thirty monks in his lifetime.[10] It is also possible that Grocheio was a priest, but I have been unable to verify the assertion of Mgr Glorieux that he was definitely a priest 'since we pos-sess some sermons by him'.[11] Those sermons – if they ever existed – are not listed in Schneyer's monumental *Repertorium sermonum*.

6 On this aspect of Grocheio's treatise see DeWitt, *A New Perspective*, passim, and M. Bielitz, 'Materia und forma bei Johannes de Grocheo', *Die Musikforschung*, 38 (1985), 257–77.

7 See the facsimile in Rohloff, *Die Quellenhandschriften*, p. 107.

8 On the de Grouchys during the Middle Ages see Le Vicomte de Grouchy and E. Travers, *Etude sur Nicolas de Grouchy* (Paris and Caen, 1878), pp. 4–9; le Marquis de Grouchy, *Mémoires du Maréchal de Grouchy*, 5 vols. (Paris, 1873-4), pp. iv-vii; *Dictionnaire de la Noblesse*, 3rd edn, 9, sv. 'Grouchy'. For the name 'de Groci' in the eleventh century see *Mémoires de la Société des Antiquaires de Normandie*, 4th series, 6 (1961), p. 374 ('Hugo de Groci').

9 For the identification of Clement's monastery see Page, *The Owl and the Nightingale*, pp. 171–2, and p. 246 note 3. The evidence in question is obliterated in Rohloff's text by his emendation of Grocheio's 'Exaquiensem monachum' (i.e. 'monk of Lessay') to '[exequiarium] monachum' (*Die Quellenhandschriften*, p. 130).

10 See the references to the community of Lessay in the celebrated *Register* of Odon Rigaud, conveniently accessible in S. M. Brown, trans., *The Register of Eudes of Rouen* (New York and London, 1964), p. 100 (visitation of 1250, thirty-six monks), p. 277 (visitation of 1256, thirty-four monks) and p. 634 (visita-tion of 1266, thirty-one monks).

11 P. Glorieux, *La faculté des arts et ses maîtres au XIIIe siècle*, Etudes de philosophie médiévale, 59 (Paris, 1971), sv. Jean de Grouchy.

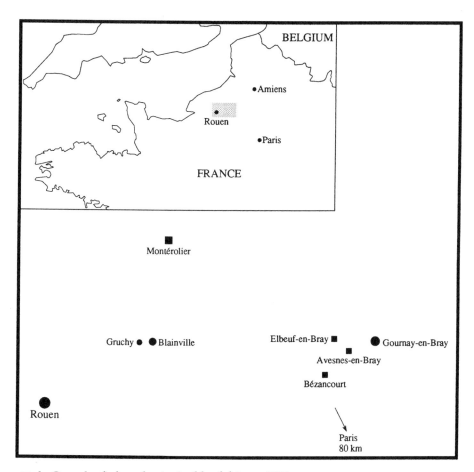

- de Grouchy fiefs and principal lordships *c.* 1300
Rouen to Gournay-en-Bray is approximately 30 km

The text given here is derived from the facsimiles of the two manuscript sources of the treatise accompanying Rohloff's edition (a most lavish provision for which the editor and his publishers are to be warmly thanked). Each extract is cued with the appropriate page number in that edition. Rohloff's text has been compared with these manuscripts, producing a significant number of new readings, signalled below. For the sake of consistency, Rohloff's classicizing orthography has been retained. It should be emphasized that what follows is not intended as a comprehensive bibliographical guide to recent research on Grocheio's text and the notes to the translation are therefore generally confined to matters of lexical or interpretative difficulty; the reader is referred to Rohloff's edition for bibliographical material pertaining to the songs and other pieces mentioned by Grocheio.

p. 124 [From the preliminary discussion of how music may be classified.] Alii autem musicam dividunt in planam sive immensurabilem et mensurabilem, per

20

planam sive immensurabilem intellegentes ecclesiasticam, quae secundum Gregorium pluribus tonis determinatur. Per mensurabilem intellegunt illam quae ex diversis sonis simul mensuratis et sonantibus efficitur, sicut in conductibus et motetis. Sed si per immensurabilem intellegant musicam nullo modo mensuratam, immo totaliter ad libitum dictam deficiunt eo quod quaelibet operatio musicae et cuiuslibet artis debet illius artis regulis mensurari. Si autem per immensurabilem non ita praecise mensuratam intellegant, potest, ut videtur, ista divisio remanere. ...Partes autem musicae plures sunt et diversae secundum diversos usus, diversa idiomata vel diversas linguas in civitatibus vel regionibus diversis. Si tamen eam diviserimus secundum quod homines Parisius¹² ea utuntur, et prout ad usum vel convictum civium est necessaria et eius membra, ut oportet, pertractemus, videbitur sufficienter nostra intentio terminari eo quod diebus nostris principia cuiuslibet artis liberalis diligenter Parisiis inquiruntur et usus earum et fere omnium mechanicarum inveniuntur. Dicamus igitur quod musica qua utuntur homines Parisiis potest, ut videtur, ad tria membra generalia reduci. Unum autem membrum dicimus de simplici musica vel civili, quam vulgarem musicam appellamus; aliud autem de musica composita vel regulari vel canonica quam appellant musicam mensuratam. Sed tertium genus est quod ex istis duobus efficitur et ad quod ista duo tamquam ad melius ordinantur quod ecclesiasticam dicitur et ad laudandum creatorem deputatum est.

Others divide music into 'plain' or 'immeasurable' music and 'measurable', understanding 'plain' or 'immeasurable' music to be that of the Church which, following Gregory, has its boundaries set by various modes. By 'measurable' music they understand the music which is made from diverse pitches simultaneously measured and sounding, as in *conducti* and in motets. But if by the term 'immeasurable' they understand music which is in no way measured, but which is entirely performed in an arbitrary fashion, then they are at fault, because every process of music – and of any art – must be calculated according to the rules of that art. If, however, by the term 'immeasurable' they understand music which is not so precisely measured,¹³ then it is evident that this division may be allowed to stand. ...There are many elements of music according to diverse usages, diverse dialects and diverse languages in different cities and regions. But if we divide it according to the usage of the Parisians, and if we treat the elements of music, as is fitting, according to how they are necessary for the entertainment and use of [Parisian] citizens, our intention will be seen to be adequately accomplished because in our days the Parisians diligently enquire into the fundamentals of every liberal art and ascertain the practice of them and of virtually every skill. We declare therefore that the music which is employed by the Parisians can be classified, as may be seen, into

---

¹² So both MSS. Rohloff: *Parisiis*

¹³ This passage has been much discussed; see H. Van der Werf, 'The "Not-So-Precisely Measured" Music of the Middle Ages', *Performance Practice Review*, 1 (1988), 42–60, and J. Stevens, *Words and Music in the Middle Ages: Song, Narrative, Dance and Drama 1050–1350* (Cambridge, 1986), p. 433 *et passim*.

three general categories. We call one of these monophonic, 'civil' or the lay public's music, and the other comprises composed, regulated or 'canon'[14] music which they call measured music. But there is a third kind which is made from these two and for which these two are structured as if for the better; it is called ecclesiastical music and has been instituted for the praise of the Creator.

p. 128 [From the discussion of the gamut]...alium modum diversitatis invenerunt dicentes unum lineam et aliud spatium, incipientes a Γ ut usque ad d la sol procedentes. Sic itaque apparet quod ponendo signa vel notas in lineis et spatiis omnes concordantias et omnem cantum sufficienter describere potuerunt. Moderni vero propter descriptionem consonantiarum et stantipedum et ductiarum aliud addiderunt, quod *falsam musicam* vocaverunt, quia illa duo signa, scilicet ♭ et ♮ quae in ♭ fa ♮ mi tonum et semitonum designabant, in omnibus aliis faciunt hoc designare ita quod ubi erat semitonus per ♮ illud[15] ad tonum ampliant ut bona concordantia vel consonantia fiat, et similiter ubi tonus inveniebatur illud[16] per ♭ ad semitonum restringunt.

[the Ancients] devised another means of distinguishing [the notes of the gamut], declaring one to be a line and another a space, beginning on gamma *ut* and proceeding as far as d *la sol*. It is therefore apparent that by putting signs or marks upon lines and spaces they were able to notate all intervals, and every melody, in an adequate manner. The Moderns, moreover, in order to produce a notated record of consonances, of *stantipedes* and of *ductiae*,[17] have added another [means of distinguishing the notes of the gamut] which they have called *musica falsa* because they extend the two signs ♭ and ♮, which they use to indicate a tone and semitone step in ♭ fa ♮ mi, to all other [degrees of the gamut] with the same meaning, so that, where there was a semitone, they make it into a tone with ♮, so that there may be good line and good harmony,[18] and in the same way, where there was tone to be found, they compress it into a semitone by means of ♭.

---

[14] The term 'canon' music (*musica canonica*) balances 'civil' music (*musica civilis*), both terms to be understood as in 'canon' and 'civil' law, i.e. as relating to the clergy and to the laity respectively. It is unfortunate that Seay's translation 'composed or regular music by rule' for Grocheio's *musica composita vel regulari vel canonica* misses this distinction (*Concerning Music*, p. 12).

[15] So both MSS. Rohloff: *illum*

[16] So both MSS. Rohloff: *illum*

[17] The passage might also be rendered 'in order to produce a notated record of the consonances of *stantipedes* and of *ductiae*', which narrows the range of purposes for which *musica ficta* was devised in what is perhaps an unacceptable way, and which also, given the meaning Grocheio attaches to *consonantia*, implies polyphonic *stantipedes* and *ductiae*, which seems out of the question in this discussion of monophonic music. On the meaning of the term 'consonantia' in Grocheio's usage see the following note, and for Grocheio's description of the *stantipes* and *ductia* see below.

[18] 'bona concordantia vel consonantia'. Grocheio distinguishes (p. 144) between *concordantia*, when one musical sound relates in a harmonious way to another (*concordantia* therefore relates to line), and *consonantia*, when two or more notes sound simultaneously (*consonantia* therefore relates to harmony). Compare DeWitt, *A New Perspective*, pp. 76f.

22

p. 130 Dicamus igitur quod formae musicales vel species contentae sub primo membro, quod vulgare dicebamus, ad hoc ordinantur, ut eis mediantibus mitigentur adversitates hominum innatae, quas magis particulavimus in sermone ad Clementem Exaquiensem[19] monachum, et sunt duobus modis, aut enim in voce humana aut in instrumentis artificialibus exercentur. Quae autem in voce humana fiunt duobus modis sunt, aut enim dicimus cantum aut cantilenam. Cantum autem et cantilenam triplici differentia distinguimus. Aut enim [cantum] gestualem aut coronatum aut versiculatum, et cantilenam [aut] rotundam aut stantipedem aut ductiam appellamus.

We say, therefore, that the musical forms or genres that are subsumed by the first category, which we have called the music of the lay public,[20] are ordained for this purpose: that they may soften the sufferings to which all men are born and which I have detailed further in a discourse to Clement, a monk of Lessay.[21] And [these musical forms] are of two kinds, for they are either performed with the human voice or with musical instruments. Those that are made with the human voice are of two kinds: we call them either 'cantus' or 'cantilena'[22] and distinguish three kinds of each. There is a *cantus gestualis, coronatus* and *versiculatus*; there is a *cantilena rotunda, stantipedes* and *ductia*.

p. 130 Cantum vero gestualem dicimus in quo gesta heroum et antiquorum patrum opera recitantur, sicuti vita et martyria sanctorum et proelia et adversitates quas antiqui viri pro fide et veritati passi sunt, sicuti vita beati Stephani protomartyris et historia regis Karoli. Cantus autem iste debet antiquis et civibus laborantibus et mediocribus ministrari dum requiescunt ab opere consueto, ut auditis miseriis et calamitatibus aliorum suas facilius sustineant et quilibet opus suum alacrius aggrediatur. Et ideo iste cantus valet ad conservationem totius civitatis.

---

[19] So MS H; MS D: *exaquiansem*. Rohloff: [*exequiarium*].

[20] There can be no fully satisfactory translation of Grocheio's *vulgare*, here rendered 'of the lay public'. It appears to denote all the laity, from working people to royalty. Seay's translation 'vulgar music' (*Concerning Music*, p. 12) is somewhat unsatisfactory – if etymologically justifiable – given the modern associations of the word 'vulgar'. Compare DeWitt, *A New Perspective*, pp. 122f (an excellent discussion), Stevens, *Words and Music*, p. 431, and Page, *Discarding Images*, Chapter 3, *passim*.

[21] The words 'quas magis particulavimus in sermone ad Clementem Exaquiensem monachum' are consistent with the view that Grocheio discussed these matters with Clement, but it may rather imply a letter or treatise, now lost. The translation offered here ('which I have detailed further in a discourse to Clement, a monk of Lessay') is designed to accommodate both possibilities which are not, of course, mutually exclusive.

[22] Perhaps modelled upon the Old French terms *chanson* and *chansonette*. Grocheio's classification of musical forms has been much discussed and paraphrased; see, for example, DeWitt, *A New Perspective, passim*; F. A. Gallo, *Music of the Middle Ages II* (Cambridge, 1985), pp. 10–13; C. Page, *Voices and Instruments*, pp. 196–201; Stevens, *Words and Music*, pp. 491–5; Stockmann, '*Musica Vulgaris*'; H. Wagenaar-Nolthenius, 'Estampie/Stantipes/Stampita', in *L'Ars Nova Italiana del Trecento: 2nd Congress* (Certaldo, 1969), pp. 399–409. A vital essay for the study of French song in Grocheio's lifetime is now L. Earp, 'Lyrics for Reading and Singing in Late Medieval France: The Development of the Dance Lyric from Adam de la Halle to Guillaume de Machaut', in R. A. Baltzer *et al.*, eds., *The Union of Words and Music in Medieval Poetry* (Austin, 1991), pp. 101–31.

We call that kind of *cantus* a *chanson de geste* in which the deeds of heroes and the works of ancient fathers[23] are recounted, such as the life and martyrdom of saints and the battles and adversities which the men of ancient times suffered for the sake of faith and truth, such as the life of St Stephen, the first martyr, and the story of King Charlemagne. This kind of music should be laid on[24] for the elderly, for working citizens and for those of middle station when they rest from their usual toil, so that, having heard the miseries and calamities of others, they may more easily bear their own and so that anyone may undertake his own labour with more alacrity. Therefore this kind of *cantus* has the power to preserve the whole city.[25]

p. 130 Cantus coronatus ab aliquibus simplex conductus dictus est, qui propter eius bonitatem in dictamine et cantu a magistris et studentibus circa sonos coronatur, sicut gallice *Ausi com l'unicorne* vel *Quant li roussignol*, qui etiam a regibus et nobilibus solet componi et etiam coram regibus et principibus terre decantari, ut eorum animos ad audaciam et fortitudinem, magnanimitatem et liberalitatem commoveat, quae omnia faciunt ad bonum regimen. Est enim cantus iste de delectabili materia et ardua, sicut de amicitia et caritate, et ex omnibus longis et perfectis efficitur.

The *cantus coronatus* has been called a 'monophonic conductus' by some; on account of the inherent virtue[26] of its poetry and music it is crowned by masters and students [of the art of songmaking] among pieces,[27] as in the French *Ausi com l'uni-*

---

[23] The 'ancient fathers' are probably not the Fathers of the Church, despite the ubiquity of *Vitae patrum* collections in the Middle Ages; no *chansons de geste* dealing with the lives of Fathers of the Church have survived. Grocheio probably means the ancient fathers of France – such as Charlemagne – whose wars and struggles brought the realm of France into being. See Page, *The Owl and the Nightingale*, pp. 30–33, and *idem*, 'Le troisième accord pour vièle de Jérôme de Moravie: Jongleurs et "anciens pères de France"', in C. Meyer, ed., *Jérôme de Moravie: un théoricien de la musique dans le milieu intellectuel parisien du XIII siècle* (Paris, 1992), pp. 83–96.

[24] 'should be laid on' translates *debet ministrari*; Grocheio sometimes chooses verbs which imply the politic provision of music for the mitigation of laymen's vices.

[25] It remains uncertain whether *civitas* should be translated 'city' here or taken in the broader sense 'State'. The former conveys Grocheio's interest in the music of a single city, Paris. However, when Grocheio speaks of the way music instils virtue and obedience his conception of the *civitas* is perhaps more expansive. See D. Luscombe, 'City and Politics Before the Coming of the *Politics*: Some Illustrations', in D. Abulafia, M. Franklin and M. Rubin, eds., *Church and City 1000–1500: Essays in Honour of Christopher Brooke* (Cambridge, 1992), pp. 41–55.

[26] The word *bonitas* demands a translation in excess of mere 'excellence', especially in the context of this imagery of crowning. Grocheio is presumably trying to convey a deeper virtue in the *cantus coronatus*, arising from the lofty subject-matter of the poetry, the excellence of its music and the high status of its composers. Grocheio's description of the *cantus coronatus* has been much discussed; for recent accounts see Stevens, *Words and Music*, p. 431, *idem*, 'Medieval Song' in D. Hiley and R. Crocker, eds., *The Early Middle Ages to 1300*, New Oxford History of Music II, 2nd edn (Oxford, 1990), p. 392, and Page, *Voices and Instruments*, pp. 196–201.

[27] A difficult passage; the sense of 'circa sonos' is not clear. Seay (*Concerning Music*, p. 16) takes it to refer to instrumental accompaniment, as does Rohloff, *Die Quellenhandschriften*, p. 131, but that seems strained. The matter is amply discussed in DeWitt, *A New Perspective*, pp. 133–4. The interpretation offered here is much the same as that of Stevens (*Words and Music*, p. 431). For a very different interpretation see C. Warren, 'Punctus organi and cantus coronatus in the Music of Dufay', in A. Atlas, ed., *Dufay Quincentenary Conference* (Brooklyn, 1976), pp. 128–43.

24

corne [see Ex. 1] or *Quant li roussignol*. This kind of song is customarily composed by kings and nobles and sung in the presence of kings and princes of the land[28] so that it may move their minds to boldness and fortitude, magnanimity and liberality, all of which things lead to good government. This kind of *cantus* deals with delightful and lofty subject-matter, such as friendship and love, and it is composed entirely from longs – perfect ones at that.[29]

pp. 131–2 Cantus versualis est qui ab aliquibus cantilena dicitur respectu coronati et ab eius bonitate in dictamine et concordantia deficit, sicut gallice *Chanter m'estuet quar ne m'en puis tenir* vel *Au repairier que je fis de Prouvence*. Cantus autem iste debet iuvenibus exhiberi ne in otio totaliter sint reperti. Qui enim refutat laborem et in otio vult vivere ei labor et adversitas est parata. Unde Seneca: Non est viri timere sudorem. Qualiter igitur modi cantus describuntur, sic apparet.

The *cantus versualis* is a species of *cantus* which is called a *cantilena* by some with respect to the [*cantus*] *coronatus* and which lacks the inherent virtue [of the *cantus coronatus*] in poetry and melody, as in the French *Chanter m'estuet quar ne m'en puis tenir*, or *Au repairier que je fis de Prouvence*.[30] This kind of song should be performed for the young lest they be found ever in idleness. He who refuses labour and wishes to live at ease has only travail and adversity in store. Whence Seneca says that 'It is not for a man to fear sweat'.[31] Thus it is plain how the various kinds of *cantus* are to be described.

p. 132 Cantilena vero quaelibet rotunda vel rotundellus a pluribus dicitur eo quod ad modum circuli in se ipsam reflectitur et incipit et terminatur in eodem. Nos autem solum illam rotundam vel rotundellum dicimus cuius partes non habent diversum cantum a cantu responsorii vel refractus. Et longo tractu cantatur velut cantus coronatus, cuiusmodi est gallice *Toute sole passerai le vert boscage*. Et huius-

---

[28] In this passage Grocheio seems determined to present a traditionalist and (by the later thirteenth century) a somewhat archaic image of trouvère monody in the High Style as an aristocratic art, rather than the increasingly urban, mercantile art that it had become with the expansion of the *puis*. In part, Grocheio's comment reflects the prominence of Thibaut, King of Navarre (*d.* 1253) in the later thirteenth-century conception of the trouvères' art. *Ausi com l'unicorne*, which Grocheio cites, is one of his chansons. In the *Chansonnier de l'Arsenal* Thibaut's songs are presented first, preceded by an illumination which shows a fiddler performing before a seated king and queen as courtiers stand nearby. This exactly matches Grocheio's remark that such songs should be performed 'in the presence of kings and princes of the land'. The *Chansonnier de l'Arsenal* continues (again, as some other sources do), to present the works of trouvères whose noble or aristocratic status was well known or assumed, such as Gace Brulé.

[29] The idiomatic translation is required to capture the quality of emphasis in the second conjunction: 'et ex omnibus longis *et* perfectis efficitur'. For discussions of this passage see J. Knapp, 'Musical Declamation and Poetic Rhythm in an Early Layer of Notre Dame Conductus', *Journal of the American Musicological Society*, 32 (1979), pp. 406–7, and Stevens, *Words and Music*, pp. 431–2, with bibliography there cited.

[30] On the distinction between the *cantus coronatus* and the *cantus versualis* see Stevens, 'Medieval Song', pp. 412 and 420, and Page, *Voices and Instruments*, pp. 199–200.

[31] *Epistulae Morales*, XXXI.

Au- si conme u- ni- cor- ne sui

Qui s'es- ba- hist en re- gar- dant,

Quant la pu- ce- le va mi- rant.

Tant est li- e de son en- nui,

Pas- me- e chiet en son gi- ron,

Lors l'o- cit on en tra- î- son

Et moi ont mort d'au- tel sen- blant

A- mors et ma da- me, por voir:

Mon cuer ont, n'en puis point a- voir.

Ex. 1

modi cantilena versus occidentem, puta in Normannia, solet decantari a puellis et iuvenibus in festis et magnis conviviis ad eorum decorationem.

There are indeed many who call any *cantilena* a 'rotunda' or 'rotundellus' because it turns back on itself in the manner of a circle, beginning and ending in the same way [i.e. with a refrain].[32] However, I only call the kind of song a 'rotunda' or 'rotundellus' whose parts have the same music as the music of the response or refrain.[33] When it is sung it is drawn out in an expansive way like the *cantus coronatus*. The French song *Toute sole passerai le vert boscage* is of this kind. This kind of song is customarily sung towards the West – in Normandy, for example – by girls and by young men as an adornment to holiday celebrations and to great banquets.[34]

p. 132 Cantilena quae dicitur *stantipes* est illa in qua est diversitas in partibus et refractu tam in consonantia dictaminis quam in cantu, sicut gallice *A l'entrant d'amors* vel *Certes mie ne cuidoie*. Haec autem facit animos iuvenum et puellarum propter sui difficultatem circa hanc stare et eos a prava cogitatione divertit.

In the kind of *cantilena* which is called 'stantipes' there is a diversity – both in the rhymes of the poem and in the music – that distinguishes the verses from the refrain, as in the French song *A l'entrant d'amors* or *Certes mie ne cuidoie*. On account of its difficulty, this [distinction] makes the minds of young men and of girls dwell upon this [kind of *cantilena*][35] and leads them away from depraved thoughts.

p. 132 Ductia vero est cantilena levis et velox in ascensu et descensu quae in choreis a iuvenibus et puellis decantatur, sicut gallice *Chi encor querez amoretes*. Haec enim ducit corda puellarum et iuvenum et a vanitate removet et contra passionem quae dicitur 'amor hereos'[36] valere dicitur.

The *ductia* is a kind of *cantilena* that is light and rapid in its ascents and descents and which is sung in caroles[37] by young men and girls, like the French song *Chi encor querez amoretes*. This [kind of cantilena] directs the sentiments[38] of girls and

---

[32] As it is a distinguishing feature of *cantilene* that they begin and end with a refrain it would appear that some musicians called them all *rotunda* or *rotundellus*, since this term denoted the rondeau (see next note), beginning and ending with a refrain.

[33] Indicating that Grocheio's *rotunda* or *rotundellus* is a rondeau, no doubt of standard fourteenth-century structure, already cultivated at this date by his Parisian contemporary Jean de l'Escurel.

[34] On this reference to Grocheio's homeland see above.

[35] 'dwell upon this [kind of *cantilena*]' renders Grocheio's idiom *circa hanc stare*, an etymologizing phrase (compare *stare*, present participle *stans*, accusative *stantem*, and *stantipes*). Grocheio employs this idiom again in his later remarks about the *stantipes*.

[36] So both MSS. Rohloff: *amor vel ερος*

[37] Seay (*Concerning Music*, p. 17) translates 'sung in chorus', but this is an error; the translation 'in caroles' is in accordance with standard usage in thirteenth-century Latin. Grocheio is referring to company dances performed in a ring or in a line. See Stevens, *Words and Music*, pp. 162–71; Page, *Voices and Instruments*, pp. 77–84; idem, *The Owl and the Nightingale*, pp. 110–33.

[38] 'directs the sentiments' (*ducit corda*); once again, Grocheio is etymologizing the name of a genre (*ductia*), or at least assaying a point of Latin style, by establishing the pairing *ductia/ducere*.

young men and draws them away from vain thoughts, and is said to have power against that passion which is called 'erotic love'.[39]

p. 133 Est etiam alius modus cantilenarum, quem *cantum insertum* vel *cantilenam entatam*[40] vocant, qui ad modum cantilenarum incipit et earum fine clauditur vel finitur, sicut gallice *Je m'endormi el sentier*.

There is also another kind of *cantilena* which they [i.e. the Parisians] call 'ornament-ed song' or 'grafted song'.[41] It begins in the manner of *cantilene* and ends or comes to a close in their fashion, as in the French song *Je m'endormi el sentier*.

p. 132 Sic igitur apparet descriptio istorum tam cantuum quam cantilenarum. Partes autem eorum multipliciter dicuntur, ut versus, refractorium vel responsori-um et additamenta. Versus autem in cantu gestuali [est] qui ex pluribus versiculis efficitur et in eadem[42] consonantia dictaminis cadunt; In aliquo tamen cantu claudi-tur per versiculum [both MSS: versum] ab aliis consonantia discordantem, sicut in gesta quae dicitur de Girardo de Viana. Numerus autem versuum in cantu gestuali non est determinatus sed secundum copiam materiae et voluntatem compositoris ampliatur. Idem etiam cantus debet in omnibus versiculis [both MSS: versibus] reit-erari.

---

[39] Unaccountably, Rohloff abolishes the readings of both manuscripts at this point and emends *amor hereos* to *amor vel eros*, breaking into Greek characters for the last word. There is no doubt about the correctness of the MS readings, however, for Grocheio's term *amor (h)ereos* (or simply *(h)ereos*) is found in numerous medical textbooks of the thirteenth and fourteenth centuries. Compare B. Lawn, ed., *The Prose Salernitan Questions*, Auctores Britannici Medii Aevi, V (London, 1979), p. 280: 'in passione que hereos dicitur'. These questions, by an anonymous English author, date from *c.* 1200. The phraseology of the passage quoted is very similar to Grocheio's and may therefore stand close to a source consult-ed by him. Grocheio had certainly read some material by the celebrated physician Galen, whom he mentions (Rohloff, *Die Quellenhandschriften*, p. 144).

[40] So both MSS. Rohloff: *entratam*

[41] 'Grafted' translates *entatam*, which is clearly the reading of both manuscripts. Rohloff's emendation to *entratam* is not necessary; there is no difficulty in regarding *entatam* as a Latinized form of the Old French past participle *enté* (from *enter*, 'to graft'), a term whose use in musical contexts during the thir-teenth century is well established. See Godefroy, *Dictionnaire de l'ancienne langue française*, sv. *enter*; Tobler-Lommatzsch, *Altfranzösisches Wörterbuch*, sv. *enter*. The term has long been used in modern scholarship to denote motet texts that begin and end with quotations of the music and/or the words of pre-existing songs. Grocheio is presumably referring to a kind of song that begins and ends with a quotation, perhaps both musical and poetic, from a pre-existing song, and therefore to one manifesta-tion of the phenomenon known to literary scholars and musicologists as the *refrain*. This is consistent with his statement that the *cantilena entata* begins and ends in the fashion of a *cantilena*, that is to say it begins and ends with a refrain or with something that, in registral terms, could be one. The song cited by Grocheio as an example of this form appears not to have survived. There may be little reason to perpetuate the musicological convention of limiting the thirteenth-century term *motet enté* to denote the texts of motets with refrain insertions split between the beginning and end of a text; as is well known, the meaning of the term *motet* was quite broad in Old French, and in Old French usage a *motet enté* may have been any song, whether monophonic or polyphonic, that contained *refrain* citations.

[42] So both MSS. Rohloff: *ex pluribus versiculis efficitur*. [*Versiculi*] *in eadem.*

28

Thus the description of these things, both of the varieties of *cantus* and of *cantilena*, is plain. Their parts are referred to in many ways, as verse, refrain or response, and the supplements.[43] The verse in a *chanson de geste* is that which is constituted from many versicles[44] which fall together with the same accord of verbal sound;[45] in some *chansons de geste* the verse ends with a versicle which does not accord in verbal sound with the others, as in the *geste* which is called 'Concerning Girard de Vienne'.[46] The number of verses in a *chanson de geste* is not fixed and may be extended according to the abundance of the raw material and the wish of the one whom makes the song. The same melody must be repeated in every versicle.

pp. 132–4 Versus vero in cantu coronato est qui ex pluribus punctis et concordantiis ad se invicem harmoniam facientibus efficitur. Numerus vero versuum in cantu coronato ratione septem concordantiarum determinatus est ad septem. Tot enim versus debent totam sententiam materiae, nec plus nec minus, continere.

The verse in a *cantus coronatus* is composed from numerous verbal constructions[47] and harmonious members producing a mutual accord. By analogy with the seven concords the number of verses in a *cantus coronatus* has been set at seven. This number of verses – no more and no less – must encompass all the subject-matter.

p. 134 Versus vero in cantu versiculari illi de cantu coronato, secundum quod potest, assimilatur. Numerus vero versuum in tali cantu non est determinatus, sed in aliquibus plus, in aliquibus minus, secundum copiam materiae et voluntatem compositoris ampliatur.

The verse in a *cantus versicularis* is made as similar to that of a *cantus coronatus* as is possible. The number of verses in such a *cantus* is not fixed, but is extended more in some, less in others, according to the wealth of the raw material and the wish of the poet.

[43] Rendering *additamenta* and denoting all the material of a refrain form which is not the refrain as fully constituted as both its text and music.

[44] Since this passage provides the only surviving description of the way *chansons de geste* were performed it is alarming that both manuscripts agree in transmitting a text that appears to confuse the crucial terms *versus* (laisse) and *versiculus* (line). The confusion has rarely been given its proper weight in discussions of Grocheio's evidence. Compare Stevens, *Words and Music*, pp. 233, 236 and 241; idem, 'Medieval Song', pp. 408–10.

[45] Literally 'in the same consonance of poetry'. Many of the surviving *chansons de geste* are constructed from assonating laisses. Some later examples, under the influence of romance, are in monorhymed laisses. Grocheio, writing *c*. 1300, may be thinking of both.

[46] Seay's translation (*Concerning Music*, p. 18) 'in the chanson de geste which is said to be by Girarde de Viana' is wide of the mark. Grocheio is referring to the *chanson de geste* of Girard de Vienne, composed, perhaps between 1205 and 1225, by Bertrand de Bar-sur-Aube. For this identification, with an extract from the text of the epic (which exactly corresponds to Grocheio's description of it), see Page, *The Owl and the Nightingale*, pp. 72–3.

[47] At first sight Grocheio's Latin ('ex pluribus punctis') suggests that he is referring to musical phrases, but throughout this section Grocheio's comments seem to relate exclusively to the poetic forms of the genres described. My translation assumes that he is referring to the pointed (i.e. punctuated) constructions of the sense. If Grocheio is using the term 'versus' to mean stanza here, then seven seems a large number.

p. 134 Responsorium vero est quo omnis cantilena incipit et terminatur. Additamenta vero differunt in rotundello, ductia et stantipede. In rotundello vero consonant et concordant in dictamine cum responsorio. In ductia vero et stantipede differunt quaedam et alia consonant et concordant. In ductia etiam et stantipede responsorium cum additamentis versus appellatur quorum numerus non est determinatus sed secundum voluntatem compositoris et copiam sententiae augmentatur.

The refrain is the part with which every *cantilena* begins and ends. The supplements differ in a *rotundellus, ductia* and *stantipes*. In the *rotundellus* [i.e. the rondeau] they rhyme and agree in their metrical form with the refrain. In the *ductia* and *stantipes* some supplements differ [from the refrain] and others rhyme and agree in their metrical form. Also, in the *ductia* and *stantipes* the refrain with the supplements is called the verse and the number of verses is not fixed but may be augmented according to the wish of the poet and the scope of the subject-matter.[48]

p. 134 Haec itaque sunt partes cantus et cantilenae diversae. De modo igitur componendi cantum et cantilenam nunc dicamus. Modus autem componendi haec generaliter est unus, quemadmodum in natura, primo enim dictamina loco materiae praeparantur, postea vero cantus unicuique dictamini proportionalis loco formae introducitur. Dico autem *unicuique proportionalis* quia alium cantum habet cantus gestualis et coronatus et versiculatus ut eorum descriptiones aliae sunt, quemadmodum superius dicebatur.

These are therefore the elements of the various kinds of *cantus* and *cantilena*. Let us therefore now discuss the manner of composing a *cantus* and a *cantilena*. There is generally one way of composing these things, as in nature,[49] for in the first place the poems are prepared beforehand, serving as the raw material, and then a correctly designed melody is introduced into each poem, serving as the form. I say 'correctly designed into each [poem]', because the *cantus gestualis, coronatus* and *versiculatus* all have their own kinds of melody just as their descriptions are different, as has been said above.

pp. 134–6 De formis igitur musicalibus quae in voce humana exercentur haec dicta sint. De instrumentalibus vero nunc prosequamur. Instrumenta vero a quibusdam

---

[48] This is a difficult passage because Grocheio is using musical terms for aspects of poetic form. It would appear that the verb 'consono' (or as a noun, sometimes reinforced as 'consonantia dictaminis') denotes rhyming, while 'concordo' (sometimes reinforced as 'concordant in dictamine') denotes identity of metrical form.

[49] Grocheio's point is that the composition of these song forms is analogous to creation in the natural world. He makes this plain by using the terms *materia* and *forma*, an ultimately Aristotelian distinction. Cf. *De anima*, II:1 'Matter is identical with potentiality, form with actuality'. Grocheio is therefore regarding the poems of these musical forms as *materia* – as matter with the potentiality to become a certain kind of song – while the music is the *forma*, transforming the raw material into a form by creating the set of musical repeats and changes that define the musical form of the genre in question. See M. Bielitz, '*Materia* und *forma* bei Johannes de Grocheo', and DeWitt, *A New Perspective*, pp. 51f.

dividuntur divisione soni artificialis in eis generati, dicunt enim sonum in instrumentis fieri afflatu, puta in tubis, calamis, fistulis et organis, vel percussione puta in chordis, tympanis, cymbalis et campanis. Sed si haec omnia subtiliter considerentur, inveniuntur a percussione fieri cum omnis sonus percutiendo causetur prout in sermonibus de anima comprobatum est. Nos autem hic non intendimus[50] instrumentorum compositionem vel divisionem nisi propter diversitatem formarum musicalium quae in eis generantur. Inter quae instrumenta cum chordis principatum obtinent, cuiusmodi sunt psalterium, cithara, lyra, quitarra sarracenica et viella. In eis enim [est] subtilior et melior soni discretio[51] propter abbreviationem et elongationem chordarum. Et adhuc inter omnia instrumenta chordosa visa a nobis viella videtur praevalere. Quemadmodum enim anima intellectiva alias formas naturales in se virtualiter includit et ut tetragonum trigonum et maior numerus minorem, ita viella in se virtualiter alia continet instrumenta. Licet enim aliqua instrumenta suo sono magis moveant animos hominum – puta in festis, hastiludiis et torneamentis tympanum et tuba – in viella tamen omnes formae musicales subtilius discernuntur et ideo de his tantummodo nunc dicatur.

These things have been said concerning the musical forms which are performed with the human voice. We now turn to consider instrumental forms. Instruments are classified by some according to the different kind of manufactured sound that is generated by them, for they declare that sound is produced in musical instruments by the breath, as in *tube*, *calami*, *fistule* and *organa*, or by beating, as in strings, *tympana*, *cymbala* and *campana*.[52] But if all these things are given careful consideration then all these sounds are found to be made by beating since every sound is produced by striking, as has been proved in the discourses concerning the soul.[53] Here, however, we do not intend to encompass the construction or classification of musical instruments unless it relates to the diversity of the musical forms that are executed with them. Among which instruments the strings hold pride of place; of this kind are the *psalterium*, the *cithara*, the *lyra*, the *quitarra sarracenica* and the *viella*.[54]

---

[50] So both MSS. Rohloff: *intendimus [notificare]*

[51] So MS H (f. 4v). MS D (f. 61v): *soni descriptio*

[52] These instrument-names cannot all be identified with certainty. *Tube* will be trumpets, while *fistula* may denote flutes and/or duct flutes. *Calami* presumably denotes wind instruments with reeds. *Organa* may safely be interpreted as organs. *Tympana* are probably frame drums of various kinds, while *cymbala* may be identified with cymbals or small bells (but perhaps not with rows of chime bells). There seems no reason to doubt that *campana* are large, tower bells or other signalling bells.

[53] The reference is to Aristotle's *De anima*, II:8, or possibly to a commentary upon it, perhaps by Grocheio himself.

[54] *Psalterium* may be safely associated with psalteries, generally of pig-snout shape in Grocheio's time and strung with metallic materials. *Cithara* is generally (but by no means exclusively) associated with forms of the Germanic word *harp(e)* in medieval word lists and translations, generally denoting a pillar harp c. 1300. The *lyra* may possibly be the lute, while the *quitarra sarracenica* is perhaps to be associated with either the gittern or the citole, although this is very uncertain. The *viella* is undoubtedly the fiddle. For the evidence on which these identifications are based see P. Bec., *Vièles ou Violes* (Paris, 1992), *passim*; Page, *Voices and Instruments*, pp. 139–50; L. Wright, 'The Medieval Gittern and Citole: A Case of Mistaken Identity', *Galpin Society Journal*, 30 (1977), 8–42 and C. Young, 'Zur Klassifikation und ikonographischen Interpretation mittelalterlicher Zupfinstrumente', *Basler Jahrbuch für Historische Musikpraxis*, 8 (1984), 67–103.

With these instruments there is a more exact and a better means of distinguishing[55] any melody on account of the shortening and lengthening of the strings. Furthermore, the *viella* evidently prevails over all the musical instruments known to us, for just as the scope of the intellective soul includes other natural forms within itself, and as the square includes the triangle and the greater number includes the lesser, so the scope of the *viella* includes all other instruments within itself.[56] Even if there are some instruments whose sound has greater power to move the souls of men – as the *tympanum* and *tuba* do in feasts, hastiludes[57] and tournaments – on the *viella* all musical forms can be discerned more exactly, and therefore it only remains to speak of those musical forms.[58]

p. 136 Bonus autem artifex in viella omnem cantum et cantilenam et omnem formam musicalem generaliter introducit. Illa tamen quae coram divitibus in festis et ludis fiunt communiter ad tria generaliter reducuntur, puta cantum coronatum, ductiam et stantipedem. Sed de cantu coronato prius dictum est, de ductia igitur et stantipede nunc [est] dicendum. Est autem ductia sonus illiteratus cum decenti percussione mensuratus. Dico autem *illiteratus* quia licet in voce humana fieri possit et per figuras repraesentari non tamen per litteras scribi potest quia littera et dictamine caret. Sed *cum recta percussione* eo quod ictus eam mensurant et motum facientis et excitant animum hominis ad ornate movendum secundum artem quam ballare vocant, et eius motum mensurant in ductiis et choreis.

A good player of the *viella* generally performs every *cantus* and *cantilena*, and all achieved musical design.[59] The genres which are usually performed before mag-

---

[55] Or possibly, following the reading of MS D, 'a better account'.

[56] The concept of an instrument which includes the scope of all others within itself is a familiar one in medieval music theory; compare John 'of Affligem' on the *musa* which, he says, *omnium [instrumentorum] vim atque modum in se continet* (J. Smits van Waesberghe, ed., *Johannis...De Musica*, Corpus Scriptorum de Musica 1 (American Institute of Musicology, 1950), p. 54). Grocheio's comments upon the *viella*, however, reveal a higher level of abstraction than those of Johannes two centuries earlier and reflect Grocheio's reading of Aristotle's *De anima*, II:3 'The types of soul resemble the series of figures. For, both in figures and in things animate, the earlier form exists potentially in the later, as, for instance, the triangle exists potentially in the quadrilateral and the nutritive soul exists potentially in the sensate soul'. The intellective soul is the highest function of the soul, standing above sensate soul (characterized by sense perception, more or less complex depending upon the species of creature at issue), and nutritive soul (characterized by the basic functions of nutrition and reproduction). This analogy between the status of the *viella* and intellective soul therefore implies the highest possible standing for the *viella* as an instrument that can encompass what every other instrument can do but which adds qualities that Grocheio compares to the distinctively human faculties of intellection and abstraction. In the context of thirteenth-century theology – much preoccupied with the nature of the soul – this analogy is less strained than it may now appear.

[57] On the distinction between hastiludes and tournaments, which is often difficult to establish, see J. Vale, *Edward III and Chivalry* (Woodbridge, 1982), pp. 57ff.

[58] Grocheio thus signals his intention to speak only of *viella* repertory. It remains unknown whether other instruments performed the musical forms he now goes on to describe, or whether other instruments were associated with specific repertoire in the same way as the *viella*.

[59] The construction is *bonus artifex in viella...formam introducit*, which might be translated 'a good player creates *forma* upon the *viella*...'. This seems a rather cumbersome and gratuitously cerebral way for Grocheio to express his meaning, but the sense seems clear none the less. The verb *introduco* here has

nates in festivities and sportive gatherings[60] can generally be reduced to three, that is to say the *cantus coronatus*, the *ductia* and the *stantipes*. However, since we have already given an account of the *cantus coronatus*, we must now therefore speak of the *ductia* and the *stantipes*. The *ductia* is a melody without words, measured with an appropriate beat. I say 'without words' because even though it can be performed by the human voice and expressed in musical notation, it cannot be written down with letters because it lacks a text and a poem. But it has 'a correct beat' because beats measure the *ductia*[61] and the movement of one who dances it, and [these beats] excite people to move in an elaborate fashion according to the art which they call 'dancing', and they measure the movement [of this art] in *ductiae* and in caroles.

p. 136 Stantipes vero est sonus illiteratus habens difficilem concordantiarum discretionem per puncta determinatus. Dico autem *habens difficilem* etc. propter enim eius difficultatem facit animum facientis circa eam stare et etiam animum advertentis et multoties animos divitum a prava cogitatione divertit. Dico etiam *per puncta determinatus* eo quod percussione quae est in ductia caret et solum punctorum distinctione cognoscitur.

The *stantipes* is a textless melody having a difficult structure of agreements and distinguished by its sections.[62] I say 'having a difficult [structure of agreements]' for, on account of its difficulty, it causes the mind of anyone who performs it – and of anyone who listens – to dwell upon it[63] and it often diverts the minds of the powerful from perverse reflection. I say 'distinguished by its sections', because it lacks the beat of the *ductia* and is only recognized by the distinction of its sections.

nothing to do with the performance of 'introductory' preludes upon the fiddle; *introduco* + accusative + *in* + ablative is Grocheio's idiom for referring to the creation of *forma* in its Aristotelian sense of actual, accomplished form rather than mere raw material (*materia*). For a parallel passage in Grocheio's treatise compare Rohloff, *Die Quellenhandschriften*, p. 114. Grocheio's point is that with the *viella* a good player can play every *cantus* and *cantilena* and can shape every kind of achieved musical design. For contrasting proposals about the interpretation of Grocheio's evidence see H. M. Brown, 'Instruments', in H. M. Brown and S. Sadie, eds., *Performance Practice*, 2 vols. (London, 1989), 1, pp. 18–23; D. Fallows, 'Secular Polyphony in the Fifteenth Century', *ibid*, p. 206; L. Gushee, 'Two Central Places: Paris and the French Court in the Early Fourteenth Century', in *Bericht über den Internationalen Musikwissenschaftlichen Kongress Berlin 1974*, ed. H. Kuhn and P. Nitsche (Kassel, etc., 1980), p. 143.

[60] The appropriate translation for 'ludi' is not easy to establish; it may encompass tournaments.

[61] 'correct beat' renders *recta percussione*. The noun *ictus* is not a common one in either the plainchant theory or the polyphonic theory of the Middle Ages, but its appearance in this context can be explained in terms of the choreography of *caroles*. There is abundant evidence that *caroles* were sometimes danced with clapping of the hands and stamping of the feet; Grocheio is here presenting such accentuation as a characteristic feature of melodies designed for the *carole*. See Page, *The Owl and the Nightingale*, p. 115.

[62] There is no adequate English equivalent of Grocheio's *puncta*, denoting a complex musical phrase capable of forming one unit of an estampie and of bearing an open or closed ending.

[63] On the etymologizing explanation *circa eam stare* see above. For commentary upon this passage see L Hibberd, 'Estampie and Stantipes', *Speculum*, 19 (1944), 222–49; K. Vellekoop, 'Die Estampie: ihre Besetzung und Funktion', *Basler Jahrbuch für Historische Musikpraxis*, 8 (1983), 51–65, and H. Wagenaar-Nolthenius, 'Estampie/Stantipes/Stampita', in *L'Ars Nova Italiana del Trecento: 2nd Congress* (Certaldo, 1969), pp. 399–409.

p. 136 Partes autem ductiae et stantipedis puncta communiter dicuntur. Punctus autem est ordinata aggregatio concordantiarum harmoniam facientium ascenden-do et descendendo, duas habens partes in principio similes, in fine differentes, quae *clausum* et *apertum* communiter appellantur. Dico autem *duas habens partes* etc. ad similitudinem duarum linearum quarum una sit maior alia. Maior enim minorem claudit et est fine differens a minori. Numerum vero punctorum in ductia ad numerum trium consonantiarum perfectarum attendentes ad tria posuerunt. Sunt tamen aliquae *notae* vocatae quattuor punctorum quae ad ductiam vel stantipedem imperfectam reduci possunt. Sunt etiam aliquae ductiae quattuor habentes puncta puta ductia 'Pierron'. Numerum vero punctorum in stantipede quidam ad sex posuerunt ad rationes vocum inspicientes. Alii tamen de novo inspicientes forte ad numerum septem concordantiarum vel naturali inclinatione ducti, puta Tassinus, numerum ad septem augmentant. Huiusmodi autem stantipedes [sunt] 'res cum septem cordis' vel difficiles 'res Tassini'.

The elements of the *ductia* and *stantipes* are commonly called *puncta*. A *punctus* is a structured collection of agreements producing euphony as they rise and fall, having two parts, similar at the beginning, different at the end, which are common-ly called 'open' and 'closed'. I say 'having two parts etc.' by analogy with two lines, one of which is longer than the other. The greater includes the lesser and differs from the lesser at its end. [Musicians] have set the number of *puncta* in a *ductia* at three, giving consideration to the three perfect consonances. There are some [*ductiae*], however, with four *puncta*, called *notae*, which can be assimilated to an imperfect *ductia* or *stantipes*. There are also some *ductiae* having four puncta, such as the *ductia* 'Pierron'.[64] Some [musicians] have set the number of *puncta* in a *stantipes* at six by analogy with the hexachord. Others, however, such as Tassin, considering the matter afresh, have enlarged the number of *puncta* to seven [see Ex. 2] perhaps by analogy with the seven concords or because they were led by natural inclination to do so. *Stantipedes* of this kind are 'the piece with seven strings' or the difficult 'pieces of Tassin'.[65]

pp. 136–8 Componere ductiam et stantipedem est sonum per puncta et rectas per-cussiones in ductia et stantipede determinare. Quemadmodum enim materia natu-ralis per formam naturalem determinatur ita sonus determinatus[66] per puncta et per formam artificialem ei ab artifice attributam. Quid igitur sit ductia et stantipes, et quae earum partes et quae earum compositio, sic sit dictum. In quo propositum

---

[64] It remains uncertain whether this is a reference to a *ductia* called Pierron or *by* Pierron. It may be both.

[65] There is a severe textual difficulty in the last sentence of the Latin. The manuscripts are unanimous in their readings for the whole sentence, save that only MS H has the *sunt*, added by a later hand and placed here in square brackets. Rohloff emends the received text in two places, reading 'Huiusmodi autem stantipedes sunt res cum septem *concordantiis*, *ut* difficiles res Tassini' (my italics). It is not cer-tain that these emendations are required; 'res cum septem cordis' is presumably the title of an estampie (or if *res* is construed as a plural, as a series of estampies), analogous to 'res Tassini'.

[66] So both MSS. Rohloff: *determinatur*

34

Ex. 2

de simplici seu vulgari musica terminatur. De musica igitur composita et regulari sermonem perquiramus.

To compose a *ductia* and *stantipes* is to shape musical sound into the *puncta* and correct pulses for a *ductia* and *stantipes*. Just as raw material in nature is given identity by natural form, so musical sound [is given identity] through *puncta* and through the man-made design that the composer gives to it. Thus we have given an account of the *ductia* and the *stantipes*, their parts and their composition. This discussion of monophonic or the music of the lay public now comes to a close. Let us turn our discussion to constructed[67] and regulated music.

p. 138 Quidam autem per experientiam attendentes ad consonantias tam perfectas quam imperfectas cantum ex duobus compositum invenerunt, quem *quintum* et *discantum* seu *duplum organum* appellaverunt, et de hoc plures regulas invenerunt, ut apparet eorum tractatus aspicienti. Si tamen aliquis praedictas consonantias sufficienter cognoverit ex modicis regulis poterit talem cantum et eius partes et eius compositionem cognoscere, sunt enim aliqui qui ex industria naturali et per usum talem cantum cognoscunt et componere sciunt. Sed alii, ad tres consonantias perfectas attendentes, cantum ex tribus compositum uniformi mensura regulatum invenerunt, quem *cantum praecise mensuratum* vocaverunt, et isto cantu moderni Parisiis utuntur quem antiqui pluribus modis diviserunt; nos vero secundum usum modernorum in tres generaliter dividimus, puta *motetos, organum* et cantum abscisum quem *hoquetos* vocant.

Some musicians, moreover, studying both perfect and imperfect consonances through experience of them, devised a kind of music composed in two parts, which they have called 'quintus' and 'discantus' or 'organum duplum', and they have devised many rules pertaining to this, as will be apparent to anyone who looks into a treatise of theirs.[68] However, if anyone is sufficiently familiar with the aforementioned consonances he will be able to have a thorough knowledge of such music, its component parts and its composition, from a few rules, for there are some who are proficient in this music and who know how to compose it through experience and innate diligence. Others, however, pondering upon the three perfect consonances, devised a form of music composed in a threefold way,[69] regulated according to a uniform measure, which they called 'precisely measured music', and it is this kind of music which the Moderns in Paris employ. The Ancients divided it in numerous ways; we, following the usage of the Moderns, generally distinguish three kinds, that is to say motets, organum and a 'cut' music that they call 'hockets'.

---

[67] 'constructed' renders Grocheio's *composita*, which cannot mean simply 'composed' because this would not distinguish polyphony from monophonic forms. The key sense here is surely that of 'assembled, put together', having reference to the scrupulous calibration of polyphonic parts in terms of intervals and duration.

[68] On this passage see K.-J. Sachs, 'Die Contrapunctus-Lehre im 14. und 15. Jh.', in *Die Mittelalterliche Lehre von der Mehrstimmigkeit,* ed. H. H. Eggebrecht (Darmstadt, 1984), pp. 161–256, especially pp. 169–70.

[69] 'in a threefold way', rendering *ex tribus*, a reference to the perfection; cf. Rohloff, *Die Quellenhandschriften*, p. 140: 'Est enim perfectio mensura ex tribus temporibus constans. ...Ista autem mensura moderni utuntur et hac totum summ cantum et cantando et figurando mensurant'.

[An account of the rhythmic modes follows, Grocheio expressing his preference for the standard division into six. The symbols of mensural notation are discussed and Grocheio emphasizes the variability of their meaning for different singers. He now begins his account of polyphonic genres.]

p. 144 Motetus vero est cantus ex pluribus compositus, habens plura dictamina vel multimodam discretionem syllabarum, utrobique harmonialiter consonans. Dico autem *ex pluribus compositus* eo quod ibi sunt tres cantus vel quattuor, *plura* autem *dictamina* quia quilibet debet habere discretionem syllabarum, tenore excepto qui in aliquibus habet dictamen et in aliquibus non. Sed dico *utrobique harmonialiter conso-nans* eo quod quilibet debet cum alio consonare secundum aliquam perfectarum cononantiarum, puta secundum diatessaron vel diapente vel diapason de quibus superius diximus cum de principiis tractabamus. Cantus autem iste non debet coram vulgaribus propinari eo quod eius subtilitatem non advertunt[70] nec in eius auditu delectantur sed coram litteratis et illis qui subtilitates artium sunt quaer-entes. Et solet in eorum festis decantari ad eorum decorationem, quemadmodum cantilena quae dicitur rotundellus in festis vulgarium laicorum.

The motet is a music assembled from numerous elements, having numerous poetic texts or a multifarious structure of syllables, according together at every point. I say 'assembled from numerous elements' because in a motet there are three or four parts; [I say] having 'numerous poetic texts' because each [part] must have its structure of syllables save the tenor, which in some [motets] has a poetic text and in some does not. I say 'according together at every point' because each [part] must harmonize with the other according to one of the perfect consonances, that is to say a fourth, fifth or octave, which we discussed above when we treated the fundamen-tals. This kind of music should not be set before a lay public[71] because they are not alert to its refinement nor are they delighted by hearing it, but [it should only be performed] before the clergy[72] and those who look for the refinements of skills. It is the custom for the motet to be sung in their holiday festivities to adorn them, just as the *cantilena* which is called 'rotundellus' [is customarily sung] in the festivities of the lay public.[73]

p. 144 Organum vero, prout hic sumitur, est cantus ex pluribus harmonice com-

---

[70] So both MSS. Rohloff: *animadvertunt*

[71] This passage has given rise to much misunderstanding. Seay's translation 'the vulgar' (*Concerning Music*, p. 26) has been highly influential but is most ill-judged, since Grocheio is contrasting the *laity* with the *clergy* at this point. See the next note and, for a full discussion of this point, Page, *Discarding Images*, Chapter 3, *passim*, and compare Stevens, *Words and Music*, p. 431 and note 50.

[72] Grocheio's term *litterati* has been translated in many ways by modern scholars ('the literati', 'men of letters', 'exclusive social circles'); see, for example, DeWitt, *A New Perspective*, p. 177. Virtually all of these authors seek to convey what they take to have been the elite audience for the motet; there can be little doubt that Grocheio is using the word *litterati* in its traditional sense of 'the clergy'.

[73] Grocheio is alluding to his own phraseology at this point. See his account of the *rotundellus* above.

positus unum tantum habens dictamen vel discretionem syllabarum. Dico autem *tantum habens unum dictamen* eo quod omnes cantus fundantur super unam discretionem syllabarum. Cantus autem iste dupliciter variatur. Est enim quidam qui supra cantum determinatum, puta ecclesiasticum, fundatur, qui ecclesiis[74] vel locis sanctis decantatur ad dei laudem et reverentiam summitatis, et cantus iste appropriato nomine *organum* appellatur. Alius autem fundatur supra cantum cum eo compositum qui solet in conviviis et festis coram litteratis et divitibus decantari, et ex his nomen trahens appropriato nomine *conductus* appellatur. Communiter tamen loquentes totum hoc *organum* dicunt et sic communis est eis descriptio supradicta.

Organum, as it is interpreted here, is a music harmoniously assembled from numerous elements, having only one poem or structure of syllables. I say 'having only one poem' because all the parts are founded upon one structure of syllables. This music is of two kinds. There is one kind which is founded upon a modal melody,[75] that is to say an ecclesiastical one, which is sung in churches or in holy places[76] to the praise of God and for the worship of the Most High, and this is appropriately named *organum*. Another is founded upon a melody composed with it and which is customarily sung at meals and festivities before clergy and magnates, and taking its name from them it is called by the appropriate name *conductus*.[77] All of this is commonly called *organum* and thus the above description relates generally to them all.

pp. 144–6 Hoquetus est cantus abscisus ex duobus vel pluribus compositus. Dico autem *ex pluribus compositus* quia licet abscisio vel truncatio sit sufficiens inter duos, possunt tamen esse plures ut cum truncatione consonantia sit perfecta. Cantus autem iste cholericis et iuvenibus appetibilis est propter sui mobilitatem et velocitatem, simile enim sibi simile quaerit et in suo simili delectatur.[78] Partes autem istorum plures sunt puta *tenor, motetus, triplum, quadruplum* et in hoquetis *primus, secundus* et ultimo eorum *duplum*. Tenor autem est illa pars supra quam omnes aliae fundantur quemadmodum partes domus vel aedificii super suum fundamentum et eas regulat et eis dat quantitatem quemadmodum ossa partibus aliis. Motetus vero est cantus ille qui supra tenorem immediate ordinatur et in diapente ut plurimum incipit et in eadem proportione[79] qua incipit continuatur vel diapa-

---

74 Rohloff: [*in*] *ecclesiis*
75 For the use of *determinare* to indicate definition according to (plainchant) mode see Grocheio's remarks in the first Latin passage given above (Rohloff, *Die Quellenhandschriften*, p. 124).
76 The phrase 'holy places' is often used in medieval Latin to denote the immediate environs of any ecclesiastical building. Grocheio may be referring to the use of organum in processions.
77 Grocheio is presumably judging *conductus* to be an appropriate name for a genre performed where the learned and powerful are gathered together because *conductus* can be etymologized as 'brought or drawn together'. See B. Gillingham, 'A New Etiology and Etymology for the Conductus', *Musical Quarterly*, 75 (1991), 59–73, especially pp. 61–2.
78 Compare Walther, *Sprichwörter*, 7418, 11012, 15304 etc.
79 Rohloff: *proportione* [*in*] *qua incipit*

son[80] ascendit, et in hoquetis ab aliquibus dicitur *magistrans*, ut in hoqueto qui dicitur *Ego mundus*.[81] Triplum vero est cantus ille qui supra tenorem in diapason proportione incipere debet et in eadem proportione ut plurimum continuari. Dico autem *ut plurimum* quia aliquoties in tenore[82] vel diapente descendit propter euphoniam, quemadmodum motetus aliquando in diapason ascendit. Quadruplum vero est cantus qui aliquibus additur propter consonantiam perficiendam. Dico autem *aliquibus* etc., quia in aliquibus sunt tantum tres et ibi sufficiunt cum perfecta consonantia ex tribus causetur. In aliquibus vero quartus additur ut dum unus trium pausat vel ornate[83] ascendit, vel duo adinvicem se truncant, quartus consonantiam servet.

The hocket is a 'cut' song composed from two or more parts. I say 'composed from more parts' because even though the cutting away or truncation can be adequate between two parts, it is possible for there to be more so that the harmony may be complete with the truncation. This music appeals to the choleric and to the young on account of its motion and speed, for like seeks like and delights in it. The elements of these [genres] are many, including the tenor, motetus, triplum and quadruplum, and in hockets the prime, the second and – the last of them – the duplum.[84] The tenor is the part upon which all the others are founded, as the parts of a house or edifice [rest] upon a foundation, and it regulates them and gives substance, as bones do, to the other parts. The motetus is the part which is placed immediately above the tenor, and as often as possible it begins a fifth above the tenor and continues in the same proportion as it began, or ascends to the octave; in hockets, some call this part the *magistrans*, as in the hocket which is called *Ego mundus*. The triplum is the part which should begin above the tenor in the proportion of an octave and which should be continued in the same proportion as often as possible. I say 'as often as possible', because it sometimes descends into the range of the tenor, or descends a fifth, for the sake of euphony, just as the motetus sometimes ascends to the octave. The quadruplum is the part which is added in some pieces to complete the harmony. I say 'to some' etc., because in some pieces there are only three parts and they suffice, since complete music can be established with three parts. In some pieces, indeed, a fourth voice is added, so that while one of the three voices pauses or ascends in an ornate fashion, or two together have rests, the fourth may preserve the harmony.

p. 146 Primus vero in hoquetis est[85] qui primo truncare incipit, sed secundus qui

80 Rohloff: *vel* [*in*] *diapason ascendit*
81 So both MSS. Rohloff: *Echo montis*
82 So both MSS. Rohloff: *motetum*
83 So both MSS. Rohloff: *ordinatim*
84 Grocheio's phraseology seems designed to exclude the possibility of four-part hockets. For an account of a four-part hocket see P. Jeffery, 'A Four-Part *In seculum* Hocket and a Mensural Sequence in an Unknown Fragment', *Journal of the American Musicological Society*, 37 (1984), 1–48.
85 So both MSS. Rohloff: *hoquetis est* [*cantus*]

secundo post primum truncat. Duplum vero est[86] qui cum tenore[87] minutam facit abscisionem et cum eo aliquoties in diapente consonat et aliquando in diapason proportione, ad quod multum iuvat bona discretio decantantis. Volens autem ista componere primo debet tenorem ordinare vel componere et ei modum et mensuram dare. Pars enim principalior debet formari primo, quoniam ea mediante postea formantur aliae, quemadmodum Natura in generatione animalium primo format membra principalia, puta cor, hepar, cerebrum, et illis mediantibus alia post formantur. Dico autem *ordinare*, quoniam in motellis et organo tenor ex cantu antiquo est et prius composito, sed ab artifice per modum et rectam mensuram amplius determinatur. Et dico *componere*, quoniam in conductibus tenor totaliter fit[88] et secundum voluntatem artificis modificatur et durat.

The 'prime' voice in hockets is the one which begins to have rests first, and the second is the one that begins to have rests after it. The duplum is the part which has minute rests with the tenor and which harmonizes with it sometimes at the fifth and sometimes at the octave, an effect which relies greatly upon the good accuracy of the performer. Anyone who wishes to compose these kinds of music should first lay out or compose the tenor and assign it both [rhythmic] mode and measure. The principal part must be formed first for it is with its help that the others are formed, just as Nature, when she forms animals, first makes the principal members such as the heart, the liver, the brain; with the help of these others are formed afterwards. I say 'lay out' because in motets and organum the tenor is derived from an old melody and is pre-composed, but it is given further definition with mode and correct measure by the composer. I say 'compose', because in *conducti* the tenor is created entire; it is modified, and its extent is set, according to the wish of the composer.

pp. 146–8 Tenore autem composito vel ordinato debet supra eum motetum componere vel ordinare qui ut plurimum cum tenore in diapente proportione resonat et propter sui harmoniam aliquoties ascendit vel descendit. Sed ulterius debet istis triplum superaddi quod cum tenore ut plurimum debet in diapason proportione resonare et propter sui harmoniam potest in locis mediis sistere vel usque ad diapente aliquoties descendere. Et quamquam ex istis tribus consonantia perficiatur potest tamen eis aliquoties decenter addi quadruplum quod cum alii cantus descendent vel ascendent ordinate vel abscisionem facient vel pausabunt consonantiam resonabit. In componendo vero organum modorum alternationem quam plurimum faciunt sed in compondendo motellos et alia modorum unitatem magis servant. Et cum in motellis plura sint dictamina, si unum syllabis vel dictionibus aliud excedat potes eum per appositionem brevium et semibrevium alteri coaequare. Volens autem hoquetum ex duobus, puta primo et secundo, componere,

---

86 So both MSS. Rohloff: *Duplum vero est* [*cantus*]
87 So both MSS. Rohloff: *qui* [*supra*] *tenorem*
88 So both MSS. Rohloff: *totaliter* [*de novo*] *fit*

debet cantum vel cantilenam supra quod fit hoquetus partiri et unicuique partem distribuere. Et potest aliquantulum rectus cantus exire cum decenti additione nisi quod eius mensuram observet. Sic enim unus iacet super alium ad modum tegularum et cooperturae domus et sic continua abscisio fiet. Volens ultimo duplum componere debet minutam abscisionem supra tenorem facere et aliquoties consonare.

Once the tenor has been composed or laid out, the motetus must be composed or laid out upon it, sounding with the tenor in the interval of a fifth as often as possible; for the sake of euphony it sometimes ascends or descends. The triplum must be further added to these, and it should sound with the tenor as often as possible in the proportion of an octave, and for the sake of euphony it may stand in medial positions or sometimes descend to the fifth. And even though complete harmony can be made from these three parts, a quadruplum may sometimes be fittingly added to them so that, when the other parts descend or ascend in an ordered fashion, or have a momentary rest or pause, [the quadruplum] will produce consonance. In composing organum [duplum, composers] produce as much variation of [rhythmic] mode as possible, but in composing motets and other genres they chiefly preserve unity [of mode]. And since there are several poems in motets, if one exceeds the other in syllables or words you can make it equal the other by the juxtaposition of breves and semibreves. He who wishes to compose a hocket in two parts, that is to say with a *primus* and *secundus*, must divide the *cantus* or *cantilena* upon which the hocket is to be made and distribute it among the two parts. And the true melody may proceed with a degree of appropriate ornamentation, unless it must keep to the measure of the original tune.[89] Thus, one part lies upon the other in the manner of tiles[90] and the covering of a house and thus continuous hocketing may be accomplished. He who wishes to add a duplum to this must make a minute 'cutting' upon the tenor and make it accord somewhat.

[Grocheio now introduces his section on plainchant, from which the following excerpts are taken, the selection being restricted to those that confirm or elucidate matters relating to secular forms.]

p. 160 Cantus autem iste [i.e. antiphona] post psalmos decantatur et aliquoties neupma additur puta post psalmos evangelistas. Est autem neupma quasi cauda vel exitus sequens antiphonam quamadmodum in viella post cantum coronatum vel stantipedem exitus quem *modum* viellatores appellant.

This kind of chant [i.e. an antiphon] is sung after the psalms, and sometimes a

---

[89] This passage, a difficult one, presumably means that when a melody is split up between different voices to make a hocket, it can be ornamented and added to in various ways, unless it is important for some reason that the hocketed version of the melody should last exactly the same amount of time as the original.

[90] Rohloff's emendation of *regularum* (in both MSS) to *tegularum* ('of tiles') can surely be accepted and is accordingly followed here.

neuma is added – as after the evangelistic psalms. A *neuma* is a kind of tail or postlude following the antiphon, comparable to the postlude which is performed on the *viella* after the *cantus coronatus*, or *stantipes*, which fiddlers call a *modus*.

p. 162 Isti autem cantus [i.e. *Gloria in excelsis deo* et *Kyrie eleison*] cantantur tractim et ex longis et perfectis ad modum cantus coronati ut corda audientium ad devote orandum promoveantur et ad devote audiendum orationem quam immediate dicit sacerdos vel ad hoc ordinatus.

These chants [i.e. *Gloria in excelsis deo* and *Kyrie eleison*] are sung slowly and from perfect longs in the manner of a *cantus coronatus*, so that the hearts of those who listen may be moved to devout prayer and to devoutly hear the prayer which the priest, or the one deputed to the task, says immediately afterwards.

p. 164 Responsorium autem et alleluia decantantur ad modum stantipedis vel cantus coronati, ut devotionem et humilitatem in cordibus auditorum imponant. Sed sequentia cantatur ad modum ductiae. ...Offertorium...cantatur ad modum ductiae vel cantus coronati ut corda fidelium excitet ad devote offerendum.

The responsory and alleluia are sung in the manner of a *stantipes* or of a *cantus coronatus* so that they may bring devotion and humility to the hearts of those who hear them. The sequence, however, is sung in the manner of a *ductia*. ...The offertory...is sung in the manner of a *ductia* or of a *cantus coronatus* so that it may inspire the hearts of the faithful to make their offerings devoutly.

INDEX OF AUTHORS
(CLASSICAL AND MEDIEVAL) AND TEXTS

INDEX OF INSTRUMENT NAMES,
RELATED TERMS AND ISSUES

INDEX OF MANUSCRIPTS